CIVIC REFORMATION AND RELIGIOUS CHANGE IN SIXTEENTH-CENTURY SCOTTISH TOWNS

Scottish Religious Cultures *Historical Perspectives*

Series Editors: Scott R. Spurlock and Crawford Gribben

Religion has played a key formational role in the development of Scottish society shaping cultural norms, defining individual and corporate identities, and underpinning legal and political institutions. This series presents the very best scholarship on the role of religion as a formative and yet divisive force in Scottish society and highlights its positive and negative functions in the development of the nation's culture. The impact of the Scots diaspora on the wider world means that the subject has major significance far outwith Scotland.

Available titles

George Mackay Brown and the Scottish Catholic Imagination
Linden Bicket

Poor Relief and the Church in Scotland, 1560–1650
John McCallum

Jewish Orthodoxy in Scotland: Rabbi Dr Salis Daiches and Religious Leadership
Hannah Holtschneider

Modern Social Christianity in Scotland and Beyond: Essays in Honour of Stewart J. Brown
Edited by Andrew Kloes and Laura Mair

Scottish Presbyterianism: The Case of Dunblane and Stirling, 1690–1710
Andrew Muirhead

The Scots Afrikaners: Identity Politics and Intertwined Religious Cultures in Southern and Central Africa
Retief Müller

The Revival of Evangelicalism: Mission and Piety in the Victorian Church of Scotland
Andrew Michael Jones

Miracles of Healing: Psychotherapy and Religion in Twentieth-century Scotland
Gavin Miller

George Strachan of the Mearns: Seventeenth-century Orientalist
Tom McInally

Bantu Presbyterian Church of South Africa: A History of the Free Church of Scotland Mission
Graham A. Duncan

Dissent After Disruption: Church and State in Scotland, 1843–63
Ryan Mallon

Scottish Liturgical Traditions and Religious Politics: From Reformers to Jacobites, 1560–1764
Edited by Allan I. Macinnes, Patricia Barton and Kieran German

John Kennedy of Dingwall (1819–1884): Evangelicalism in the Scottish Highlands
Alasdair J. Macleod

Mission, Race and Colonialism in Malawi: Alexander Hetherwick of Blantyre
Kenneth R. Ross

Protestantism, Revolution and Scottish Political Thought: The European Context, 1637–1651
Karie Schultz

Civic Reformation and Religious Change in Sixteenth-century Scottish Towns
Timothy Slonosky

Forthcoming titles

The Dynamics of Dissent: Politics, Religion and the Law in Restoration Scotland
Neil McIntyre

William Guild and Moderate Divinity in Early Modern Scotland
Russell Newton

edinburghuniversitypress.com/series/src

CIVIC REFORMATION AND RELIGIOUS CHANGE IN SIXTEENTH-CENTURY SCOTTISH TOWNS

TIMOTHY SLONOSKY

EDINBURGH
University Press

Edinburgh University Press is one of the leading university presses in the UK. We publish academic books and journals in our selected subject areas across the humanities and social sciences, combining cutting-edge scholarship with high editorial and production values to produce academic works of lasting importance. For more information visit our website: edinburghuniversitypress.com

© Timothy Slonosky, 2024, 2025

Edinburgh University Press Ltd
13 Infirmary Street
Edinburgh EH1 1LT

First published in hardback by Edinburgh University Press 2024

Typeset in 10/12 ITC New Baskerville by
Cheshire Typesetting Ltd, Cuddington, Cheshire

A CIP record for this book is available from the British Library

ISBN 978 1 3995 1022 6 (hardback)
ISBN 978 1 3995 1023 3 (paperback)
ISBN 978 1 3995 1025 7 (webready PDF)
ISBN 978 1 3995 1024 0 (epub)

The right of Timothy Slonosky to be identified as author of this work has been asserted in accordance with the Copyright, Designs and Patents Act 1988 and the Copyright and Related Rights Regulations 2003 (SI No. 2498).

Contents

Acknowledgements vi
Usage and Abbreviations viii

Introduction 1

Part One   The Burghs 11

1 The Burghs: Setting and Economy 13
2 Governance in the Burghs 30
3 The Civic Church 49
4 The Urban Clergy 86

Part Two   Discussion and Disaster 115

5 The Spread of New Ideas: 1520–1547 117
6 Plague and War: 1543–1550 145
7 Recovery and Reaction: 1550–1558 171

Part Three   Reformation from Within and Without 191

8 Reformation: 1558–1560 195
9 Creating Protestant Towns: 1560–1565 215

Conclusion 243

Works Cited 252
Index 267

Acknowledgements

This book could not have been written had not so many people freely given their time, expertise and patience. First of all of them is Margo Todd, who has supported and encouraged this project from before I arrived at Penn through to the present day. Every graduate student should be so fortunate as to benefit from her wisdom, enthusiasm and high standards. Antonio Feros, Ann Moyer and E. Ann Matter introduced me to many of the concepts discussed in the text, offered helpful comments on the dissertation stage of this project, and give much of themselves to supporting students. Philip Benedict provided crucial guidance on several key issues and I am immensely grateful to him and the rest of the Institute d'Histoire de la Réformation for allowing me to participate in their summer courses, which taught me so much about the French and Dutch reformations. Jane Dawson, Elizabeth Ewan and Roger Mason all took the time to discuss my research and make important suggestions. Though I was never his student, Robert Tittler has time and again offered career-changing advice. The readers who reviewed the book draft made many helpful recommendations on points big and small. The remaining errors and questionable choices are my own.

Many archivists and librarians offered essential help. In Dundee the staff of the Dundee City Archives not only provided expert assistance but, just as appreciated, a cheerful welcome for the many months that I sat in their office/reading room, as it was then. Iain Flett in particular shared much of his own knowledge and put me in touch with many local historians and resources. David Kett and the staff of the Local History section of the Dundee Library pointed to me to many useful sources. The staff at the National Archives of Scotland and the Stirling Council Archives were unfailingly friendly and helpful. Ruth Fyfe at the East Lothian Council Archives has patiently and diligently answered my many requests.

Financial support, without which this book could not have been written, has been provided by the Fonds Québécois de la recherche sur la société et la culture, the Social Sciences and Humanities Research Council of Canada, the Ben Franklin Fellowship and the Dissertation Research Fellowship of the University of Pennsylvania and Dawson College's Professional Development Fund.

The staff at Edinburgh University Press have been helpful and encouraging throughout the editorial and publication process, especially Ersev Ersoy, Tom Dark, Eddie Clark and Isobel Birks and their copy-editor Sue Dalgleish.

Acknowledgements

Researching and writing this work would not have been nearly as stimulating were it not for the continuing comradeship of Daniel Cheely, Matthew Gaetano, Igor Knezevic, Mathew Mitchell and Kathryn Ostrofsky, who all combine gracious warmth and relentless curiosity.

My colleagues at Dawson College all offered their support and encouragement throughout the project, and covered for me on many occasions. In particular, Isabelle Carrier, Michael Wood and Odette Dubé graciously handled my many last-minute leave requests, and I have been very lucky to have Michael Wasser just upstairs, who is always willing to read chapters and discuss Scottish history.

Finally, this work was only accomplished with the support of many people who never imagined that they would spend so much time hearing about sixteenth-century Scots. Joey Berger has been my designated non-specialist reader ever since CEGEP. Gabrielle Leadbetter along with Jane and David Wilson provided homes away from home. Victoria and Andrea Slonosky both gave, from different perspectives, immensely valuable advice on the publishing process. Anthony and Clare Slonosky spent many hours trekking to forts and castles when I was young and later spent many hours reading chapter drafts. Since the very beginning I have been supported by the love, encouragement and copy-editing of Candice Slonosky. She, Maisie and Greg have spent many evenings and summers (and one pandemic) tiptoeing past my office and keeping up their end of conversations about history and religion: I hope they understand how much that means to me.

Usage and Abbreviations

Note that dates are written with the year beginning 1 January. The lower-case 'sir' (schir) identifies a Catholic priest, as was practice in the sixteenth-century. Uppercase 'Sir' denotes someone who has been knighted.

As much as possible I have tried to keep quotes in the original sixteenth-century Scots and English, both to preserve the voices of sixteenth-century people and to minimise confusion for researchers working with the same original documents. This is especially important concerning names, where variations in spelling already make it perilous to make connections between different entries and texts, and I hesitate to add to the uncertainty with my own assumptions about how a given name should be modernised, even when the solution seems obvious (for example, Blak/Black). Shorter quotes, names and verse, therefore remain in the original spellings. However, for the sake of non-specialist readers I have modernised the spelling of longer prose quotations.

ALC	*Acts of the Lords of Council in Public Affairs, 1501–54*
BHCB	*Burgh and Head Court Book*
CSP	*Calendar of State Papers relating to Scotland and Mary Queen of Scots, 1547–63*
DCA	*Dundee City Archives*
DCA Laws	DCA Head Court Laws 1550–1612
DOST	*Dictionary of Older Scottish Tongue*
Exchequer	*The Exchequer Rolls of Scotland*
HAD/4/6/5	Haddington Court Book 1530–55
HAD/4/2/3/1	Haddington Court Book 1555–60
HAD/4/2/3/2	Haddington Court Book 1560–71
HAD/4/6/73	Haddington Treasurer's Account 1558
HAD/2/1/2/1	Haddington Burgh Minutes 1554–80
HAD/4/1/3	Protocol Book Alexander Symson 1539–42
HAD/4/1/5	Protocol Book Thomas Stevin 1548–65
LP	*Letters and papers, foreign and domestic, of the reign of Henry VIII*
ODNB	*Oxford Dictionary of National Biography*
Privy Seal	*The Register of the Privy Seal of Scotland*
RCRBS	*Records of the Convention of Royal Burghs of Scotland*
RGS	*The Register of the Great Seal of Scotland*
RPC	*Register of Privy Council of Scotland*
RPS	*The Records of the Parliaments of Scotland to 1707*
TA	*Accounts of the Lord High Treasurer of Scotland*

Introduction

On 27 May 1533, some 121 men of Haddington, a farming town east of Edinburgh, met and chose William Walson to be one of their parish clerks. In the Scottish medieval church, the clerk was responsible for various functions necessary to the running of the parish church and for assisting the priests in the saying of the daily masses. The position was one of several that the townspeople had the right to appoint, and the number of inhabitants who turned up to the meeting demonstrates the importance of the post and the sense of responsibility the burgesses felt for the proper functioning of their church.[1] Following the Protestant Reformation of 1560, Walson would again appear before his fellow townspeople in 1567, this time a smaller group of town councillors. He asked to be reinstated to the position that he had held before Protestantism, or as he called it, 'The Imitation of Religion,' was established. The councillors agreed, and specified that his duties would include keeping the church clean, opening its doors when necessary, administering the water at baptism and singing the psalms on Sundays. He was to be paid eleven shillings a year and resume his collection of 12d from every 'fine house'.[2]

Great changes had taken place during the thirty-four years between Walson's two appearances. His physical surroundings had altered, as Haddington had been devastated and then rebuilt as a result of the English invasions of 1547–9. The townspeople were different; most of the councillors he had faced in 1567 would not have been present at his initial selection, as war, plague and time created an extensive turnover, and mass meetings of the community had been replaced by governance by a small town council. From his point of view, the most significant change would have been to his duties. As parish clerk, he had played an important role in the late medieval Catholic cycle of prayers and rituals. The most important of these rituals was the mass, wherein believers held that bread and wine were transformed into the body and blood of Jesus Christ, bringing the divine presence into the profane, mundane world of the Scottish townspeople.[3] These rituals were understood to protect the townspeople in their earthly lives and aid their entry into heaven, so the inhabitants ensured that they were performed as frequently as possible. The mass and other Catholic rituals were detested by the Protestants[4] who reformed Scotland's religion in 1559 and 1560 first by force, and then by Act of Parliament, who saw them as acts of idolatry which offended rather than honoured God. The mass was prohibited, the equipment used to perform it destroyed or irreparably altered, the men who carried it out obliged to renounce it. In its place, the Protestants introduced religious practices based on Scripture reading, interior faith and a strict avoidance of sin, enforced through community discipline.[5]

The 1559–60 Reformation in Scotland was the first of three attempted Calvinist revolutions that decade, being followed by one in France in 1562 and then another in the Low Countries in 1567. The Scottish militant Protestants adapted the tactics that had originated in Swiss cities and which would be used in the subsequent Calvinist revolutions: groups of militants would establish a secret church with preaching and sometimes the administration of sacraments; then coming out into the open they seized churches for preaching, intimidated priests and friars, destroyed religious images, and where possible, pressured city officials to implement a full Calvinist church, or 'église dressé', complete with consistories and sacraments observed in the Genevan manner.[6] In France, Calvinism spread rapidly at first, before a Catholic response, organised both locally and nationally, checked and then began slowly rolling back the Protestant advances. That process ultimately took 130 years, including forty years of war and popular violence. In the Low Countries, aggressive Calvinist militance caused many of the elite to withdraw their support, allowing Philip II to repress the initial revolt. Subsequent conflict eventually allowed the Calvinists to establish themselves in regions that would become the Netherlands. Even locally however, they never became so dominant as to be able to eliminate Catholicism completely.[7] In Scotland by contrast, the Calvinists achieved near complete success, both rapidly reforming almost the whole country and ensuring that the reforms became permanent, a feat which neither their French nor their Netherlandish co-religionists accomplished and which even the Swiss reformers had realised only in limited regions.

Scotland's Reformation had begun in the spring of 1559 with an attempt by the regent, Mary of Guise, to crack down on Protestant preaching and underground churches – called privy kirks – which led first to confrontation between her and the preachers, who were backed by contingents of nobles and townspeople, and then to outright war, much of it fought by English and French soldiers. Eventually, the English-backed Protestants triumphed, Mary of Guise died, and the Protestants packed Parliament in 1560 to implement a top-down national reformation.[8] Yet even after the Reformation settlement was imposed – first by local and military violence, and then by Act of Parliament – there was no guarantee that it would succeed on the ground.[9] Several factors were working against the Protestants. The parliamentary acts that effectively banned Catholicism were not ratified by François and Mary and so were of dubious legitimacy.[10] Before, during and immediately after 1560, the majority of Scottish people were not Protestants. Despite the abolition of Catholicism, there was no immediate mass turn towards the new religious practices; in Edinburgh Catholicism was still as popular as Protestantism in the mid-1560s.[11]

Many parts of the country were not directly touched by the violence and iconoclasm of the war of 1559–60 and would have still been able to maintain Catholic religious practices. The Protestants had difficulty staffing their new church.[12] A Catholic queen was soon to rule over the country in person. These were all potential sources of conflict and division, and yet the overwhelming majority of Scots accepted the drastic changes in religion peacefully.

Various explanations have been offered for the sudden success of Scotland's Reformation. Older historiography, inspired by Gordon Donaldson's 1957–8 lecture series published as *The Scottish Reformation*, focuses largely on the failings of the institutions of the late medieval Catholic Church, including the behaviour of the church leadership and the distribution of church revenues, arguing that the clergy were corrupt, professionally inadequate and neglectful of the laity.[13] The research of Donaldson's pupil, Ian Cowan, famously pointed out that 85 per cent of Scottish parishes had their revenues diverted to non-resident clergy, ecclesiastical institutions and even laymen, who were called commendators. He argued that this weakening of the parish structure led to contempt for the church and eventually caused the Reformation.[14] Yet Cowan himself found it difficult to use this approach to explain the entire course of events of the Scottish Reformation, acknowledging that lay Scots were not as angry with the clergy as might be expected: 'parish churches were purged of symbols of idolatry, but the priests themselves were undisturbed, a fact which is difficult to explain except in terms of lack of popular opposition to the old regime despite its shortcomings.'[15] Modern historians such as Alec Ryrie and Jane Dawson are rightly cautious about accepting such a damning condemnation of the Catholic Church.[16] Ryrie offers a largely political explanation instead, arguing that the Reformation occurred because the Scottish elites chose an English, Protestant alliance over a French, Catholic one.[17] The Protestant activists of the 1550s were, in his view, 'not the makers of the revolution of 1559–60; merely its heirs'.[18] Dawson emphasises international affairs, arguing that the regent, Mary of Guise, adopted a hardline Catholic policy to improve her daughter Queen Mary's chance of gaining the English throne, which had the side-effect of creating a confrontation with Scotland's Protestants. The Protestants won the resulting conflict, known as the Wars of the Congregation, because their English allies were more effective than Mary's French supporters.[19] These studies explain how the Protestants gained military and political control of Scotland in 1560, but they are less successful at explaining why the Scottish laity, the vast majority of whom were not committed Protestants, acquiesced so easily to the elimination of their traditional religion, especially given the relatively precarious position of the Protestants and their limited resources.

The most promising research into the laity's attitude towards the Reformation comes from local studies. Two of the most influential are Michael Lynch's work on Edinburgh and Margaret Sanderson's on

Ayrshire.[20] Both point to the extent of lay control over religious practice in the towns, Sanderson going so far as to title the relevant chapter 'The People's Church' and Lynch emphasising that the church appeared to meet the needs of Edinburgh parishioners right through the 1550s.[21] When the Reformation was imposed on Edinburgh by outside political forces, most burgesses were reluctant to become members of either the hardline Catholic or Protestant factions. The innate conservatism of the townspeople limited the Protestant activists to gradual changes and in doing so made the new religion more acceptable.[22] Sanderson, for her part, draws attention away from an exclusive focus on economic, social and political factors and back to the movement for religious reform. She argues that the religious turmoil from 1530 on prepared the laity for the events of 1559–60, but when it comes to explaining why the majority supported the Reformation, she nonetheless returns to the corruption thesis, stating that the religious ferment of the sixteenth century 'can itself be seen as the laity's answer to their disillusionment with the established church which, having become self-sufficient, self-justifying and preoccupied with secular concerns, appeared to have forgotten that other people were its first responsibility'.[23]

The difficulty with explanations based on the corruption thesis or national or international politics is that the Scottish laity, whether the burgesses in the towns or the lairds (gentry) in rural areas, exercised a great deal of authority over their local churches, as demonstrated by the career of William Walson. In many places the laity exercised control over the appointment of the clergy, their terms of employment and even their retirements, and there is little evidence that they were displeased with the service they received. The behaviour of the upper hierarchy of the church and many benefice holders may have made them easy targets for criticism, but they had little direct impact, for good or ill, on the laity.

Why then did such a rapid and drastic change to a crucial part of Scots' lives and understanding of the universe take place, not only without extensive popular violence and civil strife, but in such a way that William Walson, and others like him, could keep their jobs? The answer lies in the attitudes of the ordinary Christians, who had a say in the administration of local churches but not their doctrine. The argument of this book is that the laity were satisfied with the clergy themselves, but not with the outcome of the services they were providing. In other words, the problem was not with the institution of the church but with the failure of its rituals to placate God. This dissatisfaction was deeply rooted in events of the two decades before 1560. A royal minority, religious disagreements and different foreign allegiances divided Scotland's political class. Plague in the mid-1540s terrified the inhabitants, brought trade and travel to a halt, and inspired a crackdown on all manner of misbehaviour. There was a series of devastating wars with England and the Holy Roman Empire: the Scots suffered from crippling defeats in pitched battles in 1543 and 1547 that left many dead and from the occupation of much of the East coast between 1547 and

1549 which devastated the countryside and totally disrupted normal life. These events in turn led to economic collapse, with the export trade plummeting, and caused some to warn the Scots that they had incurred divine displeasure.[24] Exposed at the same time to the spread of new religious ideas and widespread acknowledgement of the need to reform the old church, some became convinced Protestants. Just as important, many others were likely opened to the possibility of change, even if they were not committed to a particular doctrine. Few were willing to make a stand in defence of the old religion. The success of the Scottish Reformation owed as much to the acquiescence of the many as to the militancy of the few.

To understand why Scots became militantly Protestant or calmly acquiescent, we must meet them where they lived, and for many this means in Scotland's burghs.[25] A fairly small portion of Scotland's population lived in towns, though they are over-represented in surviving records and, through their ability to self-govern and represent themselves in national politics, had more opportunities for influence and self-expression than the rural inhabitants.[26] Before and after 1560, Scottish townspeople controlled much of their own religious life. They built churches and chapels; endowed them with bequests or supported them with public funds; hired the priests to staff them; oversaw their maintenance and the use of public spaces; enforced discipline through burgh courts and consistory sessions; and, of course, prayed, worshipped and listened to preaching. The burghs also played an important role in the Reformation itself. During the initial crisis of 1559 and the War of the Congregation, it was towns such as Dundee and Ayr which provided financial and military support to the Protestants, and who then helped pack the Reformation Parliament of 1560.[27] These decisions were made in meetings of the burgh courts and town councils, institutions that relied on a broad base of community support and participation. The religious beliefs and practices of Scotland's townspeople, and the structures of the towns themselves, were therefore key to the Scottish Reformation's success.

Three towns with very different levels of support for Protestantism – Dundee, Stirling and Haddington – demonstrate how people came to either join the Protestant cause enthusiastically or passively accept it, and serve as examples of similar towns throughout Scotland. In all three towns, people's attitudes were shaped not just by the theological arguments of reformers, but also by the tumultuous events of the previous decades. Dundee, as a seaport which was exposed to news and ideas from the Continent as well as the academic and theological discussions in nearby St Andrews, had a long-standing interest in Protestantism which mobilised in the late 1550s to establish a Protestant congregation. The town's support of the Protestant preacher Paul Methven made it a driving force behind the events of 1559–60. Stirling, smaller than Dundee, suffered repression of its Protestant faction in the late 1530s, and thereafter remained religiously quiet, though lingering sympathy for reforming ideas may have eased the transition to Protestantism when the burgh was reformed by force in 1559. Haddington was more isolated than the other two towns from political and intellectual developments. It was not, therefore, as fertile ground for the growth of a militant Protestant faction, yet the turbulence of the previous decades helped weaken attachment to the old church and at the same time created fear of further conflict, which reinforced the desire for communal unity. This instinct for unity and concord was at the heart of much of burgh life, and guided the response of burgesses and their leaders throughout the crisis. When Haddington's town council re-hired William Walson in 1567, they did so not as a lingering attachment to Catholicism, nor as an act of defiance towards an unpopular religious imposition. It was a sign, however, that their Protestantism was not so fervent that it caused them to renounce their obligations to their neighbours simply because of a lack of religious agreement.

The sources available for the study of urban religion in Scotland only occasionally tell us what people believed, but they often tell us what they did. The core of this study is burgh records. In theory, burghs would have both council books, which recorded laws passed at full council meetings (usually three to ten times a year, but with plenty of variance according to local practice), and court books, which recorded the sittings of the bailies (magistrates), normally held two or three times a week but again with plenty of variations. In practice, most of the records studied here combined these two forms in one volume, usually archived as burgh court books. In them are recorded the disputes brought before the courts, cases prosecuted by the town officials, and orders by the magistrates (called bailies) and councillors concerning municipal administration and expenditure. These records themselves often consist of court decisions, or statements that various individuals wished entered on the record; there is very little sense of discussion, deliberation or division. They are rich in administrative details, from the hiring of clergy to the physical upkeep of churches to the trials and punishments of misbehaving townspeople. From these, augmented with notarial records and charters, the workings of what may be called the civic church can be established.[28] Through their burgh courts Scotland's townspeople controlled much of the religious worship in their towns, especially in the collegiate churches that were established in the fifteenth century. Other foundations, such as chapels and almshouses, also came under the councils' control as the ancestors of the original donors became uninterested in continuing their commitments. The events that happened to the towns – heresy crackdowns, plagues and wars – are often not directly discussed in the burgh court books, as record keeping was not a priority during crises. Those events are recorded in Scottish government documents, contemporary narrations and correspondence collections. The burgh records pick up in the aftermath of these disasters, as people turned to the courts to help sort out the upheavals. Crude economic data can be gleaned from customs accounts, tax collections and expenditures.

A handful of literary sources let us know what some people were thinking about contemporary events, their fellow countrymen, and sometimes, about God. The nature of these records means that it is the communal aspect of religion that is emphasised. This does not mean that people were not concerned about their individual salvation, only that those worries cannot be reconstructed with the sources studied here.

In addition to representing three distinct paths to religious change, Dundee, Stirling and Haddington are also ideal for furthering our understanding of the Scottish Reformation and the dynamics of Protestant militancy because they have some of the most complete but largely unstudied or unpublished burgh records for the period in question.[29] For Dundee, these records exist from 1520–3 and from 1550 on. In Haddington, they exist from 1530 on, with a gap between 1545 and 1551. Stirling's records are more intermittent, surviving from 1519–30, 1544–50, 1554–7 and from 1560 on. The start date of this study is therefore approximately 1520, and the end date around 1565, by which time the initial structure, if not necessarily the spirit, of the Protestant church was established in the three burghs.[30] Where relevant, other Scottish burghs which have been previously studied, including Edinburgh, Ayr, Perth, Aberdeen and St Andrews, will also be discussed.[31]

Some records, particularly those from guilds, diocesan administrations and the friars, which would have been particularly important to understanding the urban Reformation, appear to be no longer extant. Just enough survives from the guild records – the occasional charter, act book or membership list – to hint at what is missing. The burgh church was perhaps the central feature of urban worship, but the contribution of other institutions to burgh worship, especially the friaries, must not be forgotten on account of the absence of evidence.[32] Also missing from the burghs are kirk session minutes for the years immediately following 1560. There was a kirk session in Dundee as early as 1559, and in Stirling not long after, but none of the early records are extant. The burgh records also provide limited information about relations between the burghs and local lairds and magnates. These men certainly exerted a firm influence over the burgesses that is not always apparent in the burgh records. The determination of the townspeople to act in their own interests, however, should not be underestimated.[33] Together, even despite the gaps, these sources give us a clear picture of the civic churches created by Scotland's townspeople, the spread of discussion about reforms to the churches, and the events that led the townspeople to reform their churches. The first part of this book, therefore, will explore the structures of burgh life, especially the remarkable scope of municipal authority over local religion, while the second will take a more chronological approach, examining the events that caused the Scots to change their minds about the best way to be godly. The third part will cover the Reformation in the burghs, showing how despite different levels of enthusiasm for religious change, all the towns actively participated in the establishment of a Protestant civic church. Finally, the conclusion will propose specific factors that explain how the Scots succeeded in reforming without religious division and violence.

Notes

1. Denis McKay, 'The election of parish clerks in medieval Scotland', *Innes Review* 18 (1967), 25–35; Denis McKay, 'The duties of the medieval parish clerk', *Innes Review* 19 (1968), 32–9; Margaret H. B. Sanderson, *Scottish Curates and Parochial Chaplains 1429–1560* (Edinburgh, 2016), xvii.
2. HAD/4/6/5 Haddington Court Book 1530–55 f40v–41, f106; Rosalind K. Marshall, *Ruin and Restoration: St Mary's Church Haddington* (Haddington, 2001), 23–4.
3. See R. W. Scribner, 'Cosmic order and daily life: sacred and secular in pre-industrial Germany' and 'Ritual and popular religion in Catholic Germany at the time of the Reformation', in R. W. Scribner, *Popular Culture and Popular Movements in Reformation Germany* (London, 1987).
4. The term 'Protestant' is used here to identify anyone who made a clear break with the mass and the authority of the Pope. The religious movement which originated in southern Germany and Switzerland in the 1520s and 1530s, distinguished by its rejection of any form of real presence in the Eucharist, a strong intolerance of religious imagery, and eventually a belief in predestination, has come to be known as the Reformed religion. However, there were many varieties of religious reformers in the sixteenth century, and it creates unnecessary confusion to reserve the term for one particular group, and so the term 'Calvinist' will be used. Though the term is now unfashionable, it is retained for the purposes of clarity. See also the remarks of Stephen Mark Holmes, though I do not follow his distinction between Catholic and Protestant Reformations. Stephen Mark Holmes, *Sacred Signs in Reformation Scotland: Interpreting Worship, 1488–1590* (Oxford, 2015), 212.
5. Margo Todd, *The Culture of Protestantism in Early Modern Scotland* (New Haven, 2002), 100.
6. Carlos Eire, *The War Against the Idols* (Cambridge, 1989); Philip Benedict, 'Dynamics of Protestant militancy, France 1555–1563', and Guido Marnef, 'The dynamics of Reformed religious militancy: The Netherlands 1566–1585', both in *Reformation, Revolt and Civil War in France and the Netherlands*, eds Philip Benedict, Guido Marnef, Henk van Nierop and Marc Venard (Amsterdam, 1999); Philip Benedict and Nicolas Fornerod, 'Introduction', in *L'organisation et l'action des Églises Réformées de France*, eds Philip Benedict and Nicolas Fornerod (Geneva, 2012), vii, lxvi–lxxiii, cvii.
7. Philip Benedict, 'Introduction', 4,19; Marc Venard, 'Catholicism and resistance to the Reformation in France, 1555–1585', 83–120; Nicolette Mout, 'The historiographical traditions of France and the Netherlands'; and Juliaan Woltjer, 'Political moderates and religious moderates in the revolt of the Netherlands', all in Benedict *et al.* (eds), *Reformation, Revolt and Civil War in France and the Netherlands*. Judith Pollmann, 'Countering the Reformation in France and the Netherlands: clerical leadership and Catholic violence 1560–1585', *Past and Present*, 190 (2006).

8. The best recent accounts of the events of 1559–60 are in Jane E. A. Dawson, *Scotland Re-formed, 1488–1587* (Edinburgh, 2007), and Alex Ryrie, *The Origins of the Scottish Reformation* (Manchester, 2006). See also Gordon Donaldson, *The Scottish Reformation* (Cambridge, 1960); Ian B. Cowan, *The Scottish Reformation: Church and Society in Sixteenth Century Scotland* (New York, 1982).
9. Donaldson, *The Scottish Reformation*, 54.
10. Peter G. B. McNeil, '"Our Religion, established neither by Law nor Parliament": was the Reformation legislation of 1560 valid?' *Scottish Church History* 35 (2005): 68–89; Keith M. Brown, 'The Reformation Parliament', in *History of the Scottish Parliament*, vol. 1, eds Keith M. Brown and Roland J. Tanner (Edinburgh, 2004); Donaldson, *The Scottish Reformation*, 67.
11. Jane E. A. Dawson, *John Knox* (New Haven, 2015), 223; Ian Cowan, *Regional Aspects of the Scottish Reformation* (London, 1978), 33; *Papal negotiations with Mary Queen of Scots during her reign in Scotland 1561–7*, ed. John Hungerford Pollen (Edinburgh, 1901), 496, 520–1.
12. John McCallum, *Reforming the Scottish Parish: The Reformation in Fife, 1560–1640* (Burlington, 2010), 10.
13. Donaldson, *The Scottish Reformation*, 1–27.
14. Ian B. Cowan, *The Medieval Church in Scotland*, ed. James Kirk (Edinburgh, 1995), 11, 12–27, 52.
15. Cowan, *The Scottish Reformation*, 71.
16. Ryrie, *The Origins of the Scottish Reformation*, 7, 19–20, 25.
17. Ryrie, *The Origins*, 1–2.
18. Ryrie, *The Origins*, 135.
19. Dawson, *Scotland Re-formed*, 200–15.
20. See also Mary Verschuur's work on Perth, which argues that the Reformation there was driven by a combination of anti-clericalism and the adoption of Protestant ideals by craftsmen looking for greater political representation. The nature of the surviving sources makes it difficult to know if this pattern applies elsewhere in Scotland. Mary Verschuur, *Politics or Religion? The Reformation in Perth 1540–1570* (Edinburgh, 2006).
21. Michael Lynch, *Edinburgh and the Reformation* (Edinburgh, 1981), 30.
22. Lynch, *Edinburgh and the Reformation*, 37, 86, 219, 222.
23. Margaret H. B. Sanderson, *Ayrshire and the Reformation: People and Change, 1490–1600* (East Linton, 1997), 142.
24. David Lindsay, *Sir David Lyndesay's Works*, eds J. Small and F. Hall (Early English Text Society, 1871; Reprint: New York, 1969); Robert Wedderburn, *The Complaynt of Scotland*, intro. A. M. Stewart (Edinburgh, 1979).
25. Understanding the attitudes of rural Scots is difficult due to the lack of sources comparable to those available for the burghs. See though the work of Margaret Sanderson, especially *Ayrshire and the Reformation*, and also Frank D. Bardgett, *Scotland Reformed: The Reformation in Angus and the Mearns* (Edinburgh, 1989) and McCallum, *Reforming the Scottish Parish*.
26. Dawson puts the urban population at less than 5 per cent of the total population of 800,000, which seems slightly low if the combined mid-sixteenth-century population of Edinburgh, Dundee and Aberdeen was about 28,000. See Chapter 1. Dawson, *Scotland Re-formed*, 8.
27. Dundee City Archives (DCA) Burgh and Head Court Book 1558–61, f73v; Michael Lynch, *Scotland: A New History* (London, 1992), 197.

28. These sources have been used to compile prosopographical databases of the inhabitants of each town, allowing the careers, interconnections and sometimes the religious evolution of the inhabitants to be traced. For Dundee, some 4000 individuals have been recorded; for Stirling, 800, and for Haddington, 700. Numbers are approximate due to the difficulty of telling apart individuals with similar names.
29. Several local studies exist for the burghs, including Alexander Maxwell, *The History of Old Dundee, narrated out of the Town Council Register, with additions from contemporary annals* (Dundee, 1884); Alexander Maxwell, *Old Dundee, ecclesiastical, burghal and social, prior to the Reformation.* (Dundee, 1891); J. H. Baxter, *Dundee and the Reformation* (Dundee, 1960); Iain E. F. Flett, 'The Conflict of the Reformation and Democracy in the Geneva of Scotland, 1443–1610: An Introduction to edited texts of documents relating to the burgh of Dundee.' Unpublished MPhil thesis (St Andrews, 1981); Elizabeth Patricia Dennison Torrie, *Medieval Dundee: a Town and its People* (Dundee, 1990); W. Forbes Gray, assisted by James H. Jamieson, *Short History of Haddington* (Edinburgh, 1944); Marshall, *Ruin and Restoration*; Craig Mair, *Stirling: The Royal Burgh* (Edinburgh, 1990).
30. From this point the story of Scotland's Reformation is ably told by Todd, *The Culture of Protestantism*, and McCallum, *Reforming the Scottish Parish*.
31. Lynch, *Edinburgh*; Sanderson, *Ayrshire and the Reformation*; Verschuur, *Politics or Religion?*; Jane E. A. Dawson, 'The Face of Ane Perfyt Reformed Kyrk: St Andrews and the Early Scottish Reformation', in *Humanism and Reform: The Church in Europe, England and Scotland, 1400–1643: essays in honour of James K. Cameron*, ed. James Kirk (Oxford, 1991); Bess Rhodes, *Riches and Reform: Ecclesiastical Wealth in St Andrews* (Leiden, 2019); Bruce McLennan, 'The Reformation in the Burgh of Aberdeen', *Northern Scotland* 2 (1976), 119–44; Alan White, 'The Menzies Era: Sixteenth-century Politics', in *Aberdeen before 1800: A New History*, eds E. Patricia Dennison, David Ditchburn and Michael Lynch (East Linton, 2002); Michael Lynch, Gordon DesBrisay and Murray G. H. Pittock, 'The faith of the people', in *Aberdeen before 1800*.
32. William Moir Bryce, Janet Foggie and Margaret Sanderson examined the friars and diocesan administration. They are able to tell us something about the institutions themselves and their place in Scottish society, but little about their liturgical and instructional functions. Janet P. Foggie, *Renaissance Religion in Urban Scotland: The Dominican Order, 1450–1560* (Leiden, 2003); W. M. Bryce, *The Scottish Grey Friars* (Edinburgh, 1909); Margaret H. B. Sanderson, *Cardinal of Scotland, David Beaton c.1494–1546* (Edinburgh, 1986).
33. Alan R. MacDonald, *The Burghs and Parliament in Scotland 1550–1651* (Burlington, 2007), 37.

PART ONE

The Burghs

Part One examines the structure of sixteenth century Scottish towns: why they existed where they did, who lived in them and why, how the townspeople governed themselves and arranged their communal life. A large part of their civic life revolved around the practice of Christianity, and the townspeople put significant thought and effort into maintaining religious worship within the town – worship provided by a large body of men who lived alongside them.

Chapter One describes the towns and outlines their economic fortunes. All three towns benefitted from the export boom of the late 1530s, but suffered heavy losses to their international trade and other economic activities during the 1540s. Recovery during the 1550s was incomplete and uncertain. Chapter Two studies the governing structure of the burghs, and finds that while at any given moment local political authority was concentrated in a handful of men, a significant proportion of the adult male population still participated in some aspect of communal government, and their opinions could not be discounted. Despite the growing trend towards oligarchy during the sixteenth century, town councils still relied on a base of public support and consensus. Chapter Three demonstrates the significant religious element to burgh administration. It argues that there existed in Scottish towns a civic church controlled by the town councils and responsive to the needs and desires of the townspeople. Municipal governments put much time and effort into administering this civic church, and were generally satisfied with the results. Chapter Four looks at the clergy in the towns, and shows that they were well-integrated into urban communities and generally respected by the townspeople.

Throughout, it is clear that the goal of the townspeople was to maintain harmony, stability, and if possible, prosperity, within the towns. Providing religious worship was an important element in securing these goals. However, external threats such as plague, war, political upheaval and economic deprivation challenged the towns, leading to economic depression and changes in their governing structure.

CHAPTER ONE

The Burghs: Setting and Economy

Sixteenth-century Scottish towns existed primarily as trade centres, oriented towards both foreign trade and the local exchange of goods and services. The townspeople were therefore sensitive to economic changes.[1] Unfortunately for them, medieval and early modern Scottish towns were victims of frequent economic disruption, with boom periods that alternated with decades of decline or depression.[2] The period between 1520 and 1565 saw both extremes. Trade in the three towns thrived during the late 1530s and early 1540s, but the plague of the mid-1540s and the wars with England and the Holy Roman Empire (which halted trade with the Low Countries) would devastate them. The brief experience of prosperity must have made the destruction especially bitter. Large towns survived by diversifying their economy, but as Scottish urban historians have pointed out, medium and small towns continued to decline throughout the sixteenth century.[3] Indeed, Dundee's recovery was helped by the trade in fish, a resource that was little affected by the war, but through to 1565 Stirling and Haddington never regained their former prosperity.

Dundee: History, Location, Economy

Settlement at Dundee, just inland from the North Sea on the Tay estuary, dates possibly to the eleventh century. The burgh grew along the route north from the harbour, which was further inland than it is today.[4] Eventually, several lanes connected the harbour to the market place, called the Marketgait. Between the harbour and the Marketgait was St Clement's church, on the site of the current city square. Connections to the rest of the country branched off from the Marketgait. The Seagait road left in an easterly direction, heading along the coast towards Arbroath and Montrose, paralleled to the north by the Cowgait. Four kilometres east was the castle at Broughty, which would play a significant role in the war of 1547–9.

Overlooking Dundee to the north was the steep hill of Dundee Law, below which lay the Franciscan friary and the Scouring burn, which went through the town's mills on its way to the Tay. To the west, between the Nethergait and the Overgait, is St Mary's church, which is now surrounded by a shopping centre but when first laid down would have been outside the settlement's built-up parts. Further west, beyond the town's gates (ports), was the hospital, the Dominican friary and a Franciscan nunnery, which shared a site with St James chapel. Also to the west were the town's fields, where plays would be performed.[5]

Dundee probably received its first charter during the reign of William I (1165–1214).[6] Originally, Dundee owed superiority to William's brother David, the Earl of Huntingdon, but became a royal burgh during the reign of John Balliol (1292–6). The Scrimgeours, a local family, held the post of constable from 1298 on, but in 1384 the townspeople bought out their right to enforce justice in the burgh.[7] Clashes over jurisdiction would nonetheless continue throughout Dundee's history. In 1359, Dundee was granted its own sheriffdom, which expanded its legal jurisdiction, and in 1360 received all royal revenues from the burgh, except for the 'great' custom on exports, for a fixed annual payment of twenty pounds.[8] Dundee's charter, like those of other burghs, granted its merchants a monopoly over the purchase of wool and skins in the nearby hinterland, and mandated that foreign goods be first offered for sale in Dundee.[9] The boundaries of this jurisdiction ran from just west of the burgh to the South Esk to the northeast and possibly included the Fife shore of the Tay estuary.[10] The town was also a shipping centre for goods customed at other burghs, especially Perth and Cupar, and a major shipping point for salmon fished in northern Scotland.[11] Dundee's prosperity began to grow significantly in the second half of the fourteenth century, despite economic stagnation throughout Europe, bringing it into conflict with Forfar, Brechin and especially Perth. Over the course of the fifteenth century, Dundee's share of the customs receipts rose from fifth to third among Scottish burghs, though it is a sign of the economic difficulties of the century that Dundee's actual customs payments declined by two-thirds even as its relative position improved.[12]

By the sixteenth century, Dundee was definitely Scotland's second-wealthiest burgh, and probably its second largest. Between 1500 and 1565, Dundee paid the second-most taxes among Scottish towns, behind Edinburgh.[13] Dundee's share of the 1539 levy for border defences was just over one-eighth of the national total (12.6%)[14] and Dundonians contributed similar amounts in 1550 and in 1556.[15] Estimates of Dundee's mid-sixteenth-century population vary, from the 4,000 proposed by J. H. Baxter to Warden's high estimate of 28,187. Perhaps the 9,000 suggested by the nineteenth-century local historian Alexander Maxwell is the most likely figure.[16] By comparison, the estimates for mid-century Edinburgh and Aberdeen are 13,500 and 5,500 respectively and so a population of 9,000 matches Dundee's relative wealth compared to other Scottish towns.[17]

While Dundee's relative position among Scottish burghs was constant during the mid-sixteenth century, its actual economy experienced significant fluctuations. The period of greatest prosperity was during the export boom of the late 1530s and early 1540s. This was a trend across Scotland, with the value of exports, in all goods, being 60 per cent higher in 1532–42 than in 1523–31. The boom was possibly driven by inflation in overseas

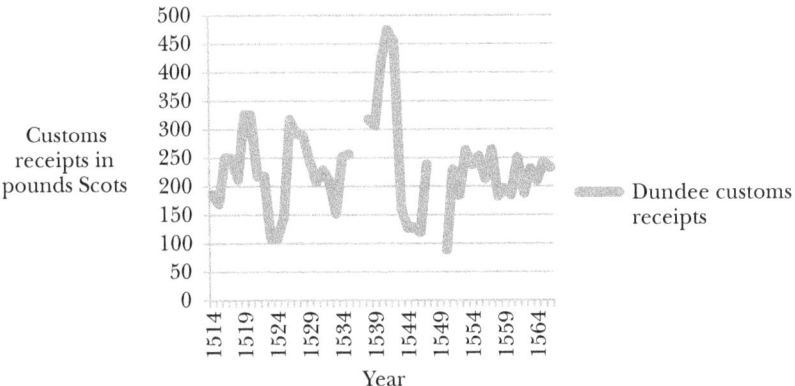

Figure 1.1 Dundee customs receipts

markets which made Scottish prices more attractive.[18] Dundee saw more than its share of the increase, as receipts increased from £152 in 1532–3 to £474 in 1540–1 and £455 in 1541–2.[19] The dual shock of war and plague ended this prosperity, and receipts fell to a low of £119 in 1546. Accounts for much of 1547–49 are missing and revenues from 1550 to 1565 did not match those of earlier years, ranging from £183 (1558) to £264 (1557).

The burgh's main exports during the sixteenth century were salmon, cloth and skins.[20] Cloth was the dominant export of the early years but declined in the 1550s. Salmon exports also fluctuated from year to year throughout the period, reaching a peak between 1538–42. After 1550, the range of fluctuation narrowed. The evidence points to a pick-up in all aspects of Dundee's economy in the late 1530s and early 1540s, which was then lost and not regained by 1565. In Scotland overall the cloth trade had returned to the levels of the 1530s by 1560, so Dundee's slow recovery was perhaps testimony to the extent of the damage done in the 1540s.[21] It is possible that the losses in buildings and livestock meant that the cloth and skin trade recovered more slowly than fishing, whose boats and wild stocks would have been less damaged by English ravaging, especially further north.

The men most immediately affected by these fluctuations were the merchants. At least forty-eight merchants, mostly but not always men, appear in the records, along with fifteen ship captains, many of whom also engaged in some trading on their own account.[22] These merchants could become quite wealthy – the four merchants whose testaments survived from between 1564 and 1575 had an average wealth of £564, compared to an average of £385 for all nineteen Dundee testaments from this period.[23] The merchants' wealth ranged from David Spens's £1330 to the £158 of Alex Donaldson. By comparison, the five craftsmen or professionals (including one surgeon, one cooper, two bakers and one maltman) had an average wealth of £355, with a range from £245 for John Kynneir (undated), a baker, to £620 for

William Leggat (1564), a maltman. These men would have been among the wealthier craftsmen, however.

The wealth in these testaments was much more than labourers could hope to accumulate. In 1523 for example, Robert Dawson, who had injured William Dougal, was ordered to compensate him twelve pence for each day that the leech (healer) said he could not work, which, assuming a work year of about 250 days would suggest an annual income for labourers of twelve pounds fifty, which may have risen slightly to between fifteen and twenty pounds by 1560.[24] Even accounting for inflation between 1525 and 1575, the amount left by the wealthy was about twenty to twenty-five times a labourer's annual income. At the lowest end of the scale, ten workmen at the common mill dared to complain, probably during the 1520s, that they were working in conditions of slavery, 'who have not consented but reclaimed against the thrall in which they are driven'. In response, the town council revoked all letters of privilege made 'or to be made' on behalf of the workmen, seemingly proving their point.[25] Though it is anachronistic to speak of class in the sixteenth century, some tensions between rich and poor were certainly present.

Evidence of manufacturing is harder to trace in the burgh court records than trade, as it was mostly merchants who brought debts and business disputes to be settled. By the mid-sixteenth century, Dundee had nine recognised trades: the bakers, the cordiners (shoemakers), the skinners/glovers, tailors, bonnetmakers, fleshers (butchers), hammermen (metalworkers), weavers and walkers (fullers).[26] Those focused on local production, such as bakers, butchers, brewers and skinners, dominate the records although these craftsmen appear more often in the records as they were closely regulated. Fewer people involved in the cloth trade appear in the records, though fullers (walkers), dyers, tailors, cutters and weavers were present. Manufacturing was nonetheless quite important, and (Dennison) Torrie notes that for much of the sixteenth century Dundee contributed proportionally more in taxes than customs, indicating that Dundee's wealth was not solely due to trade. Part of the discrepancy may be due to Dundee's manufacturing of coarse cloth, which was not subject to customs.[27] The importance of cloth workers to the burgh economy was therefore greater than the number of their appearances in the burgh court records would indicate.

By 1560, the boom of the late 1530s would have been nothing but a memory in Dundee. Nonetheless, there was still good money to be made by the merchants and ship captains, significantly more so than for the craftsmen, and the burgh was doing well relative to other Scottish towns.

Haddington: History, Location, Economy

Haddington is located just to the north and west of a bend in the River Tyne, about twenty-seven kilometres east of Edinburgh and eleven kilometres south of North Berwick, where it is surrounded by the rich farmland of East Lothian. Settled by the eleventh century or earlier, it was made into a royal burgh in 1124 by David I. The medieval layout of the town can still be discerned by a modern visitor; the Tyne, flowing from the west, first passes south of the neighbourhood of Poldrate, where the town's two mills were located. As the river bends to the north, it passes the parish church of St Mary's on its western bank. About 200 metres north of St Mary's is the heart of the burgh. The market place lay in the centre of a triangle formed by Market Street, which veers toward the north, and High Street on the southern side, with the Tolbooth forming the eastern boundary.[28] To the east, the Nungate bridge connects to the east bank neighbourhoods of Nungate and Giffordgate, the likely birthplace of John Knox.[29] North of the bridge, still on the east bank, was the Gimmersmill which belonged to the nearby nunnery, on the site of the current PureMalt plant. Past there, the river bends to the east, and the nunnery was located about three kilometres downstream.[30]

The wealth that Haddington enjoyed in times of peace was such that during the twelfth and thirteenth centuries the kings of Scotland maintained a residence there. This wealth came from the rich countryside around it, which supported mostly grain crops, with the animals pastured on the wilder lands beyond providing wool and skins for export.[31] Haddington also lay along the main route taken by invading English armies, however, and the flat countryside around it offered no natural defence, so after the royal palace was burnt in 1216 Scotland's monarchs moved elsewhere. Further English invasions would follow in 1296, 1355–6, 1384–5 and of course during the 1540s.[32] Edward III's attack in February 1356, known as the 'Burnt Candlemass', was especially devastating and destroyed both the parish and Franciscan churches. The parish church which still stands was begun about a century later and was completed in the sixteenth century.[33] Bigger than even Edinburgh's St Giles', St Mary's was a demonstration of the town's prosperity.

As a farming community, there was not a great divide between town and country, and many inhabitants either owned or worked fields in the surrounding countryside. Arguments about agricultural matters – grain owed to landlords, rent holders and business partners, passages over fields and so on – appear more frequently in the court records than they do in Dundee or Stirling's. Much of the farmland was owned by the abbeys of Haddington and Newbottle, and disputes involving their tenants were often repledged to their courts. In the mid-sixteenth century, the economy revolved around the production of grain for domestic consumption and hides and wool for export, some of which was smuggled from England.[34] Haddington's exports were shipped through Aberlady on the shore of the Forth, where the burgh maintained a customs house. By the sixteenth century, however, it appears that many of the goods customed at Haddington were actually shipped from Edinburgh, through its port at Leith.[35] In return, Haddington seems to have imported mostly timber from Fife.[36] The burgh's merchants occasionally ventured overseas but were not as active as the merchants of Dundee. Indeed, in 1558 Alexander Barnes had to be dispatched to Leith to buy wine, as it was not directly imported to the town.[37] As elsewhere in Scotland, the export trade was at a peak during the 1530s, paying around £100 a year in customs duties, reaching £139 3s 1d between August 1538 and August 1539.[38] When James V travelled to France in 1535 searching for a bride, Haddington's prosperity was such that it paid the fifth largest contribution of any of the Scottish burghs to the special tax that was collected.[39] During the wars of the Rough Wooing, however, the export trade collapsed completely. Only £4 8s 8d of customs was collected between March 1545 and October 1551, and customs receipts remained mostly around ten pounds a year for the following years. This was part of a 60 per cent reduction in woollen exports across Scotland, especially focused on regions adjoining the Forth.[40] A tax collection in July 1557 for Mary Stewart's wedding instructed the collectors to 'take consideration of the great ruin poverty and decay of the burgh of Haddington' and reduce the town's contribution.[41] With the discount, Haddington made the twelfth largest contribution. By 1563, when a tax was collected for an embassy to Denmark, Haddington had rebounded somewhat, paying the seventh largest amount.[42]

Haddington had no formal merchant's guild until 1659, but the wealthiest men in the town came from the ranks of merchants and maltmen, seventeen of whom can be identified for our period. The five testaments which survive from the late 1560s are not enough to provide a satisfactory statistical guide to the population, but they suggest some trends. The wealthiest man, by far, was Thomas Richardson, a merchant with connections on the Continent where his factors held significant amounts of cash for him - £146 13s 4d in Dieppe and twenty pounds in Flanders. The inventory at his death in 1567 consisted mostly of iron, iron goods and cloth, and he had a considerable net worth of £1464 6s 9d.[43] Despite his wealth, he was not called on to contribute to the Queen's tax in 1565. Two other merchants, Elizabeth Sinclare, the wife of merchant Patrick Lyell, and Cristell (Christopher) Galloway, had net worths of £421 18s 5d and £551 13s 4d, respectively, on their deaths.[44] Galloway contributed twenty shillings to the town in 1556–7.[45] The secret to the wealth demonstrated in these three testaments may have been that the testamentars arrived in Haddington after the difficult years of the 1540s. Thomas Richardson became a burgess in 1560, under slightly unusual circumstances, for he was not charged the usual burgess fee but was to pay an amount specially decided by the council.[46] Perhaps he made his fortune elsewhere while Haddington was suffering, and was recruited as a wealthy migrant by his father-in-law, the merchant Thomas Poynton. Patrick Lyell only settled in the burgh in 1555 or later.[47] Cristell Galloway had been in Haddington longer than the others, arriving in 1552, but still avoided the tumult of plague and war.[48] Aberdeen, in a similar circumstance following the plague

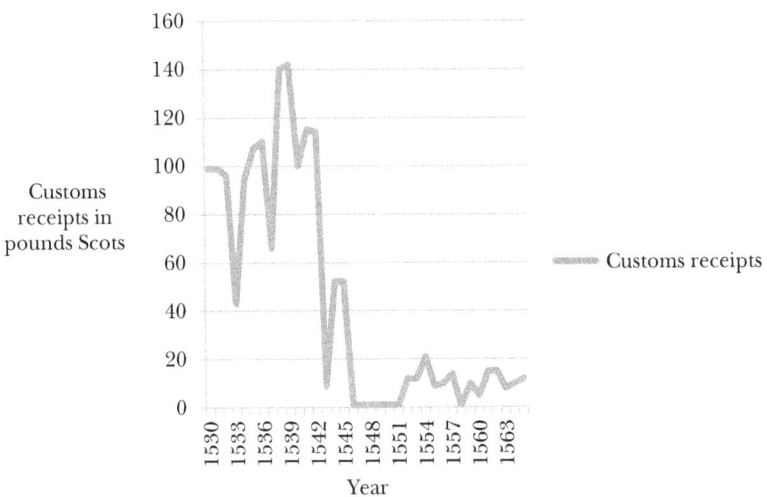

Figure 1.2 Haddington customs receipts[49]

of 1647, attempted to recruit craftsmen from other burghs, so it would not have been unusual for Haddington to restock their burgess roll after a catastrophe.[50]

The remaining two testaments reflect the more modest wealth of craftsmen, even fairly prominent ones. James Ayton, dean of the baker's guild, had a net worth of £168 6s 8d on his death in 1568. Unsurprisingly for a baker, his assets mostly consisted of grain.[51] John Douglas, a mason, was active in burgh politics, serving ten terms as councillor, two as craft representative and one as bailie (magistrate). He owned oxen and lent them out for hire, and both owed and was owed considerable amounts of money for land. On his death in 1568 he had a net worth of £58 7s 8d.[52] Both men were wealthy enough to lend money to the town in 1558, Douglas lending a modest 10s. In the absence of guild records, it is difficult to discern whether any one trade played an especially significant role in the town's economy. Aside from the unsurprising existence of bakers, tailors, masons, maltmen and smiths/hammermen, no craft appears disproportionately dominant. The butchers, barbers, furriers, wrights (builders), weavers and shoemakers were quietly present.[53] Given the exports of woollen cloth and hides there must have been some manufacturing trade in the town, but as in Dundee little trace of such activities exists in the records.

Merchants and maltmen paid a significant proportion of the extraordinary taxes and contributions levied on the burgesses. In 1556–7, three merchants, two maltmen and one baker were among the twelve men and one woman who lent the town twenty shillings (the occupations of the other seven are unknown).[54] In 1565, seven men, including two maltmen and two merchants, lent the burgh a total of £100. The impression gained from this admittedly small sample is that wealth in Haddington belonged to the merchants who collected rents in grain, exported hides and imported finished cloth, as well as to the maltmen who dealt in grain. Even the prominent craftsmen obtained nowhere near as much wealth.

The income received by the burgh council mostly came from the annual auction of the revenues from the two common mills and the small customs. Hand bells would be rung through the town to gather the 'bailies, council and community' to make their bids. Revenue also came from the customs of the tron (weighhouse), the fees from the anchorage at Aberlady and the rents from fields and urban tenements owned by the burgh.[55] For much of our period, the bids for the small customs varied from forty to sixty-five pounds. Some of the variations may be due to the bidding process, and some of the bids might have been over-optimistic, but generally bids were lower in years of disorder. As war and plague threatened, longer-term bids at lower prices were accepted and perhaps even sought by the community. It was common for several men to bid jointly; in 1545 the bid was for £170 over five years, or thirty-four pounds a year, shared by ten men. Bids shot up again in the mid-1550s, dropping in 1559, before increasing again in the 1560s.[56]

We have fewer precise amounts for the more lucrative rental of the two common mills, but the same pattern emerges. In 1554 and 1557, the winning bids, jointly made by John Ayton and John Forrois, were 310 merks.[57] Bids decreased slightly in 1558, perhaps demonstrating continuing nervousness about war, before doubling by 1565.[58] From these sources, the burgh might expect revenues of about £270 in the mid-1550s. Against this income the burgh owed every year twenty pounds to the royal Exchequer, four pounds to the abbey for the rent of the mills (which the burgh had unsuccessfully disputed in the mid-fifteenth century) and five pounds to the friars. They also paid a number of salaries and fees to their own employees and office holders, including the prebends of the college kirk, the provost, bailies, ser-

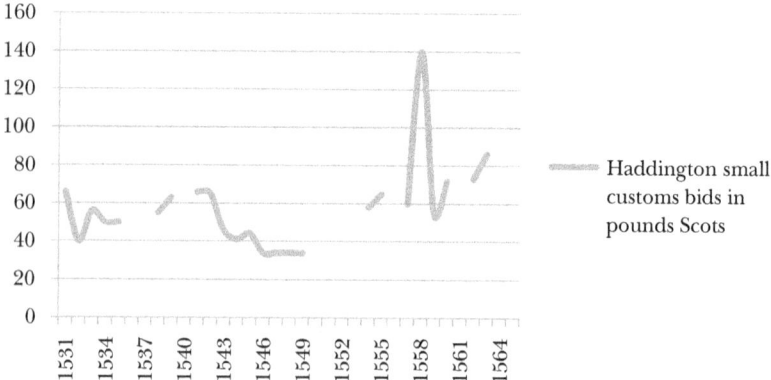

Figure 1.3 Haddington small customs bids

geants, wine tasters, the schoolmaster, clerk, hangman and clock keeper, among others. Additionally, pensions were awarded for good service: Mr William Brown, probably the former provost, received forty pounds for having secured some documents from the Earl of Bothwell. Robert Maitland received eight merks annually for saving the town's charters from the English. They also made payments to the Abbey of Dunfermline, the Hospital of Saint Lawrence and the Abbey of Haddington. Other expenses ranged from timber for the kirk to a payment to shipwrecked sailors to travel expenses for the provost. In 1555, the burgh's total expenses were £286, 18s and 2d. The gap between income and expenditures was therefore very tight and some years may have even gone into deficit, requiring loans or contributions from some of the burgesses.[59]

Sixteenth-century Haddington was a farming and exporting community whose prosperity was dependent on peace. Its relative position among Scottish burghs had been declining since the fourteenth century, partly because of the destruction of the wars, and partly because of the loss of the export trade. Like Dundee, by 1560 the boom of the 1530s was a distant memory; unlike Dundee, there was no recovery, even a modest one, in the export trade. By 1560, Haddington's customs receipts were 11 per cent of their 1540 level, compared with 44 per cent for Dundee. The bidding on the common mills and small customs demonstrates that though the agricultural economy was recovering, the burgesses were very much aware of the havoc that a new war could bring.

Stirling: History, Location, Economy

The town of Stirling occupies one of the key strategic points in Scotland, between the lowest crossing of the Forth and the castle which stood on the rock above. By the early twelve-century reign of Alexander I (1107–24), the fortification at the top of the hill seemed to have been established as one of the principle royal castles.[60] David I (1124–53) designated the settlement outside as a royal burgh and in 1140 also founded the Abbey of Cambuskenneth.[61] Originally the revenues from burgess fees had been granted to Dunfermline Abbey, but these were eventually taken over by the burgh council.[62] A charter of Alexander II from 1226 granted a market on Saturday, a trade monopoly over the surrounding region beginning at the meeting of the Forth and Avon and extending deep inland, and the establishment of a merchant guild.[63] Woolfells, hides and cloth were customed at Stirling though, like for Haddington, the actual exporting may have been done through Edinburgh and Leith, to the benefit of the merchants there.[64] Much of the town's economy likely revolved around supplying the residents of the castle, supporting the on-going construction work there, and serving the various noble residences in the town.

The town itself grew on the steep slope between the Forth river and the castle. At the bottom was the burgh gate which let out to the south and the common mill located on the Burgh Burn, a stream which flowed down to the Forth. Inside the town the High gait went up the hill and forked into the Baxter Wynd and the Back Row. The tolbooth and other buildings were built on what had been a large market place dividing the High gait from the Back Row. The parish church stood at the top of the Back Row at the intersection with the Castle Wynd.[65] At the top of the burgh, the Castle Wynd made its way past various noble lodgings. One part forked up to the castle, while Castle Hill descended towards the Bridge port and eventually the bridge, which lay below the town to the northeast.[66] In this long, narrow town, plots often contained thin houses fronting the street with a strip of backland extending to the burgh boundary. As the backlands became developed, often by craftsmen who needed extra workspace, alleys (closes) began to connect these areas with the main streets. Merchants and craftsmen also began to build in the marketplace, establishing permanent buildings where their market stalls had stood. Meanwhile, the church, tolbooth, noble residences and other large structures went up at the top end of the burgh, nearest the castle.[67] Around the edges of the burgh were the hospitals and friaries, the Franciscans to the southwest of the Back Row, the Dominicans at the bottom of the hill between the Friar Wynd and the Dirt Port Row. Spittal's hospital was built around 1540 just outside the town.[68]

Stirling's church was, and is, located at the top end of the burgh, above the market place and below the castle. Now known as the Holy Rude Church, it was originally simply known as the parish kirk. It was destroyed during the burning of the town by the Douglases in 1456 and was rebuilt over the following century. Construction took place in two phases: between 1456 and 1479 the townspeople rebuilt the western, nave end, and an initial, short tower, which were the parts of the structure maintained by the parishioners, followed in 1507–55 by the east, choir end of the church, which was the responsibility of Dunfermline Abbey, and by an extension to the tower.[69]

The town had been partially surrounded by stone walls since at least the mid-fifteenth century, a rarity in Scotland.[70] They ran down the southwest side of the burgh from the castle to the burn, from which a defensive ditch may have run down to the Forth.[71] Stirling's burgh council controlled most of the urban land within the defences and considerable tracts outside as well. The council also exercised jurisdiction, or at least influence, over some of the surrounding rural areas. In a taxation list compiled in the late 1540s, twenty-six inhabitants lived outside the actual burgh. A council order in 1550, requiring merchants to pay debts owed to fleshers, specified that the rule applied to fleshers on the land as well as in the burgh.

An inhabitant list taken in the late 1540s included 396 names. Using an estimate of 4.5 members in each household, this would give a rough population of between 1700–1800.[72] Stirling was usually around the eighth wealthiest Scottish burgh, normally paying a tax assessment that was about 10 per cent of Edinburgh's contribution, 20 per cent of Dundee's and 80 per cent of Haddington's, and roughly the same amount as Ayr, Montrose or Cupar. The burgh did slip during the 1550s, which is odd as it was not directly affected by the wars of the 1540s, and by 1557 the tax for the Queen's marriage, which saw Haddington's share distributed among the other burghs, saw Stirling in eleventh place. By 1563, however, Stirling was back up to seventh place.[73]

Stirling's pre-1540 exports were lower than Haddington's, and much lower than Dundee's. Like the rest of Scotland, Stirling's exports boomed in the late 1530s and early 1540s, with a height of eighty-five pounds in 1538–9, before decreasing to a low of thirteen pounds in 1543. In the late 1540s customs were auctioned off for just over forty pounds a year.[74] From this decline there was only slight, periodic, relief during the 1550s. Although affairs improved marginally during the 1560s, the fifty pounds received by the treasury annually was still less than the revenues collected in the 1530s. The principal exports were animal skins, though there were some cloth exports, indicating that there must have been some local weaving trade. Ten different crafts can be identified in Stirling's records, along with sixteen merchants. The records do not indicate that any one craft was particularly prominent – along with the expected bakers, fleshers and tailors there were websters, cordiners, hammermen, maltmen, masons, skinners and smiths. The unincorporated trades also appear at various points in the burgh records, which noted the oaths of ale sellers, candlemakers, grain sellers and hucksters to respect municipal regulations.[75]

The bids to collect the town's revenues also reveal some economic fluctuations. These rights, for the annual fairs, the small customs, the fishing on the Forth and others, were usually auctioned off in November. Though the records have significant gaps, the bids for the Forth fishings, the best run of records, shows a steady increase through the 1520s, from £10 in 1520 to £23.3 in 1546. Then in 1547 the council accepted a three-year bid at the lower price of £18 a year, the £54 being paid immediately and spent

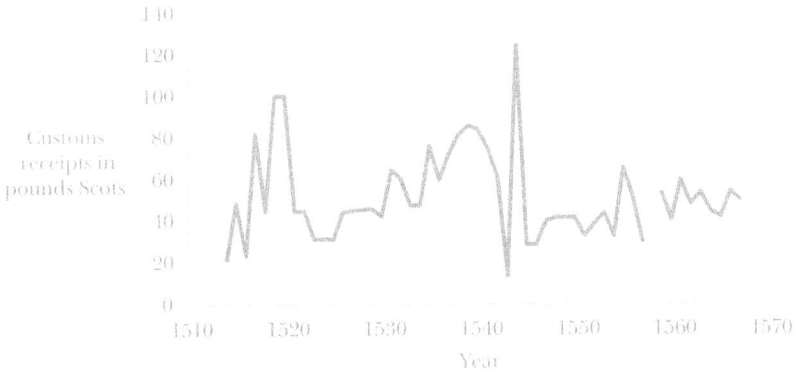

Figure 1.4 Stirling customs receipts[76]

on strengthening the town's walls.[77] By 1555, the bids had increased to £26.7, but in 1560 and 1561 declined to £16, further indicating that the Reformation coincided with, or caused, a time of economic uncertainty.

The few surviving testaments from Stirling show modest wealth. William Mentht died in 1546 with total assets of £30 12s 6d.[78] Robert Robe died in 1557 with iron, cloth hides and other goods worth £544, 14s 1d.[79] Duncan Ker had £172 worth of hides, skins, cash and small merchandise when he died in May 1559.[80] Five men, apparently all merchants, died in the late 1560s with slightly greater wealth. They mostly possessed cloth, dyes, cash in various currencies, and in the case of John Forester, grain. Forester died in 1563 with a total worth of £595, and was owed £488 and owed £381, indicating the complexity of his various business dealings.[81] John Wre, who died in Flanders in 1567, had a more diverse portfolio worth £334, including goods such as pepper and ginger. The wealthiest of the group, John Anderson, died in August 1568 with a total worth of £794 4s 4d.[82] While keeping in mind the small sample size, with an average wealth of £434 this group of burgesses was less well-off than the merchants in Haddington or Dundee.

The castle was a major presence above the town, and although it was outside the burgh's jurisdiction there was considerable overlap between the two communities. The council was sometimes called upon to help sort out disputes between local suppliers and clients in the castle or among the noble households which were occasionally resident in the town. One point of conflict was over the supply of bread; in February 1545, for example, the council relieved the bakers of any obligation to sell bread to Walter Scot, who had evidently been contracted to supply bread to Marie of Guise's household but was unable to bake the bread himself.[83] Scot was likely ill, for by July he was dead and Isabell Brouin, as his caution, was obliged to pay three pounds in lieu of the unsupplied bread.[84] Other suppliers also found themselves in burgh court, as in September 1546 when Alexander Sibbald, caution for David Sibbald, had to pay forty pounds, presumably for an undelivered order to Marie of Guise's household.[85] The council positioned themselves as mediators between the townspeople and the royal household. They ordered townspeople to first come to the council to resolve their billing disputes, rather than going directly to the Queen or other 'noble and greit men'.[86] There was sometimes conflict between the townspeople and noble retinues, as when Thomas Ryton supposedly assaulted a servant of the Earl of Argyle.[87] The council cooperated with the Queen Regent in disciplinary issues, as in March 1556 when they entered in their books her order that John Graham, who tried to steal from a French man, be banished for a year.[88] Relations between the townspeople and the castle were not always smooth, but the council consistently sought to maintain a measure of order and harmony.

Stirling, as a smaller, inland burgh, did not have a particularly well-developed export economy and local crafts were not especially important.

Like Haddington, the town was integrated into the surrounding countryside and several burgesses owned pieces of land or had business interests outside the burgh. The castle provided employment for workers and custom for merchants and craftsmen. Overall, though, it was poorer than Dundee or Haddington.

The three towns, despite their different population and economic profiles, can therefore demonstrate some common experiences. They all benefitted from the export boom of the late 1530s, experienced dramatic decline during the 1540s, and a modest recovery in the 1550s. The acceptance of lower, longer-term bids for burgh properties and rights in Stirling and Haddington in the 1540s, and again in the late 1550s, provides a snapshot of the burghers' shaky confidence in their medium-term future, and shows that they were as nervous about disruption in the late 1550s as they were during the wars of the Rough Wooing of the 1540s.

Notes

1. Gordon Jackson, 'The economy: Aberdeen and the sea', in *Aberdeen before 1800: A New History*, eds E. Patricia Dennison, David Ditchburn and Michael Lynch (East Linton, 2002), 159; Ian Blanchard, Elizabeth Gemmill, Nicholas Mayhew and Ian D. White, 'The Economy, Town and Country', in *Aberdeen before 1800*, 131; R. M. Spearman, 'Evidence of Early Industries', in *The Scottish Medieval Town*, eds Michael Lynch, Michael Spearman and Geoffrey Stell (Edinburgh, 1988).
2. E. Patricia Dennison and Grant G. Simpson, 'Scotland', in *The Cambridge Urban History of Britain*, vol. I, 600–1540, ed. D. M. Pallister (Cambridge, 2008), 729–30; T. M. Devine, 'Scotland', in *The Cambridge Urban History of Britain*, vol. II, 1540–1840, ed. Peter Clark (Cambridge, 2008), 154; Michael Lynch, 'The social and economic structure of the larger towns, 1450–1600', in *The Scottish Medieval Town*, eds Lynch, Spearman and Steele.
3. Devine, 'Scotland', 2:154.
4. David Perry, *Dundee Rediscovered: The Archeology of Dundee Reconsidered* (Perth, 2005), 8.
5. Perry, *Dundee Rediscovered*, 7–8.
6. Dennison Torrie, *Medieval Dundee*, 23; Blanchard *et al.*, 'The Economy, Town and Country', 133–4.
7. Dennison Torrie, *Medieval Dundee*, 25.
8. Dennison Torrie, *Medieval Dundee*, 25. See also DCA, CC1 no. 17.
9. Dennison Torrie, *Medieval Dundee*, 31; Blanchard *et al.*, 'The Economy, Town and Country', 131.
10. Martin Rorke, 'Scottish overseas trade 1275/86–1597,' Unpublished PhD thesis (University of Edinburgh, 2001), 76.
11. Rorke, 'Scottish overseas trade', 98, 110, 113–14, 121.
12. Alexander Stevenson, 'Trade with the South, 1070–1513', in *Scottish Medieval Towns*, edited by Lynch, Spearman and Steele, 197; Martin Rorke, 'English and Scottish Overseas Trade 1300–1600', *Economic History Review* 59 (2006): 269–70.

13. Proportionately, in 1535 Dundee paid 38.5 per cent of Edinburgh's contribution, slightly more than Aberdeen (102%), Perth (130%), and 380 per cent and 318 per cent respectively of Stirling and Haddington's contributions. By 1550, the ratio compared to Edinburgh had not changed much – but their contribution compared to the other towns increased, becoming almost twelve times Stirling's and eight times Haddington's. *Records of the Convention of Royal Burghs of Scotland, with extracts from other record relating to the affairs of the burghs of Scotland, 1295–1597* (Edinburgh, 1866): 514, 519, 526.
14. £337 9s 7d out of a total of £2666 13s 4d.
15. 304 crowns out of a total of 2454 crowns, or 12.4 per cent, raised for the peace embassy; *RCRBS*, 518, 519, 522–3.
16. Notes compiled for this study, while certainly not an exhaustive survey, indicated some 677 people who are likely to have been heads of households in 1550, after the devastation of plague and war. The figure is based only on information collected in my extracts of the burgh court records, protocol books, charters, and surviving records of various guilds and the Burgess Roll. Some individuals are also present in central government records, such as the *Accounts of the Lord High Treasurer* and *Privy Seal* records. A more systematic survey of these records would certainly reveal more individuals, and of course many individuals would not appear in any of these records. Individuals were identified as potential heads of households if they appear in the records as either being married or having children, or identified as having a trade or possessing (either through ownership or rent) a house of their own during the five years before or after 1550 (1545–55). Given an estimated figure of 4.5 people per household (a figure used by E. P. D. Torrie, 'The Guild in Fifteenth-century Dunfermline', in *The Scottish Medieval Town*, eds Lynch, Spearman and Steele, 246) this suggests a minimum population of 3046, with a true figure likely to be much higher. Alex J. Warden, *Burgh Laws of Dundee* (London, 1972), 8; Baxter, *Dundee and the Reformation*, 7; Maxwell, *Old Dundee*, 192.
17. These estimates come with their own uncertainties, of course. E. Patricia Dennison, David Ditchburn and Michael Lynch, 'Preface', in *Aberdeen before 1800*, eds Dennison, Ditchburn and Lynch, xxvi.
18. Rorke, 'Scottish overseas trade', 311.
19. Customs accounts were not always given in every 365 days. For this study every custom account has been divided by the number of days covered by the account, which was then multiplied by 365 to give a figure for the annual revenue. This method may lead to some distortion, where two years are part of one account (1523–4, for example), or where accounts may include two summers but only one winter (for example, 6 April 1524 to 7 July 1525). Nonetheless, a general trend should be apparent. Figure 1.1 is drawn from *The Exchequer Rolls of Scotland*, eds John Stuart, George Burnett and George Powell McNeill, 23 vols. (Edinburgh, 1878–1908), 14:50, 94–5, 97, 191, 264–5, 330, 371, 441–2; 15:64, 181, 268–9, 360, 440, 511; 16:39, 60, 149, 226–7, 364–5, 377–8; 17:58–9, 185–6, 303, 396, 460; 18:51, 69, 70, 85, 100, 173, 196–7, 222, 256, 282, 332; 19:4, 35–6, 83, 111, 172, 194–5, 221–2, 272–3, 291–2, 323.
20. National Records of Scotland (NRS) E71/12/1–5. Of course, this only includes goods which were customable, but, as Rorke points out, any trade which flourished became liable to customs. Rorke, 'English and Scottish Overseas Trade 1300–1600', 267.

21. Rorke, 'English and Scottish Overseas Trade 1300–1600', 275.
22. The term 'mariner' in the Dundee records often appears to mean ship captain – at any rate, many of these mariners were involved in business dealings.
23. NRS CC8/8/2/228; CC8/8/3/436; CC8/8/3/465; CC8/8/2/609; CC8/8/11/167; CC8/8/1/232; CC8/8/1/217; CC8/8/1/225; CC8/8/1/297; CC8/8/1/493; CC8/8/1/470; CC8/8/2/200; CC8/8/2/14; CC8/8/2/57; CC8/8/2/688; CC8/8/3/268; CC8/8/3/517.
24. DCA BHCB 1454–1524, f145v; Gibson and Smout indicate that Edinburgh wages for masons increased from 2s 6d in the 1530s to 3s or 4s in the 1560s. They also indicate that for urban day-labourers wages increased from 10d and over in the 1530s to 1s 6d in the 1560s – effectively doubling. The estimate of annual income here assumes less work or lower wages in winter. A. J. S. Gibson and T. C. Smout, *Prices, food and wages in Scotland 1550–1780* (Cambridge, 1995), 274, 278–85.
25. DCA Protocol Book 1518–34, t48/f30.
26. Perry, *Dundee Rediscovered*, 17.
27. Dennison Torrie, *Medieval Dundee*, 35.
28. Marshall, *Ruin and Restoration*, 7.
29. James H. Jamieson, 'John Knox and East Lothian,' *Transactions of the East Lothian Antiquarian and Field Naturalist Society* 3 (1934–8), 69.
30. National Library of Scotland. John Wood, *Map of Haddington and Nungait* (Edinburgh, 1819), http://maps.nls.uk/towns/detail.cfm?id=354, accessed 19 July 2012.
31. Haddington was one of Scotland's top five exporters of wool in the fifteenth century, although its relative position and actual exports declined over the course of the century. Stevenson, 'Trade with the South', 197.
32. *Haddington: Royal Burgh; A History and Guide* (East Linton, 1997), 4, 6; Forbes Gray, *Short History*, 2; Lynch, *Scotland: A New History*, 87, 112.
33. Richard Fawcett, *The Architecture of the Scottish Medieval Church* (New Haven, 2011), 305.
34. Stevenson, 'Trade with the South', 193; Rorke, 'English and Scottish Overseas Trade', 271. See also figure 1.3.
35. Rorke, 'Scottish overseas trade', 106–8.
36. Forbes Gray, *Short History*, 85–6.
37. NRS E82/27/1 f17.
38. Stevenson, 'Trade with the South', 193.
39. Forbes Gray, *Short History*, 6–8; *RCRBS*, 514.
40. Rorke, 'Scottish overseas trade', 312.
41. *RCRBS*, 525.
42. *RCRBS*, 514, 522, 528.
43. NRS CC8/8/1/149.
44. NRS CC8/8/2/212.
45. HAD/2/1/2/1 Burgh Minutes 1554–80, f12b.
46. HAD/4/2/3/1 Haddington Court Book 1555–60, f185.
47. HAD/4/2/3/1, f33.
48. Forbes Gray, *Short History*, 106.
49. *Exchequer*, 16:58, 147, 228, 359–60, 373, 479; 17:45–6, 59–60, 179, 299, 393, 459; 18:46, 67, 146, 197, 228, 281, 334; 19:2, 33, 84, 113, 222, 275, 291.
50. E. Patricia Dennison, Gordon DesBrisay and H. Lesley Diack, 'Health in the two towns', in *Aberdeen before 1800*, eds Dennison, Ditchburn and Lynch.

51. NRS CC8/8/1/393; HAD/4/6/73 Treasurer's Account 1558, f11.
52. NRS CC8/8/1/420.
53. HAD/4/6/5, f81.
54. HAD/2/1/2/1, f12v.
55. Henry M. Paton, 'Haddington Records: Books of the Common Good', in *Transactions of the East Lothian Antiquarian and Field Naturalist Society* VII (1958), 48.
56. Prior to 1552, the small customs changed hands from year to year, although some of the same men – Martin Wolson or Wilson, John Rycht, George Symson – reappear on multiple occasions. After 1552, the customs were taken by the same men several years running: John Ayton from 1552 to 1555, Thomas Spottiswode in 1556 and 1557, Alexander Thomas from 1560 to 1565. HAD/4/6/5, f10v, 23, 38, 47v, 66v, 98, 147, 147v, 163v, 177v, 192v, 205, 254, 274; HAD/2/1/2/1, f13v, 4, 5, 15, 19, 22v, 25v, 26, 29, 31, 34v, 39, 43v.
57. HAD/2/1/2/1, f15.
58. Paton, 'Books of the Common Good', 48.
59. Paton, 'Books of the Common Good', 48–50; for 1555, 50–1; for 1557–8, 52–4; for 1558, 55–7; for 1559, 58.
60. Mair, *Stirling*, 18.
61. *Charters and other Documents relating to the Royal Burgh of Stirling* A.D. *1124–1705* (Glasgow, 1884), 1–2, 4–5; Mair, *Stirling*, 24.
62. R. C. Fox, 'Stirling 1550–1700: the morphology and functions of a pre-industrial Scottish burgh', in *Scottish Urban History*, George Gordon and Brian Dicks, eds (Aberdeen, 1983), 63.
63. Mair, *Stirling*, 19–20; Rorke, 'Scottish overseas trade', 58, 106–8; *Charters . . . Stirling*, 6–9, 9–10.
64. For comparisons to other burghs, see Rorke, 'Scottish overseas trade', 496–7, 514–15, 555–6, 567–8.
65. Mair, *Stirling*, 67.
66. Fox, 'Stirling 1550–1700', 55; Alexander MacDonald, *Plan of the Royal Burgh of Stirling showing its condition and surroundings, about the year 1700*, National Library of Scotland, https://maps.nls.uk/view/[6144]. See also Mair, *Stirling*, 66–8 and maps, 65, 101.
67. Fox, 'Stirling 1550–1700', 57–8.
68. Fox, 'Stirling 1550–1700', 63.
69. Mair, *Stirling*, 74; Fawcett, *Scottish Medieval Church*, 298–9; Richard Fawcett, *Stirling Castle* (Edinburgh, 1995), 115.
70. E. Patricia Dennison, *The Evolution of Scotland's Towns: Creation, Growth and Fragmentation* (Edinburgh, 2018), 25.
71. Mair, *Stirling*, 69, 101.
72. Twenty-six are listed as burgesses living either to land or landward.
73. *RCRBS*, 514, 519, 521, 522, 525–6, 528.
74. The actual bids were sixty-nine pounds, from which various payments had to be deducted.
75. Stirling Council Archives (thereafter SCA) Stirling Burgh Court Book (thereafter SCBC) 1519–30 21/6/1529; SCA SBCB 1544–50 2/12/1546; 07/11/1547.
76. *Exchequer*, 14:57, 92, 189, 215, 261, 331, 345, 441, 453; 15:179, 195, 267, 283, 359, 375, 436, 453, 509, 539; 16:41, 147, 167, 291, 343, 358, 376, 388, 479; 17:46, 62, 180, 298, 392, 457; 18:45, 66, 85–6, 103, 149, 170, 196, 223, 257, 280, 333; 19:38, 83, 112, 170–1, 193, 219, 292, 324, 368.

77. SCA SBCB 1544–50 26/10/1547.
78. NRS CC6/5/1/319.
79. NRS CC8/8/1/198.
80. NRS CC8/8/1/93.
81. NRS CC8/8/1/72–4.
82. NRS CC8/8/1/160; NRS CC8/8/1/140; NRS CC8/8/1/390.
83. *Extracts from the Records of the Royal Burgh of Stirling*, ed. Robert Renwick (Glasgow, 1887–9) 1:39–40. Unless there is a discrepancy, citations will refer to the published Council Extracts rather than the originals in SCA.
84. SCA SBCB 1544–50 12/7/1546.
85. *Extracts . . . Stirling*, 44.
86. SCA SBCB 1544–50 28/2/1547.
87. SCA SBCB 1554–7 17/2/1556.
88. *Extracts . . . Stirling*, 67.

CHAPTER TWO

Governance in the Burghs

Work by urban historians has generally shown that the sixteenth and seventeenth centuries were a period of increasing oligarchy throughout Europe.[1] In Scotland this notion is particularly prominent in the work of Michael Lynch and Patricia E. Dennison.[2] Superficially, this appears to have been the case in our towns as well. The three burghs shared the same formal political structure, with three or four magistrates (bailies) governing day-to-day, supported by a council which made decisions about spending and disposing of burgh assets. Dundee and Stirling, and eventually Haddington, were controlled at any given moment by at most two dozen men who frequently served on council or as burgh officers; these men, however, depended on the cooperation and support of the townspeople, many of whom served in more minor roles. Haddington at the beginning of our period operated a more collective government, with ad hoc community meetings rather than a standing council making decisions. In 1543, however, Haddington adopted a form of government similar to the two other towns. This chapter will argue that despite a tendency towards a possibly unintentional oligarchy, there was still a meaningful degree of broader participation in and support for municipal governments. All burgesses were still able to participate in some aspect of governance, especially by serving on assizes or inquests or simply by being present in burgh court. This participation ensured that during crises, such as plague or the Reformation, in all three towns the councils had the backing of many of the inhabitants. The town councils thus governed with the support of the wider population, and usually succeeded in avoiding factional divisions, working instead to preserve communal harmony.

Haddington pre-1543: Late Medieval Communal Government

Haddington's mid-sixteenth century transition from a communal style of government to a council-based one demonstrates that more narrow administrations could still preserve civic harmony and were even preferred in times of disturbance. At the beginning of the century, it was assemblies of townspeople who made important decisions in Haddington, which was typical of the late medieval Scottish burgh.[3] During the crisis of the 1540s, however, the burgesses switched to a system similar to Dundee and Stirling's in which a stable group of less than two dozen men dominated municipal affairs. Though this inevitably reduced the extent of popular participation, the council did not lose any legitimacy, and indeed many townspeople may have welcomed the changes. This change demonstrates that narrowing the membership of the ruling group was not necessarily seen as creating an oligarchy of the wealthy, but as a welcome reduction in burdensome obligations and a practical move to establish a nimbler government in a time of crisis. The pressure and incentives which had to be invoked to fill council positions shows that many townspeople did not desire more involvement in local government.

The burgh court was administered by three bailies who were elected at Michaelmas in early October, but their role was largely limited to the procedural oversight of criminal and civil cases and property transactions. There was no standing town council; about eight council meetings would be held throughout the year, though it appears that they were simply composed of the burgesses who showed up. An assembly of the community – anywhere from two dozen to two hundred men – was sometimes gathered to make decisions regarding matters of interest to the whole burgh, such as appointments to lifetime positions.[4] It was assizes that played a significant role in Haddington's government. Assizes and inquests were minor judicial bodies, similar to the modern jury, drawn from the burghers. About a dozen times a year, at irregular intervals, an assize would be empanelled, made up of between eleven and twenty-five men. Often the assize was drawn from the men who happened to attend court that day; a man who passed judgment on a case might a short time later be pleading himself. Assizes ruled on cases brought before them, often of minor physical violence; sometimes they laid out the punishment, sometimes they left it up to the bailies.[5] Inquests were organised like assizes but dealt with much more limited questions, usually inheritances. Haddington assizes also ruled on broader burgh affairs, which, as we will see, was not the case in Dundee and Stirling. The assizes and council meetings had similar jurisdictions. Both dealt with craft affairs, burgh administration, regulation of burgesses, the behaviour of inhabitants and the spending of burgh money, an overlap which was common in the smaller burghs.[6] Haddington's informal procedures left a lot of power in the hands of men who happened to be in court on any given day. This could lead to occasional controversy (often involving a prominent but disruptive maltman named John Ayton), but the fact that it did not occur more frequently is a testament to the level of consensus in the community. Indeed, the assize itself could be seen as a symbol of burgh solidarity; as Ian Willock argued for Aberdeen, assizes represented 'what was by now coming to be regarded as the power from which the bailies derived their authority, no longer the king, but the community of the burgh'.[7] Civic unity was likely enhanced by the practice of leaving decisions open to any burgess who turned up at court.

In 1543, at the beginning of what would be several years of war with England, Haddington's governing structures suddenly changed. For the first time on record the burghers elected a provost, William Brown of

Stolencleuth, a local laird, who was presumably chosen to provide military leadership during the war. At the same time the Haddingtonians standardised the rest of their municipal government. Councils became smaller – between nine and thirteen men – and councillors were chosen for the year and often served consecutive terms, a tendency that increased over the course of the 1550s, drastically reducing the number of different men who participated in decision-making. The distinction between the role of assizes and council also became more fixed, a significant shift in how power was exercised. After 1543, assizes no longer ruled on matters of public concern but were restricted to rendering verdicts in criminal cases, ranging from insulting words to murder, as in Dundee and Stirling. The frequency of the meetings of the assize declined dramatically as well, from an average of eleven times a year between 1532 and 1542 to 0.5 times a year between 1560 and 1565. After 1543, therefore, the council took sole charge of burgh administration, leaving the assizes with criminal cases.[8] Overnight the townspeople of Haddington concentrated local power in a handful of men.

With the election of a standing council and a decline in the frequency and scope of the assize meetings came a corresponding decrease in the number of individuals who participated in burgh affairs. During the 1530s, 310 different men sat on at least one assize; in the 1550s, only 123 did so. One hundred and twenty-six men participated in council meetings at least once during the 1530s; during the 1550s, only thirty-two men became councillors. The number who served in senior positions – provost, bailie or treasurer – was roughly the same, eighteen to twenty-one. In all, 331 men were involved in some form of burgh government during the 1530s, dropping to just 142 during the 1550s.[9] Though this reduction in civic participation may seem undemocratic to modern eyes, it is possible that the Haddingtonians saw it as the reduction of an unrewarding civic duty. For many, holding office was a burden rather than a privilege. Across Europe civic office-holding was often limited to the wealthy because only they could afford to devote their time to tasks that were poorly paid, or not paid at all.[10] In the 1530s, there were cases of Haddingtonians who were extremely reluctant to serve as bailie or treasurer.[11] Men often refused or accepted only on condition that they be spared future appointments, as Philip Gibson demanded in 1534, when he agreed to be bailie on condition that he not be asked again for three years.[12] Eventually, incentives had to be offered for these positions. In 1542 each bailie was to receive three pounds, initially 'for this year only', though in 1546 John Ayton and William Gibson were each given ten pounds, and payments were still being made routinely in the 1550s.[13] These incentives could cause some squabbling, as in 1554 when James Oliphant refused to be provost because the previous provost had received a larger fee.[14]

Some men went directly to the crown seeking exemptions; the one granted to Philip Gibson (who seemed especially reluctant to participate) under the Privy Seal emphasised that he was 'heavily vexed with infirmity of the gravell and other sickness and also that is corpolent of person so that he might not goodlie endure travel without great danger of his life'.[15] Men who were only called upon to serve on council or assizes may not have had the same bargaining position as those asked to serve as bailies or treasurers but that does not mean that they were any less burdened by having to spend hours or even days sitting on council or assize meetings.[16] They may simply have not been interested in the small matters being pursued by the assizes.[17] The narrowing of the range of men who served on the town council, therefore, may have been about reducing unwanted burdens as much as it was about concentrating power in an oligarchy. As Rigby and Ewan point out, in towns with slowing economies, like Haddington, the establishment of oligarchies may have been a conscious attempt to attract and commit the richer townspeople to participate in town government.[18] If these men were oligarchs, they were very reluctant ones.

In the 1550s there were no recorded complaints from burgesses excluded from participation in the civic government. The smaller government may also have been a response to the crises; during the Reformation, the rate of participation would shrink even further, suggesting a preference for nimbler government. On the other hand, at least some people thought that burgh offices in Haddington were worth having. Controversies surrounded the elections of John Ayton and John Thomson to the position of bailie; Ayton was unable to hold onto the office after being accused of violating the burgh's anti-plague measures in December 1545, and Thomson was accused of bribing his way into office in 1552.[19] For the most part, however, the change in municipal government went unremarked upon. Haddington's experience demonstrates that reducing public participation in municipal affairs was not necessarily an elite power-grab, and that a narrower ruling group could command respect just as well as a wider one.

Government by Council: Dundee, Stirling, Haddington post-1543

From the start of our period, Dundee and Stirling and several other Scottish burghs followed the form of the Parliamentary Act of 1469 which mandated a standing council that elected its successors every October, a process Haddington adopted after 1543.[20] The municipal administration consisted of the provost, three or four bailies, fifteen to twenty councillors (nine to thirteen in Haddington), a treasurer, a variable number of craft representatives, kirkmaster and, in Dundee and Stirling, a dean of Guild. In Dundee two men served as Masters of the Almshouse, a position which was usually held for several consecutive years. Regulations were enforced by four or five sergeants or officers and two or three wine, beer and meat tasters.[21]

The provost was the leading figure in the burgh administration, responsible for the town's external relations and military leadership, and was the last resort enforcer of order within the burgh. During some periods the position went through a high turnover, but the towns were also happy to establish long-term relationships with men who suited them; in Dundee James Haliburton was elected to consecutive terms from 1550 on. Haliburton had distinguished himself in fighting against the English and was granted a pension of £500 from Mary of Guise.[22] As he was rarely recorded as making unilateral decisions it is difficult to tell what his actual influence was, though on several occasions decisions were postponed until he could be present. He did not frequently attend meetings: between April 1557 and April 1558 he attended five times out of the 112 court days. When present, he did exercise his authority – leaning on the bakers to obey the bread price regulations, for example.[23] He also attended parliaments, and signed the commission to negotiate the marriage of Mary Stewart in 1557 as one of six representatives of the burghs.[24] As provost, Haliburton appeared to suit the Dundonians perfectly, exercising his authority when necessary and representing the town on the national political stage, but otherwise not interfering with more routine burgh business.

In Stirling, the provosts were also recruited from local lairds. Through the 1540s and 1550s, John Forester of Craginelt served most frequently. Forester was part of the following of the sixth Lord Erskine, hereditary captain of Stirling Castle.[25] Stirling's provostship would turn over at the Reformation as in 1559–60 James Stirling of Keir became provost, a position which he held for three years. Alexander Forester of Garden then took over for a year in 1563, before the provostship reverted to James Stirling and then back to John Forester. While Stirling's involvement starts suddenly at the time of the Reformation, his quick rise to local dominance was not unprecedented. He appears to have been a wealthier and more prominent figure than John Forester, coming from a family that had lands in the region since the twelfth century, with holdings in Stirlingshire and Perthshire. He was often in the company of William Chisholm, Bishop of Dunblane, and took Jane Chisholm, likely one of William's several illegitimate children, as his second wife.[26]

In Haddington, William Brown served as provost for at least two years after his first appointment in 1543. He remained active in council and assizes after his term as provost. Through the 1550s, after Brown's tenure had ended, the post was rotated each year among different townsmen, none of whom had any obvious military experience or political prominence outside the burgh. Though the Haddingtonians kept the position of provost once the immediate crisis of the 1540s ended, they did not appear to attach much special significance to it or use it to build connections with local lairds.

The majority of burgh government was carried out by the bailies, council, assizes and inquests. The bailies held court to handle the day-to-day administration of burgh affairs and oversee cases relating to debts, unpaid rents, property transfers and business deals as well as 'troublance' (minor assaults and physical disturbances) and slander.[27] In Dundee they met several times a week, roughly weekly in Haddington and irregularly in Stirling, sometimes no more than once every two weeks. The council generally approved matters involving spending or renting and regulating burgh property (including the kirk).[28] The number of recorded full council meetings in Dundee varied annually, from four in 1521 to sixteen in 1551, though this variation might simply be due to the scribe's habits; often we only know that the councillors were present at the burgh court because a decision was recorded under some variation of the formula 'provost, bailies, council and community'. The term community refers to an unknown number of inhabitants present, although the extent of their participation cannot be established from the existing records. In Haddington and Stirling, the frequency of meetings per year ranged from three to eleven.

The importance of assizes varied in time and place. Assizes ruled on guilt or innocence in criminal cases or trials of undesirable people, and on violations of economic regulations, debt disputes and arguments between neighbours. Inquests generally restricted themselves to matters of inheritance.[29] There were no set rules about the relationship between town councils and assizes or inquests: in Dundee up to one-quarter of assize members might have been councillors, or none.[30] The frequency of assizes and inquests declined over the period studied; out of four sampled years for Dundee (1522, 1551, 1556, 1562) there were twenty-two in ten months in 1522, and only six or seven in each of the later years, a decline matched by the diminished role of assizes in Haddington after 1543. The use of assizes and inquests in Stirling was inconsistent during the mid-sixteenth century. In earlier years the assizes did draw on a wide representation of Stirling's community. Of the 332 male householders registered in the late 1540s, 144 (43%) sat on at least one assize or inquest. As in the other burghs, the 1560s saw a decrease in larger community participation and more power concentrated in the bailies and court with fewer assizes and inquests.

Assizes held in Stirling had the right to administer capital punishment. For serious capital cases the assize sat with the provost acting as sheriff depute (Lord Erskine being the sheriff proper until 1542) and appointed a dempster and judiciary sergeant for the occasion, as indicated by an assize in October 1525 which found that two men, Robert Murray and James Mar, had stolen a quantity of clothes, as well as a buckler, and so were sentenced to death. For such an important case the membership of the assize was of a higher than usual status, with six landed men, including one knight, and seven men from the burgh.[31] After 1542 the sheriffdom came into the council's jurisdiction.[32]

The penalties varied; for disturbances between neighbours, even violent ones where blood was drawn, a frequent punishment was to appear before the high altar, bareheaded and barefoot, ask the victim for forgiveness (or agree to be peaceful, if both parties were guilty) and offer a candle to the high altar.³³ Sometimes the offender had to pay compensation or the cost of medical treatment for the victim.³⁴ Property crimes were treated more harshly than violence. For theft, the usual penalty was to be whipped through the town and then banished, often on pain of death. Death sentences were rare, but one of the court's options.³⁵ Some cases were referred to the sheriff's court which was in the town's jurisdiction after 1542.³⁶ Many minor thieves (pikers) were also caught. Punishments could be gruesome – John Fisher who stole food and clothes was to be nailed by the ear to Stirling's tron (town weigh beam), have his ear cut off, branded on the cheek, whipped through the town and banished.³⁷ Stirling's magistrates also cooperated with landed men in administering punishments, as when council placed one Robert Dougal in the stocks on behalf of a nearby laird.³⁸

The burgh court also looked after public health matters, a responsibility shared by both bailies and members of inquests and assizes. A constant preoccupation in Stirling was preventing the spread of leprosy. The court actively sought out cases, the bailies with 'certain of nebouris' visiting those who an inquest suspected of being infected.³⁹ Christine Hunter, for example, was forbidden from attending the market until 'men of understanding' evaluated her.⁴⁰ Serious cases were exiled to a sort of leper house, 'ane desert without the burgh'.⁴¹ An inquest in Stirling also took measures against the spread of plague, in April 1545 ordering that all poor be gathered together and any strangers expelled.⁴² This concern for disease detection also extended to animals, and in 1555 the inquest reported on infected horses.⁴³ The detection and containment of disease was an ongoing task which the whole community participated in, coordinated by the burgh court.

Ballies and sometimes councils decided who would be admitted to the burgess roll and therefore eligible to participate in these bodies. The easiest way was to be the first son of a burgess, in which case there was a nominal fee – a contribution of spice and wine in Haddington, 26d in Stirling. Others, not so lucky in their birthrights, had to pay more: 40s for a second son in Haddington or four pounds for those with no family connection at all, thirteen shillings and four pence plus wax in Stirling for burgesship and up to five pounds to join the merchant guild there, and ten pounds for burgh and guild in Dundee.⁴⁴ Occasionally, someone would be made a burgess or guild member for free as a favour to an office holder or someone else to whom the council was grateful (or in debt!). Periodically the councils would complain about the bailies violating these practices, though it is unclear if the problem was that the bailies were demanding too much money or too little.⁴⁵ Burgesship was sometimes offered on condition that the recipient come and dwell in the burgh, an attempt to increase economic activity in the town. Sometimes burgess status was extended to women, as in October 1554 when Katherine Brown of Stirling was made burgess as heir to her late father.⁴⁶

Council Membership

Towns normally maintained a high degree of stability in council membership. The group of men who dominated the town council by serving repeatedly numbered about twenty to twenty-five in Dundee, and slightly fewer in other towns.[47] Membership in this group demanded consistent application; while not every member in Dundee served every year, very few returned to council after an absence of more than three years. Each year during the 1550s in Dundee, for example, the four new bailies were drawn from the old councillors, although one or two of the bailies might continue for two, though never three, consecutive years. The previous year's bailies were reappointed to the council. Normally, half to two-thirds of the councillors would repeat from one year to the next, so that, combined with the previous year's bailies serving ex-officio, two-thirds of each year's council would be drawn from the previous year's.[48] Some men served for only brief periods; it could be that they were found unfit or unwilling for future service, or that an effort was made every year to include one or two men who were not normally members of the ruling group.[49] Men did not drift in and out of council service. Out of a sample of twenty men who held a Haddington town council position at least three times between 1530 and 1565, fourteen had a political career which spanned less than fifteen years, although five men had a career of over twenty years.[50] Their periods of service were quite busy, with fifteen serving at least every second year.[51] For most, serving on the town council would mean an intense period of service, though not one that would last a lifetime – that was only for a few, either exceptionally devoted or ambitious.

Many of the councillors were merchants, though it was not exclusively a mercantile body. Of the seventeen men who served multiple terms on Dundee's council in the 1520s it is likely that at least eleven were merchants, as were ten of the twenty-six especially active members in the 1550s. Most of these merchants were involved in shipping goods back and forth to Flanders and France, principally Dieppe. At least four councillors were craftsmen or professionals, with bakers in particular being well-represented and serving as bailie and almshouse master. Dundee's vicar, John Barry, also sat as a councillor during the years 1522–4.[52] One other member of the council, Harbart Gledstanis, was a notary active at least from the mid-1540s. In 1551–2 he acted as clerk for the burgh court, and by 1557 was a councillor in his own right.[53]

Some of the councillors were well-off, but they were not necessarily the wealthiest men in the burgh. Of the group of twenty-six most active councillors in Dundee during the 1550s, at least ten also owned land or urban rental properties. This group was also well-placed to bid on the rentals of burgh revenue sources, such as the windmill and weighhouse, and lend money to cover the town's expenses.[54] James Lovell, merchant, could afford to lend approximately £133 (200 merks) to the sons of John Erskine of Dun while in France although he would be refunded by his fellow councillor George Wishart.[55] George Lovell, merchant, promised £400 to the Queen Regent in 1559, although he may have saved this expense with a £120 loan to the Lords of the Congregation later that year.[56] William Carmichael provided one-third of the £500 lent to the council to meet the 'present expenses' – the War of the Congregation – in 1559. On the other hand, the two other men who contributed did not serve as councillors at all.[57]

In Haddington, while the men who served more often on council were wealthier, there were enough exceptions to demonstrate that the burgh government had not simply fallen into the hands of its most well-off citizens. Out of the eighteen men who served on council three or more times from 1550 on, ten men paid at least one of the four financial contributions collected from the richer inhabitants during the 1550s, making a combined payment of £96 4s. Five men who served as councillors once or twice made a contribution of £22 4s 4d, twelve men who served on assizes but not councils or inquests made contributions totaling £31 11s 8d, and three people who did not serve in any way, including one woman, made a combined contribution of five pounds. Assuming that the burden was assessed reasonably fairly, the figures demonstrate that men who served more frequently on council were, per capita, the wealthiest, and that those who served on assizes were wealthier than those who did not. On the other hand, some wealthy people served very infrequently. Fifteen men who served only on assizes or not at all paid more than the twenty-three men who sat on council once or twice. Eight of the men who served most frequently on council paid no financial contributions at all.

Being wealthy created the opportunity for greater involvement in burgh politics, but there was no direct correlation – less wealthy men could serve frequently, and some well-off individuals avoided significant service altogether. Given how often people complained about holding office, or tried to avoid it, perhaps not serving was also a perk of the rich. By comparison, Willock points out that in Selkirk, between December 1534 and October 1535 thirty-seven out of ninety taxpayers sat on at least one assize, along with twenty-seven non-taxpayers, though some of these may have been the adult sons of taxpaying householders. The more frequent assize members had been or would become bailies. From this, he concludes that 'most assizes were drawn from the ranks of the more substantial citizens and their adult sons, but that not all such persons felt this obligation'.[58] When it came to involvement in burgh affairs, it was helpful to be well-off, but it was more important to be willing.

In Stirling as well it is likely that wealth made it easier to serve on council. The records there show that council members were drawn geographically and socially from different parts of burgh society within and without the physical town. Of the forty-five men who served three terms or more between 1544 and 1565, at least thirteen were merchants and thirteen craftsmen. Six were likely landed gentry from outside the burgh, while

Henry Livingston, twice a provost and once a councillor, was from Falkirk. Others, such as William Bell of Spittal, may have been townsmen who owned some land and used it as a title. Two of the men were land burgesses who lived outside the town boundary. Those who lived within the town were mostly from the Back Row quarter, though there were representatives from all quarters of the burgh.[59]

Prominent families were unsurprisingly well-represented on the councils, though it is only in Stirling that one family, the Foresters, came to form a dominant faction. Among the most involved councillors in Dundee, three of the town's prominent families – the Haliburtons, Scrimgeours, Wedderburns – each had one representative, the Lovells had two, and the Rolloks four.[60] Alexander Haliburton, who served almost continuously throughout the 1550s, was Provost James Haliburton's brother and likely represented him. In both the 1520s and 1550s, the most extensive, or most active, of these families were the Rolloks. The repetition of names within families, both immediate and extended, makes it difficult to distinguish individuals,[61] but at least five different members of the Rolloks served in various posts, though none of them served as bailie during the important years between 1550 and 1563.[62] These five individuals appear to have been descended from one man, George Rollok (I), who was treasurer of Dundee in 1520 and 1523.

Lairds were a significant presence on Stirling's council to an extent that they were not in Dundee or Haddington. As in other towns, Stirling's provosts were almost always elected from nearby lairds, who rarely had other council involvement. What was unusual was that by the mid-1550s landed men also made up a significant number of councillors. These landed men did not all necessarily belong to a single faction, and may well have been recruited as part of internal conflicts within the town. During the 1550s there was a dispute between Henry Livingston of Falkirk and John Forester of Craginelt, while the craftsmen meanwhile were apparently working to have 'some great man to landwart' elected. To end the controversies, in September 1556 Mary of Guise ordered the burghers to elect a townsman as provost.[63] Nonetheless, it appears that they chose John Forester of Craginelt.[64] Possibly as an element of this dispute, James Watson and William Norwell were accused of mutilating Craginelt, and subsequently acquitted by an assize. The two men then complained to Guise that they had been threatened and harassed by the friends and supporters of the laird. Marie directed Lord Erskine, the castellan, to investigate, and the bailies reported to him that they knew of no trouble. Summoned before an assize, both Watson and Norwell also testified that they had no complaints. They were wise to do so, as Craginelt was likely a client of Erskine's, appearing as a witness on several of his charters. Clearly some resolution had occurred behind the scenes, either agreeably or under duress. The case does show that Craginelt, and likely other lairds and nobles, possessed retinues able to apply direct pressure on burgh affairs.[65] To secure his position,

Forester recruited kin to take up council posts in 1556–7. Five Foresters would also serve between 1560 and 1565, four as bailie or provost.

In Dundee, George Rollok (II), who was born in 1498 and probably died in 1562, had a career that may be representative of the burgh's prominent men. George (II) inherited eight acres of land in Dudhop from his father, who died before 1556, and owned at least two other properties and had rights to half the tithes from Kynreiche. He also participated in the overseas trade, being one of ten merchants who had goods on a ship called the Angel.[66] He served as kirkmaster from an unknown date until 1551 and as a councillor throughout the early 1550s. He was called upon to be an auditor of the almshouse in 1560, and was able to obtain the benefice of Our Lady Altar for his son, George Rollok (III), paying five merks annually, until such a time as George (III) was fit to serve in person. Patrick Lyon appears to have been the central government's representative in Dundee. A member of the guild since 1544 and a councillor until 1553, Lyon benefitted from central government patronage, receiving various grants of non-entries and escheated goods.[67] During the war, it was he who received messages sent to the town from the governor.[68] He was customer of the burgh from 1550 until his death in January 1565.[69] Lyon was also targeted for his links to the central government, as his home was singled out by Henry Durham, who burnt it in 1549 in company with the English soldiers.[70]

The councils in our three towns also included craft representatives, and wealthier craftsmen – especially bakers and maltmen – might serve in their own right. The deacons occasionally served in more senior positions as well; for example, William Dorrocht, the baxters' deacon, served as Master of Kirkwork in 1555–6. The deacons rotated more frequently than the councillors, especially in Stirling. It may have been that, as with council service in Haddington, in a small town like Stirling being a craft deacon was a burden as much as a privilege, and therefore was an office that was shared. Serving enthusiastically or not, Stirling's craftsmen created tension on the council as they sought greater representation against the resistance of the merchants. In October 1545 the craftsmen gained four representatives on the council and were allowed to appoint one of the three bailies.[71] The crafts nonetheless selected eight deacons, but the council overrode four of the craft choices and appointed instead men 'able to serve the touin, depriving the ignorantis chosin be the craftis thairto'.[72] Little more is recorded about the conflict, perhaps as other crises focused attention elsewhere, though it indicates that relations between the council and at least some of the crafts were not harmonious, with the craftsmen perhaps being deliberately provocative. The next month, David Graham, Deacon of Smiths, brought a complaint against two men for disobeying his and the provost's commands, as not everyone appreciated the conjunction of burgh and craft authority.[73] By 1561 a more equal balance was developed as a new council committee was appointed as part of the council, with four merchants and four craftsmen.

The small groups of men who dominated burgh governments, as far as we can tell, were relatively wealthy, though not all the wealthy men participated in council. Merchants dominated, though there does not appear to have been a rigid boundary between merchants, craftsmen and professionals. The burghs' prominent families were represented in the ruling group in Dundee, and more so in Stirling, although they did not dominate the bailie posts. It appears that no particular interest monopolised town government in Dundee and Haddington, which surely helped the councils retain legitimacy and authority and helped the burgh maintain civic unity and harmony. Factions were more evident in Stirling's government, eventually requiring the intervention of Mary of Guise.

Guilds and Crafts

Merchant and craft guilds were also a significant part of municipal government. The merchant guilds in Dundee and Stirling overlapped with the town councils, while the craft guilds, also answerable to the town councils, were slightly more autonomous. The affairs of the merchants in Dundee were governed by the Holy Blood Guild which had been founded sometime between 1165 and 1214.[74] The powers of the Dean of Guild and various statutes relating to the merchant guild were formally laid out in a charter of 1515, and an arbitrated agreement sorting out the respective rights and responsibilities of the merchants and craftsmen was made in 1527. Under this agreement, the Dean of Guild was to exercise the powers he already held (likely collecting an export duty called Holy Blood Silver, regulating guild membership, and supervising and collecting fees from the market booths or stalls), but was not permitted to introduce any innovations to the detriment of the craftsmen. Craftsmen were allowed to appeal to the provost and bailies if the fines levied by their crafts were too severe. The collector of the guild duties and each craft deacon were to appear annually before the provost, bailies and other auditors to present their accounts.[75] In Stirling, the burgh court oversaw the functioning of the guild, though the members sometimes had to complain to ensure that membership was enforced.[76] Haddington did not have a merchant's guild until the seventeenth century.

The burgh council, as part of its responsibilities for the economic functioning of the burgh, supervised both the incorporated crafts and other trades, such as ale sellers or brewsters. In January 1520 for example, the deacon of Stirling's tailors had to request permission from the provost and bailies to collect money for the construction and adornment of their altar in the parish church; the council ordered them to find out what privileges the tailors of Perth had, and return for further consultation.[77] The councils, especially Stirling, were willing to be firm with the crafts, and in 1548 the websters had their privileges briefly revoked.[78] The next year, Stirling's council was in a more supportive mood and backed up the deacon of websters, ordering any person, wherever they lived, to pay a weekly penny if they practised weaving.[79] The brewsters also required regulation, and sixty-five of them were obliged to agree to keep the statues under pain of a five pound fine. With the exception of one maltman, all were women; twenty-two of them were identified as wives, an indication of the number of two-income households in Scottish burghs.[80] While the majority of the council may have been merchants, they did not always side against the crafts, and in January 1550 ordered that any merchant who owed money to a flesher (butcher) pay five pounds to the town and five pounds to the Holy Blood. Similarly, in Haddington, the council intervened in the dispute between the crafts at the Corpus Christi procession, and ordered the smith craft to pay its debt for wax.[81] While conflicts with most crafts were rare in Dundee, there were frequent disputes with the bakers over the price of bread and the use of the common mill. In 1557 Provost Haliburton made one of his rare interventions, requiring the bakers to appear before him to swear an oath to obey bread prices.[82] Council and crafts could also cooperate for the public good, as in 1529 when Stirling's council allowed the fleshers to bait a bull, creating some public entertainment.[83] There is no evidence of systemic conflict throughout the burghs though there were certainly tensions between crafts and councils in Stirling.[84]

Councils and Townspeople

Some friction between the council and the inhabitants could be expected. There were occasional incidents of men complaining about court rulings; for example, David Spanky, who was frequently in trouble for breaking various of Dundee's regulations, in July 1551 said 'there was no justice done in the tolbooth', for which he was sentenced to pay 10s to the almshouse and ask the bailies for forgiveness.[85] In Haddington in June 1535, a butcher named Robert Barnis was charged to appear before the bailies in the tolbooth to answer for not paying a fine. He spoke 'evil and malicious words' to the messengers, telling the bailies to wait until he came. The bailies then decided to go to him, accompanied by 'diverse neighbours', whereupon Robert threatened them with a halberd (battle-axe). The neighbours finally convinced him to go to the tolbooth, where he drew a knife on one of the bailies and would have stabbed him had he not been restrained. As Robert was a repeat offender, who had also tried to rouse the crafts against the bailies on Midsummer' Eve when the crafts put on plays, the bailies ordered him banished from the town and his house demolished. He may not have appreciated this application of burgh laws, but it is worth noting that the bailies were accompanied by a crowd of inhabitants, who volunteered for this risky (though doubtlessly exciting) mission, and that the craftsmen did not rally to his appeal. The weight of numbers and public opinion was on the bailies' side.

Similar incidents took place in the other towns. In Stirling in September 1546, an inquest found Thomas Carnis guilty of laying violent hands on a bailie and ordered him to ask the bailie for forgiveness, surrender his sword and dagger and pay 40s to the towns' work.[86] In 1549, the provost and bailies ruled that Margaret Tulloh was to be expelled for insulting the burgh's officers.[87] On the other hand Haddington's sergeants, who carried out the bailies' orders, caused their own share of disruption, as in 1533 when they were ordered to 'be meek in their office and use no evil words to no good man's wife'.[88]

The burgh courts also had to deal with jurisdictional issues, and in 1555 for example, Walter Steton of Tucht opposed Katherine Gray's attempt to move their dispute from the ecclesiastical court of the official of Lothian to Stirling's burgh court.[89] Plaintiffs occasionally requested that cases be transferred from Haddington to neighbouring courts, especially those of the Abbot of Newbottle and the Abbess of Haddington. These transfers were sometimes permitted, but the inhabitants were also suspicious of other courts. In a 1535 case, Patrick Eddington requested that his case be transferred back to Haddington's bailies if he did not get a satisfactory verdict in the court of the Abbot of Newbottle.[90] Some types of cases that appeared before the burgh courts, such as cases of slander and defamation, or arguments over tithes or benefices, could also be brought before ecclesiastical courts. Despite the potential for overlap, there seem to have been generally little conflict between the two court systems.[91]

Conclusion

The councillors needed and obtained the consent and cooperation of the burghers to function, as did town councillors throughout Europe. Urban government throughout medieval and early modern Europe was based on the idea that town rulers had an obligation to at least consult and preferably obtain the consent of the community (usually the burgesses), which in Scotland was referred to as 'the community of the burgh', although this consultation was certainly not equivalent to modern democratic rule.[92] Dundee and Stirling did not appear to hold large assemblies, as occasionally happened in Haddington, but council minutes often refer to the presence of 'the community', though we cannot be sure who was actually present.[93] More concretely, the two dozen or so men who dominated the town council were supplemented by a large number of men who served infrequently either as town councillors, enforcers of regulations or on assizes or inquests. During the 1550s in Dundee, in addition to the twenty-six frequent councillors, approximately fifty men served occasionally on council, a further 300 served on inquests and assizes, and many others took their turn enforcing burgh regulations as inspectors of bread, meat, ale and other substances.[94] In the smaller town of Haddington during the same period, 142 men served on councils, assizes or inquests, while in Stirling 181 male householders served on these bodies. If this broader group had not agreed with the decisions made by the core group of frequent councillors, then burgh politics would have been much more fraught than the evidence suggests. The support and active participation of the larger community was essential to the two dozen, or fewer, men who assumed a disproportionate share of responsibility for burgh government.

In Dundee and Haddington, burgh politics seemed generally harmonious, with no evidence of serious disputes or factional competition. Stirling's politics however were much more fluid, with factions developing around various lairds and more tensions around the position of the crafts. The frequent presence of the royal household in the castle also led to more attention from the central government than might have been the case in the other burghs. The activities of the municipal government or its role in burgh life do not seem, however, to have been widely disrupted by these disputes.

The councils were largely made up of merchants and wealthy craftsmen who increasingly found the duties of burgh administration concentrated in their hands, a development, that initially at least, they did not necessarily greet with enthusiasm, except possibly in Stirling. Indeed, narrowing council membership may have been partly intended to secure the participation of the wealthier burgesses. While the three towns may appear to have been dominated by these new oligarchies, the councillors still depended on the participation of the wider community to enforce their decisions and cooperate in the process of maintaining orderly and harmonious civic life.[95] The following chapters demonstrate that their responsibilities also included overseeing their town's religious worship and clergy, and they were also the mechanism through which the religious alteration of the Reformation would be implemented. Like other decisions about civic affairs, town councils required the cooperation and agreement of the broader community to implement decisions about these changes.

Notes

1. Lynch, 'The social and economic structure of the larger towns', 261–2, 264. For a more nuanced view, see S. H. Rigby and Elizabeth Ewan, 'Government, power and authority 1300–1540', in *The Cambridge Urban History*, vol. I, ed. D. M. Pallister (Cambridge, 2008); Ian A. Archer, 'Politics and government 1540–1700', in *The Cambridge Urban History*, vol. II, ed. P. Clark; Christopher R. Friedrichs, *The Early Modern City 1450–1750* (Harlow, 1995), 50.
2. Michael Lynch, 'Introduction: Scottish Towns 1500–1700', in *The Early Modern Town in Scotland*, ed. Michael Lynch (London, 1987); Lynch, 'The social and economic structure of the larger towns'; Dennison, *The Evolution of Scotland's Towns*; Patricia E. Dennison, 'Power to the people? The myth of the medieval burgh community', in *Scottish Power Centres from the Early Middle Ages to the Twentieth Century*, eds Sally Foster, Allan Macinnes and Ranald MacInnes (Glasgow, 1998).

3. Elizabeth Ewan, 'The community of the burgh in the fourteenth century', in *Scottish Medieval Towns*, eds Lynch *et al.*, 231; Ian Douglas Willock, *The Origins and Development of the Jury in Scotland* (Edinburgh, 1966), 62–8; Rigby and Ewan, 'Government, power and authority', 1:306.
4. HAD/4/6/5, f40, 264.
5. HAD/4/6/5, f17v, f94v.
6. HAD/4/6/5, f28, 29, 57v, 75v, f90, 90v, f94, 106, 116v, 118v, 122v, 136, 175v; Willock, *Jury in Scotland*, 62, 67.
7. Willock, *Jury in Scotland*, 61.
8. As examples: HAD/4/2/3/1, f43, 71; HAD/2/1/2/1, 20v, 22, 11.
9. Information for these numbers come from HAD/4/6/5; HAD/4/2/3/1.
10. Christopher R. Friedrichs, *Urban Politics in Early Modern Europe* (London, 2000), 18–19.
11. HAD/4/6/5, f90v; f121.
12. The position of treasurer was especially difficult because the holder had to take on personal financial risk. In 1542–3, Thomas Poynton complained that 'he had obeyed ye town when he had accepted the office of treasurer on him' but the bailies had discharged the feuars (of the mills and possibly small customs) from paying him. Smarting from this incident he refused to serve as treasurer again, for in April the council ordered him to take up the post of treasurer on pain of losing his freedom. By July a compromise had been worked out where he agreed to serve as kirkmaster. The problems were endemic to the position, however, and in 1544–5, John Auchar, treasurer, protested that he should not be blamed for money given out at the command of the provost or bailies or for the customars failing to enter their accounts. HAD/4/6/5, f54, 79, 108, 121, 180, 183, 205; HAD/2/1/2/1, f6.
13. HAD/4/6/5, f213v.
14. Willock, *Jury in Scotland*, 162–3; HAD/4/6/5, f276.
15. HAD/4/6/5, f207; see also Willock, *Jury in Scotland*, 162–3.
16. Willock, *Jury in Scotland*, 148.
17. Willock, *Jury in Scotland*, 72.
18. Rigby and Ewan, 'Government, power and authority', 1:312; see also Friedrichs, *The Early Modern City*, 42.
19. HAD/4/6/5, f214, 234.
20. *The Records of the Parliaments of Scotland to 1707*, eds K. M. Brown *et al.* (St Andrews, 2007–12), 1469/19 (accessed: 10 October 2012). See also Lynch, *Edinburgh*, 3, 15; Verschuur, *Politics or Religion?*, 38.
21. In the 1520s these posts tended to go to councillors or former bailies, but during the 1550s these posts as tasters went to men who were not councillors, or who served only for one term.
22. *Register of Privy Council of Scotland* (first series), eds John Hill Burton and David Masson (Edinburgh, 1877), 1:501.
23. DCA BHCB 1555–8, f152.
24. *Accounts of the Lord High Treasurer of Scotland [TA]*, eds Thomas Dickson *et al.* (Edinburgh, 1877), 9:475; *RPS*, 1558/11/21, A1560/8/7 (accessed 19 December 2012).
25. *Registrum Magni Sigilli Regum Scotorum: The Register of the Great Seal of Scotland [RGS]* (Edinburgh, 1886), 4:256, 274–5, 479, 487.

26. *RGS*, 4:3, 26–7, 28, 97–8, 192, 248, 265, 798; William Fraser, *The Stirlings of Keir* (Edinburgh, 1858), 39; Leslie J. Macfarlane, 'Chisholm, William (1493/4–1564), bishop of Dunblane', *Oxford Dictionary of National Biography* (2004) (accessed 5 January 2022).
27. For example: DCA BHCB 1454–1524, f68v, 115v; DCA BHCB 1550–4, f70, f81v; DCA BHCB 1561–2, f71v, f75.
28. DCA Head Court Laws 1550–1612, f2, 29; for a full discussion of the different categories of burgh court meetings, see Willock, *Jury in Scotland*, 53–61.
29. DCA BHCB 1550–4, f94; DCA BHCB 1555–8, f57; SCA SBCB 1519–30 16/10/1525, 9/12/1527.
30. DCA BHCB 1550–4, f94.
31. SCA SBCB 1519–30 21/10/1525, 16/10/1525; see also SCA SBCB 1544–50 30/8/1548; Fraser, *The Stirlings of Keir*, xlvii; my thanks to Michael Wasser for clarifying this point.
32. SCA SBCB 1544–50 19/12/1544.
33. HAD/4/6/5, f17v, f54v.
34. HAD/4/6/5, f129.
35. HAD/4/6/5, f66, 77v.
36. HAD/4/6/5, f130. On 19 November 1543 a combined sheriff and burgh court was held; HAD/4/6/5, f187v.
37. SCA SBCB 1544–50 17/12/1546.
38. SCA SBCB 1519–30 23/7/1527.
39. *Extracts . . . Stirling*, 37.
40. *Extracts . . . Stirling*, 39.
41. *Extracts . . . Stirling*, 33.
42. *Extracts . . . Stirling*, 40.
43. SCA SBCB 1554–7 14/10/1555.
44. SCA SBCB 1519–30 13/02/1520; DCA BHCB 1550–4, t758/f295b; HAD/4/6/5, f102.
45. HAD/4/6/5, f102; DCA BHCB 1550–4, f2/t1, f8/t16, t714/f278b.
46. SCA SBCB 1554–7 1/10/1554.
47. In Edinburgh it seems that the active ruling group included about 35–40 men. Lynch, *Edinburgh*, 15.
48. Between 1522 and 1524, nineteen men served multiple terms in Dundee, of whom ten served for all three consecutive years of 1522, 1523 and 1524. Only five men served a single term in this period. Between 1550 and 1563 twenty-nine served multiple, consecutive terms, while fourteen men served only one term (of course, some of those men may have served other terms in the years before 1550 or after 1563). A comparatively small group of six men served multiple but non-consecutive terms during this period.
49. DCA BHCB 1454–1524, f47, 105, 158b; DCA BHCB 1550–4, f2, 91, 188, 252, 340v; DCA BHCB 1555–8, f2, 71v, 144v; DCA BHCB 1558–61, f124v; DCA BHCB 1561–2, f3. The following discussion of council membership is based on these references.
50. Because of the difficulties of variant spellings, and of several men sharing a name, it is impossible to be certain that all the references have been matched to the correct individual. When a name disappears from the records for ten years or more and then reappears, I assumed that the second appearance refers to a new generation. While my assumptions may

be incorrect in some cases, I am confident that the vast majority of entries are correct.
51. This calculation is slightly complicated by the number of years with missing records.
52. *Abstract of Inventory of Charters and Other Writings belonging to the Corporation of Weavers of the Royal Burgh of Dundee [Dundee Weavers Charters]* (Dundee, 1881), 10.
53. DCA Laws, f26; *Registrum secreti sigilli regum Scotorum. The register of the Privy Seal of Scotland [Privy Seal]*, ed. Matthew Livingston. Vol. 3, *1542–1548*, eds David Hay Fleming and James Beveridge (Edinburgh, 1908–), 157; DCA BHCB 1550–4, f41/t100; DCA Laws, f3.
54. DCA BHCB 1550–4, f334; DCA BHCB 1558–61, f74.
55. DCA BHCB 1550–4, f284.
56. DCA BHCB 1558–61, 70v; DCA BHCB 1561–2, f12v.
57. The others being David Ramsay, merchant, and James Fletcher. DCA BHCB 1558–61, f73v.
58. Willock, *Jury in Scotland*, 69–70. See also Lynch, *Edinburgh*, 16.
59. Eight from the Back Row, two in the Mary Wynd, three in the North quarter and two in the South.
60. According to Friedrich, across Europe close relatives were usually banned from participating in government simultaneously. Friedrichs, *Urban Politics*, 18.
61. For this reason, when more than three individuals share a name, they will be distinguished, where possible, by number.
62. George Rollok Sr (II), James Rollok Sr, George Rollok Jr (III), James Rollok Jr and Richard Rollok. Individuals designated as 'senior' and 'junior' or 'elder' and 'younger' were not necessarily father and son, but possibly uncle and nephew or even some degree of cousin.
63. SCA SBCB 1554–7 25/9/1556.
64. SCA SBCB 1554–7 9/10/1556. Another Craginelt also served on council that year.
65. SCA SBCB 1554–7 9/12/1555; *RGS*, 4:256, 487.
66. DCA BHCB 1558–61, f137v.
67. In May 1548, Patrick Lyon and his wife Elizabeth Wedderburn received the gift of nonentries of land of Inverquheich in Perth, following the death of David Earl of Crawfurd and Dame Isabella Lundy, his wife. *Privy Seal*, 3:442; 8 August 1548 he received the goods of Alexander Thornetoun in the Hayistoun, who stayed away from the army at Haddington; on 25 August 1548 he received the goods of John Chesholme in Lunderteris, who was escheated for the slaughter of Thomas Williamson in Litiltoun. *Privy Seal*, 3:459, 462.
68. *TA*, 9:192.
69. *Exchequer*, 18:70; 19:291–2.
70. DCA BHCB 1561–2, f75.
71. SCA SBCB 1544–50 16/10/1545.
72. *Extracts . . . Stirling*, 276–7.
73. SCA SBCB 1544–50 27/11/1545.
74. Dennison Torrie, *Medieval Dundee*, 34.
75. Warden, *Burgh Laws*, 97–101.
76. SBCB 1519–30 13/2/1520; *Extracts . . . Stirling*, 2.
77. *Extracts . . . Stirling*, 1.
78. SCA SBCB 1544–50 19/3/1548.

79. SCA SBCB 1544–50 5/7/1549.
80. SCA SBCB 1544–50 nd.
81. HAD/4/6/5, f129–29v.
82. DCA BHCB 1555–8, f152.
83. *Extracts . . . Stirling*, 37.
84. See also Lynch, *Edinburgh*, 49–50.
85. DCA BHCB 1550–4, f81.
86. SCA SBCB 1544–50 17/9/1546.
87. SCA SBCB 1544–50 10/12/1549.
88. HAD/4/6/5, f44v.
89. SCA SBCB 1554–7 17/1/1555, 20/1/1555.
90. HAD/4/6/5, f66.
91. Simon Ollivant, *The Court of the Official in Pre-Reformation Scotland* (Edinburgh, 1982), 65, 76, 136–7.
92. Rigby and Ewan, 'Government, power and authority', 1:305–8; Friedrichs, *The Early Modern City*, 48.
93. See Willock, *Jury in Scotland*, 54.
94. The problem of different individuals having the same name makes an accurate count difficult, so it is possible that these numbers are slight over-estimates.
95. Even the largest of Scotland's burghs 'was too small in its size and its thinking to admit permanent divisions within it'. Lynch, *Edinburgh*, 6, 22.

CHAPTER THREE

The Civic Church

Alongside the bustle of craft work, business deals, household chores and neighbourly gossip, daily life in Scotland's pre-Reformation towns also featured almost continuous religious services. In the parish church, matins, high mass and vespers were daily events, alongside countless obit and anniversary masses. Other services took place in chapels, almshouses and friary churches. Occasional preaching and processions occurred both inside the parish church and outside in open public spaces. A constant series of rituals – baptisms, weddings, funerals, and occasional excommunications and admonishments – required the attention of clergy and lay people alike. This vigorous thread of urban religious life, described in the work of Audrey-Beth Fitch and Mairi Cowan, poses a problem for explanations of the cause of the Reformation.[1] Discussion of the late medieval Scottish church often focuses on the alleged corruption of the prelates and the lay commendators who controlled the church hierarchy and religious institutions, themes originally developed by Gordon Donaldson and Ian Cowan.[2] Cowan's research has demonstrated that up to 85 per cent of Scottish parishes had their revenues appropriated by the religious institutions and even laypeople to which they were assigned, leaving only inadequate funds for the vicars and church buildings. Subsequent historians have softened this view of the Scottish medieval church as having been fatally weakened by this system of appropriation, without wholly rejecting it either. Alec Ryrie has held that what seems like corruption was actually a close cooperation between the upper ranks of the national and ecclesiastical classes. In his view the weakness of the church was at the lower level, where it failed 'to maintain a broad defensive front in the parishes'.[3] This line of reasoning holds that such a vast diversion of revenues left the laity bereft of religious care. Most recently, Bess Rhodes has pointed out the positive effects these revenues had on the burgh of St Andrews, where they were re-invested in the university and ecclesiastical administration.[4]

This system of revenue appropriation may have been damaging for some parishes, and at times frustrating to the townspeople of Dundee, Haddington and Stirling, but it did not inhibit the development of a vigorous and extensive religious practice in many Scottish towns. The religious activities encountered by Scotland's townspeople on a daily basis were administered not by bishops and abbots but by their own burgh governments with funding both from their own revenues and, when necessary, the institutions to which the ecclesiastical revenues had been diverted.

While Ian Cowan argued that the church had a much larger role in the lives of the laity than the laity had in the church, in the towns at least it was the laity who supervised the physical churches and most of the local clergy. In Stirling, Haddington, Dundee and likely all Scottish burghs, the community, through the town council and burgh court, exercised authority over a variety of religious affairs, from the physical maintenance of church buildings to backing candidates for the parish vicarage to hiring chaplains and supervising their morals.[5] They used this authority to maximise the number of properly performed divine services in the towns. The Scottish townspeople's control and efforts constitute a form of 'civic religion'.

The concept of civic religion has been explored by a group of scholars working on continental towns, whose studies frequently focus on the two aspects for which religious devotion was used: to create a more sacred town, and to lend a sacred status to the municipal government.[6] It is the first aspect – the extent to which Scottish townspeople, through their institutions of communal government, sought to increase the quantity and quality of religious worship as a public good – which demonstrates the importance of religion to the burghers and their autonomy in shaping its forms. As André Vauchez has observed, 'divine worship, because of the repercussions that it could have on the destiny of the community, ended up by being considered as a public service, just as vital as the organization of victuals or of defence.'[7] While towns throughout Europe exercised considerable local control over religious worship, in Scotland the distance from the royal and ecclesiastical hierarchies (none of the towns studied here were the seat of a bishop), the lack of well-developed guilds and structure of a single parish in each town meant that Scottish town councils had a particularly extensive degree of control over religious affairs. Working with the secular chaplains and the friars, the provost, bailies, councillors, assize members and craftsmen of the town sought to increase, as far as possible, the daily and weekly cycles of the divine offices and to ensure their proper performance. In Scottish towns, the round of worship had several goals: getting the burgesses into heaven, or at least diminishing their time in purgatory, gaining God's favour and blessings to help the people in their daily lives, inspiring and encouraging the devotion of the townspeople and creating civic unity and harmony.[8] Civic religion in Haddington, Dundee and Stirling and other towns throughout Scotland may therefore be defined as the actions of the townspeople, often through the town council, which promoted and maintained religious devotion to benefit the inhabitants by bringing divine favour to individuals and the community.

The Church Buildings

The practice of late medieval Christianity was physical and tangible, and constructing, repairing and regulating the required spaces took up much of the efforts of burgh governments. Medieval Scottish towns hosted a variety of religious institutions, including chapels, friaries, hospitals and almshouses and they often had close relationships with nearby abbeys. All these institutions and their clergy had some links with the townspeople. It was, however, the secular chaplains at the parish church who performed the bulk of the daily and weekly cycles of divine offices. It was these services that were most heavily promoted and closely scrutinised by the townspeople. Before they could be properly held, towns had to invest a great deal of their time and money into building and maintaining a proper space. The parish church was thus the principal focus of the townspeople's efforts concerning civic religion.[9] In all three towns the inhabitants initiated the rebuilding of their parish church during the fifteenth century. Initially the townspeople maintained the nave while the religious institutions who owned the revenue of the parish were responsible for the choir. The towns then gradually took responsibility for the choir as well, after sometimes difficult negotiations with the various institutions, in order to construct buildings that met their needs for extensive worship cycles and which reflected their pride in their communities.

Churches Worthy of the Towns

Haddington's principal religious institutions were St Mary's parish church, the Franciscan friary, the nearby Abbey of Haddington and a handful of small chapels and almshouses. The parish of St Mary's had been granted to the priory of St Andrews by King David I in 1139, and ever after the priors had been responsible for the upkeep of the choir and high altar while the burghers were responsible for the nave. In practice, the burghers did most of the work, sending a bill to the prior and occasionally even being paid. In 1462 for example, when the burgh began rebuilding the church, the Prior of St Andrews agreed to contribute £100 a year for five years.[10] At other times some lobbying was required, as in February 1562 when a delegation went to Edinburgh to meet with the then-prior, Lord James Stewart, and succeeded in obtaining 600 merks for repairs.[11]

The major work rebuilding the church following the fourteenth-century razing of the town demonstrated the town's status and the devotion of its inhabitants. The rebuilt church was one of the largest parish churches in Scotland, perhaps intended to rival St Giles' in Edinburgh. The west front was particularly imposing, a feature usually seen in monastic churches and cathedrals but rarely in burgh churches. According to Richard Fawcett's survey of Scottish church architecture, there is nothing comparable to it in Scotland or England, and it was likely inspired by churches in the Low Countries, particularly the Dominican church in Bruges.[12] Perhaps it served as a demonstration of the townspeople's claims to cosmopolitanism. The relief of a scallop shell, the symbol of the famous pilgrimage to Santiago de Compostela, inside the church suggests that the church attracted pilgrims but that may simply have been hopeful thinking by its builders.[13] Inside the church, at least twenty-one altars were founded.[14] St Mary's became a collegiate church around 1539. The purpose of collegiate status, which was often sought after by towns, was to organise the priests who sang in the choir (choristers) and chaplains of the various altars in the church into a common body where they would be better supervised to ensure that they were properly performing their appointed functions.[15] In this way the burghs could enjoy a comprehensive worship cycle similar to those held in the cathedrals.[16] The inhabitants of Haddington cared a great deal about their church, building it as big as they could, and well into the sixteenth century they ensured that its status kept it in the front rank of Scottish parish churches.

Stirling hosted a parish church, Dominican and Franciscan friaries, at least four independent chapels in or just outside the town, and two hospitals. The Chapel Royal in Stirling castle and the Abbey of Cambuskenneth were prominent neighbouring institutions whose clergy also played an occasional role in burgh affairs. The parish church eventually became known as the Church of the Holy Rude, but in the sixteenth century was usually just known as the parish church, although maintenance was called the 'Rud work'. The parish was first established by David I in 1129; the monarchs held the right to appoint the vicar, though its revenues were granted to the Abbey of Dunfermline.[17] It was rebuilt at least twice in the fifteenth century, once after a fire in 1414 and again after the sacking of the town by the Douglases in 1455. The town took responsibility for the rebuilding project, and in 1507 the Abbot of Dunfermline agreed to contribute £200 to the costs of the second phase, which included the choir, high altar and ornaments. The abbey also contributed an annual rent of 40s for the maintenance of the choir.[18] The completed church included at least twelve altars.[19] The internal workings of the church were likely very similar to collegiate churches, though with the castle looming over the town there was little point in trying to make it a striking local feature on the scale of the churches in Haddington and Dundee.

Dundee, as a larger town than Haddington or Stirling, had a more extensive religious establishment. It was unusual among Scottish towns in having two parish churches, along with Franciscan, Dominican, and possibly Trinitarian friaries, a Franciscan nunnery, a hospital and a variety of smaller chapels. There was no abbey immediately adjacent to the town, although Balmerino and especially Lindores on the other side of the Tay estuary had important roles in the burgh's affairs. The parish of Dundee was likely established in the eleventh century, before the creation of the diocese of St Andrews or even the official founding of a burgh at Dundee, which would explain why it was part of the older diocese of Brechin.[20] Both parish churches, St Mary's and St Clement's, were extant by the thirteenth century but by the late Middle Ages the larger St Mary's had become the burgh's most important church.[21] The Bishop of Brechin had granted the revenues of the parish to the Abbey of Lindores, along with the right to appoint the schoolmaster.[22]

The arrangement by which the abbot and convent of Lindores held possession of the parish of St Mary's was not a happy one. As in Haddington, the burghers wanted to expand their parish church into a building which reflected their perceived status and contained space for multiple altars, a construction project the abbey was reluctant to subsidise. The resulting 'very great discord, contention, and altercation' were finally resolved in 1443 when the town and abbey agreed that the 'burgesses, council and community' of Dundee would take over responsibility for the construction, maintenance and furnishings of the choir, which normally was the abbey's responsibility, receiving in return five merks of annual rents.[23] By 1560, this had increased to ten merks, out of the 300 merks that the abbey expected to collect in tithes each year.[24] The abbey did make a substantial contribution of £500 to the rebuilding of the parish church in the early 1550s.[25] Lindores still retained the right to appoint the vicar, although the town council's support would be important when disputes occurred between the abbey and the Bishop of Brechin.[26] Once they took over the apparently decayed choir, the Dundonians roofed it with lead and constructed a new aisle and a northern transept.[27] The completed church was one of the largest medieval churches in Scotland, as long as Arbroath Abbey or Glasgow Cathedral and wider than any other Scottish church.[28] Meanwhile the much smaller St Clement's declined in importance.[29]

As in Stirling and Haddington, the arrangement left the Dundonians free to fulfil their ambitions for an expanded civic religion. The expansion created space for new altars, which allowed for more masses, and the town council held the final authority over the altars' establishment and maintenance. In 1492 for example, not long after the extension of the north aisle was complete, the weaver (Brabner) craft appeared before council and asked for permission to establish a chaplainry to St Severus the Bishop beside the altar of Magnus the Martyr, itself recently established by Robert and Thomas Seres in the north aisle. The weavers asked for, and received, certification that Robert and Thomas would not remove their chaplainry, an indication of the cooperation necessary to sustain some of these altars.[30] Other crafts and private patrons would do the same, though securing enough funding for the upkeep and chaplains for the altars was a constant struggle. The establishment of new altars would continue into the 1520s, and eventually there would be at least thirty, and perhaps as many as forty-eight, altars or chaplainries in St Mary's.[31] Of the altars whose pre-1560 patrons can be identified, four belonged to a trade or guild,[32] five to lay families[33] and four belonged to the burgh.[34] St Clement's church seems to have hosted only one altar, that of Our Lady.

The burghs all succeeded in obtaining the permission and financing to build the churches that they wanted even though the Priory of St Andrews and the abbeys of Dunfermline and Lindores controlled many of the parish revenues. The institutions took some nagging and contentious negotiations were sometimes required, but they eventually gave the towns what they asked for. The diversion of revenues did not ultimately impede the development of civic churches in Scottish towns. The church hierarchy's disinterest in the parish churches in fact gave more autonomy to the towns to build and operate the churches as they saw fit.

Churches: Maintenance and Repair

Once the initial construction was complete, the churches continued to require attention. In the three towns the physical upkeep of the kirk was the responsibility of the kirkmaster, who collected annuals and supervised repairs.[35] This kirkmaster could be a cleric – in the early 1530s Haddington's was sir[36] Patrick Mauchlin – though it was normally a layman.[37] Like the treasurer and almshouse master, the same man held the position for several consecutive years. Repairs were frequent. The never-ending nature of the work was demonstrated by Stirling's lifetime contract with the mason John Couttis, made in 1529, which promised him fifty merks a year. Shortly thereafter, Couttis was granted burgess status for 'thankful service to be done by him to the rud work'.[38] Following the occupations of 1548–9, when Haddington's church steeple was used as an artillery platform and Dundee's church was burned, even more repairs were required.[39] Despite the notion, most recently advanced by Ryrie, that the wartime damage to the churches led to the decay of Catholic worship, burgh councils vigorously set about restoring their churches, Catholic ornamentation and all.[40] In Dundee for example, on 31 December 1551, at a meeting in Provost Haliburton's lodging, the bailies, councillors and deacons of craft agreed to 'certain acts to be made touching the common well of this burgh and the repairing and decorating of their mother kirk',[41] while in 1556 Stirling ordered the Dean of Guild to collect together the funds of the Holy Blood altar into a purse, to be spent 'at the sight of the council' on new ornaments.[42]

Some of these repairs were funded directly by the town council, others by the fees and annual rents which had been donated to the parish church over the years.[43] Often these included the fees paid by new burgesses, and the kirkmasters could sometimes request that particular men be made burgesses.[44] In Haddington, the kirkmaster might also get money directly from the feuars who had rented the town's properties and revenues, while Dundee in 1550 directed fines towards maintaining the church.[45] In Stirling, a long series of ordinances and decisions made it clear that the council saw funding for the church as a priority. In February 1520 for example, they decreed that fines for violating marketplace rules were to go to the Rood work, and in 1550 a dispute among the hammermen was resolved with an agreement that future offences would be punished by a fine of 40s to the Rood work and 20s to the craft.[46] Even in normal times the large buildings were expensive to maintain, and town councils were constantly working to ensure that the necessary funds were available.

The kirkmasters, for their part, were continually warned against spending without the council's permission, and as they were responsible for such an important physical and symbolic feature, they faced constant interference and second guessing.[47] In Stirling in October 1524, a year and half after the council approved spending forty pounds on timber for the kirk, it was necessary to record an agreement that the provost and bailies would defend Duncan Paterson, the Dean of Guild (acting as kirkmaster) in the performance of his duties and that they would refund his expenses made 'within the kirk or choir in any necessary or needful things or reformation of God's service, for the honour of God and the well of the town'. The provost and bailies also agreed not to let any chaplain leave his post without the Dean's permission. Paterson for his part agreed not to interfere with the filling of lamps or lighting of candles in the church.[48] James Scrimgeour, kirkmaster in Dundee, faced similar frustrations. In April 1551 the burgh brought lumber for the church.[49] This timber however was not used right away, for in November 1551 Scrimgeour resigned his post as kirkmaster, and in doing so insisted that the new kirkmaster receive the timber 'lying in the kirk that the same be put to profit of the said kirk' declining responsibility if any of the wood was stolen or taken away.[50] The councils, meanwhile, could be picky about repairs and replacements. In September 1556, Dundee's council rejected the bell that James Rollok junior had bought in Flanders and authorised James Forester, the kirkmaster, to exchange it for a bigger one.[51]

The burghs also owned many of the ornaments, furnishings and documents in the church.[52] Dundee's agreement with Lindores specified that the council was also responsible for the ritual equipment of the church. Stirling's council received an annual of 40s from the Abbey of Dunfermline to look after the equipment. When sir James Darrow, a priest in Stirling, left a bequest that a chalice be made for the Rood loft, it was the council that supervised the arrangements.[53] During crises it was the council that took measures to protect their ornaments, often spreading them around for safekeeping. In May 1545, Haddington's provost, bailies and council handed six chalices to the priests whose altars they belonged to, with various burghers being sureties that the chalices would be returned.[54] The council's concerns for furnishing the churches continued up to and after the Reformation. In March 1563, Haddington's council authorised John Swynton to buy a basin 'for administration of baptism', and to arrange for the more routine tasks of cleaning and locking the kirk.[55] The councils also held onto the financial documents relating to the chaplainries. In Dundee the provost and bailies assigned a day in 1554 for the common chest to be opened by Andrew Annand, George Lovell and John Ferne, keepers of the keys, so that choristers could examine the 'mortifications and evidence' of the chaplainries of Saint Clement, Saint Ninian and the Rood altar.[56]

Though the specific arrangements with the official possessors of the parishes may have varied, in all three burghs the town council held primary responsibility for the structure and equipment of the parish church. Burgh governments, in fact, devoted much time and money to their parish churches and other religious buildings. As sacred spaces they were crucial pieces of civic infrastructure. The towns struggled at times to finance the necessary repairs and hoped-for improvements, but the councillors never forgot their responsibilities. The late medieval Catholicism practised in Scottish towns would simply not have been possible without the extensive time, money and administrative effort devoted by municipal governments.

The Use of Church Space

The towns exercised authority over how church space was used. While religious worship was the primary purpose of the buildings, they were also used for rituals which invoked religious emphasis for temporal use, such as punishments and debt payments, and for purely secular actions such as commerce and meetings. These were not considered insults to the churches' dignity but part of the purpose for which the parishioners built them.[57] There were limits, though. Commercial activity was sometimes a nuisance in Haddington; the craftsmen who blocked entry to St Mary's by crowding the doors with their stalls were forbidden from setting up on any day of the week except Saturday.[58] In Haddington and Dundee the minor officers were ordered to keep the poor folk (and in Haddington, dogs) out of the kirk. In Dundee it was specified that the choir should be guarded on festivals and Sundays, and the poor should be expelled on holy days, as it seems they were using the church for shelter.[59] These decrees indicate that the burgh's elites took mass attendance seriously. Access to the kirk was also regulated to limit infection. During the plague of 1545, Haddington's sick were ordered not to attend mass in the kirk but rather to go to the special mass said for them in St Katherine's chapel.[60] In Dundee, the sick were gathered outside by the East Port, where the reformer George Wishart preached to them in 1544.[61] Presumably they also heard orthodox preaching and masses at the same spot.

The church and chapels were further used as sites of announcements and even political disputes. In 1540 Sir James Mauchlin, Haddington's curate, carried out the bailies' orders to deliver a warning during 'solemn time of mass'.[62] In January 1557, Henry Campbell stood up before a 'great multitude of people' at the Saturday high mass in St Ninian's chapel to accuse John Ayton, provost of Haddington, of breaking the town's bells, finishing his declaration by saying 'and therefor I shall accuse him before an higher judge'.[63] In April 1558, an agent of Lord James Stewart, commendator of St Andrews priory, ordered Sir Thomas Mauchlin, curate of Haddington, at the 'time of high mass in presence of the parishioners' to read out an eviction order directed at John Yule.[64] Services must have been well-attended for these announcements to have had the desired effect.

Like other European towns, the assizes and bailies in the three burghs used the church as a site of punishment.[65] Crimes punished included minor acts of physical violence, theft, or disobedience of the municipal authorities. Punishments usually involved appearing in linen cloth (underclothes, essentially), bareheaded and barefoot, and offering a candle to either the high altar or the bailies. The candles were to be of a specified weight, from three ounces to two pounds.[66] The ceremonies usually took place on Sundays, either before or after high mass, and the offender would have to ask forgiveness either of the curate, the bailies or the person wronged. Additional penalties might also be applied.[67] The assizes and bailies also used processions for public humiliation; in April 1542 Haddington's bailies and council ordered John Scharp and William Mason to pass before the Corpus Christi procession, wearing only their linen cloth, before offering the bailies a pound of wax and asking their forgiveness for breaking the clock, and paying for repairs (the burghs were quite touchy about their clocks!).[68] As with the announcements, a large audience, including the bailies, must have been present for the punishments to achieve their goal of public humiliation.

The kirk and kirkyards could themselves be spaces of crime and violence; in December 1520 Andrew Walkar was found guilty of violating the statutes against pimping in Dundee's kirkyard and was ordered to offer a pound of wax to the church on the following Sunday. Having not done so, he was sentenced to offer two pounds the next Sunday, the amount doubling each Sunday he failed to submit.[69] Walker was separately convicted of 'stroublance' (disruptive behaviour) done to George Rollok (I) bailie, and because the offence was committed in the kirkyard the court ordered him to appear the next Sunday during high mass 'when the priests go in procession and offer a candle of a pound of wax and ask the bailies for forgiveness'.[70] In April 1545, James Gothra and his wife Agnes Ogill were threatened with execution should they return to Haddington without proving that a piece of iron in their possession had been bought legally and not stolen from the kirk.[71] The specific phrasing of the judgments aside, the church space does not seem to have been especially protected, as punishments were similar for crimes committed elsewhere.

The church buildings were civic institutions, used for religious and non-religious purposes. The council's responsibility for and use of church space therefore went beyond providing divine services, though that remained the primary purpose and councillors kept a close eye to ensure that services were not interfered with.

The Cycle of Worship

Having provided the physical space for worship, councils also supervised the cycle of services and the clergy who performed them. Indeed, the town councils held maintaining and increasing worship, both in quantity and quality, to be one of their primary responsibilities. Divine services consisted of a variety of sacred offices: the daily prayers of matins and vespers, the administration of the sacraments, but most importantly the performing of mass.[72] The mass was a powerful rite which was not only an essential part of obtaining individual salvation but also bound together the Christian community.[73] As Eamon Duffy points out, the consecrated host 'was the source simultaneously of individual and of corporate renewal'.[74] During an ordinary week, dozens or hundreds of masses would be said in a Scottish town, along with many prayers, and more elaborate services would be held during important holy days. Many of those masses were performed on behalf of souls in purgatory, but they were also believed to be beneficial for those still on earth.[75] Town councils worked to ensure the proper provision of these masses and prayers, and took all available chances to increase them. In a routine modification of the foundation charter of St John's altar in Stirling, for example, the council took the opportunity to specify that the chaplain should make daily service in the parish church.[76] Despite the notion that Catholicism was in decay during the 1550s, the desire for expansion continued right up to the Reformation.[77] In April 1557, it was Haddington's provost bailies and council who summoned the prebends of the college kirk 'for consultation to be had for augmentation of divine service of the said kirk', demonstrating the townspeople's focus on religious ritual as a public good.[78]

A sense of the continuous ritual cycle which was being carried out at any given moment in the parish churches of pre-Reformation Scotland's large and medium sized towns can be gained from the collegiate church of St Mary's in Biggar, whose organisation was similar to the parish churches of Haddington and Dundee, but whose records are better preserved. St Mary's was founded by Malcolm, Lord Fleming, to ensure that masses and prayers were said for the benefit of his soul, his families and 'those from whom I have taken goods unjustly or to whom I caused loss or injury'.[79] According to the 1546 foundation, St Mary's was in the charge of a provost, who exercised discipline over the prebends (called choristers in the burghs) and ensured that Lord Fleming's statutes were observed.[80] The first prebend was the master of the song school, the second was to teach grammar, and the third and fourth were the sacristans, performing the duties which in the burghs were likely performed by the parish clerk. Three prebends were responsible only for singing in services, while the eighth was vicar pensioner of the parish and administered the sacraments to the parishioners. Two of the prebends were collectors, responsible for gathering and distributing the offerings, rents, tithes and other revenues owed to the choristers. Four boys, voices unbroken, were to sing in the choir, and six poor old men, called bedesmen, were to be supported by the college in return for singing at high mass and vespers.[81]

The prebends' days were filled with services and duties and were almost as regimented as those of monks. Between 6 and 7 a.m. a prebend was to sing a mass in honour of the Virgin Mary at the high altar. The rest of the prebends were to be in their stalls for matins when the morning bell stopped ringing at 7 a.m., properly clothed in clean white surplices with red hoods, and were to assemble 'without talking, whispering and laughter, and without vain and wandering looks, in silence and quietness, and with due gravity, they are to sing, and they are to continue in that spirit to the end'.[82] Malcolm Lord Fleming, the founder, further exhorted them to

> sing the psalms slowly in the way they ought, and the singing is to be begun together, continue together, and end together, and those who fail in these things are to be severely punished, for the due honour of almighty God is not promoted by singing improperly and carelessly, the intention of the founder is frustrated, the well ordered conscience is hurt, and the edification of those present is not at all obtained.[83]

It seems that clerics were known to perform the offices quickly and carelessly, to the dismay of the lay patrons and worshippers. Lord Fleming had clear expectations of what he expected from the clergy, and placed a great deal of importance on the proper performance of the rituals. Townspeople would have been no different.

Following matins, between 7.30 and 8 a.m. each weekday and Saturdays a mass would be said. On Mondays the mass would be a requiem, held at the high altar, but on other weekdays the mass would be held at a side altar. At 10 a.m., the high mass would be sung at the high altar, after which the celebrant, 'wearing his stole and alb, will sing the Psalm "de Profundis" and the Collects and Prayers for the soul of the founder and all faithful departed'.[84] Between services the prebends were expected to attend to their assigned duties, as well as study and recite private prayers at the altars for the soul of the founder and his family. At 5 p.m., vespers would be sung, followed by compline, both at the high altar. In the burgh churches, only one service at the end of the day, evensong, would be held. On the eve of the observed feast days the Vespers of the Dead and the Matins of the Dead were to be sung, along with the Nine Lessons and the Nine Psalms.[85] The provost was to sing the mass on 15 August, The Assumption of the Blessed Virgin Mary, the patronal feast of the college. A requiem mass for the soul of the founder was to be sung on the four days following each feast day.[86]

The burgh parish churches would have followed similar schedules and rules creating a constant flow of services. In addition to the masses said at the high altar and the daily performance of matins and evensong by the choristers, there would have been a variety of masses sung by chaplains at the side altars; some would have been regularly scheduled, on a weekly or annual cycle, others would have been performed for the recently deceased.[87] The burghs organised the choristers of their parish churches in the same manner as St Mary's in Biggar. In Haddington, one chorister was chosen as master (or President) and was responsible for enforcing order, and one chaplain was designated to collect the annuals and take on responsibility for the records and court appearances which were involved.[88] Another was assigned as a teacher, and in May 1535 the council gave him four pounds and ten shillings for expenses related to the children and books.[89] Dundee, Stirling and other Scottish burghs would have done likewise.

Within the burgh churches many masses were sponsored by individual bequests. One example from Haddington was left by John Mertyne in 1482, which called for eight choristers and the clerk to sing a placebo and dirge annually, likely on St Andrew's Day, for a requiem mass to be sung by fourteen priests annually, and a yearly service to be held in the friars' kirk. For this he left annual rents of 33s, as well as 6s 8d for the friars, 10d for bread, wine and lights in the high kirk, and 23s 2d in alms for the poor.[90] As these bequests from burghers and clerics accumulated, the required masses must have taken up much of the day (though possibly with a lull in the afternoon); for any burgher who went into the parish church the divine offices would have been a constant background. High mass was sung at the chapels as well, adding to the overall number of masses in the burgh.[91]

Urban religion also included other practices beyond mass and prayers, even if few records of these activities survive. Towns placed a high importance on preaching, and in England and Germany benefices were devoted to funding preachers.[92] There is no evidence that the three burghs did this, though Aberdeen supported preachers on at least one occasion, and sermon notes from Dundee indicate that preaching of some sort did occur.[93] The various friars also preached.[94] The clergy would also have been involved in administering the sacraments, sometimes in the church, as with communion, other times inside homes, as with anointing the sick. We have no records of these kinds of activities, and no way of knowing how they were divided between the vicars, curates, chaplains and the friars.

Clergy as Municipal Employees

Many of the clerics in the towns were effectively municipal employees, especially the choristers of the principal churches and the chaplains of the altars in the town's patronage. It was the burgh governments who hired the clergy for these posts, ensured that they were qualified and performed their duties properly, supervised the collection of their annuals and topped up the income of those priests whose benefices were insufficient. The councils managed these employees to ensure the maximum performance of divine services, in quantity and quality. They were firm but fair employers, willing to ensure a reasonable income but expecting diligent and loyal service in return.

The most important group of clergy in the towns' employ were the choristers. They were essentially salaried employees, as demonstrated by an agreement between Dundee town council and three priests in 1527 that they would receive 'half of the common allowance of the said weekly choristers' in return for their daily service over the next year.[95] In July 1553, John

Mertyne (conspicuously not identified as 'sir John' – perhaps he was too young to be in orders) was hired to be a chorister in Dundee's choir for ten merks a year, to be renewed annually 'so long as the council thinks expedient'. He was required to serve at matins and evensong, and the council gave to sir James Kinloch, parish clerk, the chaplainry of St Thomas the Martyr to help fund Mertyne's salary.[96] In Stirling as well the council employed choristers, agreeing to pay four merks annually to Sir Robert Cristeson.[97] The low pay suggests that services were less elaborate than Dundee's.

It was the town councils or even the whole community which made important clerical appointments. Typical was the meeting in 1525 of Stirling's whole council in the lodging of Sir Duncan Forester of Garden, 'to advise on the gift of the altar of Saint Katherine' in the parish kirk.[98] The councils were constantly managing a sort of waiting list for vacancies as one vacancy could create a whole series of openings. In June 1544, the provost, council and community of Haddington gathered to make appointments following the death of sir Patrick Mauchlin, chaplain of the Rood altar. Sir Archibald Borthwick, previously holder of half the parish clerkship, was promoted to the Rood altar and to the choir stall attached to it. Sir Adam Brown, an unbeneficed priest who had been receiving a pension to sing in the choir, was promoted to sir Archibald's half of the parish clerkship. Sir Robert Symson was given sir Adam's pension of ten merks, with the promise of being given the next vacant benefice. A proviso promised to increase his salary by five merks if he did not eventually receive a benefice.[99] This management of posts continued right up until the Reformation: in October 1558, Dundee's council promised Master Andrew Cowper that they would grant him the next chaplainry available in the town's gift. These sometimes elaborate arrangements demonstrate that the councils were trying not simply to fulfil minimal obligations but to fill their churches with as many competent choristers and chaplains as they could, and to treat the priests in the town, especially the young ones, fairly. Councillors were willing to devote the necessary time to carry out these dual obligations as best they could.

The council also supervised many of the clergy who served at the side altars or chapels. An example of an altar granted to the council, and the obligations that went with it, is the young James V's grant of some revenues to the altar of St Michael the Archangel in Stirling in 1516. The king (or his regent) appointed the 'provost, bailies, councillors and community' of Stirling as patrons of the altar, giving them full authority to hire an ordained priest who resided in the burgh and did not have any other benefice. The appointee was to be present with the other chaplains in a 'clean and decent supplice' 'at all vespers, compline, matins and high mass'. Finally, the chaplain was to keep no concubine.[100] Many other altars were founded by individuals or families but over time became the responsibility of the town council. A less regal example came from Haddington: when William Kemp set up a benefice for a chaplain to perform an obit at the

St James altar in Haddington in 1520, he specified that the patronage was to go to his successors, and if they failed, to the town council, as indeed happened in 1541.[101] The priests who served at these altars were employees of the town council, just as much as the choristers.

The towns all preferred to hire locals, but this favouritism did not lead to a lessening of standards. In September 1532, the 'Provost, bailies, councilors and a multitude of the deacons and community of Dundee' agreed that in future if the son of a burgess and an outsider were both equally qualified for a benefice in the town's gift, that the local man would be nominated. To ensure that this agreement was kept, the assembly delegated the vicar, John Barry, and two others 'to enact them in the act book of the Bishop of Brechin, or his commissaries under pain of excommunication'.[102] In Haddington, as William Walson and Archibald Borthwick were appointed parish clerks, the town specified that should either of them die while holding the benefice, it was to revert to the town, who would appoint 'whom they please and in special to a neighbour of the town most able'.[103] In 1541, when William Kemp handed over his patronage of St James altar to the town in exchange for an annual pension of ten pounds, the agreement specified that after the decease of the incumbent, sir James Mauchlin, the benefice would go to a child of either Thomas Waus or John Kemp, if the child is 'found qualified for the said service'; whoever received the position was to 'make service in the choir as the other chaplains do'.[104] No matter how well connected, the priests were actually expected to do their jobs.

This preference for locals meant that sometimes boys who were not yet properly qualified were appointed, though they were expected to fulfil the requirements as soon as possible. In 1528, Robert Wedderburn, son of James Wedderburn (b. 1450), was appointed to the chaplaincy of St Katharine the Virgin, made vacant by the decease of sir Robert Lam, but had to promise that 'he should immediately receive ordination of the presbytery, and abide continually in the daily service of the said parish church of Dundee'.[105] On 7 November 1558, the bailies George Lovell and Andrew Fleshour required George Rollok (II), himself a former bailie, to agree to pay five merks yearly to the town because his son, having been appointed to the benefice of Our Lady altar, was not yet qualified to serve at the altar.[106] In Stirling, Robert Ferny, son of Robert Ferny, burgess, lost his turn at St Ninian's altar because he was not yet properly qualified when it became vacant.[107] The council and the choristers cooperated to ensure the qualifications of the office holders. Before appointing sir James Erskin to the chaplainry of St Agatha and Erasmus, martyrs, Dundee's councillors 'for observance of their act made by them to the choristers of the said church', had sir John Fethy, master of the song school, 'and expert chantors of the said choir' examine him. He passed.[108] In 1556, Stirling's council granted the Rood altar to sir John Stoddart, on condition that sir John continue to study at music and be present at services. William Smart was caution that sir John would indeed fulfil his commitments.[109] The councils cared that the divine services be properly conducted, and it was widely accepted that they were right to do so, even by well-connected parents and patrons.

The burgesses were specific in their expectations of their clerical employees, and willing to admonish them for failing to perform their duties properly. Parish clerks came in for particular scrutiny, as they had to perform the tedious, menial tasks necessary for the services to be held properly. Stirling had a particularly frustrating relationship with their clerk. In February 1520, John Bully appeared and presented to the provost and bailies a document granting him the parish clerkship and responsibility for clock keeping.[110] That he had to present this document at all shows that the council was dubious of his claim to the post. Apparently, his subsequent performance was not satisfactory as, in September 1520, the council ordered him to sing in the choir at high mass, matins and evensong, specifying that he was to wear the surplice, as he did in the time of the late James of Mentecht.[111] Perhaps Bully took advantage of the death of a patron to attempt to relax his obligations. Bully further brought a case before the official of Lothian to claim an annual fee from the common goods for the upkeep of the clock, a claim which the town opposed.[112] It is perhaps as a result of the rejection of this claim that in August 1521 Bully freely renounced his claim to the keeping of the clock 'and never to claim any right to the same'.[113] In February 1530, when the question of appointing the clerk came up again, the 'provost, bailies, counsall and community present' agreed that 'in all times coming' the clerkship would be granted to 'the most cunning chaplain that can be had to sing in the choir' and that it would be given to 'no secular in all times coming'. The council acknowledged that this grant be made 'without prejudice to John Bully, possessor for the time'. Nonetheless, the act and their determination to hire 'the most cunning chaplain' was clearly a sign of dissatisfaction with Bully, who was not a chaplain. He had intended for his post to become hereditary, as he dissented to the act unless the clerkship was given to his son, sir Thomas Bully, after his death, which the town refused.[114]

The other burghs also supervised their parish clerks carefully. When in 1533 Walson and Borthwick were appointed to be Haddington's parish clerks, it was specified that both were to do daily service in the choir, at matins, high mass and evensong, and were to become priests as soon as they were of age. The townspeople threated to undo the appointment if they failed in any of these points, and three sureties were found for each youth to ensure that he would follow the prescribed conditions.[115] Sure enough, in 1539, the two were brought before the assize for neglecting their duties of bell-ringing and lamp lighting. The assize ordered them to ensure that the oil lamp over the choir was lit by 5 a.m., and that it stayed lit until high mass, and that it be lit again at the second bell for evensong and until the doors were locked. They were also ordered to ring the bell in the morning, for which the inhabitants of the burgh were to pay them thirty-two shillings, and if they would not do so the inhabitants would hire someone else.[116] In April 1551, Dundee's parish clerk sir James Kinloch was accused of 'suffering of little wool to be laid in ye kirk'. In time honoured fashion, sir James blamed his servant and promised to dismiss him.[117] In June 1554, the chaplains of the choir complained that John Corntoun did not ring the bells properly and did not lay out fire and water in time for mass and divine service. Corntoun agreed that should he fail again he could be dismissed without 'delatour [denunciation] or further process'.[118] Parish clerks may have borne the brunt of the communities' frustrations, but other clergy were closely watched as well. In 1540 Haddington's council told the master of the college kirk 'to punish and correct the faults within it'.[119] In Dundee the council ordered John Mertyne, the singer hired for the choir, to stop living with Elene Ramsay. He complied, and a short time later the unhappy couple came before the burgh court to argue over the ownership of a blanket.[120] More positively, in December 1555, the council instructed the kirkmaster to pay James Blyth, beadle and common servant in St Mary's, 40s a year for his good service.[121]

The townspeople's desire that their appointees serve in person was challenged by those who tried to build a career beyond the town, such as Archibald Borthwick. When Borthwick was summoned to royal service in 1540, Haddington's council agreed to James V's request that he be allowed to supply a substitute for his half of the parish clerkship, but reacted angrily when another chorister asked for the same arrangement, proclaiming that they 'utterly repelled the said protestation and plainly declared [that] they would receive none by substitute for any of the prebends without they be compelled and coacted for fear'.[122] The community felt unable to turn down the king's request, yet was worried about the prospect of their choristers leaving them, replaced by inferior substitutes. As it was, Borthwick's arrangement would frequently cause tension. In January 1541 the council withheld Borthwick's half of the clerkship's income, causing him to dispatch a messenger to proclaim royal letters from the market cross demanding payment.[123] Likely they paid up, but still pressured sir Archibald to serve in person; in May 1541, sir Patrick Mauchlin, president of the college kirk of Haddington, obtained a decree from the Archbishop of St Andrews ordering sir Archibald's substitute, sir John Story, to remove himself from the choir; sir John demanded that his contract with sir Archibald be honoured nonetheless, for he was ready to perform service.[124] A year later, in April of 1542, the bailies and council again ordered Borthwick to come and demonstrate his service, resolving to appeal to the king if he did not. These disputes came to a satisfactory conclusion with the death of James V and in 1544 the provost council and community gathered and promoted sir Archibald to the Rood chaplainry, one of the most prestigious in the town.[125] Not all priests who sought leave had such a hard battle. In June 1545, when sir Robert Symson, a pensioned but unbeneficed chorister, requested a two years' leave, the councillors agreed provided that a qualified man could be found to replace him. The substitute was to be chosen by the 'provost bailies and council with advice of the choir', demonstrating the burgesses' determination that everyone who served in the church, even substitutes, be vetted and hired by them alone.[126]

The inhabitants' demands for proper clerical performance also drove disputes with outside authorities. In the autumn of 1531, a dispute broke out between Dundee and the Bishop of Brechin, John Hepburn, over the appointment of the parish clerk. The parish clerk was normally elected by the parishioners, as in Stirling and Haddington, and confirmed by the bishop, but in this case Hepburn refused to appoint any but his own candidate, who evidently refused to serve in person.[127] A meeting was held on 6 September 1531 in the vestibule of the parish church at which Robert Myll, on behalf of the bailies and councillors of Dundee, demanded that sir William Silver prove his rights to the parish clerkship of Dundee and either show up and serve, or resign. Sir William defended his right to the office and offered to provide documentation on a day appointed by the bishop.[128] Growing impatient with the delay, which would have hindered the proper functioning of divine services in the church, on 2 October Dundee's kirkmaster David Rollok 'required the provost, bailies and councillors under peril of their souls' to ensure that the chaplains serving under the council's patronage, presumably including the parish clerk, fulfil their obligations. Rollok's request was seconded by William Rog, the collector of the crafts.[129] In response the bailies insisted they had already done so and were not to blame because they had already brought the matter before the bishop. The concerns of the burgh officials demonstrate that the dispute was not over patronage but rather the proper provision of divine services.

On 16 October, the forty days within which sir William was supposed to produce his evidence had expired without him producing the documents, and so on 10 November the council appointed William Drummond as their parish clerk. They expected some opposition from the Bishop of Brechin, and so their proclamation was an assertion of the town's right to appoint the parish clerk:

> Alexander Lovell, bailie, in name of the whole community of Dundee presented to John bishop of Brechin, William Drummond clerk of the parish of Dundee, elected by the provost, bailies and community to the said office, according to the tenor of their gift under the common seal of the Burgh, requiring the said bishop to admit the same William as it behoved by law, in and to the said office, and if he would not admit him the said Alexander protested that he should of right be admitted by the bishops of St Andrews, or judges competent.[130]

Despite the defiant tenor of Lovell's declaration, the council did not make a firm stance in defence of Drummond, for on 27 November they tried again, with a different candidate, sir John Fethy, a noted organist.[131] Again the bishop refused to admit the council's candidate.[132] It is not known how the dispute was resolved but by the following May he was master of the song school, not parish clerk.[133] The council may have failed to get their preferred candidates appointed, but the doggedness with which they pursued the matter is an indication of their determination that clerical posts actually be held by the men who carried out the duties. The councillors evidently took the responsibility of ensuring proper worship in the towns more seriously than the bishop.

Dundee's council was also willing to intervene in benefices which were indisputably not in their gift, once again opposing the appointments of the Bishop of Brechin. On 11 August 1553, Master John Rolland appeared before the council and appealed on behalf of himself and his patrons – the abbot and convent of Lindores – and the parishioners of Dundee against Bishop John Hepburn for refusing to collate him to the vicarage of Dundee, despite the presentation of the Abbot of Lindores, patron of the vicarage. The bailies and councillors asked Master John to leave the room, and then called him in again for further questioning, before they, on behalf of themselves and the parishioners, 'ripely advised determinedly answered that they would adhere and inhere to the said master John Rolland appellation'.[134] This time the council eventually had their way and in September 1554 John Rolland, vicar, requested the key to the vicar's chamber from the burgh treasurer.[135]

The town council got dragged into disputes involving the local clergy as well. In 1522, sir Robert Gray, chaplain of Dundee's Holy Rood altar, faced a claim on the altar's revenues from sir John Barry, vicar. The council had generally good relations with sir John (in fact, he sat as a councillor), but in this case as patrons of the altar they took up sir Robert's defence.[136] The disputes were not always financial: in August 1523 the choristers appeared before Dundee's bailies and announced that they would not sing mass in the presence of Hector Richardson, who they claimed was excommunicated 'for violently laying hands on Mr. Robert Fife'; it is not known what the bailies made of their announcement.[137] The councillors took care to ensure good order in the service and appointments of the town's clergy, always with an eye to the proper and frequent performance of divine service.

Management of the Civic Church

The town councils put considerable attention into the financial and personnel administration necessary to support the churches and services. The altars, whether in the patronage of the town council or not, acquired revenues through donations which were often in the form of annuals or rents from lands or tenements. The bailies supervised these transactions: a routine example took place in November 1524 in Dundee when Robert Halys resigned a tenement to Thomas Carale, bailie, who then transferred seizin of the land to sir James Barry, chaplain of the altar of Jesus, the exchange being witnessed by James Wedderburn, bailie.[138] The councils further supported the clerics in their attempts to collect payment, though usually the tenants who had to pay up were not the owners who had made the donation.[139] On 13 January 1556, for example, Dundee's bailies ordered the officers to make a sweep collecting for all the annuals owed to St Mary's, an order which apparently had little effect because it was repeated the following March.

These donations had accumulated over the fourteenth, fifteenth and sixteenth centuries, and reflect the commitment of generations of townspeople to their churches. Some evidence of sixteenth-century donations to Haddington altars survives. Although there is not enough evidence for a detailed chronological analysis, the records reveal some patterns.[140] Between 1520 and 1535, fourteen donations were made by twelve different people, eleven of them laymen. For the most part people gave either a whole merk or a half merk (13s 4d or 6s 8d), though others gave annual rents of 10s, 16s or 20s. This got the donor a yearly annual, usually for one's self, parent or spouse. The records reveal no difference between the service performed for 6s 8d or 13s 4d; perhaps there were different rates for different incomes, or it was simply understood that there was a different level of service for different donations. After 1535, there is only one donation whose date is certain: Philip Gibson left 20s for 'suffrage to be done', as well as 6s 8d to be given to the poor folk, in February 1542.[141]

Given that between 1520 and 1535 donations were made at a rate of one a year, but that there are few surviving documented donations from before 1520 or after 1535, it can be assumed that the surviving records are most likely simply a fraction of those that once existed, and we should not assume that donations dried up after 1535. What the records do indicate is that donations were largely simple donations to the parish church; elaborate bequests were either out of style or beyond the means of those in the surviving records. Most donors did not have particular attachments to a given altar – the main civic effort was to support the choir. These donations would have contributed to the effort to ensure that an extensive series of divine services would have been performed almost every day in Haddington. This accords with Bess Rhodes' findings for St Andrews, where 47 per cent of all donations to religious institutions between 1500 and 1560 went towards funding masses.[142]

Chaplains sometimes alienated the properties belonging to their benefices and required the council's permission to do so. They usually feued the land, which meant giving tenants secure possession of property for a lump-sum payment and a fixed annual payment.[143] In May 1552, for example, sir James Wicht, chaplain of St Colanis[144] chaplainry, which was attached to Dundee's almshouse, received permission from the council to feu lands belonging to his chaplainry in the Argylis gait, feuing it to John Wicht, his brother, for twelve merks annually, on condition that John spend forty pounds repairing the tenement.[145]

Councils also collected revenues from other uses of the church space. In Dundee in 1521 those who wanted the great bells rung for 'any psalms or dirges' paid 40d, and ten merks for burial in the choir, while in Stirling the council set the mason's fees for burials: 12d for each grave dug and 8d for each pavement stone moved, though the mason was responsible for repairing any stone that was broken in the process.[146]

In cases where the altars were insufficiently funded the town council provided subsidies and pensions. In practice, the basic minimum for a beneficed priest during the first third of the century seemed to be around twenty-three to twenty-five merks (£15–16), only slightly better than a labourer could expect to earn.[147] When Stirling appointed Sir John Spotiswode to the Holy Rood altar, they also gave him a pension of six merks (£4) to supplement the revenues from the lands and annuals owned by the altar. His pension was to be reconsidered after a year of good service.[148] In November 1533, Haddington granted a subsidy of five merks to sir William Cokburn, chaplain of the St Thomas and the John the Baptist altar, and promised to supplement his income further if the benefice turned out to be not worth eighteen merks annually.[149] Clerical income could be augmented with payments for participating in obit masses, or for performing sacraments.[150] Even so, sir William Cokburn was obliged to seek further financial assistance from the town and in 1536 an assize granted him a further £1.5 to build his house, a demonstration of the willingness of the burgesses to assist their priests in securing a basic standard of living.[151]

Councils might also support a priest in his retirement, though even then they tried to squeeze out as much service as they could. In April 1558, Sir James Mauchlin reached an agreement with Haddington whereby he made the council 'his procurators, actors and factors' with power to administer his tenements as they thought best, in return for an annual pension of four pounds and a promise 'to do service in the college kirk of Haddington at his power during his lifetime', a requirement that might also have been made of other retired priests.[152] In September 1560, sir James' pension was increased to ten pounds in return for renouncing the chaplainry of St James, whose revenues would now go directly to the town council.[153] A similar retirement arrangement, supervised but not funded by the town council, was made in Stirling in 1556, when sir James Nicolson resigned St Katherine's altar to the provost, in the expectation that he would in turn grant it to sir Andrew Hagy. Sir James retained the liferent of the house 'that he [had] biggit himself'.[154] These arrangements demonstrate both the good relations between towns and their clerics, and their desire to fill their divine services with as many participants as possible.

The subsidies could add up to fairly significant amounts for the townspeople to pay. In both 1554 and 1555, Haddington's council paid forty-one pounds to the prebends, likely to compensate them for the annuals that were uncollectable following the destruction of the town in 1548–9.[155] Their generosity was not unlimited though for in 1539 they had demanded that sir John Lytle produce evidence that he was owed light (likely in the form of candles) as part of his altar service, saying that if evidence was not produced 'they will not compel the said altar to find him light'.[156] Providing the priests with fire and light was a recurring problem and in 1540, in the midst of the long November nights, the council agreed to deliver to the choristers 'fire yearly as they had before'.[157] Stirling's council could also take a hard line: in October 1525 for example, an inquest determined that there would not be any pension granted to a chaplain to supplement their altarage fees for a year.[158] This stinginess more likely reflected the state of Stirling's finances than their willingness to support their priests. In 1529 the bailie John Aikin agreed to personally contribute 6s 8d of the four merks pension granted to Sir Robert Cristeson, who served in the choir of the church but did not have a benefice of his own.[159]

The willingness of councils to support chaplains also extended to those who served in municipal institutions other than the parish church. Dundee granted the chaplain of the hospital the altar of St Columba to support him, as well as an annual rent of one pound.[160] Master John Rolland, Dundee's grammar school teacher, was originally assigned the chaplainry of St John and a pension of two pounds, but these posts were then replaced by his appointment to the chaplainry of St Michael the Archangel. Rolland agreed that should he leave his post at the grammar school he would resign the chaplainry back to the town council.[161] When Master William retired as Stirling's schoolmaster, the council gave him the proceeds of St Leonard's altar, specifying that he would not have to perform any services at the altar. They also granted him the right to live in a tenement which had originally been donated to the council to pay for a daily mass in the parish church. In return, Master William gave up the twenty-four pounds annual salary he collected as grammar school master.[162] The councils kept tight control over these posts, ensuring that they did not become personal sinecures.

Ensuring that there was a sufficient, competent and respectable clerical workforce to sustain the worship cycle was clearly a major preoccupation of the town councils. They managed elaborate arrangements to ensure that priests got a fair turn at the benefices, they used public and sometimes personal funds to supplement insufficient revenues, they devoted municipal resources to ensure that the priests collected the money due to them, and they were willing to stand up to the bishop over unsatisfactory appointments. Burgh governments clearly and willingly held the supervision and support of their clergy in the provision of divine services to be one of their principal tasks.

Religious Institutions not Directly Controlled by the Town Council

Institutions such as friaries and crafts also contributed to a burgh's cycle of divine services. Even though they were not under the town council's direct supervision, municipal governments still exercised some authority or influence over them, ensuring that they were adequately sustained and resolving disputes among members of these bodies or between them and other townspeople. Notably absent from the records are any mention of confraternities unrelated to crafts or merchants. It is likely that such confraternities did not exist in the towns; even if they were not under the direct jurisdiction of the town council, it is hard to imagine that such communal organisations did not create a single dispute that had to be brought before the burgh court, or a property transaction requiring the bailies' attention. The simplest explanation for such a complete absence of references is that there were no non-craft or merchant confraternities.[163]

The crafts in the burghs supported a significant number of altars, though securing proper funding for these altars was a continuous struggle, especially in the smaller burghs. The crafts and councils nonetheless cooperated to ensure that the altars and chaplains could be sustained as well as possible, as part of the effort to maximise divine services in the burgh. The craft altars were funded, like other altars, by annuals, but they also received fines and dues from the craftsmen.[164] These funds went towards the books, ornaments and vestments of the altar and to the salaries of the craft chaplains. The craft chaplains, like the choristers, were regarded as hired employees rather than beneficed priests, though they had even less security as their position had to be renewed every year.[165] Dundee's walker craft, for example, reserved the right to remove their chaplain if 'his demerits require'.[166] Serving as a chaplain was not especially lucrative: Stirling's websters hired the curate to sing two masses a week for an annual salary of twenty-six shillings and eight pence; Dundee's weavers agreed in 1529 to pay their chaplain, sir William Lwyd, six pounds annually and sir Thomas Wedderburn, chaplain of the bakers, one of Dundee's most prominent crafts, held two additional benefices, St Michael's altar and the chaplainry of Our Lady in the Cowgait – a rare example of pluralism which may indicate how poorly funded any one of those positions was.[167] The responsibilities of the craft chaplains included saying mass, though the frequency would have varied; the Holy Blood altar in Dundee, run by the merchants' guild, required their chaplain to say divine service on a daily basis, with a solemn mass on Thursdays; it is hard to imagine that the weavers received the same from sir William for six pounds annually.[168] Craft chaplains were also responsible for administering the altar and helping sort out the affairs of the crafts. Sir William Lwyd was responsible for supervising the accounts of the weavers and for his 'Writings', presumably account-keeping.[169] Furthermore, the weavers decided, 'in consideration of the ruinous state of their Altar', to hand over all their documents to sir William so he could take on the burden of collecting his own fees.[170] Lwyd was also given the power to call a meeting over the behaviour of any of the five guild supervisors.[171]

Despite the low wages paid to the chaplains and the elaborate schedules of fines and fees, the crafts had great difficulties in adequately funding their altars, which caused frequent disputes, re-foundations and even mergers, all of which came before the town councils. Dundee's weavers first made arrangements to establish an altar in 1492 for 'the growth of grace, and for the honour of St Severus the Bishop'.[172] They collected donations of annual rents, but in 1512 they returned to the council to ratify a new series of statues 'for the supplying and upholding of divine service and repairing of their Altar of Saint Severtne'.[173] In January 1520, for example, Stirling's tailors also requested the council increase their privileges to augment their altar's funding; the council in turn instructed them to find out what privileges their craft had in Perth.[174] Shortly after, the council also granted the smiths permission to collect a penny from any person who sold competing products in the burgh, the money going 'for help of God's service to be done in the said parish church, in honour of God, the blessed Virgin, St Eloi, and all saints'.[175]

In Haddington, the 1530s saw the tailors, cordiners, bakers and the smiths gain the approval of the town council to modify the regulations surrounding the craft altars.[176] Not all of the modifications were rubber-stamped by the council: in July 1535 the council refused the butchers of Haddington permission to gather a weekly penny, and told them that any future collection would require a special licence.[177] In March 1544, Haddington's council felt comfortable ordering the skinners and furriers to be joined to the tailors' altar and to pay their weekly penny to it.[178] The skinners and furriers may not have been happy about this, for the order was repeated in April 1545. The series of re-foundations of Haddington's craft altars in the early 1530s, before the crises of plague and war, followed by mergers in the 1540s, reflects the difficulties that many crafts had supporting these altars, but also highlights the attention paid to the problems by the burgh councils. They issued unpopular but necessary orders, demonstrating their concern with all aspects of divine worship in the burghs and their determination to sustain as much of it as possible.

The burgh council and court were sometimes called upon to resolve disputes within the crafts concerning the administration of the altars. In October 1537, for example, Gilbert Robison had to promise, before the Haddington burgh court, to repay 11s 3d to the furriers' craft box of St James.[179] The burghs might also restrain over-zealous crafts. In Stirling, not long after the smiths were granted the right to collect a penny from non-guild members who sold competing products, their deacon was reprimanded by the burgh court for trying to collect 22s 4d from George Smith. The deacon claimed that it was owed for their priest's board and weekly penny, but the assize ruled otherwise.[180] Disputes between chaplains and crafts were also resolved with the community's assistance. An arbiter resolved a dispute between Haddington's wrights and masons on one side and sir William Cokburn, chaplain of St John's altar, on the other, by ruling that the craftsmen could have the image of St John the Evangelist as their patron, as long as they provided it with wax and mass-cloths for masses and festivals. In exchange for the image of St John they were to make an image of St Doicho to be placed at the altar of St John the Baptist and finally they were to return to sir William 11s 6d of offerings collected at Yule.[181]

The crafts were therefore significant contributors to the civic religion in the burghs, and the town councils worked with them to maximise the provision of divine worship. The importance of the craft's contributions to the whole community is hinted at by a complaint from Haddington's malters. When they wanted to object, in February 1540, to unlicensed malters competing with them, they phrased their complaint in terms of the hurt being done to their altar of St Andrew.[182] It is easy to read this as a cynical attempt to eliminate economic competition, but in order for the crafts to be able to contribute to the burgh's cycle of divine worship, they had to be economically successful. If divine worship was considered a public good, then there was a legitimate case to be made against these freeloaders who were not only not contributing, but hindering the viability of those who were. The divine services provided by the crafts did not simply benefit the guild members, though they may have been the primary beneficiaries; as such, it was of concern to all that the services be properly provided.

Public Plays and Festivals

Religious plays, processions and festivals likely took place in most burghs, though as with other routine events not much evidence has survived.[183] In both Haddington and Dundee religious plays and processions were put on under the supervision of the council. The Corpus Christi procession was of great importance to Haddington's crafts. Dundee had a Corpus Christi procession in the fifteenth century, and there is no reason to think it had been discontinued in the sixteenth century. In Haddington, as in towns throughout Catholic Europe, the crafts argued over precedence in the Corpus Christi procession, which was resolved by the council. In 1532 the masons and wrights claimed that they, and not the bakers, should have the position of greatest prestige, nearest the host. The council decided to resolve the matter by deferring to Edinburgh, requiring the masons and wrights to acquire a document describing the practice there. This precedent did indeed favour the masons and wrights, placing them directly before the host, and nothing more is heard of the matter in Haddington.[184] Though the council, sensibly, deferred to outside practice rather than side with one craft over the other, the careful consideration and costly documentation involved demonstrates the importance the townspeople placed on the procession. Corpus Christi was not the only festival: the burgh did keep 'play coats' in the common chest, plays may also have been supervised by the Abbot of Unreason, who was usually associated with May games, and the crafts put on plays.[185] These craft plays were likely what George Wishart had in mind when he complained about the 'vane Clerk play' which attracted a much bigger audience than his preaching.[186] The council did often find it difficult to find someone willing to take on the expense of the position of Abbot though, and the crafts were also sometimes reluctant to put on the plays, and so the traditions finally died out in the 1550s.[187] There must have been frequent plays in Dundee, for there was a designated play field outside the town where at least two of the Wedderburn plays, one about the beheading of John the Baptist, the other about Dionysius the tyrant, were performed.[188]

Poor Relief

Church space and religious services were also used for collecting poor relief. The bailies organised the kirkboard collection held during high mass to gather alms for the poor. In all towns those who refused to take up the collection were to be fined: in Haddington, 8s and an amount equivalent to the next day's collection, while in Dundee and Stirling, only the previous day's collection was demanded.[189] The need to pass such laws indicates that this duty was not always popular. In October 1540 Haddington's council ordered the bailies to find 'famous and honest men' to pass with the kirkboard, repeating a similar injunction made in 1531. Each man was to collect in person as substitutes were not accepted.[190] Between October 1557 and November 1558 the receipts in Haddington's treasury accounts record that fifty-three different men took a turn, with the bailies passing in person at Yule and Easter. Only once, Trinity Sunday, did no one pass with the kirkboard. In all, £8 6s 7d was collected in just over a year.[191]

In Dundee, burgesses were also expected to take turns contributing bread to the almshouse. In September 1553 John Spens, merchant, failed to provide bread to the almshouse and was ordered to supply as much bread as had been contributed the previous day; John Duncan, who had provided that, swore an oath about the quantity he supplied.[192] Alms collection would occur after the Reformation as well, when the inhabitants were selected to take turns collecting money at the kirk door; just as with the kirkboard, if one missed his turn he was obliged to pay as much as had been collected the Sunday before.[193] These collections may have taken place in the church, but were the responsibility of the civic, not religious, authorities.[194] The burghs also had almshouses and hospitals which served as residences for the poor as much as places of healing. Dundee's mid-sixteenth century almshouse may or may not have been a successor to the various hospitals which are listed as having been established in the town.[195] A separate leper's hospital existed, possibly in the east of the town.[196] Stirling also had an almshouse and a leper colony.[197] In Haddington, the almshouses and hospital were associated with the friars, though the burgh took on administrative responsibility. When it came to looking after the poor, the burgh and clergy divided the responsibilities between them, a situation that would continue after the Reformation, as will be seen in Chapter Eight.

Friars

Friars were present in each of the three towns, and were the most significant element of urban religion not established or administered by the townspeople. All three towns had major Franciscan friaries, and Dundee and Stirling had Dominican houses as well, although much less evidence survives about the relations between the Dominicans and the burghs.[198] Although they were not under the councils' direct supervision the friars contributed to the towns' cycle of divine services and were linked to the burghers through a series of agreements and bequests. The most extensive evidence for the place of the friars in burgh life comes from Haddington where the friars enjoyed good relations with the town. In the other two burghs the friars were less connected to the daily affairs and spirit of the burghs, leading to more distant relations between them and the councils.

Haddington's Franciscan friary was just north of the parish church and included its own large church with at least five altars.[199] As Conventuals, they were allowed to own property, and received ground rents worth at least £48 9s 4d.[200] In return for these rents they, like the chaplains of the parish kirk, were required to perform obit and commemorative services. Sir William Haliburton in 1389, for example, donated a rent worth ten merks annually to fund an altar to St John the Baptist at which he expected daily mass to be performed and an annual mass to be sung on the obit day of his grandfather.[201] People were also buried in the friary church: Sir John Congilton's parents were buried next to the altar of St Duthac, and in 1514 he endowed the altar with a supply of bread and wine in return for an annual service, specifying that the arrangement was to be observed as long as three friars remained in the convent.[202] This doubt about the ability of the friars to keep up services predicted the gradual decline in the number of friars in Haddington during the sixteenth century; there were nine friars in 1478, seven in 1539 and 1543, four in 1555, and possibly only two by 1559.[203] This matches the general decrease of the Conventuals in Scotland during the sixteenth century, from a high of about fifty to only thirty by 1559.[204] The decline in Haddington seems to have taken place in conjunction with the growth of the collegiate church, which may explain the lack of tension between the secular chaplains and friars, as services the friars were unable to provide were taken over by the town's choristers.[205]

Though the friars were not under the town's direct authority, they were still tied to the community by various agreements and obligations. As part of their effort to increase divine worship within the burgh, Haddington's council gave the friars an annual payment of six merks for 'furnishing of wine, wax, bread and other necessaries things within their kirk of the said burgh to the uphold of divine service'.[206] The emphasis on wine, wax and bread points to a definition of divine service focused on the mass, as the agreement is silent about preaching and pastoral care. The contract, originally made in 1287, was renegotiated in 1527 to ensure that payments would be more reliable, with the burgh throwing in another set of annuals for good measure, and promising payment directly from burgh funds if the friars were still unable to collect.[207] The burgh was flexible and generous in upholding the agreement; in 1539, the friars asked for and received an advance of three years on their annuals to help them repair their dortor which had fallen down.[208] In 1559, the friars apparently again sought to be paid in advance, and the council ordered the treasurer to pay five pounds and sixteen shillings, in addition to the twenty-four shillings already given to the friars, for their 1560 and 1561 rents.[209] The council could give out spontaneous alms to the friars as well, especially under the pressures of the Reformation; in August 1559 the council ordered the treasurer to deliver three pounds of money to Friar Lawrence Bell.[210] In 1564 however, they disallowed a payment of twenty merks given to Friar Flock, though it is unclear whether they disapproved of the payment or the lack of a receipt.[211] Haddington's council, over the centuries, treated the friars in much the same manner as the burgh priests and subsidised them just as they would their own employees.

Friars also served other functions in the town, too; in October 1556 Friar John Blackburn received fifteen shillings for maintaining the town's clock.[212] The friary kirk was open to the public, and used by the burghers as a meeting place. It was the customary location in the burgh for disputes to be settled; parties would nominate one to three representatives who would meet at an appointed hour to arbitrate an agreement.[213]

The town also sponsored candidates to the Franciscans – or perhaps more accurately, hoped the order would take care of some problematic inhabitants. In January 1540 the council ordered the bailies 'and certain honest neighbours to pas to the friars and commune with them' about accepting John Fleming, who was apparently unable to support himself, as a friar.[214] This mission was unsuccessful, for burgh records indicate that Fleming was later issued clothing and six pence a day by the treasurer, followed ultimately by an allowance of fifty shillings yearly, after the bailies had gone through the town collecting for him.[215] A year earlier, however, George Lyngon, son and heir of John Lyngon in Haddington, joined the friars with no council intervention, though his widowed mother paid the order twenty shillings.[216]

Haddington's friars were responsible for supervising an almshouse and the Hospital of St Lawrence. The almshouse, located in the Poldrate, had been founded by sir John Haliburton, Vicar of Grenlaw, in 1478, and featured two beds reserved for the poor of Dirleton and one put aside for the warden to offer a night's shelter to any poor person. These institutions were also responsible for contributing to divine worship in the burgh. Haliburton specified that the inmates were to recite the psalter of Our Lady three times, and say five Pater Nosters, five Aves, and a Credo each night, as well as the De profundis if they could read. A friar was to say mass every Sunday, and when the endowment increased, on Fridays and Wednesdays as well. On Candlemas Day a mass was to be said by six priests in the friary and parish churches, before forty pence of bread was distributed among the poor.[217] About half a mile west of the town was the leper hospital. It was originally founded in 1312 or earlier, and by the early sixteenth century it was the Franciscan wardens who were responsible for pastoral care and who received payments made to the hospital, including twenty shillings of annual rent from the royal ferms. From 1532 on however, the town council appointed an official for the day-to-day administration of the hospital, as municipal officials began the process of taking on responsibilities that the friars could not.[218]

In the other two burghs, the friars were less connected to the daily affairs of the burghs, leading to more distant relations between them and the councils. In Dundee, the Franciscans also belonged to the Conventual wing, who were allowed to own property. Their friary was possibly the largest in Scotland and was the normal residence of the Conventual Provincial Vicar, and may have housed a school for the friars.[219] Dundee was also home to houses of Observant Dominicans and Franciscan sisters. Not much is known about their relations with the burgh council, although it is likely that they too performed religious observations that contributed to the town's worship.[220]

The Franciscans in Stirling were clearly connected to the royal household. James V's confessor was based at their friary, and the friars in return received royal alms and contributions towards building expenses. James V was in the habit of donating ten pounds annually and Arran as regent eventually matched his generosity, providing fifty-three pounds in 1548 and another seven pounds in 1552.[221] Their connections to the town were a little more tenuous, though the burgh did grant them a piece of the common land 'at the south part of their yard' in 1524.[222]

The role of the friars, then, varied from burgh to burgh. Haddington maintained good relations with the friars and incorporated them into the burgh's civic religion. It is striking that so much of the surviving evidence relates to their role in performing masses rather than preaching or providing pastoral care to the inhabitants. It is likely that they performed these functions, which were largely their *raison d'être*, but the lack of references suggests that the tasks may not have been a priority for the burgh authorities. Dundee and Stirling, meanwhile, appear to have had cooler relations with the friars than Haddington; in Dundee this was likely because of the association of the local Conventual friary with the church hierarchy, and in Stirling the friars may have been more focused on their relations with the royal household than with the town. Neglecting their links to the municipal authorities would come back to haunt the friars, as we will see in Chapter Seven.

Conclusion

Peter Brown has memorably described early medieval monasteries as 'powerhouses of prayer'.[223] With divine services held in expanded parish churches, chapels, friaries and almshouses, the same might be said for the mid-sixteenth century Scottish burgh. Increasing the quantity and quality of divine services was a constant goal of the burghers and their municipal administrators. Such concerns were not limited to Scotland, of course.[224] A case study of south-west France by Michelle Fournié has demonstrated that there, the consuls – equivalent of Scottish bailies – took care of the ecclesiastical buildings in the town, owned the religious ornaments and equipment, organised liturgical life, especially processions, paid salaries to the parish clerk, the bell-ringers, the organ blowers and to the chaplains, and ensured that the clergy fulfilled their obligations. Fournié concludes that the involvement of the municipal authorities was 'justified by their acute consciousness of their responsibilities'. Like Scottish municipal authorities, 'the consuls considered themselves to be the guardians of the community's spiritual and material goods'.[225]

The Scottish urban conception of spiritual good relied heavily on divine services, especially the mass, to an extent remarkable even in the context of late medieval Christianity. Though preaching did occur, it does not appear to have been of particular concern to the burgh council or the laity. Likewise pastoral care and the administration of the sacraments are never referred to. Even if the burgh council did not consider these activities to be part of their responsibility, and complaints were more likely to be found in diocesan records, it is still remarkable that no disputes or complaints surfaced in the burgh courts or notarial protocol books. The absence of evidence must not be used a proof of satisfaction, but the lack of complaints or conflict is striking. The church that Scotland's townspeople encountered on a daily basis answered not to the prelates, but to themselves. There was certainly potential for corruption without careful, close supervision, but careful close supervision was precisely what the town governments offered.[226] An explanation for the Reformation of 1559–60 therefore cannot rely heavily on the idea that townspeople were fed up with the corruption of their local church, nor can it be claimed that the Scottish laity were indifferent to Catholic religious ritual. Nor, as the next chapter will argue, can an explanation rest on corruption's sibling, anti-clericalism.

Notes

1. Audrey-Beth Fitch, *The Search for Salvation: Lay Faith in Scotland, 1480–1560*, ed. Elizabeth Ewan (Edinburgh, 2009); Mairi Cowan, *Death, Life and Religious Change in Scottish Towns c. 1530–1560* (Manchester, 2014).
2. Donaldson, *The Scottish Reformation*, 1–4, 20, 27, 36; Cowan, *The Medieval Church in Scotland*, 27–8, 52. See also Alex Ryrie, 'Reform without frontiers in the last years of Catholic Scotland', *English Historical Review* 119 (2006): 30–2, 51, though Ryrie argues that the Catholic reformers recognised doctrine rather than discipline as the key division with Protestantism.
3. Ryrie, *The Origins*, 14–16, 24.
4. Rhodes, *Riches and Reform*, 33.

5. Cowan, *The Medieval Church in Scotland*, 170. For other Scottish towns, see Lynch, *Edinburgh*, 3, 28, 30, 222; White, 'The Menzies Era', 230; Verschuur, *Politics or Religion?*, 21–3; Sanderson, *Ayrshire and the Reformation*, 10–22; M. Cowan, *Death, Life and Religious Change*.
6. André Vauchez, 'Introduction', in *La Religion Civique à L'Époque Médiévale et Moderne (Chrétienté et Islam)*, ed. André Vauchez (Rome, 1995), 1; Andrew Brown, *Civic Ceremony and Religion in Medieval Bruges, c.1300–1520* (Cambridge, 2011), 23, 280. Other works focus on Italy, though the nature of Italian city-states and Italian ecclesiastical politics make comparisons with Scotland difficult; see Nicholas Terpstra, *Lay Confraternities and Civic Religion in Renaissance Bologna* (Cambridge, 1995) and Augustine O. P. Thompson, *Cities of God* (University Park, PA, 2005), 3.
7. Vauchez, 'Introduction', 4.
8. David S. Rutherford, *Biggar St Mary's: a medieval college kirk* (Biggar, 1946), 27, 33; Denis McKay, 'Parish life in Scotland, 1500–1560', in *Essays on the Scottish Reformation, 1513–1625*, ed. David McRoberts (Glasgow, 1962), 97–9; Fitch, *The Search for Salvation*, 101: M. Cowan, *Death, Life and Religious Change*, 86. On the dual functions of the late-medieval mass, see Eamon Duffy, *The Stripping of the Altars: Traditional Religion in England 1400–1580*, 2nd ed. (New Haven, 2005), 100; Scribner, *Popular Culture and Popular Movements*, esp. 40.
9. See also Brown, *Civic Ceremony*, 6.
10. Fawcett, *Scottish Medieval Church*, 305; Marshall, *Ruin and Restoration*, 7.
11. Forbes Gray, *Short History*, 24–6; Marshall, *Ruin and Restoration*, 24; Paton, 'Books of the Common Good', 51; HAD/2/1/2/1 f31b; HAD/4/6/73, 13b.
12. Fawcett, *Scottish Medieval Church*, 305–7.
13. *Haddington: Royal Burgh*, 4–5.
14. Known altars include the High Altar (Our Lady), St Andrew, St Anne, St Aubert (Cowbert), St Eloi (Blaise), St James the Apostle, St James the Great, St John the Baptist, St John the Evangelist, St Catherine the Virgin, St Michael the Archangel and Saints Crispin and Crispian, St Nicholas, St Ninian, St Peter, Saints Severus and Bartholomew, St Thomas, the Trinity/Holy Blood/St Salvator, The Three Kings of Cologne, St Peter's, and St Ninian the Confessor; Marshall, *Ruin and Restoration*, 10; HAD/4/6/5, f45, 101v–102, 213b; HAD/4/2/3/1 (1555–60), f8b; HAD/4/6/73, f19; Barbara L. H. Horn, 'List of References to the Pre-Reformation Altarages in the Parish Church of Haddington', *Transactions of the East Lothian Antiquarian and Field Naturalist Society* 10 (1965): 64, 72, 77, 84; Forbes Gray, *Short History*, 25–6; Ian B. Cowan and David E. Easson, *Medieval Religious Houses: Scotland*, 2nd edn (London, 1976), 180.
15. Forbes Gray, *Short History*, 25.
16. Sanderson, *Ayrshire and the Reformation*, 14.
17. *Privy Seal*, 1:390; Mair, *Stirling*, 24.
18. *Charters . . . Stirling*, 71–3.
19. Fawcett, *Scottish Medieval Church*, 298–9.
20. Perry, *Dundee Rediscovered*, 24.
21. Maxwell, *Old Dundee*, 13, 47; Perry, *Dundee Rediscovered*, 24; Dennison Torrie, *Medieval Dundee*, 60–1.
22. *The Chartulary of the Abbey of Lindores*, ed. John Dowden (Edinburgh, 1903), lv xlvi, 116; *Registrum episcopatus Brechinensis [Brechin Registrum]*, eds Patrick Chalmers, John Inglis Chalmers and Cosmo Innes, 2 vols (Edinburgh, 1856),

The Civic Church

I: 62–3; Perry, *Dundee Rediscovered*, 24; Dennison Torrie, *Medieval Dundee*, 69.
23. *Charters, Writs and Public Documents of the Burgh of Dundee*, ed. William Hay (Dundee, 1880), 20; Flett, 'The Conflict of the Reformation and Democracy', 7–8, 19–20.
24. *The Books of Assumption of the Thirds of Benefices*, ed. James Kirk (Oxford, 1995), 32.
25. DCA BHCB 1550–4, f197v.
26. DCA BHCB 1550–4, f244v.
27. Perry, *Dundee Rediscovered*, 25; Fawcett, *Scottish Medieval Church*, 311, 313.
28. The church was 87 metres long and 53 metres wide in the transept. Dennison Torrie, *Medieval Dundee*, 62.
29. St Clements was probably about 13 by 6 metres. Maxwell, *Old Dundee*, 48; Dennison Torrie, *Medieval Dundee*, 61.
30. *Dundee Weavers Charters*, 2, 7–10.
31. Dennison Torrie, *Medieval Dundee*, 89; Maxwell, *Old Dundee*, 18, 36.
32. St Severin, Weaver Trade; St Martin, Glover Trade; St Mark, Walker/Fuller Craft; Holy Blood, the Merchant Guild; Torrie adds St Duthac for the Skinners; Dennison Torrie, *Medieval Dundee*, 89.
33. St Anthony, St Sebastian, the Scrimgeour family; Magdalen Altar, the Barrie family. Torrie adds St John, the earls of Crawford; St Margaret the Virgin and St Thomas the Apostle, the Spaldings; and St James the Apostle, the Scrimgeours. Dennison Torrie, *Medieval Dundee*, 89.
34. St Michael the Archangel, St Agatha and Erasmus, St Ninian's, and St Thomas. The chaplainry of St Salvatours appears to have been in the combined patronage of the King and the Abbey of Cambuskenneth. *Privy Seal*, 1:157.
35. Although sometimes these tasks were taken over by the treasurer.
36. Catholic priests are identified with a lowercase 'sir'.
37. HAD/4/6/5, f16, 41v.
38. HAD/4/6/5, f50v, 91, 166–7; HAD/2/1/2/1, f5v. In 1557–8, expenses also included fees for nails and cutting holes in the wall to set the timber. HAD/4/6/73, f13–13v; SCA SBCB 1519–30 26/8/1529, 21/10/1529, 27/04/1523.
39. Paton, 'Books of the Common Good', 49. In Dundee, a slater was hired immediately in 1550 to start work on the roof, and in 1552 a wright was hired to install a coupled rafters in the choir; DCA BHCB 1550–4, f7v, 190v.
40. See Donaldson, *Scottish Reformation*, 21–3; Ryrie, *The Origins*, 78–9.
41. DCA BHCB 1550–4, f126.
42. *Extracts . . . Stirling*, 70.
43. See Rhodes for a discussion of the system of annuals, or rent charges, collected from urban properties. Rhodes, *Riches and Reform*, 38–9.
44. Some fees owed to altars in the town's patronage were paid directly to the town's treasurer, though these seem to be exceptional cases: HAD/4/6/5, f11v, 21v, 54, 85v, 114v, 168; HAD/4/6/73, f1v; HAD/4/6/5.
45. HAD/4/6/5, f16v, 60; DCA BHCB 1550–4, f3.
46. SCA SBCB 1519–30 13/2/1520; 1544–50 11/01/1549–50.
47. HAD/4/6/5, f98v, 183.
48. SCA SBCB 1519–30, 23/10/1524; *Extracts . . . Stirling*, 20.
49. DCA BHCB 1550–4, f54.

50. DCA BHCB 1550–4, f114.
51. DCA BHCB 1555–8, f69v; DCA BHCB 1454–1524, f3–5.
52. HAD/4/6/5, f173.
53. SCA SBCB 1519–20 5/11/1520.
54. HAD/4/6/5, f210–211v.
55. HAD/2/1/2/1, f31v.
56. Also present at this examination were George Wishart, James Lowell, George Spalding, James Forester and two craftsmen. DCA BHCB 1550–4, f339v.
57. St Ninian's chapel in Stirling, for example, was where Katherine Miller received a batch of linen from Sande Thomson. SCA SBCB 1544–50 17/11/1549. See also Thompson, *Cities of God*, 23–4.
58. HAD/2/1/2/1, f5v.
59. HAD/4/6/5, f38; DCA BHCB 1454–1524, f46v.
60. HAD/4/6/5, f213v.
61. John Knox, *The Works of John Knox*, ed. David Laing, 6 vols. (Edinburgh, 1895), 1:62–3.
62. HAD/4/1/3 Protocol Book Alexander Symson 1539–42, f84.
63. HAD/2/1/2/1, f11v.
64. HAD/4/1/5 Protocol Book Thomas Stevin 1548–65, f207.
65. See Brown, *Civic Ceremony*, 14, for such rituals in Bruges; in France, Philip Conner, *Huguenot Heartland: Montauban and Southern French Calvinism during the Wars of Religion* (Burlington, 2002), 29; for Scotland, see Gordon DesBrisay, Elizabeth Ewan and H. Lesley Diack, 'Life in the towns', in *Aberdeen before 1800*, Dennison, Ditchburn and Lynch, 52.
66. In 1556, the cost of candles in Haddington was set at 8d for a 'ragweik' or 'caddess' (wool or fabric) candle, and presumably more for wax. HAD/2/1/2/1, f9. Augustine Thompson has pointed out the careful attention paid to the quality of wax used in votive candles in Italian communes, where 'votive wax quality affected the integrity of a corporate act of worship and devotion. Inferior wax shamed the commune.' Thompson, *Cities of God*, 164.
67. HAD/4/6/5, f2, 17b, 54v.
68. HAD/4/6/5, f167.
69. DCA BHCB 1454–1524, f10.
70. DCA BHCB 1454–1524, f10v.
71. HAD/4/6/5, f202v.
72. For a detailed discussion of the ceremonies that made up the weekly round of worship in medieval Italy between the twelfth and fourteenth centuries, a cycle that would have been very similar to the one practised in Scotland, see Thompson, *Cities of God*, 242–59. Duffy, *The Stripping of the Altars*, 123–6, details the ceremony of the mass, distinguishing between weekday masses and the weekly Sunday high mass.
73. On the Eucharist, see John Bossy, 'The mass as a social institution 1200–1700', *Past and Present* 100 (1983): 29–61; John Bossy, *Christianity in the West 1400–1700* (Oxford, 1985); Virginia Reinburg, 'Liturgy and the laity in late medieval and Reformation France', *The Sixteenth Century Journal* 23 (1992): 526–47; Miri Rubin, *Corpus Christi: The Eucharist in Late Medieval Culture* (Cambridge, 1991). For a Scottish perspective, Fitch, *The Search for Salvation*, 151, 157–81. See also Brown, *Civic Ceremony*, 130–1.

74. Duffy, *The Stripping of the Altars*, 92–3.
75. Duffy, *The Stripping of the Altars*, 100–1.
76. SCA SBCB 1519–30 8/7/1527.
77. DCA BHCB 1550–4, f205v.
78. HAD/2/1/2/1, f12v. The same was true elsewhere in Scotland. Many of the donations made to St Andrews religious institutions were devoted to improving the endowment of the choir. Rhodes, *Riches and Reform*, 73.
79. Rutherford, *Biggar St Mary's*, 27.
80. Rutherford, *Biggar St Mary's*, 27.
81. Rutherford, *Biggar St Mary's*, 29–30.
82. Rutherford, *Biggar St Mary's*, 33.
83. Rutherford, *Biggar St Mary's*, 33.
84. Rutherford, *Biggar St Mary's*, 33–4.
85. Special services were held on the feast days of All Saints (1 November), The Purification of the Virgin Mary (2 February), Saints Phillip and James (1 May) and the feast of St Peter ad Vincula.
86. Rutherford, *Biggar St Mary's*, 33–4.
87. HAD/4/6/5, f40, f48v.
88. HAD/4/6/5, 142v; HAD/4/1/3, f101.
89. HAD/4/6/5, f60v.
90. Haddington Charters, HAD 1/16 (formerly B30/21/40/5), some parts of the passage are illegible. Other examples can be found at HAD 1/16 (formerly B30/21/40/7). The dating of 1494 is from Marshall, *Ruin and Restoration*, 9.
91. HAD/2/1/2/1, f11.
92. J. J. Scarisbrick, *The Reformation and the English People* (Oxford, 1984); Francis Rapp, *L'Église et la vie Religieuse en Occident à la fin du Moyen Âge* (Paris, 1971), 131.
93. It is unclear if the burgh actually paid them or simply provided them with an opportunity. White, 'The Menzies Era', 226; NRS GD45/13/119.
94. Rapp, *L'Église et la vie Religieuse en Occident*, 130.
95. DCA Protocol Book 1518–34, f90.
96. DCA BHCB 1550–4, f239.
97. SCA SBCB 1519–30, 21/11/1529.
98. *Extracts . . . Stirling*, 23.
99. HAD/4/6/5, f198v, 209v; HAD/4/1/4 Protocol Book Alexander Symson 1542–44, f97v; Horn, 'List of References', 58.
100. *Charters . . . Stirling*, 195–6.
101. HAD 1/16; HAD/4/1/3, f95–95v.
102. DCA Protocol Book 1518–34, f174.
103. HAD/4/6/5, f40–41.
104. HAD/4/1/3, f95–95v.
105. DCA Protocol Book 1518–34, f113.
106. DCA BHCB 1558–61, f28v.
107. *Extracts . . . Stirling*, 21, 23.
108. DCA BHCB 1555–8, f30.
109. *Extracts . . . Stirling*, 70.
110. SCA SBCB 1519–30, 13/2/1520.
111. *Extracts . . . Stirling*, 5.

112. *Extracts . . . Stirling*, 10.
113. *Extracts . . . Stirling*, 11.
114. *Extracts . . . Stirling*, 39.
115. HAD/4/6/5, f40–41.
116. HAD/4/6/5, f106.
117. It is unclear what the wool was to be used for. DCA BHCB 1550–4, f52.
118. DCA BHCB 1550–4, f307.
119. HAD/4/6/5, f142v.
120. Maxwell, *Old Dundee*, 40; DCA BHCB 1550–4 (n.p., 18 December 1554).
121. DCA BHCB 1555–8, f19v.
122. HAD/4/6/5, f134–134v.
123. HAD/4/1/3, f87–87v.
124. HAD/4/1/3, f101–101v.
125. HAD/4/6/5, f198v.
126. HAD/4/6/5, f210v.
127. Bishops would have had to confirm candidates in any case, and would have wanted to see evidence that the clerk election had been duly elected by the majority of the townspeople. See McKay, 'The election of parish clerks in medieval Scotland', 25–35.
128. DCA Protocol Book 1518–34, f211.
129. DCA Protocol Book 1518–34, f211.
130. DCA Protocol Book 1518–34, t273, t274.
131. Cowan, *The Scottish Reformation*, 14.
132. DCA Protocol Book 1518–34, f216.
133. In other parishes the clerk was responsible for the song school as well, but this does not appear to be the case in Dundee, as it was not among the duties specified in the burgh's contract with Richard Barclay, appointed parish clerk in 1543. DCA Protocol Book 1518–34, f231; McKay, 'Duties of the medieval parish clerk', 35, 39.
134. DCA BHCB 1550–4, f244b.
135. DCA BHCB 1550–4, f336.
136. DCA Protocol Book 1518–34, t66.
137. DCA Protocol Book 1518–34, f27/t41.
138. DCA Protocol Book 1518–34, f47/t68.
139. DCA BHCB 1550–4, f20v, f39; DCA BHCB 1558–61, f159.
140. For a comparison, see St Andrews, where fifty-seven sixteenth-century donations to the Holy Trinity were recorded between 1500 and 1559. Bess Rhodes, 'Property and Piety: Donations to Holy Trinity Church, St Andrews', in *Scotland's Long Reformation: New Perspectives on Scottish Religion c. 1500–1660*, ed. John McCallum (Leiden, 2016), 33–9.
141. HAD/1/15; HAD/4/1/5, f159v; NRS B30/21/40/7.
142. Rhodes, *Riches and Reform*, 71–2.
143. HAD/4/1/3, f119.
144. Possibly St Columba.
145. DCA BHCB 1550–4, f154, 333v. This supports Rhodes' argument that feuing could often be used to improve properties. Rhodes, *Riches and Reform*, 88. Chaplains often handled the administration of their chaplaincies, although their transactions often had to be approved by the patrons of their chaplaincy. Similar arrangements were quite common in England, though they became

infrequent in the later Middle Ages as doubts about the financial acumen of the chaplains grew. Marie-Hélène Rousseau, *Saving the Souls of Medieval London: Perpetual Chantries at St Paul's Cathedral c.1200–1548* (Burlington, 2011), 56–8. Not so in Scotland, it seems.
146. *Extracts . . . Stirling*, 66.
147. See the discussion in Chapter 2. Gibson and Smout, *Prices, food and wages*, 274, 278–85.
148. *Extracts . . . Stirling*, 19.
149. HAD/4/6/5, f45.
150. See Rhodes for a discussion of some of the smaller payments offered to clergy in St Andrews. Rhodes, *Riches and Reform*, 35–6.
151. HAD/4/6/5, 75b.
152. HAD/2/1/2/1, f18; HAD/4/6/73, f17–19.
153. HAD/2/1/2/1, f24v.
154. *Extracts . . . Stirling*, 69.
155. Paton, 'Books of the Common Good', 48, 50.
156. HAD/4/6/5, f102.
157. HAD/4/6/5, f140.
158. *Extracts . . . Stirling*, 23.
159. SCA SBCB 1519–30 21/11/1529.
160. DCA Protocol Book 1518–34, f266.
161. DCA Protocol Book 1518–34, f175/t232–3.
162. SCA B66/25/133.
163. See M. Cowan, *Death, Life and Religious Change*, 101–2.
164. DCA, Baxter Craft Lockit Book, 7.
165. DCA, Baxter Craft Lockit Book, 5.
166. Warden, *Burgh Laws*, 543.
167. *Extracts . . . Stirling*, 16; DCA BHCB 1555–8, f102, 165.
168. Warden, *Burgh Laws*, 93–6.
169. *Dundee Weavers Charters*, 10–14.
170. *Dundee Weavers Charters*, 14.
171. Warden, *Burgh Laws*, 510–11.
172. *Dundee Weavers Charters*, 2.
173. *Dundee Weavers Charters*, 7.
174. *Extracts . . . Stirling*, 1.
175. *Extracts . . . Stirling*, 3.
176. Horn, 'List of References', 64, 65, 71; HAD/4/6/5, f16; St Crispin and St Crispianus were the patron saints of shoemakers. Marshall, *Ruin and Restoration*, 11.
177. HAD/4/6/5, f61.
178. HAD/4/6/5, f194v.
179. HAD/4/6/5, f84; St James is assumed for St Ames.
180. SCA SBCB 1519–30 3/2/1522.
181. Possibly 'the Celtic St Duthac'. Marshall, *Ruin and Restoration*, 11–12.
182. HAD/4/6/5, f118.
183. For a calendar of festivals and rituals in St Andrews which was likely similar to those held in other Scottish towns, see David Ditchburn, 'Religion, ritual and the rhythm of the year in later medieval St Andrews', in *Medieval St Andrews: Church, Cult, City*, eds Katie Stevenson and Michael Brown (Woodbridge, 2017).

184. HAD/4/6/5, f28.
185. Anna Jean Mill, *Mediaeval Plays in Scotland* (Edinburgh, 1927), 21; HAD/4/6/5, f28–29v, f81, f101v.
186. Mill, *Mediaeval Plays in Scotland*, 74.
187. John McGavin, 'Drama in sixteenth century Haddington', in *European Medieval Drama* 1, ed. Sidney Higgins (Turnhout 1997).
188. Mill, *Mediaeval Plays in Scotland*, 71; David Calderwood, *History of the Kirk of Scotland*, ed. Rev. Thomas Thomson, 8 vols. (Edinburgh, 1842–9), 1:142.
189. HAD/4/6/5, f21v; DCA BHCB 1454–1524, 149v; *Extracts . . . Stirling*, 68.
190. HAD/4/6/5, f139.
191. HAD/4/6/73, f3–6.
192. DCA BHCB 1550–4, f250.
193. HAD/2/1/2/1, f35.
194. Current research, especially John McCallum, *Poor Relief and the Church in Scotland 1560–1640* (Edinburgh, 2018), focuses on poor relief administered by kirk sessions. A fuller consideration of the role of burgh governments is still necessary.
195. One, run by the Trinitarian order, existed in the late fourteenth century. *RGS*, 1:331. Perry, *Dundee Rediscovered*, 29. There was a hospital of St John the Baptist in the mid-fifteenth century; *Brechin Registrum*, 1:93.
196. Perry, *Dundee Rediscovered*, 30–1; Maxwell, *Old Dundee*, 16.
197. SCA B66/25/114 Charters by Burgh, Protocol and Saisines, 1544–90.
198. See Foggie, *Renaissance Religion*, especially chapter 4.
199. John Mair (Major), for one, complained that the original church was too large for their Order, and seemingly approved of its destruction during the 'Burnt Candlemas': 'Now I for my part do not think it well that the Minorites should possess churches of this sumptuous magnificence; and it may be well that for their sins, and the sins of the town itself, God willed that all should be given to the flames.' John Major, *A History of Greater Britain*, trans. Archibald Constable (Edinburgh, 1892), 297. Bryce, *Scottish Grey Friars*, 1:168, 197.
200. Bryce, *Scottish Grey Friars*, 1:197.
201. Bryce, *Scottish Grey Friars*, 1:178.
202. Bryce, *Scottish Grey Friars*, 1:175.
203. Cowan and Easson, *Medieval Religious Houses*, 126 (from Bryce, 1:193–4) (1478). HAD/4/1/3, f26v (1539), 134 (1541–2); HAD/4/1/5, f110b (1555); HAD/1/15.
204. Bryce, *Scottish Grey Friars*, 1:157. The Observant Franciscans seemed to be the more vigorous order during the sixteenth century.
205. Bryce, *Scottish Grey Friars*, 1:182.
206. 'ble' has been transcribed as wheat, thus bread, HAD/1/15.
207. HAD/1/15; HAD/4/6/5 f74v, 168.
208. HAD/1/15.
209. HAD/2/1/2/1, f23.
210. HAD/2/1/2/1, f21v.
211. HAD/2/1/2/1, f40.
212. HAD/2/1/2/1, f8v.
213. For example, HAD/4/6/5, f288v.
214. HAD/4/6/5, f116v.

215. Bryce, *Scottish Grey Friars*, 1:185 (from HAD/4/6/5, 116v).
216. HAD/4/1/2, f110; Bryce records his name as George Hugo: Bryce, *Scottish Grey Friars*, 1:184.
217. Bryce, *Scottish Grey Friars*, 1:178.
218. Bryce, *Scottish Grey Friars*, 1:181. In 1532 its lands were transferred to the nuns of St Katherine's of Sciennes, outside Edinburgh, and leased to local inhabitants to farm. Cowan and Easson, *Medieval Religious Houses*, 181.
219. Bryce, *Scottish Grey Friars*, 1:15, 219; Perry, *Dundee Rediscovered*, 28.
220. Foggie, *Renaissance Religion*; 6, 60, 143–4; Dennison Torrie, *Medieval Dundee*, 67; Perry, *Dundee Rediscovered*, 28; *RGS*, 2:560; *Privy Seal*, 2:413.
221. *TA*, 6:32, 82, 444; 7:159; 9:217–18; 10:77, 8–90.
222. *Extracts . . . Stirling*, 19.
223. Peter Brown, *The Rise of Western Christendom*, 2nd edn (Oxford, 2003), 219–31, especially 226.
224. See Friedrichs, *The Early Modern City*, who uses the German city of Braunscheig as an example, 67; for Britain, Gervase Rosser and E. Patricia Dennison, 'Urban Culture and the Church 1300–1540', in *The Cambridge Urban History*, vol. I, edited by D. M. Pallister (Cambridge, 2008), 366.
225. Michelle Fournié, 'Confréries, bassins et fabriques dans le Sud-Ouest de la France: des oeuvres municipales', in *La Religion Civique à L'Époque Médiévale et Moderne (Chrétienté et Islam)*, edited by André Vauchez (Rome, 1995), 258.
226. See Lynch, *Edinburgh*, 22.

CHAPTER FOUR

The Urban Clergy

'Droukin Schir Johne latyneless' was Sir David Lindsay's memorable skewering of the typical Scottish priest.[1] This impression of the clergy was shared by the sixteenth-century church's own councils and repeated by many historians, but it would not have been shared by the priest's neighbours.[2] According to the burgh records, the townspeople saw the clergy as important and respected members of the community. They supported them financially, protected their interests, relied on their knowledge and abilities and generally valued their service.

Modern historians have been ambivalent in their assessments of the pre-Reformation Scottish clergy, on one hand acknowledging the often good relations between clerics and lay people, as in the work of Mairi Cowan, on the other hand being drawn to the evidence of inefficiency and corruption among some sectors of the church, particularly as emphasised by Donaldson and Cowan.[3] A focus on the criticisms leads to the assumption, seen in Ryrie, that there was 'widespread' anticlericalism which led some to Protestantism.[4] A closer examination of the criticisms directed at the clergy by Lindsay and others reveals that there were three main targets: the bishops and senior clergy, who were judged for their luxurious living and for neglecting their religious duties; the parish vicars, who were condemned both for their avariciousness and for their failure to preach; and the friars who were criticised for having excessive influence over kings and housewives alike and for taking alms that should have gone to the needy poor.[5] Many of these criticisms did not apply to the chaplains and unbeneficed priests who made up the bulk of the urban clergy. Bishops had almost no apparent role in religious ceremonies in the towns, and only a small role in the administration of the civic church, although many individual burghers may have found themselves before the bishop's court at one point or another.[6] Urban vicars may have been as rapacious as their rural colleagues but could also play a positive role in town life. The fact that Scottish towns had only one parish, and thus only one vicar, also meant that burghers were more likely to interact with chaplains. As to the friars, the criticisms levelled at them may in fact have indicated their popularity, though their relations with the townspeople varied from burgh to burgh.[7] In all, the lives and behaviour of the clergy in the towns were less controversial than one would expect based on the literary and historiographical criticisms of the late medieval Scottish church.

The urban clergy, like the burgh's churches, were products of the community they served. The surviving records have few references to their pastoral duties, and none to their sobriety (or lack thereof) but enough material survives to trace their careers, their family connections, their litigiousness and to some extent their education. This material indicates that many priests served diligently at their posts, were not especially litigious and many of them were not particularly well-off. They maintained close family and social links with the townspeople, and as many as half of the priests active between 1520 to 1560 may have attended university.

The lack of evidence about the clergy's pastoral care means their activities must mostly be assumed. There are occasional glimpses of priests officiating at services, and almost nothing of their duties; performing baptisms and funerals, administering the Eucharist, hearing confessions, visiting the sick or simply praying. These activities surely took place, but there was no reason for anyone to have written about them in the surviving records.[8] Curates were normally at death beds to record testaments, receive last confessions and performs last rites.[9] It is a dispute in Haddington which provides a rare example of a priest interacting with the laity outside of court; in June 1532 an assize heard a dispute about the sale of a horse to John Stane. As evidence in the case, sir William Lawson, along with Patrick and Robyn Schort testified that 'they heard a wife say in birth that Gawin delivered the horse to a boy'.[10] We cannot say if sir William was on the scene as a witness, to comfort the woman, or to provide last rites and an emergency baptism during a difficult delivery, but it seemed expected that the priest be present at this dramatic yet commonplace event.

Vicars

Like provosts, individual vicars varied in their involvement in local affairs, with little note being taken of their routine duties.[11] In our three towns the vicar was appointed by nearby religious houses.[12] In Dundee the vicar was a local figure, with a residence and a role in the burgh's affairs. Dundee's vicar from 1518 or earlier through to the early 1550s was Master John Barry, who had attended the University of St Andrews around 1510.[13] He was evidently a respected and active member of the community, sitting on the burgh council in the early 1520s. The townspeople respected his honesty and competence, asking him to perform sensitive tasks. In 1527 he was nominated by the merchants to serve as an arbiter in their dispute with the craftsmen, and in 1529 the weavers chose him to be one of the auditors of their accounts.[14] He was willing to express his opinion on burgh affairs, as in 1530 when he objected to the admission of a woman, Marion Ker, to Dundee's guild.[15] Master John also had family connections in Dundee, including his sister Janet and his brother Andrew.[16] Janet had married James Wedderburn (b. 1450) and was the mother of Robert, Master John's successor as vicar, and of James and John who were early Protestants.[17] Master John was tutor to William Barry in the early 1520s, and following the occupation of 1549, became responsible for three young orphaned Barry boys.[18] A sir James Barry, likely a relation, was chaplain of the Jesus altar in the parish church in 1524.[19]

Master John did bring people before the courts, as vicars were notorious for doing.[20] He pursued Alexander Davidson, cutler, for the dues owed on his wife's death (called the 'kirkright'), after Alexander failed to prove himself a burgess, and pursued another couple for their tithes.[21] While the clergy were often criticised for over-avariciousness in collecting tithes, these disputes were under the jurisdiction of the ecclesiastical courts and appear rarely in burgh courts.[22] Burgesses also had less onerous obligations than non-burgesses, which may have blunted some resentment. Barry also pursued John Fell, butcher, for a stone weight[23] of tallow, though it is not clear if this was owed to him as vicar or was a business transaction gone wrong. In 1522, Master John tried to claim some of the revenues of the Holy Rood altar, held by sir Robert Gray. The council sided with sir Robert, even though Master John was a fellow councillor, demonstrating that connections with the burgh's elites did not necessarily grant advantages in court.[24] Barry was certainly willing to use the court system to pursue what he was owed, but there is no evidence that he was particularly favoured or that his position carried any special weight.

Following Master John's death, three other men filled Dundee's vicarage in the eight or so years until the Reformation: Robert Wedderburn did not long survive his uncle Master John, and he was followed by Master John Rolland. From 1558 on the vicar was Master John Hamilton, who complained in January 1561 that he had not received any income from the altar for three years past. At that point, the benefice was worth forty pounds annually.[25] Given that Dundee's council respected their obligations through the Reformation changes, it is possible that this was a personal or administrative dispute. There was also a curate present, who would be responsible for pastoral care in the absence of the vicar; in 1554 it was sir William Lwyd.[26] Other vicars and parsons were an occasional sight in the burgh courts, collecting rents owed to them from tenements in the burgh. Sir Patrick Graham, Vicar of the Mannis, for example, appeared in Dundee burgh court in July 1558 to secure a payment of four pounds from John Boyes for his 'entry', the fee due to him upon a tenant's occupation of a property.[27]

Stirling's vicars did not develop the same respectful relationship with the council and townspeople as the vicars of Dundee did and were not as involved in town life. Master William Hamilton, vicar in 1521, along with John Bully brought a claim to ownership of four acres of the burgh's common land before the ecclesiastical court of the official of Lothian. The town councillors decided to defend themselves against this claim vigorously, as the actions 'pursued by the said vicar and clerk were unjust and that they had no just title to the said acres nor money'.[28] The claim, and the fact that the vicar and clerk brought it before the ecclesiastical court system, indicates a lack of cooperation and goodwill between the vicar and the town. While bringing financial disputes to court may have been routine for vicars, taking on the burgh council was rare and contrasts with the support Dundee's council gave to Master John Rolland. The case also demonstrates why it was important for town councils to try to have some say over the appointment. One of Master Hamilton's successors in Stirling, sir Robert Wemys, did not succeed in establishing a better reputation, being excommunicated in his own parish church at the behest of the abbot of Cambuskenneth. The process took place over the course of a month during the late spring of 1531, during which sir Robert does not seem to have been present.[29] Alas, despite the dramatic rituals of excommunication, there is no sense of what caused this drastic step, although it was possibly part of the never-ending dispute over fishing rights in the Forth.

An exception was sir John Crag, who was vicar portioner in Stirling during the 1550s, substituting for Robert Auchmurty, the vicar perpetual.[30] As vicar portioner, Crag would have received a portion of Auchmurty's income as his salary.[31] Amongst the townspeople he helped to arbitrate disputes, offering evidence about arrangements made between them. In 1556, for example, he testified that five years previously he had been present when an annual obligation was fixed at six capons. He was also responsible for collecting the tithe from the fisheries on the Forth. He was one party in a complex dispute over the proper division of the land on which he lived, which was resolved when he and his neighbours split the parcel four ways. The evidence indicates that he was a neighbour who lived among the people, however it does not indicate that he played a role in official burgh affairs.[32] The records say little about the vicars of Haddington.[33] There it was apparently the curate who performed the high mass, as demonstrated in 1530 when sir James Mauchlin spoke from the pulpit concerning a theft of iron.[34] In sum, vicars could play a positive role in town affairs, but much depended on personality, and it was in the interest of the town councils to influence the appointment as much as they could.

Chaplains, Choristers and Priests in Search of a Position

The remainder of the urban clergy was made up of stipendiary priests who were hired to say mass and administer the various altars and chapels, choristers who sang the main daily services at the parish church, and priests without positions.[35] Some of these in the last group would have required financial support from the town councils while they waited for a vacancy, others would have scrambled at a variety of odd jobs, of which working as a legal representative, known as a procurator or prolocutor, is most apparent in the records. There were friars based at each of the towns studied, and monks and priests from elsewhere visited on a regular basis. In addition to the Abbey of Lindores, the priory of St Andrews and the abbeys of Scone, Balmerino, and Coupar Angus all owned annual rents in Dundee.[36] In Stirling, the Abbey of Cambuskenneth and the Chapel Royal were prominent rent and annual holders. In Haddington, it was the provost and priests of the college church at Bothans and the church at North Berwick who had interests in the burgh.

In the towns, therefore, clerics would have been a common presence among the inhabitants. In Aberdeen, which hosted both a university and an episcopal administration, clerics were as much as 25 per cent of the adult male population in Old Aberdeen and 5 per cent in New Aberdeen.[37] In the three towns studied here the ratios were not so high, but still noticeable. During the period 1530–65, about sixty-one priests and friars were likely residents of Haddington and another ninety or so would have visited occasionally.[38] At any given time, then, there were probably thirty to forty resident clerics, and several dozen others who made occasional appearances in the burgh. There may well have been many others who simply do not appear in the surviving records. In Stirling, some seventy clerics have been identified from the records as being resident at some point in the years between 1520 and 1565, although this figure does not include all the clergy at the Chapel Royal or nearby Cambuskenneth abbey. Of these, thirty-one were chaplains of a particular altar, and a further nineteen were chaplains without known attachments. Six were vicars or curates of the parish church. Six Dominican friars were also noted. Two clerics were notaries and one was an apparently well-regarded prolocutor. Forty other clerics were present in the burgh at least briefly during that period. In Dundee, the burgh records reveal at least fifty-two clerics resident or especially active in burgh life during the 1550s alone.[39] Thirty-nine of them held at least one benefice or stipend during the decade and a further four were collecting annuals and probably had an unidentified position. Of the remaining nine, one was a notary public and three appeared as procurators or litigants on behalf of others (which did not exclude them from holding a benefice or stipend). One Dominican friar also appeared. Though several friars lived in the burghs, usually only one was tasked with appearing in the burgh court to collect rents owed to the order and settle other financial disputes. Townspeople would thus have been familiar with a variety of clergy on their streets, though the secular clergy who served in the town's parish churches and chapels would have been the most common sight. The familiarity was more than just superficial, as these clerics were also integrated into the social fabric of the town.

Clerical Careers

Many urban priests were deeply rooted in their burghs, though they may have left to attend university or engage in business in other towns. Brief sketches of five priests from the towns indicate that the typical burgh priest retained family connections, which brought opportunities to supplement his clerical income, and spent his ecclesiastical career slowly moving up to more lucrative positions. Sir Adam Brown first comes to our attention in February 1534, when Haddington town council granted him an annual worth eight merks to perform a daily service in the parish church.[40] It was standard practice for councils to give modest salaries to young priests to participate in worship at the parish church while waiting for a vacant benefice or altar. He must have soon been given an altar, albeit not a very well-endowed one, for just over a year later the council decided to supplement his income by ten merks a year.[41] In 1544 he received sir Archibald Borthwick's half of the parish clerkship, his previous stipend of ten merks being assigned next to sir Robert Symson.[42] He supplemented his income with the inheritance he received from his father (which included two tenements shared with his siblings) though it took him prolonged legal wrangling to obtain it.[43] In 1542 he acted as surety (guarantor) for his sister's dowry of £100. As his modest income would not have been sufficient if he was called on to redeem the debt, his property, possibly inherited, must have been significant.[44] In 1557 sir Adam would fail in his attempt to be named his niece's heir.

At some point during these years sir Adam had a son named William, who in 1567 would get the bailies' agreement to reduce the payments owed on his property. Unlike other clerics, sir Adam did not go to the trouble of having William legitimated.[45] Scottish townspeople were somewhat resigned to clerical relationships. Through foundation charters and ordinances they made clear their preference for celibate priests, and as seen in the example of the forced break-up of John Mertyne and Elene Ramsey they were willing to be firm with younger clergy. They seemingly found it hard to be equally harsh with more established relationships.[46] Likely, once children were fathered, the most important concern was to ensure that the man responsible acknowledged and looked after them.

Later on in his career, sir Adam developed some administrative experience. In the mid-1550s he was procurator for the priests of the college kirk, which meant that he appeared frequently in the burgh court to feu land and pursue rents.[47] He also sometimes served as procurator for relatives.[48] In 1555 he rented one of the town's mills, though it is not clear if he did this for himself or on behalf of the choristers.[49] In January 1557, Master William Brown, presumably a kinsman, appointed him as chaplain of the Holy Blood altar.[50] As time went on he increasingly shared the job of procurator for the kirk, especially with sir Thomas Mauchlin, and served as procurator for the prominent burgess Barnard Thomson.[51] He was also chamberlain to the Bishop of Moray, collecting crop tithes.[52] These activities would also have brought some extra income and his dealings became extensive enough that on occasion he would appoint procurators himself.[53] More dramatically, he also apprehended a pair of Englishmen, who filed a claim against him in February 1557 for a horse, a dog and their weapons.[54] By 1561 he was still pursuing annuals either on his own tenements or as chaplain of the Holy Blood altar, and appearing as procurator for Margaret Brown, who was likely a relation. He died sometime before 1567.[55]

Sir William Wolson or Wilson, who appeared in the Introduction, was appointed to Haddington's parish clerkship along with Archibald Borthwick in April 1533. He would have been a young man or even a teenager at that point, and he and Archibald promised to become priests as soon as possible. In 1539, a William Wolson matriculated at St Andrews, and that same year William Wolson was first designated as 'sir' in the burgh council minutes, indicating that he had been ordained as a priest.[56] In 1540, he was appointed to the St Salvator's/Holy Blood altar by its patron, George Crosar. This arrangement appeared to simply have secured his right to succeed to that altar (and possibly some of its income), for he immediately agreed to pay the previous chaplain, sir John Crosar, ten merks annually to serve at it.[57] Meanwhile, sir William appears to have continued as parish clerk.

From time to time he served as a procurator for others and witnessed documents, especially those involving other clergy.[58] He briefly took a turn as procurator for the chaplains of the choir and for sir John Crosar.[59] Following the Reformation, sir William continued to receive support from the town council; in 1563 the council ordered the sergeants to seize an annual rent of eight merks which he was attempting to collect on behalf of the prebends.[60] In 1567, he asked the town council for permission to resume his collection of twelve pence from each house, as he had done from 1535 until 1560. He had previously agreed that his duties in the Protestant church would include ministering water at baptism, cleaning the church and keeping the church door open at proper times. The council agreed, adding psalm singing to his responsibilities along with a payment of eleven shillings.[61] These functions were quite similar to the parish clerk duties he had been performing since his youth, when he was told off for not ringing the morning bell and lighting the lamps on time. He seemed a little bitter about Protestantism, however, referring to it as 'the "Imitation of religion"'.[62]

The final Haddington priest to be examined, sir James Mauchlin, first appears in the records in 1520, when as curate he received an annual rent in exchange for performing an anniversary.[63] In 1530, he intervened from the pulpit in a dispute over some iron which had supposedly been stolen from a ship; sir James spoke on behalf of the alleged thief, George Ryklington, and was contradicted by William Kemp who spoke to the curate in the pulpit 'in presence of all the parishioners'. The incident was controversial enough that the parties immediately had their claims recorded in Alexander Symson's protocol book.[64] Sir James acted as procurator for the chaplains of the choir throughout the 1530s and on occasion acted as procurator for lay people as well.[65] In 1541, he became chaplain of St James altar, whose patronage William Kemp, who had argued with him in the church a decade earlier, had just delivered to the bailies in exchange for payments of ten pounds yearly.[66] Kemp likely had some idea of who the altar would go to, so this may be a sign that the previous decade's acrimony had faded. It is not known if sir James remained as curate. Throughout the 1540s and 1550s sir James appeared in the burgh records pursuing various rents, witnessing transactions and testifying about annuals paid in the past.[67] Finally, in 1558 he began a form of retirement, handing over the administration of St James altar to the town council and agreeing to continue to serve in the choir in exchange for a yearly pension of four pounds, which was increased to ten pounds in September 1560.[68] That the council was willing to increase his pension after the Protestant regime had been established and his service would no longer be necessary demonstrates Haddington's good relations with their priests, and that the religious changes of the Reformation did not alter their perception of their responsibilities to their neighbours and employees. Thereafter nothing was recorded about him.

Master James Wilson, alias Cristeson, was a typical Stirling priest. He was chaplain of St Anne's altar in the parish church, and first appears in the burgh records as claiming an annual rent from an unidentified piece of land in October 1524. He would go on to make ten court appearances, concerning four different annuals or dues he claimed, in the surviving records up to 1546. As procurator for the chaplains of the church he would make a further thirteen appearances. In 1529, the provost agreed to be guarantor for an annual that he was owed. For that annual, disputed between him and Sir Archibald Watson, the two clerics agreed to have their claim adjudicated by the warden of the Franciscans and the prior of the Dominicans. He also partnered with at least one merchant relative, as in 1549 he and John Cristeson in Dieppe agreed to pay forty pounds to Jonet Geichay, so he had some income from non-clerical activities.[69]

The scanty records between 1523 and 1550 make it difficult to trace the lives of the Dundee priests. The career of sir William Lwyd, nonetheless, can be traced back to 1529, when as chaplain of the weavers he took on the oversight of their accounts, with his brother sir David as his designated replacement.[70] In 1553, he, his brother and Margaret Wenton, the widow of George Rolland, were guarantors for eight pounds owed by John Rolland and David Aldcorne.[71] Aldcorne would ask him to be guarantor again in 1560.[72] The modest sums in these transactions do not hint at any great personal wealth, but they do demonstrate his place in the networks of personal connections that made up burgh life. In April 1554, sir William served as the curate of Dundee and appeared in burgh court to testify about the amount owed from a tenement to the chaplain of the Rood altar.[73] Between 1554 and 1556 he appeared in court several times to collect annuals.[74] His final appearance in the records occurred in 1561 when Lord Oliphant demanded that Lwyd produce the protocol book of sir William Robertson, which he had apparently been keeping.[75]

It is evident from the above accounts that many priests stayed in the burgh for most of their lives. They held a few different positions throughout their careers, and were available to friends and family to help with legal affairs and financial transactions. They commonly had some business dealings or sources of income unrelated to their clerical careers including inherited income, which brought with it the usual and eternal family entanglements. Though they sometimes became involved in a legal or business dispute, in small towns disputes and bad feelings eventually had to be settled, as shown by the case of sir James Mauchlin and William Kemp. Their relations with their fellow townspeople thus seem to have been generally cordial, and the priests were trusted to witness transactions, help resolve disputes or act as guarantors. Of course, the nature of the available evidence means we can say little about the lives of the quieter clergy, who may not have had reason to appear in court.

Education and Wealth

As a group, the clergy were reasonably well-educated. It is possible that about a third of the total clergy in the three towns had attended the university at St Andrews, which was fairly close to Dundee and Haddington and reasonably accessible from Stirling.[76] In Haddington, as many as twenty-six priests, out of thirty-nine resident secular clergy, may have attended St Andrews, while in Dundee as many as twenty-six out of fifty-two secular clergy could have gone. St Leonard's, whose principal Gavin Logie was an early supporter of Protestantism, appears to have been the preferred college, with twenty-two identified attendees as opposed to only eight for the more conservative St Salvators.[77] This perhaps accounts for what would be, if not necessarily support for the Reformation among the clergy, at least enough sympathy to mute strong opposition. In Stirling, possibly thirteen of the resident clerics had attended St Andrews, and likely more attended Glasgow or Aberdeen than in the other burghs.[78] The rest would have been trained through the local song and grammar schools; while the grammar schools were in the charge of professional schoolmasters, albeit sometimes supported by benefices, the song schools were often taught by one of the choristers.[79]

Serving in the local clergy was not a road to significant financial comfort, except for the few who were lucky enough to get the better benefices or to supplement their income by working as notaries or procurators. The Dundee rental roll of 1581, which inventoried the altars owned by the burgh, lists how much income some of the altars and chaplainries would have brought.[80] The incomes provided by the altars ranged from £7 13s 4d to over £22, comparable to the range of £5 6s 8d to £13 6s 8d found in Ayr.[81] Many did not reach or exceed the 1559 Provincial council's minimum for curates of £13 6s 8d.[82] Few would have matched the twenty-pound annual salary promised in July 1559 by Dundee council to Master John Young for his combined services as reader in the congregation and chaplain of the song school.[83] In Stirling, daily service at the Holy Blood altar, belonging to the merchant's guild, was worth twenty-five merks in 1524 (about sixteen pounds), rising to twenty-two pounds in 1557.[84] However, there as well, many altars provided less, and the incomes did not always go to one man. St Michael's altar, which had received a grant of a tenement from King James V in 1516, was worth £8 11s 10d in 1540. This amount was to support two chaplains, one to say daily mass and another to fulfil 'the burdens and services according to the custom of the said church every week'. Sir William Robesoun, who was appointed to this altar in February 1541 upon the resignation of sir Alexander Forsitht, was also expected to serve as master of work as part of his appointment.[85] St James's altar, according to a charter of 1492, was worth £9 16s 8d, which was to fund one chaplain to perform daily private mass and prayers, and a yearly celebration, likely by all available chaplains, of a requiem mass and nine private masses on the obit day of Richard Crystysone.[86]

As a yearly salary for a skilled labourer in the 1550s would have been about ten to fifteen pounds a year, we can see that many of the altars would have provided a living below that level.[87] The sixteenth century was a time of rapid inflation in Scotland, though less so in the first half, and the clergy were relying on fixed rents and annuals which led to a gradual decrease in their relative worth. It is unclear, furthermore, if the chaplains kept all this income for themselves; in 1560 sir John Murray, chaplain of the Magdalene altar in Dundee, got into trouble with the young Mark Barrie, the altar's patron, for deducting part of an annual rent without his permission, although the deduction appeared to be in keeping with the Act on Burnt Lands. Clearly, Barrie thought he had a financial stake in the collection of annuals – either he expected a portion of the collection or, as this took place in 1560, he was hoping to reclaim all of the income with the abolition of the mass.[88] Those with the charge of an altar also had expenses – wax, lamps, cloths, hosts and cleaning.[89]

Priests had other sources of income to augment the revenues of their altars. Evidence from England demonstrates that many priests had greater personal wealth than one would expect based on their stipends.[90] Some of this wealth might be from inheritances or from participating in obits and funerals. On Candlemas, for example, six Haddington priests and the parish clerk would each receive one shilling for participating in mass, paid for with funds left by John Haliburton, Vicar of Grenlaw.[91] They may have also received offerings and small payments for performing various sacraments.[92] In Stirling, the royal household provided some lucrative opportunities. Twenty-two pounds were distributed to the chaplains annually for participating in the anniversary mass of Queen Magdalene.[93] Another unidentified 'poor priest' received a shilling a day for saying mass daily to Mary of Guise.[94] Appearing as procurators also probably brought in some extra income. Three Dundee clerics served as procurators for others, as did three of ten non-stipendiary clergy in Haddington. In Stirling, nine priests took a turn as a procurator or prolocutor, though only sir Thomas Swynton was likely able to earn a living at it. This demonstrates that a fair number

Table 4.1 Rentals owed to Dundee chaplaincies[95]

	Sum owed
Choristers:	£83 18s 2d
Chapel of St Salvator	£22 11s 2d
Chapel of St Agatha	£11 6s 8d
Chapel of St Andrew	£13 13s 6d
Chapel of St John the Baptist	£17 13s 4d
Chapel of Our Lady in the Cowgait	£7 13s 4d
Chapel of St Ninian	£8 14s 10d
Chapel of St Catherine	£10 4s 10d
Chapel of the Rood or Holy Cross	£9 16s 8d
Chapel of St Thomas	£8
Church of St John the Evangelist (Slateheughs)	£8 3s 11d
Church of St Clement	£21 14s and 16 bolls of victual meal and wheat

of clerics had a reasonable education and professional demeanour and were trusted by the inhabitants to represent them fairly and competently: it is unlikely that many burghers would have entrusted their legal affairs to 'drouken Schir John latynless'. Rather, the clergy were an important local resource, able to put their learning and status at the disposal of people who would have had only limited access to the small number of professional lawyers practising in the sixteenth century.

After the vicar, the curate and the chaplain of the Holy Blood altars, the most important priests were the choristers. Though at least one singer who was hired was probably in minor orders, all those who had endowed positions were priests and were referred to as 'the choristers'.[96] According to the 1581 rental roll, Dundee's choristers collectively were due annuals worth £83 18s 2d. It is unclear how many choristers this money was divided among; however, in 1527, the council promised to three men, sir Thomas Bell, sir Thomas Ducher and sir James Ramsay, 'half of the common allowance of the said weekly choristers' in return for their daily service.[97] Presumably, more than six men performed service weekly, otherwise the three priests would not have gained any advantage by this arrangement. The share of each would have been about fourteen pounds, a barely liveable income as inflation increased.

Given the disparities in incomes, it is not surprising that the chaplains frequently manoeuvred for better positions. Clerics were allowed to serve at least two less well-endowed benefices, but they were expected to resign wealthier benefices before accepting another post. Sir Thomas Wedderburn served as chaplain of Dundee's bakers throughout the 1550s, and in 1557 and 1558 was also chaplain of Our Lady in the Cowgait and St Michael's.[98] Our Lady in the Cowgait earned only seven pounds and thirteen shillings, so evidently the patrons permitted sir Thomas to find other sources of income.[99] Sir James Kinloch, Dundee parish clerk, also had to scrounge for income; in addition to what he received as parish clerk the council gave him the chaplainry of St Thomas Martyr in 1553, and then added the job of keeper of the town's clock for five merks annually.[100] Out of his revenues from these posts, however, he had to fund a stipend of ten merks annually to John Mertyene chorister.[101] It is also likely that the smaller stipends were for positions where daily mass was not required. As priests were only allowed to say one mass a day, perhaps some combined several posts which only required mass a few times a week.[102]

If some Dundee clerics were busy serving at a variety of poorly paid positions, some benefices saw a high turnover as well. St Salvator's chaplainry saw three incumbents (Master James Scrimgeour, Master David Lyall and sir John Wilson) between 1549 and 1557.[103] Though St Salvator's is one of the wealthier altars for which we have records (£22 2s 4⅓d), Master James resigned it to take up St Traduan's, which must have been even more lucrative. Similarly, St Michael's altar went through three incumbents during the 1550s: Master John Phillip (1553), sir Thomas Wedderburn (1557–8) and Master John Balsom (1559).[104] Some priests, though, stayed in a given benefice for most of their careers. Master Richard Jakson served as chaplain of St Clement's from at least 1540 until 1558, when he apparently retired and resigned the altar in favour of George Rollok (III).[105] St Clements held a relatively comfortable income of twenty-one pounds fourteen shillings and sixteen bolls of grains, which explains why Master Richard did not need to secure a more lucrative benefice and why George Rollok was so anxious to secure the post for his son. Some chaplainries, moreover, were in the hands of outsiders who were not among the burgh's clergy, such as the chaplaincy of St James the Apostle and the chapel of the Virgin in the Welgait in Dundee. Town councils were, nonetheless, determined to ensure residency in positions under their control.

Family Connections

Many of the clerics had close connections to the town and townspeople. As burghs favoured locals for benefices and private patrons favoured kin, many families had several representatives among the clergy. These connections ensured that priests remained entangled in worldly affairs, which may have reduced respect for the sacredness of the clergy and sometimes created acrimony, but also preserved valuable ties between the clergy and the laity, and possibly eased resentment at the clergy's special status.

In Dundee, a few families had multiple members in the clergy. The Wedderburns had several clerical members, some of whom had dramatic careers. Robert Wedderburn was the chaplain of St Matthews in 1528, and Vicar of Dundee in 1551, although in between he spent some years overseas in France. John Wedderburn, his brother and the reputed author of the *Gude and Godlie Ballatis*, may also have been a priest, but there is no surviving evidence about whether he had any religious posts in the burgh.[106] Sir Thomas Wedderburn, relation uncertain, was more present in Dundee, serving as chaplain of the bakers and of Our Lady in the Cowgait and St Michael's altar. The Scrimgeours, the prominent local family who occupied the hereditary post of Constable, also had two representatives among the local clergy.[107] The surname Gray was common in the Dundee area, belonging to important lairdly families and ordinary burgh residents, as well as four chaplains in the burgh.[108] Of other prominent Dundee families, no Lovells or Rolloks appear among the known clerics, although George Rollok (III) appeared to be destined for the clergy when his father obtained the benefice of St Clement's for him, and Charles Rollok, possibly a cousin, was similarly provided for, but chose to become a merchant instead, as in 1554 he gave up his claim to the Rood benefice in favour of sir Thomas Ducher. That one of the most important merchant families in Dundee was determined to place their children in the priesthood well into the 1550s indicates the respect with which the townspeople viewed the clergy right up to the Reformation.

In Haddington, at least eight clerics are known to have had kin in the burgh. Sir Thomas Mauchlin, sir James Mauchlin and sir Patrick Mauchlin were likely related to Robert Mauchlin (I), who served on a handful of assizes in the 1530s, and Robert Mauchlin (II), who had his expenses paid for travelling to Edinburgh on town business in 1558.[109] Sir Thomas was also related to the Lauta family, who had several members in Haddington, though none of them were especially prominent.[110] Sir Adam Brown also had extensive family connections: his brother-in-law was John Auchar, a mason who was treasurer in 1544. Sir Adam feued two tenements of the Trinity aisle to one William Brown, likely a relative, and was appointed to the Holy Blood altar by the patron Master William Brown. Master William was married to Janet Oliphant, who in her turn was likely related to James Oliphant, who served as provost and in many other town council positions during the 1550s. Sir Adam also acted as procurator for Friar Gilbert Brown of Pebbles, possibly another relative. Sir Adam, along with his sisters, was further involved in a dispute with his mother and step-father. It is not surprising to find these connections in a small town like Haddington, but they emphasise that the local clergy were not an alien occupation force but part of the kin and social network of the burgh.

Some of the clergy of Stirling also maintained family connections. Three Cristesons, David, James and Alexander, were clerics: sir David was the steward of King James V's bedchamber and became a burgess and guild member in 1529 on the death of his father; sir James had business dealings with a John Cristeson in Dieppe.[111] There are three examples in the Stirling records of priests serving as curators for orphaned children, all from the 1520s. A typical arrangement comes from 1520, when Robert Moles chose Sir Andrew Lammanson, along with James Moles, as his curators.[112] More contentious were disputes over inheritances. Six such cases were recorded in Stirling's burgh records, along with two cases of clergy inheriting burgess status. An example was 1521 when the burgh court assigned Isabell Norrocht to bring her evidence over some possessions of Sir James Crag, which was claimed by James Reduacht as an inheritance. In four of these six cases, however, clergy inherited from each other, indicating that not all clergy had close family connections to leave their belongings to.[113]

The lives of the priests remained intertwined with their families even after their ordination. In 1521, during the early days of his career, sir Thomas Ducher in Dundee tried to claim fifteen merks he asserted were owed to him by his sister, Eufame Silver, from the land she inherited from their parents. The parents had been accustomed to providing sir Thomas with meat and drink, and obliged Eufame to give him five merks every year to buy a gown, which she did until their death. However, the documents demonstrating this had been taken away from Thomas when he had been sick and 'wrongfully held from him to his great skaith [damage]', and Eufame refused to pay him a penny without the documentation. She further claimed that 'what her father and mother did for themselves she would do for herself' and remained firm, despite Thomas's plea that

> she knew perfectly that her mother when she lay on her deid bed and her father stretched beside, that they said both, that they had great concern that they had not provided a way for the said Thomas to live upon, nor could comely, and therefor sought the said Eufame to be kindly to him, and labour for some way for his living, because they got his heritage from him that he should have lived on.

It is not known whether Thomas was able to obtain any more justice than his curse that 'all damage and skaith would come upon her and her heirs'.[114]

There were several similar though less dramatic cases. Sir Adam Brown, who we met above, and his siblings – John, Alexander and Janet – sued their mother Marion Mur and her new husband John Loigan for the possession of two tenements which they thought they should have inherited from their father, William Brown, in a case that dragged on for a year and a half. The episodes demonstrate that priests could count on (or hope for) substantial financial support from their families, including portions of inheritances. Sir Thomas Ducher's case also demonstrates the poverty that priests, especially young ones, could suffer. For all the criticism of clerical greed, sir Thomas' parents did not seem to expect that his priestly career would be especially lucrative, and many chaplains may have been more pitied than resented.

Clerics could also count on the support or assistance of family members in furthering their career or carrying out their duties. Sir James Kinloch, parish clerk in Dundee, likely owed a great deal of his career success to his brother, William Kinloch, who was kirkmaster between 1550 and 1553 and a member of the town council throughout the 1550s. William was guarantor for sir James when he became keeper of the clock in 1554; both William and sir James were the victims of stroublance by John Leuch; both William and sir James were made responsible for paying John Mertyne a stipend of ten pounds for service in the choir; indeed, sir James was not permitted to do much without William sharing responsibility, and seeing as the first reference to sir James is the accusation that he did not provide enough wool for the kirk, perhaps the council was dubious about his competence.[115] The parish clerkship seems to have been a position essentially in the possession of William Kinloch, for in 1558 his son Robert was appointed clerk, although William was obliged to pay five merks annually until Robert was qualified to serve.[116] It is unclear why James was no longer clerk as he was still alive and collecting annual rents in 1560.[117] Chaplains sometimes sold, rented or feued lands belonging to their chaplainry to their kinsmen, and it is difficult to tell if their relatives paid an honest price. One suspects that they sometimes did not. On 8 November 1527, for example, sir James Ramsay, the chaplain of St Columba in Dundee, set to his kinsman William Carale 'a chamber with loft of the east land of the said chaplainry, for his lifetime', for which William was to pay yearly one pound of wax.[118] Whatever the going rate for a single room, it was likely higher than a single pound of wax.

At least one pair of brothers were both priests. In the charter of the Dundee weaver craft in 1529 sir William Lwyd was appointed as chaplain for six pounds annually, but should sir William be dismissed as chaplain of the weavers, the post was to go immediately to his brother. This suggests that the post was promised to the family, who perhaps had links to the guild (in 1529 a John Lwyd is listed as having borrowed forty shillings from the weaver craft box) rather than to the individual.[119]

The network of family connections among the clergy and laity reminds us of just how many Scots had an interest in the late medieval church. The clerical estate was not removed from and opposed to the laity: for some, a clerical career was a family concern, with the resources of a given position being administered by different family members. For others, having a cleric in the family meant having someone with the education and status to appear in court on their behalf. The benefits of clergy extended well beyond the individual priests themselves. This deep integration and familiarity partly accounts for why the violence of the Scottish Reformation was directed against objects and property, not people.

Litigation

Most of the extant evidence about the clergy comes from property charters, court records of financial disputes and literary works so it is not surprising that the adversarial nature of these documents, and a couple of well-placed jibes by their literary critics, have given the pre-Reformation clergy their reputation as being overly worldly and avaricious. In her study of Perth, for example, Verschuur argues that 'indications of continued faith in the clergy and in the services they performed were far outnumbered by the many public disputes between burgesses and priests which surfaced in the various courts'.[120] The burgh court records, however, do not simply reveal a grasping, legalistic clergy.[121] Many clerics rarely appeared in court. Those clerics who did pursue legal cases were treated no differently than anyone else; evidence of their claims, either written or through the testimony of others, was treated as sceptically by the judges as lay people's were. Priests testified as witnesses, but admitted ignorance rather than inventing evidence favourable to each other. Clerics even went to court against each other.

While many priests were certainly prepared to go to court to obtain money they thought they were owed, comparing them to the laity suggests that they did not particularly deserve their notoriety for litigiousness.[122] For comparative purposes, samples of court cases in all three burghs have been examined.[123] These disputes were mostly rents owed, payments not made and other uncollected debts. The results demonstrate that while overall the clergy accounted for about half the cases, most of these cases came in sustained bursts after crises. In most months, the clergy accounted for just a small handful of cases. From the combined samples, the clergy accounted for 141 out of 302 cases, or 47 per cent. Many of these cases, however, came from a surge of clerical collection in Stirling during the 1520s. During that decade, Stirling's clergy were very active, bringing 107 cases to the laity's twenty-one. In subsequent years there were many fewer cases in Stirling. In Dundee and Haddington, the numbers are strikingly different, with just twenty-six clerical cases out of a total 132 claims related to property. After all, laypeople were very capable of suing each other without the clergy's assistance.

Haddington's clergy were not particularly aggressive compared to the lay people. In the combined four sample months of 1532, the clergy brought three cases before Haddington's courts to the twenty-two brought by the laity. In 1542, clerics brought four, laypeople fourteen. In 1552, it appears that the laity got a head start on sorting out the arrears following the upheavals of the 1540s; they brought thirty-nine cases before the courts, compared to four for the clergy. That said, beyond the sample months and years, we find that there was a delayed effect of the plague and wars. Beginning in October 1554, Haddington's clergy, along with some of the more prominent landowners, began a concerted effort to start collecting back rents and annuals. In January 1555, the clergy dominated the court; forty-nine of the seventy obligations claimed were by clerics, either the college kirk (24), the other chaplains (9), the friars (9) or the Abbey of Haddington (7). Of the twenty-one claims brought by lay people, six were brought by crafts seeking rents owed to their altars.[124] The Act on Burnt Lands, passed in February 1552, gave owners two years to repair their tenements before the lands could be repossessed, so it is not surprising that 1554 saw a wave of repossession processes.[125] Twenty-three of thirty-one tenements for which debts were pursued were listed as belonging to dead tenants, so the wave of claims was not the result of a lay refusal to pay clerics but more of the devastation of plague and the war, which killed many of the inhabitants and left the clerics without the revenues which made up their living. As it was, many of the tenements were redeemed, likely by surviving kin, towards the end of the repossession process – probably much to the relief of the clergy, who must not have been excited at the prospect of owning a portfolio of burned-out tenements. Despite this burst of legal proceedings, it is hard to imagine that this process did serious damage to the clergy's reputation, given that many of the lands were unclaimed and that the laity were even quicker to start collecting their own debts.

In Dundee as well the laity brought more cases before the courts than the clergy. In total, over the ten months examined, fifteen cases were brought by the clergy and thirty-one by the laity.[126] Of the ten sample months between 1550 and 1557, only two had more cases brought by clerics than non-clerics. No pattern directly relatable to the Act on Burnt Lands is apparent in Dundee, suggesting that war damage to ordinary homes was not as severe there as in Haddington. Though the clergy were certainly present in court, these figures do not suggest that as a group they were overly aggressive in collecting rent. While it is impossible to know exactly what proportion of the population were clerics, and thus whether they were overrepresented, it is hard to imagine any Dundee court-watcher coming to the conclusion that during this period it was the clergy who were overly litigious and rapacious, oppressing the laity.

In Stirling, through the 1540s and 1550s, there were very few cases where either lay people or clerics appeared in courts over unpaid rents. There were, however, many during the 1520s. During that decade, the clergy were much more active in pursuing unpaid rents than were the laity. Whether the discrepancy was due to the clergy owning disproportionately more land or being better organised in the record-keeping, it is certain that priests,

Table 4.2 Haddington: monthly samples of litigation

Month	Lay	Clergy
January 1532	0	0
May 1532	8	1
October 1532	7	2
December 1532	7	0
January 1542	8	2
May 1542	2	2
October 1542	2	0
December 1542	2	0
January 1552	missing	missing
May 1552	22	2
October 1552	9	0
December 1552	8	2
Total	70	11

Table 4.3 Dundee: monthly samples of litigation

Month	Lay	Clergy
October 1550	6	1
April 1551	1	4
November 1551	4	0
May 1552	1	2
December 1552	4	0
June 1553	3	0
January 1553–4	3	3
July 1554	2	1
February 1555	4	2
March 1556–7	3	2
Total	31	15

monks and friars claiming rents were a common sight in Stirling's burgh court. Of the sixty clerics resident in Stirling at the time, thirty-five made court appearances pursuing rents or other money owed, twenty appearing more than three times.

Individually, the majority of priests in the three towns were not especially litigious. Out of forty-three secular clergy who were likely resident in Haddington during the years studied only twelve had personally appeared in court more than three times. Three others did not appear personally but had more than three appearances made on their behalf by a procurator. It took at least four court appearances to repossess a property, so the number of appearances is greater than the total number of rents pursued. The vast majority of court appearances were made by those who took turns as procurator for the choristers; sir Thomas Mauchlin made eighty-five personal appearances and had eighty-seven appearances made on his behalf; sir Adam Brown made forty-three personal appearances and had forty-five appearances made on his behalf. On the other hand, at least seven priests never appeared at all. Of the thirty-eight stipendiary chaplains in Dundee during the 1550s, fifteen do not appear to have engaged in any litigation to collect rents. Another seventeen clerics appeared in the burgh court to collect rents three times or less. Thirty-two of thirty-eight beneficed clergy, therefore, were not especially litigious, and other clerics who did not engage in litigation very likely never appeared in the burgh records. Of the remaining six, by far the most frequent presences in the burgh courts were sir Thomas Ducher and Master James Scrimgeour who appeared twenty-eight and fifteen times, respectively, as collectors for the rents owed collectively to the choristers. According to the 1581 rental roll, the choristers were owed rents from ninety different properties, so it is not surprising that they were frequently involved in court cases. Five other clerics appeared between four and nine times.[127] The bulk of the cases that appeared before the burgh courts therefore revolved around the many different annuals

Table 4.4 Stirling: annual litigation cases

Year	Laity	Clergy
1520	0	7
1521	0	4
1522	4	9
1523	5	13
1524	0	4
1525	0	16
1526	2	14
1527	4	20
1528	4	17
1529	0	4
1530	2	0
1545	0	1
1546	0	0
1547	1	0
1548	0	0
1549	0	0
1554	0	5
1555	0	1
1556	2	1
1557	1	0
1558	1	0
Total	26	116

owed collectively to the choristers. The vast majority of those annuals were apparently paid without dispute.

The friars are difficult to measure in the same way, for the warden would represent the whole friary, and entries sometimes refer to 'the friars' without specifying an individual. Franciscan Friar John Congilton of Haddington appeared thirty-six times on his own behalf and also had thirty-six appearances made on his behalf. No other friar appeared a significant number of times there, and in Dundee Friar William Gibson represented the Dominicans and appeared only once. The frequency with which the Franciscans pursued cases in Haddington, where they had good relations with the townspeople, demonstrates that there was no straightforward connection between the litigiousness of the friars and their popularity.

When clerics did appear in court to claim annuals, they had no inherent advantage over lay people. Lay people had no hesitation about contesting their claims, and clerics often had to submit proof to diligent and cautious judges. In 1530, for example, sir John Young claimed twelve shillings in rent from Haddington's Marion Cok; the case was heard in burgh court on four separate occasions before, in the absence of any evidence produced by sir John, the court accepted Marion's oath that she owed him nothing.[128] One of the cases where the Dundee clergy were refused took place in June 1552, when Wat Curmannow produced evidence that he owed no annual to the choristers.[129] After the siege of Haddington in 1548, however, other measures had to be resorted to if evidence had been lost or destroyed. The records of the Holy Blood altar must have been in particular disarray, and sir John Crosar had to rely on the testimony of other clerics about what the altar had paid in the past; sir James Mauchlin and sir William Cokburn testified that Cristiane Kello and John Barnis paid two merks to the altar before the English came, while sir Thomas Mauchlin testified that he knew sir John collected an annual from Cristiane and John 'bot he knawis not how meikle [much]'.[130] In another case, sir John Crosar accepted the oath of his tenants about what they paid before the burning of the town.[131] The same process applied to the rents owed by the clergy as well. In 1549, when sir John Crag, soon to be vicar portioner of Stirling, was ordered to pay the annual owing to Henry Reidheuch, he was discharged from paying an annual on another house, which was occupied by one Thomas Couson.[132] Without written documentation, however, witnesses had to testify, as in 1563 when several testified that the late sir William Litstar had paid two shillings annually on land of Marion Bruce.[133]

The careful consideration of evidence does not mean that the clergy were especially distrusted, however. In one case Haddington's bailies accepted the statement of sir William Cokburn, 'on his conscience' that Alex Barnis owed him twelve shillings and ten pence.[134] In some cases which were closely disputed the parties might agree to arbitration. On 6 August 1551, Dundee's bailies put off the case between the collectors of the choir and Robert Barry and John Burne 'in howpe of aggreeans'.[135] In December 1552, sir Robert Lawta became involved in a disagreement with William Langlandis over the rent owed by William. The case was to be arbitrated by sir Thomas Mauchlin and Haddington's bailies, but in effect, it was sir Thomas who decided that William should pay two merks, and be absolved of all other claims, the bailies simply ratifying the decision.[136]

Some disputes could become more acrimonious. On rare occasions, tenants refused to pay the annuals. In November 1541, John Hawschaw was found guilty of wronging sir Patrick Mauchlin while he was seizing an annual, and was ordered by the bailies and council to ask forgiveness of both sir Patrick and of the bailies.[137] For their part, clerics might also evict tenants. On 12 July 1538, John Clerk in Haddington agreed to leave the tenement owned by sir Cuthbert (probably sir Cuthbert Lynd), in return for a payment of ten merks.[138] Given that evictions were usually issued for Whit Sunday in May, this dispute must have been dragging on for a couple of months.

A priest might also agree or be obliged to reduce annuals, particularly after the passing of the Act on Burnt Lands which mandated reduced rents on tenements damaged by war.[139] In Haddington in December 1557, sir Thomas Gethrason, chaplain in Preston, agreed to refund three shillings to Thomas Punton after the annual was reduced from fifteen shillings annually to twelve shillings by the arbitrators, who were both clerics.[140] Thomas Syld succeeded in October 1558 in reducing the rent on his tenement, which had apparently been completely destroyed, to one shilling, owed to Master Alex Leviston chaplain of the Holy Blood altar in Haddington, although he had to promise to build on the plot.[141] The laity might also be called upon to determine what a rent should be worth. In Dundee, a delegation of three bailies and six councillors visited a tenement on the north side of the market gait, and determined that it was worth sixteen merks, and therefore, under the Act on Burnt Lands, owed five merks four shillings and five pence to St Gregory's chaplainry.[142] In April 1558, ten Haddington men, 'at command of John Ayton provost' appraised the goods of George Symson, which had been seized as payment for the ten merks he owed to Dene James Abircromby, canon of Holyroodhouse.[143]

Nor were the clergy determined to protect their interests as a group against the laity. Clerics could represent their clients against other clerics: in Dundee, for example, sir Duncan Makynare defended his client, James Adam, against the claims of the chaplains of the parish church.[144] At one point Friar William Gibson, procurator general for the Dominicans, appeared in court to defend a woman, presumably a tenant, from an annual claimed by another chaplain.[145] In March 1550, Dundee's choristers even summoned the vicar, Master John Barry, to court to claim unpaid annuals from him.[146]

Clergy were also involved in financial disputes with townspeople over other matters than rent: in 1520 for example, Stirling's Gilbert Johnson went to court to prove that he had paid twenty-four shillings for a cow to sir John Paterson, chaplain of the Rood altar.[147] Sir Lawrence Ramsay, chaplain, became embroiled in a case over a horse that he bought for twenty-two shillings from William Tasker. At least five men had witnessed the transaction, indicating both the social nature of commercial transactions and the need to have many witnesses for each deal.[148] Some disputes were personal, as that between sir William Myrton and George Gardineris, which ended with a ruling in June 1560 that sir William avoid Gardineris's walkway.[149] Other transactions were more purely financial. In 1529, Master James Wilson agreed to be guarantor for nine shillings that William Cristeson had borrowed from sir Thomas Bully.[150] Though these disputes were on occasion bitter, they are further evidence of how integrated the clergy were with normal town life, and of the perceived fairness of the burgh courts in resolving disputes between the clergy and lay people. The laity had no fear of using the burgh courts to protect themselves against unjust claims, while the burgh courts showed no particular favour or animosity towards the clergy. The courts, in doing so, not only provided basic justice but, as far as they were able to, preserved communal harmony.

It is difficult to use the burgh court records to build a case against the grasping, avaricious clergy. Certainly, they appeared to claim annuals they felt they were owed, but they do not appear to have been any more aggressive than lay people, nor do they appear to have used deceit or collusion to gain an advantage. The vast majority of rents were paid on time and without any evident acrimony. Indeed, many of the repossession cases were served against vacant and apparently abandoned tenements. Finally, it appears that many priests never appeared in court at all.

Conclusion

In all three burghs, priests resided in the towns, performed religious services and acted as community resources. They retained close connections to families in the burghs, and several members of an extended family might be clerics. Several of the important leading families had members among the clergy, possibly as a deliberate strategy of family advancement. Clerics cooperated with the laity by serving as procurators or financial agents, and served as a resource to assist family members. In return the burgh also looked after them, offering top-ups if the revenues from their benefices were insufficient and granting them pensions after their retirement, or after the Reformation had taken away their incomes. Clerics were willing to go to court to defend their rights, against the laity and even against each other, but were not especially litigious. In short, the clergy were respected members of the community who largely did their jobs well, and in return received the support of their fellow townspeople, even after the Reformation. There were no signs at the burgh level of a widespread resentment of the clergy that could be considered a cause of the Reformation.

Notes

1. David Lindsay, 'Kittis Confession', in *Works*, 582. The author of *The Complaynt of Scotland* criticised the clergy for their lack of teaching and for failing to show a good example to the people. Wedderburn, *The Complaynt*, 125. Lindsay of Pittscottie reported that the Vicar of Dollar had accused priests of spending their tithes on 'harlattis and houris and delicat clething, ryottous babcatting and wantoun playing at cairttis and dice, and the kirk rewin and the pullpit doun and the pepill nocht instructit in godis word, nor the sacramentis trewlie ministrat to thame as the scriptour of Christ commandis'. Robert Lindsay of Pittscottie, *The historie and cronicles of Scotland: from the slauchter of King James the First to the ane thousand fyve hundreith thrie scoir fyftein zeir*. Robert Lindsay, Ae. J. G. Mackay eds. (Edinburgh, 1899–1911), 348–9.
2. Donaldson, *Scottish Reformation*, 11, 15; Cowan, *Medieval Church in Scotland*, 2; *Statutes of the Scottish Church 1225–1559*, ed. David Patrick (Edinburgh, 1907), 28. Ryrie claims the main problem for the church was the perception, rather than the reality, of abuse: Ryrie, 'Reform without frontiers', 51; *The Origins*, 16, 19–22. See the more positive view of M. Cowan, *Death, Life and Religious Change*, 157, and the balanced take of Sanderson, *Ayrshire*, especially 31–2.
3. Donaldson, *Scottish Reformation*, 1–27; Cowan, *The Scottish Reformation*, 5.
4. Ryrie, *The Origins*, 36.

5. Lindsay, 'The Dreme', in *Works*, 269; Lindsay, 'An Dialogue', in *Works*, 152–3; Lindsay, 'Ane Satyre', in *Works*, 451.
6. Ollivant, *Court of the Official*, 65; see Rhodes for indications that bishops and archbishops were more involved in town life in St Andrews. Rhodes, *Riches and Reform*, 14.
7. Foggie argues that the Protestants targeted their attacks on the friars to break the link between townspeople and Catholicism. While the friars were generally popular, she supposes, the literary tradition denouncing them and their financial litigation meant that Protestants could easily arouse discontent. Foggie, *Renaissance Religion*, 231, 235, 237.
8. In Peebles, for example, housing was provided to the fifteenth-century curate on condition that he be available on call for the parishioners. Sanderson, *Scottish Curates*, xiv.
9. Sanderson, *Scottish Curates*, xxii.
10. HAD/4/6/5, f30. The woman was not identified or asked to testify in court, although apparently her statement delivered at a moment of great peril carried some evidentiary weight.
11. See Sanderson, *Scottish Curates*, though her examples are often from rural parishes.
12. Stirling: Dunfermline Abbey; Mair, *Stirling*, 16; *Privy Seal*, 1:390. Haddington: the Priory of St Andrews; Marshall, *Ruin and Restoration*, 7. Dundee: Lindores Abbey; *Charters, Writs and Public Documents Dundee*, 7–8, 19–20.
13. James Maitland Anderson, *Early records of the university of St Andrews; the graduation roll, 1413–1579, and the matriculation roll, 1473–1579* (Edinburgh, 1926), 201, 207.
14. Warden, *Burgh Laws*, 97; *Dundee Weavers Charters*, 10.
15. His protest may have been due to his fear of losing her guild dues, as he asserted that her admission should not 'be any prejudice to his privilege upon the vestments of whatever women are so admitted'. DCA Protocol Book 1518–34, f174/t232.
16. DCA Protocol Book 1518–34, f19/f31.
17. J. K. McGinley, 'Wedderburn, James (*c.*1495–1553)', *ODNB* (accessed 26 June 2013).
18. In the early 1520s he was tutor of William Barry; in the early 1550s he became curator for James Barre, son of Andrew Barre, tutor to Marcus Barry, son and heir of William Barry, and the nearest relative to James Barry, pupil, William's second son.
19. DCA Protocol Book 1518–34, f47/t68.
20. Lindsay, *Works*, 152; 'The Satyre of the Three Estatis', 451.
21. DCA BHCB 1550–4, f27b, f28.
22. Ian B. Cowan claims that disputes over tithes were a major conflict between laity and clergy, more so than rents owed. Cowan, *Scottish Reformation*, 22. See also Sanderson, *Ayrshire*, 20. Tithe disputes made up 26 per cent of the sentences passed by the court of the Official Principal in St Andrews, and 11 per cent of those passed by the official of Lothian. Ollivant, *Court of the Official*, 77. In England, Christopher Haigh has pointed out that while people did not want to pay more tithes than necessary, they did not object to tithes themselves. Christopher Haigh, *English Reformations: Religion, Politics and Society under the Tudors* (Oxford, 1993). See also G. W. Bernard, *Late*

Medieval English Church (New Haven, 2012), 155; Lindsay, *Works*, 'Dialogue Betwix Experience and ane Courteour', 152; 'The Satyre of the Three Estatis', 451.
23. A stone, or 'stane', was normally sixteen pounds, slightly heavier than the modern stone weight. *DOST*, 9:481.
24. DCA Protocol Book 1518–34, t66.
25. Bardgett, *Scotland Reformed*, 69; *Books . . . Thirds of Benefices*, 394.
26. DCA BHCB 1550–4, f297.
27. DCA BHCB 1558–61, f14.
28. As part of the same case, John Bully, parish clerk also brought a claim for money for upkeep of the parish clock. *Extracts . . . Stirling*, 10.
29. *Extracts . . . Stirling*, 266.
30. Sanderson, *Scottish Curates*, xvi.
31. Sanderson, *Scottish Curates*, xii.
32. SCA SBCB 1554–7 25/02/1555, 13/5/1555, 1/7/1555, 7/7/1556; Sanderson, *Scottish Curates*, 131–3.
33. In August 1559, sir George Reid, vicar, appointed sir Thomas Mauchlin and Thomas Spottiswode his procurators, suggesting a prolonged absence from the town.
34. HAD/4/1/2, f22v.
35. Chaplains are generally considered to be in possession of stipends rather than benefices, although many chaplains were appointed for life and were responsible for collecting their own annuals. Durkan refers to them as altarists. John Durkan, 'Chaplains in Late Medieval Scotland', *Records of the Scottish Church History Society* 20 (1979), 91–103, 94.
36. *Books . . . Thirds of Benefices*, 12, 29–30, 57–8, 331, 352–4, 369.
37. Lynch *et al.*, 'The faith of the people', 289.
38. As always, different spellings and transcription errors mean some individuals may have been entered twice, or more rarely, different individuals conflated under the same name. Residents were identified by either by having a benefice, a relationship with the town council or residents in the burgh, or by appearing frequently enough in the burgh court that they may as well have been residents.
39. All men listed as 'sir' ('schir') were counted as clergy, unless specifically identified as a knight or gentry. 'Masters' or 'Misters,' however, were only included if the context or other evidence made it clear that they were clerics. The count excludes those who lived or held benefices outside the burgh and occasionally appeared in the records to claim annuals owed or submit disputes to the burgh council.
40. HAD/4/6/5, f48v.
41. HAD/4/6/5, f60v.
42. HAD/4/6/5, f198b.
43. HAD/4/6/5, f92, 104b, 108, 129.
44. HAD/4/1/3, f155.
45. Horn, 'List of References', 90.
46. Sanderson, *Scottish Curates*, xxvi; McKay, 'Parish life in Scotland 1500–1560', 95; M. Cowan, *Death, Life and Religious Change*, 156.
47. HAD/4/6/5, f266.
48. HAD/4/6/5, f197b, 289b.

49. HAD/2/1/2/1, f6v.
50. HAD/4/1/5, f163v.
51. HAD/4/1/5, f219. He was bailie five times during the 1550s and later treasurer.
52. HAD/4/1/5, f167v, 107, 215v.
53. Especially William Brown, Master William Brown and Barnard Thomson. HAD/4/2/3/1, 74, f99.
54. HAD/4/1/5, f168v.
55. Horn, 'List of References', 90.
56. HAD/4/6/5, f106; Anderson, *Early records of the university of St Andrews*, 243.
57. HAD/4/1/3, f83–83v. Six years earlier sir Adam Brown received eight merks for a year's service. HAD/4/6/5, f48v.
58. HAD/4/1/3, f30b, 100b; HAD/4/6/5, f264b.
59. HAD/4/2/3/1, f144.
60. HAD/2/1/2/1, f35v.
61. Marshall, *Ruin and Restoration*, 23–4.
62. Marshall, *Ruin and Restoration*, 23–4.
63. NRS B30/21/40/17.
64. HAD/4/1/2, 22v.
65. HAD/4/6/5, f33.
66. HAD/4/1/3, f95–95b.
67. HAD/4/6/5, f170, 213b; HAD/4/2/3/1, f29; 39v.
68. HAD/2/1/2/1 f18, 24b.
69. SCA SBCB 1519–30, 2/8/1529; 1544–50 26/2/1549.
70. *Dundee Weavers Charters*, 13.
71. DCA BHCB 1550–4, f225b.
72. DCA BHCB 1558–61, f157b.
73. DCA BHCB 1550–4, f297.
74. DCA BHCB 1555–8, f61.
75. DCA BHCB 1558–61, f182.
76. It is impossible to know the exact number, as students with common names – John Wilson, for example – were not necessarily the same men who became priests in the burghs.
77. Anderson, *Early records*; R. G. Cant, *The University of St Andrews: A Short History* (Edinburgh, 1946), 41.
78. At least two, Sir David Cristeson and Master William Hamilton, can be plausibly identified in the surviving Glasgow records, though as always the problem of common names makes certain identification impossible. Not all who attended graduated. *Munimenta alme Universitatis glasguensis: Records of the University of Glasgow from its foundation till 1727*, 4 vols, eds Cosmo Innes and Joseph Robertson (Glasgow, 1853) 2:125, 136. These numbers are higher than Sanderson has reported for Ayrshire, where she found that only 9 out of 133 identified chaplains had graduated university. Possibly urban clergy were more likely to have attended university, or Haddington and Dundee were simply close to St Andrews. Sanderson, *Ayrshire*, 26.
79. McKay, 'Parish life', 151–5; Durkan, 'Chaplains in Late Medieval Scotland', 92–3.
80. Assuming, of course, that the council had not sold off any of these rents between 1560 and 1581.
81. Sanderson, *Ayrshire*, 27; M. Cowan, *Death, Life and Religious Change*, 157.

82. Sanderson, *Scottish Curates*, xi.
83. DCA BHCB 1558–61, f74b.
84. *Extracts . . . Stirling*, 19; SCA SBCB 1554–7 21/2/1557.
85. *Charters . . . Stirling*, 85–9.
86. *Charters . . . Stirling*, 49–52.
87. Gibson and Smout, *Prices, food and wages*, 274, 278–85.
88. DCA BHCB 1558–61, f142.
89. Durkan, 'Chaplains in Late Medieval Scotland', 100.
90. John Pound, 'Clerical Poverty in early sixteenth-century England: some East Anglian evidence', *Journal of Ecclesiastical History* 37 (1986): 392, 393.
91. HAD/1/15 (NRS B30/21/39/3); McKay, 'Parish life', 89.
92. Rhodes, *Riches and Reform*, 35–6; Sanderson, *Ayrshire*, 27.
93. *TA*, 7:466.
94. *TA*, 8:342.
95. DCA Transcript of Rental Roll, ed. Cosmo Innes.
96. DCA BHCB 1550–4, f239, 249b.
97. DCA Protocol Book 1518–34, f90.
98. DCA Baxter Craft Lockit Book, f5, 11, 14.
99. DCA Baxter Craft Lockit Book, f5; DCA Transcript of Rental Roll, 142.
100. DCA BHCB 1550–4, 239, 349b.
101. DCA BHCB 1550–4, f249b.
102. J. Schmidt, 'A case of Bination Extra Loca Sacra', *Jurist* (1945), 221–4; Andrew Meehan, 'Bination', in *The Catholic Encyclopedia* (accessed 15 August 2013 from www.newadvent.org).
103. DCA BHCB 1550–4, f86, f230.
104. DCA BHCB 1550–4, f284b; DCA BHCB 1555–8, f164v; DCA BHCB 1558–61, f71. Other benefices which saw a turnover were St Nicholas chapel (Master John Balfour, 1556 or earlier; Master John Watson, 1558), St Matthews altar (sir John Spens, 1554; Master Thomas Seres, 1557), the Rood altar (sirs George and Robert Gray, 1554; sir Thomas Ducher, 1558).
105. DCA Protocol Book of Alexander Wedderburn, vol. 1 (1554–65), f12b.
106. Margaret H. B. Sanderson, *Early Scottish Protestants 1407–1560* (Edinburgh 1560), 137; McGinley, 'Wedderburn, James (*c.*1495–1553)'.
107. Anderson, *Early records*, 115, 177, 133, 134, 233; DCA BHCB 1550–4 f86/t219, f180/t465; DCA BHCB 1555–8, f73.
108. DCA BHCB 1550–4, f297; DCA BHCB 1558–61, f62b; DCA Protocol Book 1518–34, f27/t41; DCA Baxter Craft Lockit Book, f32; Bardgett, *Scotland Reformed*, 4.
109. HAD/4/6/73, f16.
110. Sir William Gibson was the brother of Philip Gibson (I), who served constantly as bailie or councillor throughout the 1530s and 40s, and was the uncle of Philip Gibson (II) who also served as a councillor and bailie during the 1550s and 60s. There is no indication that sir William ever held a benefice in the burgh.
111. *TA*, 6:47, 7:125.
112. SCA SBCB 1519–30 30/7/1520.
113. SCA SBCB 1519–30 8/11/1521, 4/4/1524.
114. DCA Protocol Book 1518–34, f36/t54.
115. DCA BHCB 1550–4, f5, 232v, 239, 249v, 349.

116. DCA BHCB 1558–61, f2, f18b.
117. DCA BHCB 1558–61, f154.
118. DCA Protocol Book 1518–34, f104/t139.
119. *Dundee Weavers Charters*, 10.
120. Verschuur, *Politics or Religion?*, 25.
121. Some of these cases may have also appeared in church court records. Between 1541 and 1553 twenty-three cases involving fees due clergy were brough before the Official Principal of St Andrews. Ollivant, *Court of the Official*, 80.
122. See Christopher Dyer, 'Trade towns and the Church: ecclesiastical consumers and the urban economy of the West Midlands 1290–1540', in *The Church in the Medieval Towns*, eds Terry Slater and Gervase Rosser (Aldershot, 2018), 70.
123. All the court cases in Haddington for May, October, December and January in 1532, 1542 and 1552 have been studied – a set of months which allows us to capture the two head courts in October and January, as well as the more ordinary but still busy months of May (when rents were collected for the Whitsunday term) and December. The years chosen are intended to be typical years without too much drama, although that might be too much to ask of any year during the 1540s. For Dundee, with a more limited run of records, ten months from the 1550s were selected in order to give a picture of activity year-round. They were October 1550, April 1551, November 1551, May 1552, December 1552, June 1553, January 1553, July 1554, February 1555 and March 1557. In Stirling, April, October and January were examined in each year for the periods 1519–30, 1544–50 and 1554–7.
124. HAD/4/6/5, f283b–286.
125. *RPS*, A1552/2/30 (accessed 2 February 2021).
126. DCA BHCB 1550–4, f2b, 4b, 5b, 47b, 48, 117, 117b, 152b, 155, 157, 201, 203b, 232b, 281b, 320, 322, 323b; DCA BHCB 1555–8 f30b, 33, 33b, 107, 107b, 108, 112v, 113.
127. Master Andrew Cowper, who appeared four times to claim rents owing to the chapel of St Ninians (nine annuals, worth f8 14s 6d); Master George Scot, who appeared six times to collect the rent owing to the Chapel of Our Lady in the Welgait; Master Richard Jakson, who litigated seven times to collect rents owing to Our Lady Altar in St Clement's Church (eight annuals, worth £28 2s); sir James Wright, who pursued four rents owing to St Colanis chaplainry; and sir John Murray, who appeared nine times to collect annuals owing to the Magdalene altar.
128. HAD/4/6/5, f13, 13b, 14b, 15b.
129. DCA BHCB 1550–4, f161.
130. HAD/4/2/3/1, f13b.
131. HAD/4/2/3/1, f10.
132. SCA SBCB 1544–50 20/05/1549.
133. SCA SBCB 1560–4 22/4/1563.
134. HAD/4/6/5, f273.
135. DCA BHCB 1550–4, f84, 278v.
136. HAD/4/6/5, f236, 237v.
137. HAD/4/6/5, f160, 167.
138. HAD/4/6/5, f89.
139. DCA BHCB 1550–4, f84, 155v.

140. Master Alex Forrof, priest of the Kirk of the field, and James Balfour, parson of Knawis and official of Lothian. HAD/4/2/3/1, f110.
141. HAD/4/2/3/1, f136.
142. DCA BHCB 1550–4, f176, f361.
143. HAD/4/2/3/1, f125b.
144. DCA BHCB 1550–4, f270b.
145. At other times references were simply made to rents owed to the 'friars'. DCA BHCB 1550–4, f361.
146. DCA BHCB 1550–4, f42. Ollivant points out the few cases of disputes between priests in ecclesiastical court records. Ollivant, *Court of the Official*, 83.
147. SCA SBCB 1519–30 3/9/1520.
148. SCA SBCB 1519–30 6/2/1523.
149. *Extracts . . . Stirling*, 72–3.
150. SCA SBCB 1519–30 22/1/1529.

PART TWO

Discussion and Disaster

The Reformation of 1559–60 was not the inevitable result of a Catholic Church doomed to fall. It did fall nonetheless, as the events of the previous decades had created the conditions for many Scots to be accepting or even receptive to changes in religious worship. Part Two examines these developments, focusing on those which had an impact on the townspeople. Chapter Five emphasises that Protestant or reforming ideas, of different theological emphases, had been circulating in Scotland since the 1520s. Though repression kept an organised Protestant movement from gaining a firm base and momentum until the late 1550s, there was enough discussion of the new religious ideas that most urban Scots would have been familiar with the proposals for reforms. Where possible, Scots banded together to protect each other from heresy persecution, demonstrating that they feared attacks upon their neighbours more than they worried about the potential disruption or divine punishment from new ideas.

Chapter Six examines the devastation and trauma that was inflicted on the Scots by the overwhelming impersonal forces of plague and war which arrived during the 1540s. These placed a heavy burden on the townspeople, killing many, forcing others to flee, leveling towns and ruining local economies. As part of their invasion strategy, the English worked to gain the allegiance of Protestant Scots, turning them against their loyalist countrymen. The eventual defeat and withdrawal of the English set back the Protestant cause by several years, and ensured that when the Reformation did come it would have a strongly Genevan, Calvinist inclination.

Chapter Seven surveys the reaction of the Scots to those events. The 1550s were outwardly calm, a time when the Scots worked hard to recover from the damage of the previous decade, to understand the causes of their suffering, and brace themselves for the next round of disaster. There is little evidence of an organised Protestant movement in the first years of the decade, but there was a growing worry, expressed on all points of the religious spectrum, about the sins which had triggered God's punishments. This was the uncertain and worried landscape in which Protestant activists spread their message in the late 1550s. Their quick success would be possible in part because Scots were expecting change but were wary of yet more division and conflict.

CHAPTER FIVE

The Spread of New Ideas: 1520–1547

In May 1537, sir Mungo Millar knelt before the altar of Haddington's parish kirk during high mass and asked for forgiveness from sir John Tait. Sir Mungo had accused his fellow priest of saying that the Virgin Mary 'had no more power than any other woman to do for man', thus denying that she had any ability to work miracles or help humans achieve salvation.[1] This was a touchy point in Reformation-era Europe, as Protestants denied the sacred status of Mary and the saints, insisting that only God had divine powers. Millar's accusation against sir John was quite specific, however, and not the sort of general insult one might expect in a moment of anger, such as being a heretic or Lutheran, thus causing the modern historian to suspect that sir John had actually said something controversial. The move backfired for sir Mungo, however, and he was the one ordered to apologise.[2] At a time when new ideas were spreading, and James V beginning sporadic but deadly heresy persecutions, such accusations could bring unwelcome attention to more than one person. It is just possible that it was sir Mungo being punished because whoever reported the case to his superior perceived that attention as being more dangerous than the idea sir John might have been discussing. As reforming ideas spread throughout sixteenth-century Scotland, many Scots expressed only cautious interest. When forced to choose, however, the townspeople opted to protect, rather than turn against, dissenters such as sir John.

Historians tracing the origins of the Reformation of 1559–60 have often dwelt on Scotland's committed Protestants, attempting to determine their numbers, beliefs and political influence. This work has given us an invaluable picture of Scotland's first generations of Protestants, their theological influences and the dynamics of their activism.[3] This research has also revealed that these Protestant groups remained small, and it is not clear how united they were in theology or level of commitment. What ultimately allowed the Reformation to take place therefore was not simply the triumph of a faction inspired by Calvin's Geneva but the sense which must have been growing among the population at large during the four decades before 1560 that some kind of reform would eventually occur. Many Scots heard reforming ideas from the 1520s on, became accustomed to intense criticism of the church, rubbed shoulders with their more convinced neighbours and often did their best to protect them from prosecution.[4] The more committed Protestants should not be isolated as members of a particular faction but should be understood as part of their broader communities, along with 'protestantizing Catholics' who were interested in new ideas and rejected aspects of contemporary Catholic practice but who were not eager for drastic changes such as eliminating the mass or rejecting the Pope's authority.[5] After all, even among those who were accused of heresy or labelled as Protestants there were a variety of theological positions and degrees of interest.[6]

In Dundee, Stirling and Haddington, reforming ideas were circulating from at least the late 1520s to 1547, when the English occupation began. Both the nature of the surviving records and different sequences of events mean that direct chronological comparisons are not always possible, but nonetheless distinct patterns are clear. In Dundee, the town council made strong efforts to protect those who held these new ideas while the councillors continued to maintain and promote their own Catholic civic church. Religious disputes often involved the friars, leaving the burgh's own church and clergy untouched. In Stirling, a network of Protestants and reformers flourished in the town and surrounding regions until it was broken up by anti-heresy prosecutions in the late 1530s. Civic efforts to protect the accused were less successful than in Dundee, though those who were accused and recanted remained prominent members of the community. Haddington did not experience as much religious controversy as the other two burghs, but even in the quiet agricultural town the laity became familiar with the reforming ideas in circulation.

1520–40

Dundee

Dundee was both a major seaport with links to Denmark, northern Germany, the Low Countries and France and the closest large town to the university and ecclesiastical centre of St Andrews.[7] It is no surprise then, that supporters of reforming ideas came to the town relatively soon after Martin Luther posted his theses in Wittenberg in 1517. Much of the discussion was started by Patrick Hamilton, who picked up the new ideas while he was in France, where there was significant discussion of reform among humanistic circles prior to Francis I's crackdown in the 1530s.[8] Hamilton returned to St Andrews where Gavin Logie, principal of St Leonard's, and canons such as John Duncanson and Alexander Allane became interested in discussing the Bible and Lutheran texts.[9] Hamilton's interests demonstrate the blurred lines between Catholicism and Protestantism in this period; while he was an adherent of justification by faith alone, he also composed a choral mass.[10] He was initially protected by his kinship to James Beaton, the Archbishop of St Andrews, and the King, but in 1527 the archbishop finally summoned him on heresy charges. He fled to the continent for a few months but then returned to Scotland. He was arrested and burnt for heresy in February 1529.[11] An observer, John Lindsay, was said to have told

Archbishop Beaton 'the reik of Maister Patrick Hammyltoun hes infected as many as it blew upoun', and the execution did nothing to stop discussion of reform at St Andrews, although those subsequently accused were quicker to flee and stayed away longer, if not permanently.[12] By 1534, Protestant ideas had become sufficiently entrenched that the annual feast at the Faculty of Arts was abandoned because some members were offended by the accompanying mass.[13] It is not surprising that many of these reformers made the short trip to Dundee to preach, to lose themselves in the bigger town when they came under pressure, or to flee on one of the ships which frequently left for Protestant parts of the continent. These same ships also brought books, both Protestant tracts and texts such as Tyndale's New Testament translation.[14]

Around 1528, a friar named William Arth was possibly the first to preach in Dundee against the decadence of the bishops, abuses of the use of excommunication, and false miracles. Arth was harassed by the servants of the Bishop of Brechin and went on to St Andrews, where his propositions received the support of John Mair.[15] Even in Knox's telling there is nothing Protestant about the ideas presented; Arth held that cursing was a powerful sanction if used properly and not trivialised (cursing was used by the laity as a way of ensuring that agreements would be respected), complaints against the failings of bishops were commonplace and medieval Catholics were often concerned with distinguishing false from true miracles.[16] Indeed, after the Scottish friars, fearing that he had gone too far in his criticisms of the bishop, forced Arth to flee to England, he would be imprisoned by Henry VIII for supporting the Pope.[17]

The pace of the circulation and discussion of these new ideas increased in the 1530s. Knox specifically singled out Dundee and Leith as places where there were 'merchants and mariners who, frequenting other countries, heard the true doctrine affirmed, and the vanity of the papisticall religion openly rebuked'; many towns in the Baltic, frequently visited by Scots merchants and sailors, converted wholly or in part to Protestantism during the 1520s, including Malmo, Danzig, Hamburg and Lubeck.[18] England moved towards Protestantism, in fits and starts, from the 1530s on. These discussions caused the Dominicans and Franciscans to complain to the Lords of the Council in May 1534. The Scottish leaders of these orders asked the king to extend the Act of 1525 banning Lutheran books and to act against those who harboured 'strangers and others of that sect coming forth of other countries'. They also requested that the king deal with apostate friars who were preaching publicly and order the heads of religious houses to keep a close watch on their members; clearly the church leaders did not feel that they had enough control over the diverse institutions and individuals that composed the medieval Catholic Church.[19] In total, at least seven friars, mostly Dominicans, left Scotland for more Protestant-friendly areas during the 1530s.[20] In response to these pleas James V wrote to the burghs emphasising the dangers of books translated out of Latin into Scots, which had appeared primarily in seaports, with Dundee being one of the towns specified.[21] The Lords of Council also sent letters to the burghs instructing them to forbid strangers and their hosts 'to argue, disput or commune [with] of any of the said Luther's or his disciples opinions'. The lord chancellor turned the other matters back to the religious orders, requiring them to ensure that the friars not spread 'any new opinions' to the people.[22] The need for these various measures makes clear that by the mid-1530s new ideas were spreading among the lay people as well as the clergy.

Much of the evidence for their spread comes from judicial actions, which in the early 1530s targeted clerics and lay people. The timing of these bursts of persecution had more to do with the concerns of the royal and ecclesiastical hierarchy than with the actual spread and popularity of heretical ideas.[23] The crackdown in the early 1530s for example, which would see five executions in 1534, may have been inspired by James V's wish to impress the Pope with his defence of orthodoxy in order to secure papal approval for his plan to tax the clergy.[24] It is likely that much more discussion of reform was taking place than is apparent in the surviving records.

In Dundee the judicial prosecutions began with a more systematic hunt for another friar, the Franciscan Alexander Dik. Although not much is known about Dik's opinions other than that he left the Aberdeen cloister as a heretic, the search for him brought suspicion on the inhabitants and authorities of Dundee. On 7 May 1532, the King's advocate began proceedings against James Scrimgeour, who was provost and constable of Dundee, and the burgh's bailies (James Wedderburn, James Rollok, Alexander Craile). The charges were that Dik, having left Aberdeen, stayed with his friends in Dundee. There, the constable, bailies and others were aware of his presence, for they met and talked with him. The magistrates apparently refused to turn him over to the Bishop of Brechin or to the friars, though they did promise to deliver him to the Archbishop of St Andrews if he be accused of heresy. Having accompanied Dik to St Andrews, however, the Dundonians decided not to give him up after all. They then returned home, where they ignored royal letters to surrender the friar.[25] The bailies, through their procurator, claimed that they had in fact diligently search for Dik. This claim was apparently rebutted by Friar Laing (later the confessor to James V), who testified to the Lords of Council that people in Dundee (who, or how many, is unknown) 'threatened him and his order, saying . . . they should pull their cowls over their heads'. Laing went on to insist that if trouble came to him or his order, 'the wit thereof should be imput' to the people of Dundee, 'and they to be accused'.[26] The final verdict by the Lords of Council was to order the magistrates to hand Dik over to the friars in either Aberdeen or St Andrews, but to absolve them of contempt for royal authority, because it could not be proved that they disobeyed the royal letters. It is not known what actually happened to Dik.[27] This incident demonstrates that the Dundonians, as a civic body, were willing to meet with and protect suspect preachers, as well as to defy both the friars and the archbishop. While the resident clergy in the town appear to have kept quiet, it was church authorities from outside the burgh who pushed the issue of heresy.[28]

The government began to act against lay people during the winter or spring of 1532, the same time as they started searching for Friar Dik. The goods of James Watson in Invergowrie, an hour or two's walk from the centre of Dundee, were escheated (confiscated by the crown) for Lutheranism and given to Walter Scrimgeour. However, Watson cleared himself of the charges, probably by paying a fine, and his goods were returned to him.[29] He cannot have changed his opinions too much, for over a decade later he would host the Protestant preacher George Wishart.[30] On 23 June, a month and a half after the trial of the magistrates for sheltering Friar Dik, James Wedderburn younger and John Wait were obliged to appear in the Franciscan friary and, before Mr James Scrimgeour chanter of Brechin, deny several erroneous points, purging themselves 'by their great oath'. They were supported by the testimonials of 'twenty honest burgesses' of Dundee.[31] As James Wedderburn would continue to criticise the church publicly and eventually flee from renewed heresy charges, the testimonials were not so much affirmations of his innocence as an effort to protect a fellow townsman. This incident may have caused further discontent with the Conventual Franciscans in Dundee. Although it was a cleric from Brechin cathedral who conducted the hearing, it was held in the Franciscan friary and not in the burgh's own church. The friary served as the base for the hierarchy, while St Mary's was the townspeople's territory, even if the divine services held in both were essentially the same.

Friar Alexander Seton, who had been James V's confessor and the prior of the St Andrews Dominicans, was also known to have been in Dundee, though it is unclear if he preached there. In 1536 he delivered a controversial series of Lenten sermons on the Commandments in St Andrews, complaining that God's Law had been obscured by traditions. His teachings, according to Calderwood (following Knox), were an attack on the ability of good works to achieve salvation, specifically

> that Christ was the end and perfection of the law; that there was no sinne where God's law was not violated; that remission of sin cometh by unfeigned repentance, and faith apprehending God, the Father, merciful in Christ, his Sonne, and that it lyeth not in man's power to satisfie for his sinnes. He made no mention of Purgatorie, Pardouns, Pilgrimages, Prayers to Sancts, or suche trifles.[32]

He thus avoided directly criticising key Catholic beliefs but emphasised the Lutheran justification by faith. Having given his sermon Seton left for Dundee, but when challenged by another friar in St Andrews returned and defended his preaching, claiming that there was no bishop in Scotland who behaved as Paul had prescribed. The bishops and Franciscans, according to Knox, convinced James V that his confessor was a heretic and so Seton fled to England.[33] At around this time James Hewat, who had been sub-prior of the Perth Dominicans and was supposedly inclined towards Protestantism, also moved to Dundee.[34] The fact that these men, along with Dik, were friars would have emphasised to the laity that reform could come from within the current church.

In the mid-1530s, more Dundonians were targeted for their Protestant or reformist ideas, and George Lovell and John Black (Blacat) were accused of hanging an image of St Francis in 1536. Their action likely combined unhappiness with the friars, who were held to live elite lifestyles at odds with their profession of poverty, with a rejection of the cult of saints and a display of support for Protestantism. Royal letters instructed the provost and bailies to search for the two men.[35] No further reference to the case has been found, suggesting that some sort of informal arrangement was made to cover for the two. George Lovell had become a burgess in 1535 and was the son of a former treasurer and Dean of Guild, and could probably have been found easily had the provost and bailies bothered to look.[36]

The cases of Lovell, Black and Friar Dik demonstrate the Dundonians' determination to defend their burgh and neighbours from persecution. This determination did not interfere with their desire to maintain Catholic worship practices within the burgh; after all, Lovell and Black had attacked the friary, not the burgh's own church, as even the more militant reformers were not about to attack burgh property. There was a distinct tension between the burgh and the Conventual Franciscans. The council and townspeople did not have the same cordial relationship with the Conventuals that they had with the clergy of the civic church, and the Franciscans for their part seem to have been willing to take on the role of enforcers of orthodoxy. The Dundonians could accept discussion and criticism of religious practices while at the same time maintaining their existing forms of worship. This implies that civic unity was not threatened by discussion or the spread of new ideas, but that the townspeople did see heresy investigations by outside authorities as threats to their community. It also hints, though with less certainty, that the criticisms were not yet focused intensely on the mass and daily services which were at the heart of the civic worship cycle.

As the Dundonians had not been intimidated into staying away from discussing reform, a heavier wave of persecution began in 1538. Several men were accused of heresy and forced to pay fines. These persecution were led by Abbot, soon to be Cardinal, David Beaton, who would have received a share of these fines as keeper of the Privy Seal, giving him an incentive to cast his net widely.[37] James Annand, George Annand, Robert Anderson, John Fleshour and Alexander Fleshour were convicted of heresy by a church court and had their goods confiscated by the king, though each paid twenty pounds for pardons.[38] James Hay was also escheated for heresy and as he was apparently unable or unwilling to buy a pardon, his goods were given to David Wod in the Crag. In February 1548 his goods would once again be escheated, this time for cooperation with the English invaders.[39] These convictions did not affect his standing in the burgh, and he sat as a councillor on five occasions during the 1550s.[40] Eight men were fined lesser amounts for heresy, ranging from about £2 to £6 13s 4d. Others, who may have fled to avoid persecution, had their fines paid by family members.[41] There is no specific reference in the surviving records to any ecclesiastical punishments, though these were likely the same Dundonians who Knox claimed abjured and burned their bills.[42]

The Dundonians got off lightly, for in 1539 David Beaton would mark his appointment as Archbishop of St Andrews with five executions, with most of the victims coming from central Scotland. At least one man escaping this round of persecution, Robert Logie, a canon regular at Cambuskenneth and a friend of the Vicar of Dollar (one of those executed), fled to Dundee and then left on a ship, destination unknown.[43] Though a strong anti-Protestant, Cardinal Beaton's ability to persecute was always limited by his need to avoid losing the support of his vassals and tenants throughout Fife, Angus and the Mearns, some of whom belonged to families sympathetic to reform.[44] In Dundee itself, two Rolloks were among those fined but Beaton also paid a presumably friendly visit to the house of George Rollok (II).[45] Ironically, it may have been their very closeness to Scotland's most determined opponent of heresy that helped save the Dundonians from more deadly persecutions.

The accused were mostly young and reasonably prominent in burgh society. Nineteen Dundonians suspected or convicted of heresy during the 1530s can be identified. Ten were burgesses, another four were the sons of burgesses and possibly burgesses themselves, and Master John Wedderburn was a chaplain.[46] At least six of this group were probably merchants.[47] Of the other four, John Black appears to have been involved in merchant activity, Alexander Fleshour served on several inquests, and John Wait, the only confirmed craftsman, was a baker. Twelve of them belonged to one of five families: three Annands, three Wedderburns, two Fleshours, two Rolloks and two Patersons, though it is not known what the exact relationships were.[48] The accused were relatively young – eleven of the eighteen were made burgesses between 1527 and 1540.[49] Given that most men appear to have become burgesses in their late twenties, this suggests that many (fourteen of nineteen) of those suspected of heresy were probably well under forty.[50] It would be this generation that would reach the height of their influence around 1560. The pattern, then, is that young but established men, many linked to the merchant trade, developed an interest in new ideas, although we do not know anything about the content of their beliefs or how firmly they were held. It must be kept in mind that possibly only records of the more prominent cases survive. As long as the penalties were mostly financial, the opinions of women or the poor may not have been as interesting to the authorities. The accusations did not affect the men's reputations within the town. Six of the group would serve on the town council before 1559, where among other tasks they would oversee Catholic civic religion.[51] On the other hand, George Lovell and James Rollok would sit on council during the crucial year 1560, when they would finally have the opportunity to put these Protestant ideas into practice. The Dundonians did not ostracise one another on the basis of religious belief or interest, and there is no evidence that they divided themselves on religious lines. No one, at this stage, whatever their individual inclinations, was threatening the common worship of the civic church, and so there was no reason for there to be political divisions in the town along religious lines, though there must have certainly been discussion and disagreement. The townspeople were not convinced that their neighbours were heretics or dangerous idolators.

The security of their position in the burgh, and the financial, rather than physical, nature of the penalties meant that few accused Dundonians fled. This was not for lack of opportunity; others under suspicion used Dundee as their way out of Scotland, and several of the accused were merchants who regularly travelled overseas. It seems that they felt secure enough in the company of their fellow townspeople.

The Wedderburns

Two Dundonians who did flee, probably because they were in greater danger, were James Wedderburn (b. 1495) and Master John Wedderburn. The three Wedderburn brothers – Robert was the other – played important roles in Dundee's religious history. Robert was the Vicar of Dundee in the early 1550s and was possibly the author of the *Complaynt of Scotland,* a text that called for reforms in Scotland's government and church. James and John became Protestants, whose biographies were briefly sketched by Calderwood. James had been educated at St Leonard's college in St Andrews, where he likely encountered the reformist ideas of Gavin Logie. He spent some time trading in France and then returned to Dundee where he encountered further reforming ideas from James Hewat, the Dominican, and was forced to purge himself of heresy in 1532.[52] James turned his hand to play-writing. Though the texts are now lost, Calderwood reports that the plays 'nipped the abuses and superstition of the time'.[53] He ridiculed 'the abuses and corruptions of the Papists' in a tragedy about the beheading of John the Baptist and in a history of Dionysius the tyrant of Syracuse.[54] Both these plays were put on in the fields around Dundee, outside the west port. He also showed up Friar Laing, the confessor to James V, who had apparently been conjuring a ghost near Kinghorn. This was probably the same Friar Laing who complained of being abused by the Dundonians in 1532 (indeed, it may have been the same incident).[55] Without knowing more about the plays or the incident with Friar Laing, it is clear that James popularised criticisms of the existing church. These were some of the ways theological ideas picked up at St Andrews and elsewhere were explained to the broader laity. In 1540 he was informed on; a relapsed heretic faced a very real threat of execution, and he wisely fled to France, where he stayed in Rouen and Dieppe until his death.[56]

His brother, Master John Wedderburn, also studied philosophy under Gavin Logie at St Andrews.[57] According to Calderwood, he became a priest reluctantly but soon became interested in Protestantism and was convicted of heresy in 1538.[58] As a priest he likely faced more severe punishments than a layman, and so he fled, probably to Germany, and left it to relatives to try and buy back his goods.[59] In Germany he became more fervent after hearing Luther and Melancthon. He then converted some popular songs into spiritual hymns, which are believed to be the source of the *Gude and Godlie Ballatis*. He also translated some works of Luther and some psalms into Scots. He briefly returned to Scotland after the death of James V in December 1542, but left again after coming under scrutiny from Cardinal Beaton.[60]

The first surviving edition of the song collection attributed to him, known variously as the 'Psalms of Dundee', the 'Psalms of Wedderburn', the 'Godlie and Spiritual songs' or the 'Gude and Godlie Ballates' dates to 1567.[61] An edition may have been printed as early as 1542 and individual songs could have been printed or distributed separately as from the 1540s on there were references to religious songs in circulation.[62] Knox claims that George Wishart, when arrested in 1547, sang the fifty-first psalm in Scottish metre, which is included in the collection.[63] Some of the songs make strong criticisms of the church hierarchy and spread the basic tenets of the Protestant message; for example, 'Allace that same Sweit Face' criticises the presumed usefulness of works and Catholic ritual, emphasising instead the importance of justification by faith:

> Na kynde of outward deid,
> How haly that euer it be,
> May saue us at our neid,
> Nor zit vs Iustifie,
> Nor zit can mak vs remedie.[64]

The bluntly titled 'Ane Carrell Contrair Idolatrie' unsurprisingly criticises the worship of physical objects, as

> Contrair it is to Goddis command
> To trow that help may cum,
> Of Idolis, maid by mennis hand,
> Quhilk ar baith deif and dum.[65]

Other songs targeted the church itself:

> Thocht thow be Archebishop or Deane,
> Chantour, Chanslar, or Chaplane,
> Resist thow God, thy gloir is gaine,
> And downe, thow sall cum downe.[66]

Traces of traditional faith also remained, however. 'The Conception of Christ' emphasises the Virgin Mary:

> Thir wordis to hir he did reheirs,
> Haill Marie full of grace,
> The Lord God is with the[67]

Demonstrating that a total elimination of late medieval devotion was not yet on the table. Even if these songs were in popular circulation during the 1550s, it is unlikely that many people would have heard the whole repertoire. Many of the songs included in the printed source were also translated psalms. Heard in bits and pieces, the songs would not necessarily have convinced their listeners of a coherent alternative religion, but emphasised the problems with current religious practice and emphasised a faith based on scripture and devotion to Jesus. Combined with the play and later on the *Complaynt*, the message received by a general audience would have been about the need for religious reform, without necessarily specifying the shape of that reform.

Stirling

Reforming ideas were also present in Stirling, though government repression in the late 1530s and the later presence of the household of Mary of Guise in Stirling Castle suppressed open activity more successfully than in Dundee. As was the case elsewhere our knowledge of the spread of new ideas comes mostly from the records of prosecutions. Just as in Dundee, prominent men in the town had close connections to the reformers, and there was likely latent sympathy for the new ideas that muted opposition to the Reformation of 1559.

The group of reformers active in the Stirling region during the 1530s included burgesses, regular clergy and secular priests. At the very least it is likely that members of this group read and possessed the scriptures in English. Some went as far as attending the wedding of a priest who was the Vicar of Tullibody, a parish a few kilometres outside of Stirling. There they also ate meat during Lent, a typical Protestant act of defiance against Catholic rules about fasting. This group was targeted by Cardinal Beaton, and five of its members, mostly clergy, were executed, while others, largely burgesses, recanted and paid fines. Yet others fled. The origins of the group are unknown, but its unravelling began in 1538. According to Calderwood, in that year Robert Logie, who was a canon at Cambuskenneth and in charge of novices and teaching grammar at the abbey, fled on fear of being imminently apprehended. Calderwood recounts a dramatic escape, in which Logie recovered some money hidden by friends in a horse stall in Tullibody, about four kilometres east of the abbey, and then avoided his pursuers by hiding in a sheepfold. He eventually went on to Dundee, from where he took ship out of the country, reappearing some years later in

England.[68] Soon after another canon at Cambuskenneth, John Richardson, also fled, as did a Franciscan named John Lyne.[69]

The first group of clergy may have been outed by their fellows, and a subsequent investigation directed by Cardinal Beaton and the Bishop of Dunblane, the firmly orthodox William Chisholm, led to several arrests in February 1539, which included inhabitants of Stirling, Dominican friars, and priests.[70] The most prominent member of the group, or at least the one who most appealed to martyrologists, was the Vicar of Dollar, the Augustinian Dean Thomas Forret. He had been worrying the Bishop of Dunkeld for some time on account of his refusal to accept the death due of cow and best cloak from each deceased parishioner and for preaching on Sundays. The vicar apparently made a point of memorising Paul's Epistle to the Romans, a key Protestant text justifying salvation by faith alone, and had possibly attended the wedding of the Vicar of Tullibody. Such an event would definitely have been a Protestant act but as it is unclear who attended it is difficult to ascribe these outright Protestant beliefs to the Vicar of Dollar. Forret comes across in Calderwood's recounting as a reformer, but with no specific evidence that he taught anything unorthodox or broke with the rites of the Catholic Church. It appears that he was summoned several times by the bishop, who had been tipped off by the friars who perhaps detected a rival to their preaching. Eventually he was included in the round-up of suspected heretics.[71]

Also summoned were the Dominicans John Killore and John Beveridge, sir Duncan Simson, a priest of Stirling, and several inhabitants of Stirling. Friar Killore, according to Calderwood, had written a passion play that drew parallels between the pharisees and bishops, who both blinded the people and persuaded the authorities to persecute Christ. The play was performed before the king at Stirling and the bishops took offence as a result.[72] The lay people from Stirling included Walter Cousland, a burgess who had previously served as bailie and councillor, Robert Forester the brother of Thomas Forester of Arnegibon, William Forester the son of burgess John Forester, James Watson, David Graham, and possibly five others. The burgesses were accused of reading heretical books, perhaps simply meaning English scriptures. These men appear to have been the younger generation of the burgh's prominent families, and their connections are demonstrated by those who stood surety for them: Alex Forester of Killemuke the Laird of Arngibbon, who would take a turn as councillor in Stirling in 1560–1; John Forester, who served as bailie repeatedly from the 1520s through to the 1560s; John Forester of Craginelt, who would serve as provost through much of the 1540s and again in the 1560s; Archibald Spittell who was frequently bailie during the 1540s.[73] Important men in the community were willing to stand by their kin and neighbours who had been accused of heresy.

This support notwithstanding, Killore, the Vicar of Dollar, Beveridge, sir Duncan Simpson and one burgess, Robert Forester, were burnt at

Edinburgh at the end of February 1539.[74] Nine others recanted according to Buchanan, and many more fled.[75] Walter Cousland abjured his heresy and paid a fine of twenty pounds, in return for which he received his own goods back, while William Forester had his goods confiscated and given to John Cowan, a Stirling burgess.[76] The friars of Stirling continued to be interested in new ideas regardless, and in 1543 it was the Dominican John Rough who was appointed by Arran first to be his own chaplain and then to preach reforming ideas throughout Scotland.[77]

The accusations made in 1539 did not taint the accused within Stirling. As was the case for those accused of heresy in Dundee at the same time, these men would go on to public careers in the burgh in the next two decades: William Forester would be a bailie in 1545–6 and again in 1566–7 and Walter Cousland would continue to serve on various posts until 1557, including as treasurer and dean of guild.[78] During the wars of the Rough Wooing he would have various business arrangements with the French present in the town. James Watson would serve several terms on the burgh council, including as bailie, dean of guild and treasurer: he would also serve as a councillor during the crucial year 1560–1. David Graham would serve as representative of the smith's guild. Stirling's leading group of citizens were thus long familiar with reforming ideas, which would have primed them for the rapid transition to Protestantism that took place in 1559 and 1560.

There is not much evidence of interest in reforming ideas in Stirling after this episode, though the presence of nobles, diplomats and French personnel with the royal household surely brought some news of outside developments. At the same time, the presence of the Queen's household in the 1540s and 1550s may have discouraged excessive public interest in Protestantism. Within the burgh accusations of unorthodoxy remained sensitive: in 1545, Agnes Hendersoun was ordered to offer a wax candle to the Rood light and ask forgiveness for having called Annapill Garheme 'ane freirs get and freris yawde [whore[79]] and ger her mother to come to me and I shall tell her how she burnt her faggot [recant heretical beliefs]'.[80] Allegations of unorthodoxy and sexual relations with clergy were serious enough to require the slander to be disproved and abjured in court.

The example of Stirling shows that even in towns which appear religiously quiet in the two decades preceding the Reformation, there would have been knowledge of and familiarity with reforming ideas and new ways of organising the church and the obligations of the clergy. As in Dundee, the connections among the community, both the burgesses and the surrounding networks of lairds, meant that even those not personally interested in the new religious ideas still supported those who were. Unlike in Dundee, however, this support was not enough to save some lay people in Stirling from suffering severe punishment. This might partly account for the frosty relations between Stirling and its resident clergy, if those friars and priests were perceived to have not stood with their fellow reforming clerics, or to have even informed on them.

The 1540s

Dundee

After the death of James V in December 1542, the regent, the Earl of Arran, briefly flirted with a more reformist policy during his 'Godly Fit'. On 21 March 1543, a messenger was dispatched to Dundee and elsewhere with letters proclaiming the act of Parliament permitting possession of the New Testament in English.[81] Arran also relaxed the ban on heresy, promised some church revenues to the lairds, detained Cardinal Beaton and appointed reformist friars to tour Scotland.[82] These measures are regarded as having been pro-Protestant, but it is worth noting that apart from the relaxation of heresy laws there was nothing that suggested adherence to a specific alternative doctrine to Catholicism. The appointed preachers, John Rough and Thomas Gwilliam (Williams), for example, would become Protestant but at the time were still members of their orders; Knox said of Gwilliam that his doctrine was 'wholesome, without great vehemence against superstition'.[83] Reform within the Catholic Church was still very much a possibility. Arran soon abandoned this movement as Scots rallied against the pro-English political position that accompanied it and Cardinal Beaton regained his position of influence.[84] The few months that the measures were in place, nonetheless, would have seen the spread of reforming ideas even further among the general population, and many of the vernacular Scriptures likely remained discreetly in circulation. Even if Knox doubted the sincerity of many who took to carrying the New Testament around, saying that some who 'had never read ten sentences in it, had it maist common in thare hand', there certainly would have been widespread discussion and knowledge of new ideas.[85] After 1543, Protestant books continued to be imported. In 1545, James Rollok in Veere, likely the same James Rollok who fled from Dundee in 1538–9 after being accused of heresy, bought seven Scots pounds worth of books from John Mailer, a London printer associated with Protestantism.[86] Very few books came from England to Scotland, so it is interesting that Rollok went out of his way for these items.[87]

Before Arran's pro-Protestant period ended, he took the opportunity to sponsor the sacking of several Catholic institutions, including both the Franciscan and Dominican friaries in Dundee.[88] Much of our evidence about this assault dates from a trial in 1553, during which 193 men were charged with the attack on the friaries on 30 August 1543, as well as with giving aid and support to the occupiers of St Andrews who murdered Cardinal Beaton in 1546 and giving assurance to the English in 1547–8. It is impossible to know if those accused participated in all the events described or just some of them.[89] What is surprising is that only five of the nineteen Dundonians accused of heresy in the 1530s appear on the 1553 list of accused.[90] For many, being interested in Protestant or reforming ideas did not necessarily mean involvement in acts of violence. The assailants concentrated on the interiors of the friaries, destroyed 'the ornaments, vestments, images, and candlesticks', and they stole 'the friars' bedclothes, cowls, napery, pewter plates, tin stoups, and their "meal, malt, flesh, fish and coals"'.[91] James Williamson, Alexander Makinlay and 'several other persons' were murdered, possibly when the attackers moved on to Perth.[92] Going in the other direction, the attackers were thwarted in their attempt to sack the Abbey of Arbroath but succeeded in damaging two nearby parish churches.[93]

According to the court document, the attack was led by Henry Durham, the brother of Michael Durham who was physician to James V and one of Arran's circle of pro-Protestant advisors.[94] Henry Durham had become a burgess and guild member of Dundee in 1535, and was made customer of Dundee on 26 March 1543 – very likely a patronage appointment by Arran's newly installed regime. Durham was a member of the faction loyal to the Gray family, and would hold Broughty Castle for them. He was also an associate of James Scrimgeour of Dudhop, who was the constable of Dundee and the provost who helped shelter Friar Dik.[95] Scrimgeour and Patrick Lord Gray, who were kin, were two local lairds who were responsible for shielding the region's Protestants. In 1546, Henry Durham paid a fine of £133 6s 4d, presumably for staying away from the army or cooperating with the English.[96] He was likely related to the other Durhams in Dundee, as he appointed James Durham his procurator. James was made a burgess in 1552, and was the son of John, also a burgess. He was connected to William Durham, Laird of Grange, who in 1548 would buy a remission for assisting the English at Broughty Castle. Of the other Durhams listed in the Dundee records, only Patrick Durham, a dyer, was also on the list of 1553.[97]

The political and religious dimensions of the 1543 attacks on the friars were therefore closely entwined. This attack was probably part of Arran's campaign against the anti-English, pro-Catholic party in Scotland; the commendator of Arbroath Abbey, who received the bulk of the Abbey's revenues, was Cardinal Beaton, the head of the Catholic hierarchy and political rival to Arran.[98] The friars – at least those who had not apostatised – were important opponents of the Protestants. As in 1536 the target was the friaries and not the burgh church; the attackers left Dundee's civic church alone, either because they wanted to keep the burgh on their side or because a move against the parish church would provoke resistance, as it did near Arbroath. Iconoclasm was already a part of Protestant tactics, but at this early stage, militant Protestants chose targets that were ideologically powerful but physically vulnerable. Parish churches were more likely to be defended by the townspeople, or at least the damage would be resented; at the same time they were less potent sources of opposition. This is similar to Protestant acts of iconoclasm elsewhere: in Geneva, in 1530, Bernese troops attacked friaries and occupied the cathedral for preaching, but did no physical damage there or at any of the parish churches though as Carlos Eire notes, 'had they really wanted to, the soldiers could have caused more trouble.'[99] The primary targets were the inhabitants of the buildings, the contents only secondary.[100] If destroying religious ornamentation had been the main goal, then surely the burgh churches would have been attacked as well. After Arran had shifted his political allegiance to the Catholic faction, Durham, Gray and their associates continued to back the Anglophile, Protestant cause. They evidently supported the Protestants who occupied St Andrews in 1546 and collaborated with the English in 1547.[101]

In late 1543 and early 1544, Arran and Cardinal Beaton, freshly reconciled, marched on Dundee to punish heretics. During an expedition in November 1543, seven or eight Dundonians were reportedly arrested and taken with Arran and Beaton to Stirling, though their names and fates are unknown.[102] At the same time, two priests from the surrounding rural areas, John Wigton and David Lindsay, were arrested.[103] Arran and Beaton returned in January, hoping to apprehend the Earl of Rothes, Lord Gray and Master Henry Balnaves. On a similar mission to Perth, they had executed five accused heretics and removed the provost to eliminate the protection offered to reformers by the burgh council. They faced more opposition in the region of Dundee, however. Although Arran came with a number of soldiers, the suspect nobles themselves brought three hundred followers, and after a confrontation just west of Dundee persuaded the governor and the cardinal to withdraw to Perth.[104] Arran subsequently succeeded in isolating Rothes and Gray from their followers and arrested them, although the show of force may have been sufficient to convince him and Beaton to be less brutal in dealing with heresy than they had been in Perth.

Once safely back in Edinburgh, Arran summoned several unnamed inhabitants of Dundee to appear on 18 March 'for breaking the gates and doors of the Black Friars, carrying away chalices, vestments, and the Eucharist'.[105] Although several arrests were made, once again nobody from Dundee was executed. As in the 1530s, it seems that local Protestants and reformers were shielded from the full wrath of the central government and church hierarchy, this time by the local nobles and lairds rather than the burgh council.

By the late 1540s, many Dundonians would have been exposed to varieties of new religious ideas.[106] Some of them had enough interest to be accused of heresy, although many of the accused were flexible enough to recant. A few men were members of a violent, militant Protestant faction led locally by Henry Durham and associated with Lord Gray, and others fled to England or Europe. Many of them may also have been saved from the stake by the protection of their fellow burgesses and local lairds and by Beaton's reluctance to tread too heavily in the regions that were his power base. The gap between the townspeople, and authorities such as Cardinal Beaton and the friars, widened. The religious and political schemes of the lairds did not always serve the town's interests, however, as the events of the late 1540s will demonstrate. For the townspeople of Dundee, these new ideas did not shake their attachment to their civic church. Even those who were attracted by the new ideas continued for the time being to support the Catholic civic religion based on the mass.

The Preaching of George Wishart

The attacks on images in Dundee in 1536 and 1543, as well as expressing discontent with the friars, may be an indication that Zwinglian ideas, which were more intolerant of perceived idolatry than Lutheranism, were beginning to take hold in Scotland.[107] A more coherent exposition of the ideas being developed by the Swiss Protestants was expressed by the preacher George Wishart in the mid-1540s. Wishart, an ordained priest, had graduated in Arts from Louvain in 1532. By 1535 he was the schoolmaster in Montrose.[108] He was subsequently summoned to appear before the Bishop of Brechin for teaching the New Testament in Greek and so fled to Bristol.[109] He created controversy there as well with his preaching, being eventually forced to recant by Archbishop Cranmer.[110] After leaving Bristol, Wishart spent a year at Cambridge, returning to Scotland in 1543 in the company of the Scottish commissioners who had been in England negotiating the marriage of Queen Mary and Prince Edward. Through Henry Balnaves, one of the commissioners, he may have been associated with the faction of militants around Henry Durham.[111] Once back in Scotland, Wishart returned to Montrose where he preached inside a private house.[112]

Wishart then moved on to Dundee, where his preaching, according to Knox, was on the Epistle to the Romans.[113] Initially, his preaching from the pulpit in St Mary's had the support of the town council, who allowed him to defy the orders of Arran and the Bishop of Brechin to cease preaching. The pressure on the burgh mounted, however, and the council eventually ordered Wishart to leave. Their willingness to fend off central government pressure could only be pushed so far. The man who issued the order was Robert Myll, who had served repeatedly as councillor and bailie. Knox claims that Myll acted 'by procurement of the Cardinal' and spoke 'in the Queen and Governor's name'.[114] If we are to believe Knox, Myll 'of old had professed knowledge'. It is probable that like many Dundonians, Myll was willing to permit the discussion of new ideas and even express an interest himself, but was not a member of an ideological faction. The Earl Marischal and other lairds offered their protection, but it was declined by Wishart who opted to preach publicly in the west. The presence of the nobles suggests that this preaching was an advertised, public event.[115] Wishart would also preach from the pulpit in Haddington, as would Knox in Perth. It is possible that it was common for itinerant preachers,

The Spread of New Ideas: 1520–1547

emphasising one message or another, to claim the pulpits of Scotland's medieval churches. Perhaps they were tolerated by the clergy and councils who ran the churches because most of them were not considered to be unorthodox or even unusual.[116]

Wishart returned some months later when plague struck Dundee. He preached the day after he arrived, this time setting up near the East Port, with the sick outside the town boundary and the healthy inside. According to Knox, he based his sermon on Psalm 107, emphasising that God 'sent word and healed them'. Wishart used this text to emphasise scripture, the importance of faith in God, and the consequences of neglecting them, as he 'most comfortably did entreat the dignity and utility of God's word: the punishment that comes from contempt of the same; the promptitude of God's mercy to such as truly turn to him'. He visited the sick and gave out food and drink.[117]

It seems that one of the priests who had been arrested by Arran and Beaton in 1543, John Wigton, was offered his freedom if he would assassinate Wishart. In Knox's retelling, Wishart perceived that the man was about to attack him, gently disarmed him, and then protected him from the anger of the mob.[118] Assuming Knox's account is accurate, Beaton's covert assassination attempt indicates his wariness of acting directly in Dundee, fearing either renewed resistance or increased unpopularity in his home territory. Once the plague subsided, Wishart left Dundee, heading to Montrose and then the west. On his way back from Montrose he passed by Dundee and stayed in Invergowrie with James Watson, who had previously been accused of heresy.[119]

George Wishart also preached in Haddington during the winter of 1545–6, spreading his reforming ideas. While in Haddington Wishart first stayed with David Forrest, an apparently committed reformer, and then with the Laird of Lethington who was civil to him, 'albeit not persuaded in religion'.[120] His stay with Lethington demonstrates that even men who were not committed followers could be sympathetic and support religious discussion. Wishart initially went to Haddington because some of his supporters among the lairds thought he might get a good audience there. The first morning Wishart spoke to a 'reasonable' number of listeners, but apparently not as many as would usually be in the church.[121] That afternoon, and the next day, there were so few listeners that 'manie wondered' and thought that the Earl of Bothwell had prohibited people from attending.[122] By the third day, the lack of interest from the population provoked Wishart to preach, if the Protestant historians are correct, that

> I have heard that in thee, Hadington, would have been at any vain clerk play two or three thousand people; and now, to hear the messinger of the Eternall God, of all thy town and parish there cannot be numbered an hundred persons. Sore and fearefull sall the plagues be that sall insue for this thy contempt.

Wishart went on to list dire yet prescient predictions of violence and destruction.[123] As with the reports of his predictions about Dundee, either Wishart truly had a gift for prophecy, or his chroniclers, notably John Knox and David Calderwood, had some assistance from hindsight when they recalled his words. The next night, Wishart was arrested by the Earl of Bothwell at the house of the Laird of Ormeston, and was subsequently tried, convicted and executed on heresy charges.

Wishart's translation of the Helvetic Confession, printed in London in 1548, and the records of his heresy trial provide an indication of the kind of ideas he was introducing to the Scots.[124] The Helvetic Confession was a compromise document written by Swiss Protestants as part of an effort to unify Swiss and German Protestantism.[125] It is difficult to know if it exactly matched Wishart's own opinion, or if he simply thought it would be useful as a central point of agreement for various Protestant movements.[126] It highlights the importance of Scripture and God's grace (man has free will to do evil but not good) and recognises two sacraments, baptism and the Eucharist, the bread and wine being regarded as 'tokens' to be 'a nourishment and meat of eternal life', but not containing God within them, as Catholic doctrine held.[127] The Confession firmly rejects images and ceremonies that 'serve to subverte the trewe relygion of God', meaning the mass, along with clerical celibacy.[128] The Confession also emphasises the duties of the magistrates, whose power is granted by God to defend true worship from blasphemy, ensure preaching and instruction of the word of God, be liberal towards the ministers of the church, care for the poor, 'judge the people by equal and godly laws' and to defend the commonwealth.[129] Whether or not Wishart preached this particular message, it well describes how the town councils perceived their role, especially as they introduced reforms to the burghs during the late 1550s and early 1560s. Wishart's answers during his interrogation for heresy, as reported in an account printed in 1548, are evasive in his support for these doctrines.[130] He denied the sacrament of confession, was non-committal on the sacrament of extreme unction and was unconvincing in refuting the charge that he had said that the sacrament was a piece of bread. Accused of saying that it was permitted to eat meat on the fast days of Fridays and Sundays, he replied by quoting Paul's statement that all things are clean to the clean. In regards to denying prayer to saints, Wishart said that it was certain that one should pray to God but uncertain that one should pray to saints. He refused to preach about purgatory as it was not in the Scriptures.[131] His evasiveness was not enough to save him from the stake.

It cannot be known how closely the trial reflected Wishart's preaching, though the accusations may have been based on spies sent to listen to him.[132] It is likely that his hearers would have heard a more comprehensive attack on the mass than had yet been common in Scotland, at least among the laity.[133] He also probably criticised the cult of saints, images and several sacraments. More clearly than previous preachers (though admittedly our knowledge is very limited) Wishart was proposing major changes to Christian beliefs and worship.[134] The church hierarchy evidently realised that the discussion was moving beyond suggesting reform towards a rejection of the mass itself, and with it the structure of the medieval church. In March 1547, a delegation of 'Bishops, Prelates and kirkmen' complained to Arran of the spread of the 'pestilencious hereseis of Luther', and specified that some of them were beginning to criticise the Catholic conception of the 'Sacrament of the Altar'. Perhaps thinking of men like James Watson of Invergowrie or James Hay, they complained that some of those previously converted were relapsing, unpunished. By identifying their opponents as those who were against 'the Sacrament of the Altar' the senior clergy indicated that the main battleground of the dispute was the mass.[135] Until the very late 1550s, however, Protestants did not in fact physically target the masses in the burgh church or the priests who performed them.

Haddington

Haddington may have been more isolated from European developments than the other two burghs, but over the two or three decades preceding the Reformation the townspeople would still have had opportunities to become familiar with reforming ideas. In addition to Wishart's preaching some of these ideas, as in Dundee and Stirling, may have come from the clergy themselves.

The dispute among priests discussed earlier shows that the status of the Virgin Mary, particularly whether she had any power to intercede on man's behalf before God, was a controversial topic. In May 1537, at high mass sir Mungo Millar asked forgiveness from sir John Tait for having accused him of denying the Virgin Mary's power. The apology was witnessed by several clergy, including the curate, and 'many others diverse'.[136] The accusation was a dangerous one in a time of increasing heresy persecutions, and sir Mungo certainly did not get the benefit of the doubt from either his fellow priests or the bishop for defending orthodoxy. What the incident does indicate is an awareness in Haddington of attacks on the cult of the Virgin Mary and of the saints, and the seriousness with which such criticisms were taken. Moreover, even if many of the townspeople did not hear the alleged initial statement or sir Mungo's accusation, certainly those who attended the high mass would have heard his apology, which would still have had the effect of broadcasting the basic questioning of the Virgin's intercessory power. For those who may not have attended the high mass, the sight of a priest apologising on his knees would have been an important tidbit of local news. Whatever the Haddingtonians may have thought of this attack on the Virgin's powers, from this point on they would certainly be aware that the criticism existed. Nothing else is known about sir Mungo, but sir John Tait would continue to have a quiet career as chaplain of the altar of St Michael, Crispin and Crispianus. He collected a number of rents through procurators, and was still collecting debts in 1564.[137] A very tentative Protestant connection might be identified if he was related to Helen Tait who assisted the English during the siege of Haddington and then fled to England with them.[138]

Wishart's preaching, like the dispute between sir Mungo and sir John, would have increased familiarity with Protestant ideas even if the townspeople appeared unenthusiastic. Wishart and his supporters apparently expected that people would show up in the kirk, morning and afternoon, three days in a row to listen to preaching. Even if not as many people turned up as Wishart hoped, even a hundred people was a good crowd in a town the size of Haddington, and certainly enough to ensure the local circulation and discussion of his ideas. If they were the same hundred people each time, then it demonstrates the existence of a core group who were curious and dedicated enough in reforming ideas to take a certain amount of risk; if it was a different crowd each time, then his total audience can be multiplied. Even the accusation that people stayed away is suggestive: either the inhabitants decided of their own accord because they were sophisticated consumers of sermons who knew what they did and did not like, or, as Calderwood suspects, they were warned against attending, which would likely pique the same sort of curiosity that may have been aroused by sir Mungo's apology. Certainly, the dramatic circumstances of Wishart's arrest and trial would also have inspired some discussion.

While the general population would have been at least somewhat aware of Protestant ideas by the mid-1540s, a few individuals became more deeply committed. The first is of course John Knox himself, a Haddington native. Knox was probably born in Giffordgate, across the Tyne from St Mary's and the burgh mills, and attended the Haddington school.[139] One reference survives to his start as a local notary as he represented Richard Dikson in a dispute over a chalder of grain in 1542.[140] He claimed to have been introduced to Protestant ideas by Thomas Gwlliame (Williams), a Dominican friar initially from nearby Athelstaneford, who was one of those appointed to preach by Arran in 1543.[141] Knox spent the early 1540s working as a tutor, probably staying with William Brownfield at Samuelston, about four kilometres from Haddington, in 1540–3, and later as tutor to the sons of Hew Douglas at Longniddry, about eight kilometres from Haddington, until he left to join the Castillians in St Andrews.[142] It was in the company of Hew Douglas that Knox heard Wishart preach in Leith.[143]

Another man who may have been converted by Wishart's preaching was David Forrest (II), who Knox identified as a long-standing Protestant.[144] Forrest belonged to a prominent local family who had bought the Gimmersmill from the Abbey of Haddington. David Forrest (I) had founded the altar of the Virgin Mary and the Three Kings of Cologne sometime before 1522, and owned several properties and been involved in the wool trade and in brewing.[145] His eldest son, William, inherited his properties and served as burgh treasurer. Another son, George, was a sheriff in the Haddington constabulary in 1543, a bailie and wine inspector in the burgh, and along with John Riclington (husband of Helen Tait), assisted the English during the siege of 1548–9.[146] Wishart stayed with the third son, David (II), his first night in Haddington. David (II) served as bailie and as kirkmaster during the 1530s, and Knox describes him as being one of Arran's counsellors in 1543, before being driven from court around 1546.[147]

David (II) subsequently joined up with the Castilians who avenged Wishart's execution, escaped severe punishment, and assisted the English during the invasion of 1548.[148] He returned to England for a period, but returned to Scotland after Mary Tudor ascended to the throne.[149] In 1554, he was made General of the Mint.[150] Forrest would encounter Knox on his return to Scotland in 1555, and in 1559 he was deposed from his position as General of the Mint, probably on account of his Protestant sympathies. That winter he travelled to England, along with William Maitland of Lethington and Henry Balnaves, as an emissary of the Lords of the Congregation. He was later nominated as an ambassador to England, but never appointed because Mary Stewart seemed to not care for him. In 1562, however, the new Protestant regime restored him as General of the Mint and auditor of the Exchequer.[151]

The range of opinions present in one family, like Dundee's Wedderburns, is indicated by David (II)'s brother Alexander, a priest with a career in church administration. He received an MA from St Andrews in 1534 and then received several benefices, the most important of which was the provostship of St Mary's in the Fields outside Edinburgh. He was appointed to the altar of the Three Kings of Cologne in Haddington by his father, though he resigned it in 1553.[152] In 1547, he benefitted from government patronage by receiving two tenements in Haddington confiscated from Elizabeth Clapen, who had fled to England during the war.[153] He became the secretary to Archbishop Hamilton, and it was Alexander who oversaw the 1557 investigation, ordered by Hamilton, into the grant of the Gimmersmills to John Forrest, his nephew, by the abbey. This grant was apparently done without proper sanction, but the investigation carried out by Alexander's subordinates unsurprisingly found no wrongdoing.[154] He also had two sons, James and William, and James at least was legitimised in 1553. There is no evidence that Alexander recanted his Catholicism at the Reformation.[155] The fluidity of religious opinions in this period was such that families contained committed adherents of both sides.

There was clearly knowledge of, and interest in, reforming ideas in Haddington and the surrounding countryside. The discussions of these ideas did not seem to have aroused intense passions, and most Haddingtonians may have been content with traditional practices, but some committed converts were made. There are no reports of iconoclasm or attacks on the clergy, but by the time of the Reformation in 1559–60, many of the ideas discussed by the Protestants were familiar to the Haddingtonians, having been in circulation for over twenty years.

Conclusion

In Dundee, Stirling and Haddington, the burghers would have been exposed to much religious discussion in the years before 1547. Many of these ideas were criticisms of clerical abuses; others involved access to vernacular scriptures and doubts about purgatory and prayer to the saints. Justification through faith alone was also emphasised. It was not until George Wishart's preaching in the mid-1540s that the mass was directly targeted. These discussions would have gone a long way to creating what, during a similar process in the Low Countries, has been called a 'plastic' middle group who were interested in reform, especially of the most egregious abuses.[156]

The different experiences of the three burghs were also becoming apparent during this period. The size and connections of Dundee to both the University of St Andrews and to Europe attracted some reformist thinkers, who attracted the attention of church authorities, which in turn obliged the council and townspeople to defy the authorities to protect passing preachers and their own people. Certainly, the reaction to the intervention of Cardinal Beaton and the Conventual Franciscans in Dundee demonstrates that they were losing the support of the townspeople. The civic church, however, was unaffected by these divisions. Militant Protestants were careful to direct their attention to institutions not under control of the townspeople, and the Dundonians did not let these reformist ideas deter them from maximising the number of masses said in the town. Early Protestantism was perhaps even more developed in Stirling, at least among clerical circles and those connected to them. Stirling, however, experienced a more severe repression than Dundee, which deprived the local movement of its leadership. The harsh punishments, and the proximity of the royal government in the castle, sufficed to discourage further public interest, though it does not mean that support for the local Catholic church increased in proportion. In Haddington, Protestant ideas were clearly circulating in the region, but the few local converts – such as John Knox and David Forrest – did not long remain in the town, and so the council was never called upon to defend its own, which meant that the circular dynamic of repression and protest that occurred in Dundee never began, and the townspeople had no reason to be alienated from the religious authorities. As events would demonstrate, many of them too had nonetheless absorbed enough reformist ideas to be sufficiently 'plastic' when the Reformation began. We cannot know how many people were persuaded by Wishart, but the devastation which followed his execution may have convinced many of the truth of his warnings about following false religion. The small numbers of committed Protestants were only part of the shift that was taking place in Scotland's religious landscape during the middle years of the sixteenth century. At least, if not more important, was the exposure of the population as a whole to spirited religious discussion, and the acceptance of the idea that some type of church reform was inevitable.

Notes

1. HAD/4/1/2, f95v.
2. Likely at the orders of Archbishop of St Andrew, James Beaton, not to be confused with his successor, David Beaton.
3. Alec Ryrie, 'Congregations, conventicles and the nature of early Scottish Protestantism'," *Past and Present* 191(2006): 45–76; Sanderson, *Early Scottish Protestants*; Cowan, *The Scottish Reformation*, 89–114; John Durkan, 'Heresy in Scotland: the second phase 1546–1558', *Records of the Scottish Church History Society* 24(1992): 320–65; James Kirk, 'The Religion of Early Scottish Protestants', in *Humanism and Reform: The Church in Europe, England and Scotland, 1400–1643: essays in honour of James K. Cameron*, ed. James Kirk (Oxford, 1991).
4. Verschuur, *Politics or Religion?*, 18; Sanderson, *Ayrshire*, 48.
5. For a discussion of the idea of 'protestantizing Catholic' see Guido Marnef, *Antwerp in the Age of Reformation, 1550–1577*, trans. J. C. Grayson (Baltimore, 1996), 56.
6. Ryrie, 'Congregations', 48.
7. Thomas Riis, *Should auld acquaintance be forgot: Scottish–Danish relations c.1450–1707*, 2 vols (Odense, 1988), 1:40.
8. Sanderson, *Cardinal of Scotland*, 77; Nancy Roelker, *One king, one faith: the Parlement of Paris and the religious reformations of the sixteenth century* (Berkeley, 1996), 181.
9. Sanderson, *Cardinal of Scotland*, 76.
10. William Stevenson, 'Patrick Hamilton's nine-part mass', *Records of the Scottish Church History Society* 36 (2006): 29–39; Gerhard Muller, 'Protestant theology in Scotland and Germany in the early days of the Reformation', *Records of the Scottish Church History Society* 22 (1985): 103–7; Martin Dotterweich, 'Sacraments and the Church in the Scottish Evangelical Mind 1528–1555', *Records of the Scottish Church History Society* 36(2006): 41–71.
11. Sanderson, *Cardinal of Scotland*, 75–7.
12. Knox, *Works*, 1:42; Sanderson, *Cardinal of Scotland*, 82–3. See also Jane E. A. Dawson, 'The Scottish Reformation and the Theatre of Martyrdom', in *Martyrs and Martyrologies*, ed. Diana Wood (Oxford, 1993), 259–70.
13. Cowan, *The Scottish Reformation*, 94.
14. Sanderson, *Cardinal of Scotland*, 75; *Letters and papers, foreign and domestic, of the reign of Henry VIII [LP]*, 21 vols, eds J. S. Brewer, R. H. Brodie and James Gairdner (London, 1862–1910), 4:1296.
15. Knox, *Works*, 1:37; Cowan, *The Scottish Reformation*, 94.
16. See Ryrie, *The Origins*, 20.
17. Knox, *Works*, 1:41.
18. Knox, *Works*, 1:61; Ole Peter Grell, 'Introduction', in *The Scandinavian Reformation*, ed. Ole Peter Grell (Cambridge, 1995), 4; Riis, *Should auld acquaintance be forgot*, 40; James Larson, *Reforming the North* (Cambridge, 2010), 204, 219, 226; David Kirby, *Northern Europe in the Early Modern period: The Baltic World 1492–1772* (London, 1993), 82–6; Philip Dollinger, *The German Hanse*, trans and eds D. S. Ault and S. H. Steinberg (London, 1970), 32.
19. *RPS*, 1525/7/32 (accessed 26 July 2012); *Acts of the Lords of Council in Public Affairs, 1501–1554: Selections from the Acta dominorum concilli [ALC]*, ed. Robert Kerr Hannay (Edinburgh, 1932), 424–4.

20. Except for the Dominican John Craig, who oddly went to Italy. Sanderson, *Cardinal of Scotland*, 82.
21. Leith, Edinburgh, Dundee, St Andrews, Montrose, Aberdeen and Kirkcaldy being the others.
22. *ALC*, 424–4.
23. Sanderson, *Cardinal of Scotland*, 74.
24. 1534 was also the year when François I of France turned firmly against the Protestants as a result of the 'Affair of the Placards', which doubtless left an impression on both James V, his prospective son-in-law, and the future Archbishop David Beaton. Sanderson, *Cardinal of Scotland*, 77, 88.
25. One bailie, Alexander Craile, asked for and received an exemption from the proceedings, as he was away in business in Perth when the King's letters were received. It is difficult to say whether this was a sensible move to dodge certain punishment, or a deliberate rejection of solidarity with his fellow magistrates. *ALC*, 371–2; *TA*, 6:58.
26. *ALC*, 371.
27. Mostly likely Alexander Wedderburn the elder. *ALC*, 372.
28. See Flett, 'The Conflict of the Reformation and Democracy', 21–2.
29. *Privy Seal*, 2:173.
30. Calderwood, *History*, 1:189; John Spottiswood, *The History of the Church of Scotland*, 3 vols (Edinburgh, 1847–51; reprint: New York, 1973), 153.
31. DCA Protocol Book 1518–34 f233/t292; not much is known about John Wait, except that he was listed as an apprentice baker in 1521, which would probably place him in his mid-20s in 1532. The number of James Wedderburns present in Dundee at the same time makes any positive identification of that individual impossible, but it is likely that he was James, brother of John and Robert.
32. Knox, *Works*, 1:45–6; Calderwood, *History*, 1:87.
33. Knox, *Works*, 1:46–8.
34. Sanderson, *Cardinal of Scotland*, 81; Calderwood, *History*, 1:142.
35. *TA*, 6:307. See also Foggie, *Renaissance Religion*, chap. 6.
36. DCA Burgess Roll f29v; DCA BHCB 1454–1524, f46v, 75, 89v–90, 105, 158v, 169v. There is no trace in the records of a John Blacat, though a John Black was involved in some trading activities in the 1550s, which would possibly have made him a contemporary of George Lovell. DCA BHCB 1550–4 f152; DCA BHCB 1558–61, f3v
37. Sanderson, *Cardinal of Scotland*, 88–9.
38. *Privy Seal*, 2:396.
39. *Privy Seal*, 3:419. An older James Hay was a signatory of the charter establishing the merchant guild in 1516, and served as treasurer at around the same time. Warden, *Burgh Laws*, 96; DCA BHCB 1454–1524, f68v.
40. *Privy Seal*, 3:419.
41. Gilbert Wedderburn and John Paterson were convicted and received remissions in the same manner as James Annand and company (on 8 September 1538), though they only paid £6 13s 4d each. Thomas Kyd, Robert Paterson, Alexander Annand and John Paterson also went through the same process, although they only paid ten pounds (£2 10s each, if the sum was divided equally). Robert Cant paid £6, 13s 4d for his remission. Nothing is known about how much Richard Rollok paid for his remission. *TA*, 6:377, 7:74, 77, 78, 79; *Privy Seal*, 2:403, 407, 408.

42. Knox, *Works*, 1:61.
43. Calderwood, *History*, 1:124.
44. Sanderson, *Cardinal of Scotland*, 89.
45. Sanderson, *Cardinal of Scotland*, 131.
46. Gilbert Wedderburn, James Wedderburn, Richard Rollok and James Rollok were the sons of burgesses.
47. George Lovell, John Black, James Annand, George Annand, Robert Anderson, James Hay.
48. The Wedderburns – Gilbert, James and Master John – were probably all sons of James Wedderburn (1450), and James and Master John are the brothers supposed to have written the *Gude and Godly Ballatis*. Richard Rollok was either the brother or uncle of James Rollok, depending on which James Rollok was cited in the accusation. Calderwood, *History*, 1:143.
49. With the constant caveat that the similarity in names among different individuals makes it difficult to be certain exactly which individual is under discussion, the identifications made above are those I believe to be most likely. Although the Burgess Roll is not especially accurate in regards to dates (having been complied around 1580), the discrepancies are not likely to be more than five years or so.
50. For the age at which men became burgesses, see for example Andrew Kynneris, described as 'skinner boy' in 1539, made burgess in 1541 (*Privy Seal*, 2:471); Edmund Brown listed as apprentice baker in 1553, made burgess 1561 (DCA Burgess Roll, 35; DCA BHCB 1550–4, f267v). Of those who were not necessarily burgesses, Master John Wedderburn was born around 1500, and so would have been around thirty-seven at the time of the accusation against him; James Wedderburn, his brother, if the birthdate of 1495 is correct, would have been thirty-eight at the time of the accusation; John Wait, also accused in 1532, was listed as an apprentice baker in 1521; if he was in his teens then, he would have been in his twenties at the time of his accusation.
51. George Lovell, James Annand, Robert Anderson, James Rollok, Richard Rollok and James Hay.
52. DCA Protocol Book 1518–34, f233/t292.
53. Calderwood, *History*, 1:142.
54. Calderwood, *History*, 1:142.
55. *ALC*, 371.
56. Calderwood, *History*, 1:141–2.
57. Anderson, *Early records*, 118, 121, 222.
58. Calderwood, *History*, 1:142.
59. *TA*, 7:79.
60. Calderwood, *History*, 1:143.
61. A. F. Mitchell, 'Introduction', in *A Compendius Book of Godly and Spiritual Songs*, ed. A. F. Mitchell (Edinburgh, 1897), xiv. *Ane Compendious Buik of Godlie Psalmes*, Dundee City Library Rare Books Collection: my thanks to David Kett for allowing me to view this fragile document.
62. *ALC*, 527; *Statutes of the Scottish Church*, 127.
63. Mitchell, 'Introduction', xxxv.
64. *Godly and Spiritual Songs*, 64.
65. *Godly and Spiritual Songs*, 71.
66. *Godly and Spiritual Songs*, 178.

67. *Godly and Spiritual Songs*, 84.
68. Calderwood, *History*, 1:124.
69. Calderwood, *History*, 1:124.
70. Macfarlane, 'Chisholm, William'.
71. Calderwood, *History*, 1:124–6.
72. Calderwood, *History*, 1:125.
73. James Watson was probably about thirty-five years old at the time; SCA SBCB 1554–7 10/05/1555; Robert Pitcairn, *Ancient Criminal Trials in Scotland*, 3 vols (Edinburgh, 1833), 1:210, 216.
74. *A Diurnal of Remarkable Occurrents that have passed within the country of Scotland since the death of King James the Fourth till the year MDLXXV*, ed. T. Thomson (Edinburgh, 1833), 23; Pitcairn, *Ancient Criminal Trials*, 1:211–12. There are references to a Robert Forester in the burgh records following 1539, though it may also have been a common name in Stirling.
75. Calderwood, *History*, 1:125; George Buchanan, *History of Scotland*, 3 vols, trans. John Watkins (London, 1900), 354.
76. *TA*, 7:77; *Privy Seal*, 2:435, 441.
77. Calderwood, *History*, 1:160.
78. SCA SBCB 1544–50, 13/4/1548, 7/5/1548.
79. *DOST*.
80. *Extracts . . . Stirling*, 40–1.
81. *TA*, 8:179.
82. *RPS*, 1543/3/25 (accessed 4 November 2013); Calderwood, *History*, 1:155–8; Knox, *Works*, 1:95–100; Ryrie, *The Origins*, 57–65.
83. Sanderson, *Early Scottish Protestants*, 76–7, 123.
84. See Sanderson, *Cardinal of Scotland*, 160–78.
85. Knox, *Works*, 1:100.
86. DCA BHCB 1555–8, f9v/t17. A John Mailer was a London bookseller, accused of Protestant sympathies in 1540; Diarmaid MacCulloch, *Thomas Cranmer: A Life* (New Haven, 1996), 281.
87. Marcus Merriman, *The Rough Wooings: Mary Queen of Scots 1542–1551* (East Linton, 2000), 59.
88. Foggie, *Renaissance Religion*, 43, 143–4; Ryrie, *The Origins*, 66; *The Hamilton Papers: Letters and Papers Illustrating the Political Relations of England and Scotland in the XVIth Century*, 2 vols, ed. Joseph Bains (Edinburgh, 1890–2), 2:38.
89. The names listed on the document, except for those specifically mentioned as leaders of the attacks, should not be taken as a list of participants in the events of 1543. More likely the list includes many people associated with the charge of assuring with the English. As will be seen, this was hardly a voluntary act for Dundee's inhabitants. 'Indictment of Certain Dundee Burgesses on Charges of Riot and Treason', trans. Alexander Maxwell, in Maxwell, *Old Dundee*, 393–5.
90. George Lovell, John Paterson, James Hay, James Rollok (possibly a different man of same name), John Black. Three of the men (Gilbert Wedderburn, Master John Wedderburn, James Rollok) left Dundee in the meantime.
91. While the damage was clearly significant, Ryrie's claim that the two houses were 'destroyed' appears overstated, as is his claim that the parish churches in the town were also assaulted. As will be evident in later sections, the friaries survived both these attacks and the later English occupation. Ryrie, *The*

The Spread of New Ideas: 1520–1547 143

      Origins, 66; Foggie, *Renaissance Religion*, 143–44; 'Indictment', 395; Bardgett, *Scotland Reformed*, 28.
92. 'Indictment', 395.
93. Bardgett, *Scotland Reformed*, 28.
94. Bardgett, *Scotland Reformed*, 28.
95. DCA Burgess Roll, 30; *Privy Seal*, 3:27; Bardgett, *Scotland Reformed*, 28–30.
96. *TA*, 9:12.
97. *Privy Seal*, 2:482, 4:14; *TA*, 7:237, 9:13.
98. Bardgett, *Scotland Reformed*, 28; *Hamilton Papers*, 2:38.
99. Eire, *The War Against the Idols*, 126–7.
100. Ryrie, *The Origins*, 66.
101. *Hamilton Papers*, 2:38; 'Indictment', 393–5.
102. Sanderson, *Cardinal of Scotland*, 174; *LP*, 18, part ii, no. 425.
103. Cowan, *The Scottish Reformation*, 101–2.
104. Buchanan, *History of Scotland*, 2:371; Calderwood, *History*, 1:169; Knox, *Works*, 1:113–16; *A Diurnal of Remarkable Occurrents*, 30; *TA*, 8:247–8, 252, 258–64.
105. *TA*, 8:266; Calderwood, *History*, 175.
106. See Flett, 'The Conflict of the Reformation and Democracy', 23.
107. Iconoclasm took place throughout Scotland in this period, including in Perth, Ayrshire, Edinburgh and possibly Aberdeen. Sanderson, *Ayrshire*, 49–50, 68; Ryrie, *The Origins*, 66, 124; Foggie, *Renaissance Religion*, 43; David McRoberts, 'Material Destruction', in McRoberts, *Essays on the Scottish Reformation*, 417–18.
108. According to Alexander Petrie, who wrote in the seventeenth-century. Martin Holt Dotterweich, 'Wishart, George (*c*.1513?–1546)', in *ODNB* (accessed 7 November 2013).
109. Dotterweich, 'Wishart'.
110. Dotterweich, 'Wishart'.
111. Dotterweich, 'Wishart'; Bardgett, *Scotland Reformed*, 30.
112. Dotterweich, 'Wishart'; Knox, *Works*, 1:125.
113. Dotterweich, 'Wishart'; Knox, *Works*, 1:125; Calderwood, *History*, 1:205.
114. Knox, *Works*, 1:125–6.
115. Knox, *Works*, 1:126.
116. Wishart also preached in a church in Ayrshire, though there he did so with the protection of a local laird. Knox, *Works*, 1:127; Sanderson, *Ayrshire*, 66.
117. Knox, *Works*, 1:129–30.
118. Knox, *Works*, 1:130–1; Maxwell, *Old Dundee*, 87; Calderwood, *History*, 1:189.
119. *Privy Seal*, 2:173; Knox, *Works*, 1:132.
120. Calderwood, *History*, 1:193–5; Knox, *Works*, 1:137.
121. Knox, *Works*, 1:136.
122. Knox, *Works*, 1:136–7.
123. Calderwood, *History*, 1:194; Knox, *Works*, 1:138.
124. *The Miscellany of the Wodrow Society*, ed. David Laing (Edinburgh, 1844), 6.
125. Philip Benedict, *Christ's Churches Purely Reformed: A Social History of Calvinism* (New Haven, 2002), 65; Bruce Gordon, *The Swiss Reformation* (Manchester, 2002), 146–9.
126. Dotterweich, 'Wishart'.
127. 'The Confession of Faith of the Swezerlandes', trans. George Wishart, in *The Miscellany of the Wodrow Society*, Laing, 11–23.
128. 'Confession of Faith', 11–23.

129. 'Confession of Faith', 11–23.
130. This account by John Daye was 'incorporated verbatim' by Knox and Foxe; Dotterweich, 'Wishart'; Ryrie, 'Congregations', 74.
131. Knox, *Works*, 1:149–67.
132. Franciscans came to hear his preaching in Inveresk, for example, where they tried to dissuade people from attending. Knox, *Works*, 1:135–6.
133. Though some at St Andrews university had been refusing the mass since 1534.
134. Although his actions can be read in different ways. On one hand Ryrie points out that Wishart tried to stick close to Catholic teachings, but it also appears that Wishart held a eucharistic ceremony prior to his execution which was not a mass, although he had requested, and been denied, the Catholic sacrament. Ryrie, 'Congregations', 74; Sanderson, *Cardinal of Scotland*, 219. For the centrality of questions concerning liturgy and worship to the Reformation, see Holmes, *Sacred Signs*, especially 160–4.
135. *RPC*, 1:61.
136. HAD/4/1/2, f95v.
137. HAD/4/6/5, f277v; HAD/4/2/3/1, 274v, f28v, 32, 115, 169v.
138. *Privy Seal*, 4:183.
139. Jamieson, 'John Knox and East Lothian', 62, 69.
140. HAD/4/6/5, f174v.
141. Forbes Gray, *Short History*, 32.
142. Jamieson, 'John Knox and East Lothian', 70–1; Knox, *Works*, 1:139.
143. Jamieson, 'John Knox and East Lothian', 71.
144. Forbes Gray, *Short History*, 32; Martin A. Forrest, 'David and Alexander Forrest and their part in the Scottish Reformation', *Transactions of the East Lothian Antiquarian and Field Naturalists Society* 25 (2003), 22; Knox, *Works*, 1:137.
145. Forrest, 'David and Alexander Forrest', 14–15.
146. Forrest, 'David and Alexander Forrest', 15, 17–18.
147. Along with David Lindsay of the Mount, Henry Belnaves, Sir William Kirkcaldy of the Grange, Thomas Bellenden, David Bothwell, Michael Durham, David Borthwick. Knox, *Works*, 1:106.
148. Forrest, 'David and Alexander Forrest', 17–18.
149. *Calendar of State Papers relating to Scotland and Mary Queen of Scots, 1547–1563 [CSP]*, 12 vols, eds Joseph Bain *et al.* (Edinburgh: 1898–), 1:265.
150. Forrest, 'David and Alexander Forrest', 19.
151. Forrest, 'David and Alexander Forrest', 20.
152. 'Documents relating to Haddington', *Transactions of the East Lothian Antiquarian and Field Naturalists Society* 5 (1952): 68.
153. *Privy Seal*, 3:340.
154. 'Documents relating to Haddington', 68; Forrest, 'David and Alexander Forrest', 20.
155. Forrest, 'David and Alexander Forrest', 17–22.
156. Marnef, *Antwerp in the Age of Reformation*, 57.

CHAPTER SIX

Plague and War: 1543–1550

'The cruel invasions of our old enemies, the universal pestilence and mortality, that has occurred merciless among the people, and the contention of diverse of the three estates.'[1] These were the three 'vehement plagues' that afflicted Scotland in the mid-sixteenth century, according to *The Complaynt of Scotland*, a polemic attributed to Robert Wedderburn, Vicar of Dundee. War and plague struck Stirling, Dundee and Haddington particularly hard during the 1540s. Disease spread fear and tension through the towns, and questions of English and French allegiances and minority power politics divided the Scottish political class. The scars would be felt for decades; many people were killed, the survivors exhausted, whole tracts of buildings destroyed, and the local economies crippled. How these upheavals reshaped Scottish politics is well known, as the eventual defeat of the English and subduing of the Anglophile faction meant the firm establishment of a pro-French government. This chapter shifts the focus and demonstrates the cumulative toll these successive events had on the townspeople of Stirling, Haddington and Dundee, a toll which would shape their thinking during the 1550s and 1560s.

Wars and War Scares 1520–47

War was a constant presence in Scotland during the first half of the sixteenth century, punctuated by heavy defeats at Flodden in 1513 and Pinkie Cleugh in 1547. In between these battles less intense warfare kept the Scots on edge. After the disastrous Scottish defeat at Flodden both England and France continued to use the border as a second front to the main theatre of war in France. The Scottish regent, the Duke of Albany, tried in 1521 and again in 1523 to rouse the Scots to play an active part in their alliance with France and retaliate against English raids, but his efforts were stunted by Scottish reluctance.[2] These conflicts ended with a decade of tense peace, but a new crisis broke out in 1532 and 1533, with heavy border raids on each side and clashes in Ireland and on the Irish sea. Though the initial crisis eased as a result of an Anglo–French detente on the Continent, tensions remained high through the 1530s. The storm would finally break in 1542, as Henry VIII tried to secure his northern border. James V, a firm adherent of the French alliance, refused to cooperate in negotiations, and so Henry launched a series of assaults intended to secure hegemony over Scotland.[3] Throughout the period the recurrent crises kept Scots on the alert, but the burdens placed on the townspeople increased dramatically in the 1540s.

Haddington

As Haddington was situated on the main route between the English border and Edinburgh it was frequently caught up in war. Sometimes the town was attacked or occupied by the English, more often it was an assembly point for Scottish forces, and frequently its inhabitants were called up to military musters. These summonses occurred whenever there was sabre-rattling, a royal expedition against unruly subjects or actual war. In the period between the battle of Flodden and the wars of the 1540s, these crises threatened Haddington once a decade, during the war scares of 1522–3 and 1532–3. During the first episode, it was the Scots and French, some of whom mustered at Haddington, who were on the offensive as part of a French–English war.[4] In the 1530s the Scots prepared to defend and expected Haddington to be attacked, though the English invasion never materialised.[5] The disturbance caused by these war scares is reflected in the customs receipts, which in 1532–3 were less than half of what was collected in the preceding and subsequent years.[6]

War became an unavoidable reality from 1542 on, however. In August of that year, the men of Haddington were summoned to join an army at Lauder, probably the same one which defeated an English raiding force at Haddon Rigg.[7] The burghers of Haddington took the threat very seriously, and placed a watchman on the tolbooth, every man in the town either taking his turn or hiring a replacement.[8] In late October the English burned Kelso, and in November the Lords of Council met in Haddington, possibly as a result of measures taken to see off this invasion.[9] On 12 December 1542, a little more than two weeks after the disastrous defeat at Solway Moss and two days before the death of James V, a renewed English invasion to take advantage of Scottish weakness was feared. All men in Haddington and the other sheriffdoms along and near the eastern border were ordered to be ready 'at the height of this next morning' 'to pass forward for resisting of the Englishmen'.[10] Haddington increased its level of preparation, ordering a ditch to be constructed on the north side of the town on 19 December.[11] The burghers tightened their watch system, posting a man on each gate, and in December 1542 and again in October 1543 fines for lax participation were mandated.[12] In spite of these invasion fears, 1543 was fairly quiet as a truce with Henry VIII had been bought with the Treaty of Greenwich, which promised the marriage of the infant Queen Mary to the English prince Edward.[13]

War resumed in 1544 as the Scots refused to follow through with the treaty and marriage. In January 1544, the town authorised a detachment of twenty-four men to be sent to Edinburgh to join the Earl of Bothwell, each man to be paid two pounds.[14] Men were again summoned to be ready to join the army in April 1544, presumably to meet the invasion of the Earl of Hertford which departed Newcastle on 1 May.[15] This force was not successful in fending off the English, and Haddington, along with much of the rest of the Lothians, was burnt by the invading army.[16] During this invasion, the English left placards informing the Scots that they could 'thank their cardinal for this', a reference to the role of Cardinal Beaton in governing Scotland and ending Arran's pro-English Protestant reforms.[17] This propaganda may not have actually turned many Scots against Beaton, but it likely strengthened the mental connection between religious discord and disaster.

The invasion of 1544 was just a prelude to the wars to come. The men of Haddington were mustered again in November and December 1544, as well as February 1545, when the Scots won a minor victory over a small English invading force at Ancrum Moor.[18] Several more levies were organised in 1545 with summonses going out to Haddington in March (this army was to assemble at Haddington), May, July, August and September.[19] The repeated summonses probably helped spread the plague that was contagious that year. In August 1546, men were ordered to join the army at St Andrews to participate in the siege of the castle which had been occupied by the assassins of Cardinal Beaton. Frequent summonses continued throughout 1546: in September and October the men were placed on alert to join Arran in St Andrews, and in November and December they were once again ordered to join the siege.[20] In May 1547, the Haddingtonians were ordered to Edinburgh to resist the English.[21] Oddly, no record exists of any summons to the disastrous battle at Pinkie Cleugh, in September 1547, which took place about eight kilometres to the west of Haddington. Perhaps the record was simply lost, or the men of East Lothian were left to organise their own defence along the main English invasion route. After seeing little actual fighting for thirty years, the wars of the 1540s must have placed a heavy burden on the Haddingtonians, with repeated tours on field armies, a constant rota for local defence and added expenses. The worst was yet to come for Haddington, however.

Dundee

Dundee was also called on to mobilise men, money and supplies in response to the war scares of the 1520s and 1530s and the actual fighting in the early 1540s. In October 1523, for example, the Dundonians were ordered to provision a boat with bread, butter, cheese, ale and fish to be sent to the camp at Eyemouth.[22] In January 1533, Dundee was ordered to provide thirty-six men and £108 a month to the army gathered to defend against the English, the second highest contribution after Edinburgh.[23] In 1539 Dundee also contributed £337 for border defence.[24] The wars of the early 1540s created less urgency in Dundee, which was further away from the border, than in Haddington. In May 1544, 220 soldiers were raised or passed through Dundee and Perth, heading to Glasgow.[25] As the crisis intensified in 1545, at least two summonses were issued for men to join the armies at Roslin Muir and Lauder, and presumably Dundonians were involved (possibly on both sides) at the siege of St Andrews Castle in 1546.[26] As in Haddington, few references survive to a muster for Pinkie in September 1547, but when the English captured Broughty Castle in September 1547 war truly came to Dundee.

Stirling

Stirling was not to be directly affected by the scares of the 1520s and 1530s or by the wars of the 1540s, although the inhabitants did not know that at the time. Like other burghs, they sent men and money, shored up their defences, and suffered losses on the battlefield. Likely some men served in 1542 at Solway Moss, and in September 1545 the 'fiery cross', summoning men to the army, was brought to Stirling.[27] The burgh also had to contribute taxes to the national war effort, paying £67 7s 6d in 1546.[28] Aside from their direct contribution to the war, Stirling was a frequent mustering place for armies. Though there seem to have been few direct conflicts, there were dealings with the soldiers who had to be supplied, especially the French. Early in January 1543, for example, James Dog raised a band of 300 soldiers, who gathered at Stirling to await the earls of Lennox, Cassilis, Glencairn and others, before proceeding to Leith.[29] The band then returned to Stirling, before heading off with Beaton and Arran on their anti-heresy sweep through Perth and Dundee.[30] It was only in the later 1540s that the townspeople felt directly threatened by the wars.

Plague

In the midst of these military confrontations plague arrived in Scotland. It appears that both bubonic plague and typhus hit Scotland in the mid-1540s. Bubonic plague mostly struck during the summer, with peaks in mortality in late summer and early autumn, but other epidemic diseases, such as typhus, could occur year-round.[31] Plague outbreaks usually killed between 10 and 50 per cent of the population of an infected area, and 60 to 80 per cent of those infected, but also seemingly spread randomly, striking some towns, households and individuals but not others, depending on whether the rats in a particular house became infected or not.[32] The plague which affected Scotland was likely the same outbreak which struck London in 1543, spread throughout southern England in the following year and peaked in 1546–7. Plague was reported in Berwick in 1543, Newcastle in 1544 and then in towns throughout Scotland.[33] The *Diurnal of Remarkable Occurrents* reported that 'In this time the pest was wonder great in all burghs towns of this realm where many people died with great lack and want of victuals.'[34] As late as 1550, Ayr was still paying expenses incurred during the outbreak.[35]

The very randomness of the disease inclined people to interpret it as God's will, inflicted on the population because of sin of either a national or local variety.[36] Gilbert Skene, who wrote Scotland's first medical treatise in 1568, explained that the first cause of plague 'is ane scrurge and punishment of the maist just God, without quhais dispositioun in all thingis, utheris secund causis wirkis no thing', before going on to list such secondary causes as stagnant water and filth.[37] In line with this thinking, towns implemented a variety of public health measures such as quarantines and travel bans, but prayer, repentance and moral reformation were the first line of defence.[38] These responses were constant throughout the medieval and early modern period. European Christians responded to the Black Death of 1348–51 with religious remedies such as intercessory prayers and the Flagellant Movement, as well as slowly developing a public health apparatus; two centuries and one Reformation later, in 1574, the kirk session in Edinburgh ordered a public fast against the plague.[39] These various measures would all be invoked during the 1540s as well.

Haddington

Haddington's burgh records note several plague scares, demonstrating the townspeople's perpetual nervousness about epidemic diseases as well as the practical measures available to them. Concern about plague appears in 1530, when the Saturday market was cancelled on account of fears of the pestilence raging to the west.[40] Plague had been reported north of the Forth in 1529, and in 1530 in Edinburgh, but there is no further evidence that this epidemic severely affected Haddington.[41] In 1538, the council again took preventative measures and ordered that any inhabitant of the town who had any sickness in his house should immediately 'schwa it to ye bailies' under pain of banishment from the town. The bailies also cancelled the fair of St Mythawell, and all dogs were to be put out of the town. Possibly thanks to these measures, Haddington once again was spared a major plague outbreak.

The plague did strike Haddington in the spring of 1545.[42] On 23 April, the council took a series of anti-plague measures, expelling all poor folk except for those born in the town who were to receive a token allowing them to receive alms.[43] Proclamations such as this suggest that even a medium-sized town like Haddington received a fairly large influx of poor immigrants. In October, all sick people were ordered to be moved outside the town, to the south side of St John's port (gate).[44] No sick person was to return inside unless proven to be cured, under threat of death. At least one execution in Edinburgh demonstrates the seriousness with which townspeople enforced these regulations.[45] Sick people were also to be inspected by the provost and bailies.[46] Another act called for all those suspected of being infected to leave the town within forty-eight hours, on pain of having their goods seized, half going to the provost and bailies and half to the informant. In December 1545, George Forrois (likely Forrest) accused John Ayton and 'his complices' of breaking the act. Whether they did so by concealing a sick person or by keeping the seized goods for themselves is unknown, but the scandal was serious enough for Ayton to be deprived of his office of bailie.[47] Though we have no record of how many people died, the 1545 plague was devastating enough to still be remembered in 1564 when the town again enacted preventative measures, 'the whole council having in their remembrance the great and unrecoverable damage hurt hardship and despoliation of this burgh and of the great ruing of the inhabitants there of in the year of God (1545) be the pest'.[48]

Stirling

Stirling first took action against the plague in April of 1545, when an inquest ordered the bailies to summon the poor of the town and expel all the strangers, though, as in Haddington, not 'our awin puir'.[49] The townspeople of Stirling were especially worried about the plague because, in addition to the concern that everyone had for their own life, Stirling Castle was also home to the toddler Queen Mary, and the burgh was responsible for enforcing 'proclamations maid and defendit in our Soverane Ladyis names for keping of hir maist nobil persoun'.[50] The town strictly enforced travel and entry restrictions. That June John Henderson was convicted of letting two strangers into the town.[51] In August. six men were found guilty of having left the town without permission, leaving at 3 a.m. 'without licence of the touin and contrair the will of the wache'. Though the penalty for this act was death, the men had evidently escaped the bailies' jurisdiction, and so the authorities contented themselves with stripping the men of their burgess status, banning them from the town for life and condemning to death anyone who would receive them.[52] Perhaps as a result of these strict measures, Stirling seems to have made it through 1545 unscathed. Their continued vigilance was demonstrated by the issuing of a licence to seven men in September 1546 to travel to Renfrew to deliver some herring. The licence specified that their mission was to proceed only 'as lang as it [Renfrew] is unsuspect of the pest', that they were to bring with them only enough food for their sustenance, and that they were to stick together and visit no other town on pain of loss of life, land and goods.[53]

The threat of plague continued to close in on the town regardless, and on 13 October 1546 the council met to prepare for its arrival, especially by agreeing to use the burgh's resources to help sustain the poor 'if God sends ye infirmity of pest amangis yame', as the poor would be unable to work if quarantine measures were put in place. The councillors agreed 'to be in readine to serve ye saidis provost and bailies in all actions concerning ye common wele'.[54] This declaration was made just in time for the plague seems to have infected the burgh almost immediately. Nine days later, Andrew Clune was accused of having sent plague-infected goods into the town to his wife, who had then died of the plague, infecting the rest of the town as well. Clune confessed 'sayand [he] had put ane blok in Striveling of the pest that suld nevir gang furth of it, with many otheris evill wordis to that effect, as the hale cuntray knawis'.[55] Clune's fate is unknown, though the council seems to have been quite inclined to carry out the death penalty. In December, two men arriving from Leith and Edinburgh with merchandise were initially prevented from entering the town, but were eventually granted permission to enter 'on pain of death if any fault'.[56]

No further reference to the plague is found in the burgh records, although it is notable that in this period there was an increased crackdown on misdemeanour offences, both in the number of cases prosecuted and the severity of the punishments. In August 1546, for example, Marion Ray was convicted of slander: telling William Cuniggame that she had seen him 'swiff Henry Thomson wiff vj times' telling Henry Thomson that 'wer you worthie to swiff thi wiff thiself you wald nocht let otheris swiff hir' and for calling Agnes Hendersoun 'a common huir and that scho wust hir xx tymes swivit, and tha scho [saw] Wille Cuniggame swiff her vj times'. For these various insults and accusations, she was to ask forgiveness on her knees, and then to remain in the tolbooth 'while the claspis and calvill of iron [manacles and a gag] devisit of before be made'. Evidently the burgh had planned to increase the severity of their punishments, and now in the midst of a plague scare, they resolved to go ahead and have the devices actually made. Once ready, they were to be locked on Marion Ray for twenty-four hours, without any relaxing.[57] Neither this punishment, nor the plague, ended Ray's feud with Agnes Hendersoun, and in April 1547, after a further round of insults, the council decided to add to their instruments of punishment, ordering the construction of a creill, or basket, to be hung outside the tolbooth, and Ray to be placed there 'during the will of the provost and bailies'.[58] Shortly after, William Duchok, having called Merion Aikman a whore, was ordered to ask forgiveness and then to drink only water for twenty-four hours, as he was drunk at the time of the offence, and to be put in the creill for forty-eight hours if he faulted again.[59] The council continued to make full use of the creill, sentencing Ray to a further term after she called another woman a whore.[60] These more severe punishments may simply have been a response to Ray's unstoppable verbal onslaught. The timing, however, just as the townspeople worried about the plague, is striking, and it is quite plausible that these measures were an attempt to ward off God's wrath.

Dundee

Most of what we know about the 1545 plague in Dundee comes from Knox's account of George Wishart's presence in the burgh. An associate of Wishart's, Knox can be considered a near if not direct witness. According to him, Wishart had first preached in Dundee in 1544, but was expelled from the town, prophesying as he left that

I am assured that to refuse God's Word, and to chase from you his messenger, shall not preserve you from trouble; but it shall bring you into it. For God shall send you messengers who will not be afraid of horning, nor yet of banishment . . . If it be long prosperous with you, I am not led with the spirit of truth. But and if trouble unlooked for apprehend you, acknowledge the cause and turn to God, for he is merciful. But if ye turn not at the first, he shall visit you with fire and sword.[61]

According to Knox, the plague began only four days after Wishart issued this prediction. Knox, of course, had his own motives for playing up Wishart's prophetic talents, as he sought to demonstrate proof of Wishart's divine calling.[62] The historian can only hope that Knox, while selective in his narrative, would not dare to utterly fabricate such a dramatic story within the lifetime of eyewitnesses. In any case, once the news reached Wishart in Kyle, he returned to Dundee to aid the afflicted, and hoped that they would pay more attention to his message, reportedly saying: 'Perchance this hand of God will make them now to magnify and reverence that word which before (for fear of men) they set at light price.' He preached to the sick quarantined outside the town's East port and gave physical assistance, visiting, comforting and supplying food and drink.[63] As with the other towns, we do not know how many inhabitants died, as the burgh records for this period have not survived and there is no way of separating out the deaths caused by plague from those caused by the English invasions. This next trial descended on Scotland almost immediately, giving the people little time to regroup and recover.

War 1547–1550

No sooner had the worst of the plague passed than Protector Somerset of England renewed the war on Scotland. The 'War of the Rough Wooing' was intended to secure the marriage of the Scottish Queen Mary to the English Edward Tudor in order to create a British dynastic union. Having agreed to the marriage at the Treaty of Greenwich in July 1543, the Scots reneged later that year. Henry VIII, and following his death Somerset, were determined to gain the marriage one way or another, and by 1547 Somerset had developed a strategy of military occupation. By establishing fortified strongholds at key points, the English could control important areas of Scotland and secure the allegiance of some local Scots by a process known as 'assuring.' An 'assured' Scot promised to obey the King of England and oppose his enemies.[64] The English hoped that promoting Protestantism would gain the support of like-minded Scots, and the oath of assurance also included a pledge to 'utterly Renownce and forseik the usurped pour of the Bysshope of Rome and his successours for ever'.[65] This strategy of persuasion was soon set aside by more immediate military needs, with unfortunate consequences for both Dundee and Haddington.

Haddington

Along with predicting misfortune for Dundee, George Wishart may have also foretold the Haddingtonians about the tribulations which were to fall on them in 1548 and 1549. Despairing that only a hundred or so people came to his preaching, Wishart had reportedly predicted in early 1546 that

> Fearful shall the plagues be that shall ensue for this thy contempt. With fire and sword shall thou be plagued, even thou, Hadington, in speciall. Strangers will possess thee; and yee inhabitants, for the present, shall either in bondage serve your ennemies, or else be chased from your own habitations, and that because ye have not known, nor will not know, the time of God's merciful visitations.[66]

According to Pittscottie, just before his execution Wishart had a vision of a great cloud which rested above Traprain Law, a prominent hill just north of Haddington, for half an hour. This cloud then divided into two: 'the one half, passed west above Haddington and there moved above the town and turned in fire: the other half passed north-west above Inveresk kirk and there appeared to him as if it had been blood descending out of the lift'. It is worth noting that Inveresk kirk would be the site of the disastrous battle of Pinkie Cleugh in September 1547. Wishart, when asked the meaning of the vision, said

> the cloud that rose above Dumpender [Traprain] law signified to him that [there] should come a council and be held in the said law, which should devise much trouble in Scotland and cause much blood to be shed and in special should wreak and destroy Hadingtoun for were [ever?] and many of the inhabitants thereof.[67]

This prophecy was either uncannily accurate, or embellished by later writers who had the advantage of observing subsequent events – Knox probably wrote his version around 1566 and Pittscottie sometime before his death in the 1570s.[68] Even if Knox and Pittscottie took some liberties, it is possible that versions of the stories were circulating as early as the 1540s and 1550s. Given the strong prophetic tradition of the sixteenth century, such a warning would have added to the sense contemporaries had that Scotland was suffering from God's wrath.[69]

The English marched on Haddington in February 1548, beginning an occupation that would last for nineteen months, during most of which Haddington itself would be occupied. Haddington was chosen as the main garrison point for the English forces in south-eastern Scotland, from which they could hinder the operations of the Franco-Scottish forces based at

Edinburgh, harass the surrounding countryside and persuade or compel the Scots in the Lothians. A garrison at Haddington could also be supplied by land from England or by sea through the port at Aberlady. Supply, nonetheless, would prove to be a constant problem for the English.[70] The invaders began fortifying Haddington at the end of April 1548.[71] The tolbooth was reinforced to serve as a central keep, and a gun platform placed on top. An earth wall was built around the town, with gun bastions placed at each corner. The size of the garrison varied but was usually about 2500 soldiers.[72] Haddington's parish church, to the south of the town, was outside the fortifications and partially demolished by the English – the walls and steeple remained standing, but the English commander claimed to have broken the vaults of the steeple and the church, torn down the roof and cut and under-propped the pillars. Houses near the Tyne river were cleared away to deny cover to besiegers, and the town's gates were closed up.[73] The occupying army collected grain and meat from the surrounding countryside, though it is unclear whether the food was given, taken or bought.[74]

By the end of June 1548, the French and Scots had begun to besiege the English base.[75] It was then, on 7 July 1548, that a parliament was held at the Abbey of Haddington, outside the range of the guns. The Scots delegates agreed to the marriage of Mary Stewart to the French dauphin, a complete reversal of the Treaty of Greenwich.[76] The siege at first went well for the French and Scots, but English reinforcements slipped into Haddington around 8 July.[77] A second English resupply expedition was driven off, but a further effort in August succeeded, forcing the French to lift the siege in the process.[78] After clashing with the townspeople in Edinburgh, the French soldiers were sent back to Haddington in October. On arrival they almost took the town by surprise assault but were ultimately repulsed with heavy casualties.[79] Thereafter the siege lightened and the English were able to resupply their garrison at a level of bare subsistence.[80] The French and Scots slowly began to gain regional dominance, causing many previously assured Scots to reconsider their loyalties and making it difficult for the English to gather supplies.[81] In August 1549, the French occupied the port of Aberlady, cutting the English garrison off from the sea. Facing the need to supply Haddington by costly overland convoys, and suffering from disease and hunger, the English finally evacuated the town in September 1549, leaving a devastated town and local population in their wake.[82]

Dundee

War came to Dundee in full force immediately after Somerset's decisive victory at the battle of Pinkie Cleugh in September 1547. The English quickly occupied Broughty Castle at the mouth of the Tay, a position which allowed them to dominate Dundee, some three kilometres distant, tax or blockade goods travelling along the Tay to Perth and points further inland, and use the river to raid the surrounding countryside, monasteries and nunneries. This strategic, though small and badly maintained fortification, was turned over by two pro-English Scots, Lord Gray and Henry Durham. It was these two men who had led the sacking of Dundee's friaries in 1543.

Initially, the English commander, Andrew Dudley, did not devastate the countryside and demand from civilians the exactions common in sixteenth-century warfare, hoping to win the Scots to the English cause through persuasion. He reported to Somerset 'I use the country gently as ordered. Diverse gentlemen who favour the word of God would come in if they durst, but wait "till they see how the world go".'[83] Dundee, however, did not respond to Dudley's first request to assure, and so he resorted to force. On 27 October 1547, the English bombarded Dundee with two ships and threatened to burn the town. The inhabitants surrendered and a delegation of the town council assured to Dudley, promising to practise and promote Protestantism (specifically, 'to be faithful setters forth of God's word'), to sell provisions to the English at fair prices, to pay duty to them, and to resist the Scottish governor as far as they could, unless he came with an army in which case they would do 'as they are able and think best'.[84] Dudley attempted to carry out the English strategy of using Protestantism to create a pro-Protestant, pro-English faction, and requested bibles from Somerset. The repetition of his requests, especially in January 1548, when he wrote that he was 'daily "cried" on by Dundee and the lords and gentlemen, for a good preacher, and bibles, testaments and other good books', suggest that the books and preacher never arrived.[85]

A Scottish army led by the Earl of Argyll duly arrived at the end of November, re-took Dundee, and used it as a base for an unsuccessful siege of Broughty.[86] It was probably to reinforce this army that the Scottish Privy Council ordered 300 soldiers to be raised: the church prelates and the inhabitants of Dundee were each to raise fifty hagbutmen and fifty spearmen for one month, an expense for which the prelates were to pay £600; presumably the Dundonians paid the same. The region's lairds were to raise 100 horsemen.[87] Argyll's army left by 18 December. Having been briefly occupied by Scottish soldiers, Dundee, an essentially unfortified town, once again surrendered to the nearby English garrison after fighting in which two or three Scots were killed. On 20 December 1547, Dudley issued a proclamation in Dundee, in the presence of Lord Gray and the lairds of Grange and Balumbie (Henry Lowell), as well as the town council.[88] The councillors took an oath to the English, but not very convincingly. As Thomas Wyndam, the commander of the English fleet wrote, 'me thought [their oath] very weekly at the Scots hands, but putting there whole trust to the lord Gray, I think chiefly for fear of the Governor and other of his affinite, for disowning of them when we be absente with the ships.'[89] This was the high point of Gray's influence, as the town looked to him as a dependable local source of protection. They sent two hostages to Dudley and again agreed to the previous terms of assurance.[90] The English also started to ravage the countryside, burning crops, villages and the Abbey of Balmerino, although they seemed careful to leave some sustenance for Dundee.[91]

The townsmen were caught between two sides, easily threatened by the nearby English who were nevertheless too weak to hold Dundee against significant opposition from Scottish and French forces. Exposed and having assured with the English, the townsmen feared the arrival of vengeful Scottish forces, and asked for help from Broughty's garrison in preparing their defences.[92] The English knew that the Scots, both the townspeople and those in the surrounding countryside, would give their loyalty to whoever could offer protection. Dudley therefore worried that a victory by Argyll would discredit the English in front of Gray, the Dundonians and the assured Scots, begging Somerset 'I beseech your grace rather discharge me than let me lose my credit with Scotsmen'.[93] The English made the best of their position regardless, and on 12 January 1548 they sent a small force, twenty to fifty men, to Dundee, and placed guns in the church steeple. Despite the threat of destruction from the Earl of Argyll, at this point the townspeople were still sticking with the English, according to Dudley.[94] The attempts at making the unwalled town defensible were clearly deemed inadequate, however, as the townsmen fled 'with sorrowful hearts' before the return of Argyll's Scottish troops later in January 1548. Where they fled to is unknown; nonetheless, four or five men loyal to the English remained, indicating the persistence of a small but resolutely pro-English faction.[95] As the English evacuated the undefended town, they stripped St Mary's of bells, brass and copper, and burned the Catholic ritual figures ('idols') within it (although many valuable ornaments had been hidden by the inhabitants before the war began), as well as the steeple which could be used as an artillery position. They left the rest of the town intact, however, hoping eventually to recapture it.[96]

After withdrawing from Dundee, the English literally bought time by paying Argyll 1,000 crowns in return for a twenty-one-day truce, during which they received 400 men in reinforcements. As part of the truce, Dudley was allowed to buy necessities from Dundee and enter the town with a 'sober' number of men.[97] As well as selling provisions to the English, the local inhabitants were paid five pence (English money) a day to work on building fortifications for them, and Dudley reported that many Scots were willing to do the work and accept English money. These fortifications were built with timber and frames from houses in Dundee.[98]

As 1548 progressed, Dundee's loyalties increasingly turned away from the English. When a Scottish force passed through they found support from the town, though not from the surrounding region.[99] In March 1548, Argyll ordered a muster at Dundee of all men between the ages of sixteen and sixty, though he did seem to be having difficulty recruiting men.[100] In May 1548, Governor Arran sent letters to Patrick Lyon (the customer) in Dundee, further demonstrating the government's efforts to control the region.[101] Lyon was likely responsible for organising the Scottish effort inside Dundee, and indeed he would be targeted by Henry Durham, who would burn his house in November 1548.[102] Around this time, James Dog, military captain, became Dundee's provost, a sign of the militarisation of the town.[103] Dudley himself received a warning from the English general Grey of Wilton in June 1548 that local Scots 'having liberty there to by your over great familiarity' were planning on killing him.[104]

The English in Broughty Castle hung on, and on 8 November 1548 made a renewed effort, entering Dundee, expelling the townspeople and spoiling the town. They were initially driven out by a counter-attack of local troops led by Captain Dog, but they returned the next day and completed the destruction.[105] Of all the destruction inflicted on the town, this seems to have been the most severe, for the council records state that November 1548 was the month 'the said land was burnt and destroyed be our old Ennemies of England like as the whole remanent of the said burgh was or the most part thereof whom to they [the inhabitants] might not resist'.[106] After the burning the English continued to make daily raids, cutting off the supplies to the Scottish soldiers who had re-occupied Dundee, who the English estimated to include 120 infantry and eighty cavalry, 'beside the Scotish men that inhabit with them, who indeed are not many – only such poor people as serve to bake and brew'.[107] By December 1548, the Scots had responded in force, the governor being present and French troops being sent.[108] This army did not stay long, and the following March the English spoiled the town again, seeking building materials for their fort, and the Scots responded by dispatching yet more French troops.[109] The standoff continued through the year, and Broughty Castle was finally retaken in January 1550, when the treasury records a series of expenses incurred by the governor in recovering the castle, including guides, transportation workers and food.[110]

The fallout from the wars continued for some time. In March 1550, the governor made a payment of forty-six shillings to men hurt at the siege of Broughty who were recovering at the Gray Friars gate.[111] A Dundonian named Ramsay was still holding an Englishman captive, possibly for ransom, in March 1552. The prisoner was only freed after repeated requests from the crown, who paid the captive three pounds for his trouble.[112]

Stirling

With the resumption of war in 1547, the people of Stirling had to increase their preparations and contributions. The burgh, firstly, had to look after its own defences, which required both money and physical labour. In October 1547, they rented the fishing grounds in the Forth to John Forester for a term of three years, at eighteen pounds a year. The fifty-four pounds was paid immediately, 'to be expendit upon the strenthing and bigging of ye wallis of ye town in yis perilous tyme of neid for resisting of our auld ennemies of Ingland'.[113] The following February, the town council called for labour, requiring all inhabitants to be ready with servants and horses to work on the town's defences. They tried to ensure participation by ordering that no one was to be permitted to leave the town on pain of losing their goods and to be never allowed 'place, fredoom nor dwelling' in the town again.[114] The town arranged as well for the workers to be fed 'to support and furniss the towns labouris for resisting of the Inglismen now in time of need'.[115] William Bell, treasurer, was assigned to buy artillery for the burgh, the council generously agreeing to be taxed 'gif neid beis' to reimburse him.[116] Alas, this does not seem to have been resolved satisfactorily, for as late as 1554 William Bell was deemed to owe £359, 19s 10d for the defences.[117]

As well as working on the town's defences, men continued to be mustered to fight at the front. Proclamations were made in August 1547 and February 1548 recruiting men to go to the siege at Haddington.[118] In July, Provost John Craginelt received the right to all the goods of those who did not go.[119] In January 1549, 'all maner of horsemen' in Stirling were ordered to join the army and in January 1550 the men of Stirling were again ordered to muster with the army gathered against the Englishmen.[120] That men responded to these summonses is revealed by the arrangements made for, or by, their widows. Stirling's burgh court ordered Janet Kay to pay sixteen shillings to John Tailor for the sword that Tailor had lent to her, by then deceased, husband.[121] Agnes Smith, whose husband Alexander died at Pinkie Cleugh, was granted his goods by the Queen Regent, a step made necessary by the fact that Alexander was illegitimate.[122] In 1548, a case involving Robert Hobe came before the burgh court; being away with the army at Dundee, Hobe appointed Robert Drummond to represent him.[123]

The burgesses of Stirling who remained at home had various dealings with the soldiers using the town as a base. Walter Cousland, William Bell and Alexander Watson had several business arrangements with the French, and on at least one occasion were refunded by the regent's officials.[124] In February 1548, the provost and bailies deemed the French treasurer to owe eight pounds to Andrew Anderson for a horse 'because it was clearly proven by diverse witnesses that the said horse was worth as much', and designated Walter Cousland as guarantor.[125] Not all encounters were so peaceful, and two Dutch men were arrested by the council for gravely wounding William Wright and recklessly shooting his pistol.[126]

While Stirling avoided the destruction that occurred in Dundee and Haddington, like the rest of Scotland the townspeople suffered from losses of men and money and lived with the constant fear that war might come to their doorstep. The efforts of preparing the town's defences, being on alert, fighting in the frontline armies and warily hosting 'friendly' soldiers all took their toll.

Collaboration

The townspeople of Dundee and Haddington were faced directly with English invasion and occupation, and many chose, or were forced to choose, to collaborate with the occupiers. Stirling's inhabitants, further away from the front lines, were spared such difficult choices. This collaboration often took the form of assuring, a tactic classically described by Marcus Merriman, whereby Scots were encouraged or compelled to pledge themselves to the English cause.[127] A key part of this English strategy included trying to gain the support of Scottish Protestants; English defeat however led to the suppression of the most militant Scottish Protestants, which contributed to the decline in overt Protestant activity through the early 1550s and cleared the way for a new generation of Protestant preachers to arrive in the second half of the decade.

The behaviour of both the Dundonians and Haddingtonians during the English invasions perfectly matches the findings of a report sent to Mary of Guise, dated 3 June 1548. The anonymous author reports that the principal reasons why people assured with the English were

> In the first, part of the lieges has taken new appointment of the scripture and has gone against the law and ordinance of holy kirk. Secondly, others [of] the lieges has for fear – them on borders and dry marches, and others upon the shores of the sea or burghs upon the sea of this realm – for safety of them, their wife barnis and goods has favoured and been familiar and assisted to [the] English. Thirdly, others of the lieges has through insolence and regard of particular profit has assisted and taken part with English. [Fourthy], others [of] the lieges has upon less understanding and imprudently taken consent that they might live at more quietness and justice under the English nor [than] our own nation.[128]

Collaborators for religious reasons were certainly present in Dundee, and possibly in Haddington, and in both towns there were those who sought profit or a quieter life under the English. Many, however, likely cooperated for the second reason, fear. Those who collaborated too enthusiastically either fled or were discredited after the war, while many who had cooperated out of fear remained and paid substantial penalties. Many of those who were interested in Protestantism remained loyal to the Scottish cause throughout, and the English efforts to create a faction of allied Protestant Scots succeeded only in driving a faction of militant reformers out of the country.

Haddington

Many Scots in East Lothian supported and assisted the English, though it is difficult to know how many of them did so under compulsion. Some Scots were allied to the English from the start of the Rough Wooings, with confiscations beginning as early as February 1547 when the goods of the late William Clapen, burgess of Haddington, and of his sister Elizabeth were escheated because they lived in England in time of war. Faced with overwhelming English military dominance, it is not surprising that in early 1548 many more Scots assured with the English. How many of these assured Scots were inhabitants of Haddington, and how many were from the surrounding countryside, is difficult to establish. In February 1548, the English general Grey of Wilton reported from his headquarters in Haddington that almost 1000 Scottish horse had assured with him.[129] At the end of April, as he began work on the fortifications, Grey reported that he had 'required the dwellers here about to bring in all they can, and find them "so well willing or so well afraid" that I doubt no want of grain'.[130] The Scottish government did its best to stamp out this collaboration, and not long after the invasion of late winter 1548 began, four men of Longniddry had their goods seized for travelling to Haddington to join up with Grey of Wilton.[131] A particularly active collaborator was John Riclington, who had already purchased a remission from the Scottish government for not joining the army gathered at St Andrews in 1546. In 1548 he and George Forrest were praised by the English general James Wylford as having 'served very honestly during this siege, and have suffered great losses'.[132] Riclington evidently saw no future in remaining in Haddington after the English defeat, and fled into England, dying soon after. His Scottish goods, and those of his wife, Helen Tait, were subsequently seized by the crown.[133]

Others moved in the opposite direction; Philip Gibson (I) apparently fled Haddington just before the English arrived, leaving behind some skins, which the English captured and intended to ship to Berwick. Along the way they fell into Scottish hands again, and were confiscated by the crown. Fleeing did not do much good for the ill Gibson, for he was dead by the time the letter of eschete was dated, 20 June 1548.[134] It is impossible to know how many Scots stayed in Haddington, but there surely must have been many refugees.

The English hoped to appeal to those who remained through religion. In June 1548, Grey urged Somerset to send some Scottish preachers to join him. The preachers were originally supposed to arrive earlier in the winter but had been 'unwilling to risk their bodies'. The situation, Grey reported, had since improved and he expected that the preachers would find many converts.[135] There is no evidence that the preachers were sent, but at least there were enough Scots left to preach to. They were not necessarily enthusiastic Protestants but do seem to have been open to different ideas; at least, perhaps some inhabitants thought it politic to express such an interest to their new masters. These inhabitants probably did not remain long as the siege intensified; Calderwood reports that when the English finally left, the French soldiers found only 'some few ancient inhabitants'.[136]

It was only once the English evacuated Haddington that most Scots began either to buy remissions – essentially, paying a fine – or to suffer the forfeiture of goods. Men from all over Scotland were sanctioned for cooperating with the English in Haddington, the accusations normally being variations on fortifying, assisting and partaking with our old enemies of England in perseuing of the lieges of this realme, and in convoying of powder and victualis to the fort of Haddingtoun, and taking assurance with them, and otherwise dealing, communing and taking with them to the subversion of this realm and lieges thereof.[137]

In Haddington, the process began with the remission of John Forrous (Forrest) in October 1549, and at least three more inhabitants had their goods seized or bought remissions the following year.[138] Others would have bought remissions at the justice-ayre held in Haddington in January 1554, when the justice general arrived to hold court, as the Dundonians did at theirs.[139] Apart from the handful who fled to England, most of those sanctioned likely cooperated out of fear or profit, there being no evidence that they were supporters of a Protestant, anglophile cause.

Dundee

In Dundee, unlike Haddington, there was an organised pro-English party under the leadership of Patrick Lord Gray and his man Henry Durham. These two men had been active and militant leaders of the Protestant faction since at least 1543.[140] The position of many of the townspeople was more ambivalent, as they had been caught between the two sides. With the defeat of the English, the more active collaborators fled to England, leaving everyone else to face the punishment of the Scottish government.

The leaders of the pro-English faction did not gain much from their collaboration with the losing side and lost their local prominence. Lord Gray had assured with the English after being captured at Solway Moss, and apparently agreed to hand over Broughty Castle in March 1547.[141] Gray was rewarded by the English, who paid him £1,000 that November.[142] The most important Scottish collaborator in the region, he was captured by the Scots late in 1548, and was imprisoned in Edinburgh Castle from January 1549 on. The government was determined to keep him secure, buying four locks to prevent him escaping.[143] Paying a fine of £1,912 10s did not hasten his release, which did not come until 1554. It was only Arran's intervention that saved him from the French, who had wanted to execute him as a traitor.[144] He was then captured by the English in 1557. In between, the burgh of Dundee sued him for damages caused by his collaboration.[145]

Henry Durham eventually fled to England, though not before assisting the English in burning the town in November 1548. In March 1549 he would petition Somerset, complaining that for his efforts on behalf of the Gospel and the English king he was exiled from his country, and had lost one hundred merks in annual revenue when he surrendered Broughty Castle.[146] Somerset's response, if any, has not survived. In February 1562, perhaps thinking he might get a sympathetic hearing under the new Protestant regime, Durham hired a legal representative to pursue John

Fothringham for a payment for a barrel of salmon, dating back to 1549. Patrick Lyon interrupted the proceedings, claiming that during the attack of 9 November 1548 Durham had appeared 'in company with Englishmen' and 'spoiled his house and burned the same his loss extending to four (pounds)'. John Fothringham also complained that his house had been burned by Durham. The court refused to hear the case until Durham appeared in person to defend himself against the accusations, an opportunity he apparently declined.[147] Joining the English cause had transformed Durham from a prominent local figure into an outcast.

Other men who fled after the English defeat included Alexander Whitelaw, Thomas Steward, and possibly David Gardin and Robert Curmannow. Whitelaw was an eager ally, offering in December 1547 to 'ride on' those who refused to take assurance.[148] Whitelaw's goods were ordered confiscated by the Scots in February 1548. The crown found it difficult to enforce this particular condemnation as the summons was again issued in March, with the directive that the messenger bring two witnesses with him.[149] Whitelaw left Broughty in early 1549 to join the English on the Borders.[150] Like Durham, Thomas Steward sailed away with his wife and children on English ships (though he left earlier, in January 1548), and the following March the crown gave all his goods to Mathew Hamilton of Mylburn, Captain of Blackness Castle.[151] After fleeing Dundee, Stewart wrote John Lutrell, an English officer, thanking him for his help but asking to be refunded the money he had lent or spent in Broughty.[152] He wrote again to ask for Lutrell's assistance in regards to his brother, who had been taken prisoner.[153] Stewart tried to maintain his contacts in Dundee, and in March 1550 the burgess and merchant Thomas Thane had his goods confiscated for communicating with Stewart, still considered a fugitive.[154] Stewart had not returned in 1552, when his mother was forced to give up the goods of her late husband, which would have gone to Thomas but instead passed to Mathew Hamilton.[155] He may have returned by February 1559.[156]

David Gardin, burgess of Dundee, had his goods seized for his joining with the English in burning and plundering the town in November 1548.[157] He may also have fled, for there is nothing about him in the records following 1550.[158] In April, the goods of Robert Carmannow were confiscated, also for supplying the English, participating in the burning of Dundee and for 'showing of the secrets of this realm to them'.[159] Robert was perhaps the son of the Robert Carmannow who signed the charter establishing Holy Blood altar in 1515, and therefore belonged to a significant family in the burgh. Like David Gardin, perhaps he also fled from vengeful neighbours. The cost of joining the losing side was high, and most of those who actively collaborated with the English would not play a further role in local politics.

Other Scots stayed behind and had to come to terms with the authorities. Some of these were lairds: Andrew Balfour of Monquhany paid £240, William Durham of Grange £225, and Thomas Maule, junior of Panmuir, £144 10s.[160] Henry Lovell of Ballumby and his brother David also obtained remissions, though it is not known how much they paid. Whatever the amount, David's actions cannot have been too detrimental to the Dundonians, for he was admitted to the burgess roll in 1551.[161] John Scrimgeour, who as provost had signed the assurance with the English in 1547, saw his lands and his castle at Dudhope seized by Arran and retired to Argyll.[162]

Townspeople also helped the English occupiers. In the summer of 1548, Luttrell found a (unnamed) wealthy Scotsman, the 'King's servant' who had a pension of fifty pounds, who lent cloth and seventy pounds to build the fortifications.[163] Over the winter of 1548, Scots were happy to work for the English. Many of these burgesses were penalised for their cooperation, but remained in the town after the war. Some of them were eager to rejoin the Scottish side. Thomas Forester, a merchant who had been Dean of Guild, was the first on record to receive a remission in June 1548.[164] He was then sent back to Dundee in the company of Master John Forsyth to recruit military pioneers (proto-engineers), but died soon after.[165] Next, in January 1549, a messenger summoned certain men in Dundee who 'spoiled the town after the burning'.[166] Perhaps as a result of this mission, James Lovell paid a fine of one pound, his remission specifying that he had traded with the English.[167] He had also assured as a member of the town council. He was a merchant who had earlier been accused of heresy, which perhaps explains his desire to quickly get back into the crown's good graces. This payment of one pound, however, did not save him from further prosecution during the trial which would take place in 1553.

Other Dundonians were fined as the fighting eased but nonetheless kept their place in the burgh community. In February 1549, the crown seized the goods of James Hay. Hay would serve on the town council in 1550 and thereafter throughout the 1550s, so his activities were not held against him by his fellow burgesses. The following March, the crown also confiscated the goods of Andrew Myln, the second son of the prominent burgess Robert Myln.[168] Poorer men had to account for their activities as well. In 1551, David Daw, John Daw, John Davidson, James Davidson and William Annand paid small fines for assisting the English.[169] John Davidson may have been the same man who was admitted burgess in 1552. It is possible that these men either traded with the English, or perhaps some of the poorer men were among those who worked on their fortifications. Their collaboration was minor enough that they were not ostracised by their neighbours.

The town council had also made an agreement with the English, albeit at gunpoint. Many of the councillors who assured to Dudley, promising to assist the English and promote Protestantism, would dominate burgh politics throughout the 1550s, and at least three of them were sympathetic or supportive of new religious ideas.[170] Their initial delay in assuring with the invaders suggests that for them, an interest in religious reform did not necessarily imply support for the Protestant English. Despite a report by Dudley in 1547 that 'most of the honest and substantial men favour the Word of God and would be glad to become English' (although in the same letter he asks whether Dundee men could still travel to France, or Frenchmen to Dundee), the activities of many of the townspeople, forced to collaborate with the English and to make the best of a bad lot, should be distinguished from the willing collaboration of Durham, Gray, Stewart and others.[171] Many of them likely assured out of fear or hope for a 'quiet' life. The Dundonians may have been willing to hear the Bible preached and listen to ideas about religious reform, but there is no indication that the militantly Protestant, pro-English faction around Durham and Gray had broad support. What support there was had certainly disappeared by November 1548, when Durham's supporters and the English burned the town.

The final reckoning for the Dundonians came in March 1553 when the Earl of Argyll, as Justice General, spent twenty-two days in Dundee, eventually charging and fining 193 men for a variety of acts dating back to 1543. Principally they were charged with assuring with the English in Broughty Castle and assisting the men who murdered Cardinal Beaton, principally by 'entertaining' and 'providing them with victuals'. They were further charged with the attacks on the friaries in 1543 'in company with Henry Durham and his accomplices', going on to besiege Perth and killing several people there, and for assisting the 'late John Charteris of Cuthelgurdy and his accomplices' in their attack on the castle of Kirkhill, after which they drowned 'the lady thereof'. They were also accused of killing seven French and Italian soldiers of the company of the Prior of Capua after the siege of St Andrews.[172] Those accused denied the charges 'and were by a worthy assize acquitted', though they did collectively pay the staggering sum of £3,938, or about twenty pounds per person if the fines were spread out equally.[173]

The nature of the collective accusation makes it difficult to discern the extent of the participation of any given individual. The most militant Protestant leaders had already fled, and the accusation was careful to emphasise that the Dundonians had participated in acts led by others: they 'accompanied' Henry Durham and his 'accomplices'; they assisted John Charteris; they provided Beaton's assassins with supplies. The only acts the Dundonians were solely responsible for were the killing of the seven soldiers and assuring with the English.[174] Skirmishes between townspeople and marauding soldiers, even though nominally on the same side, were quite common during the period; and, as we have seen, the assurances with the English were hardly voluntary. Of course, faced with such serious charges it was an easy escape to accuse absent men of being the ringleaders.

A significant number of the influential men in the town were not charged (only fourteen of the twenty-six most prominent men were charged), so the accusations must have had some basis in fact and were not simply a shakedown of the wealthiest and most prominent. Many of those accused were bakers (twenty-five), butchers (twelve) and ironworkers (five), and it is likely that they were accused of provisioning the English and the assassins of Cardinal Beaton without necessarily participating actively themselves. Only five of the eleven men who signed the assurance with Dudley on 27 October 1547 were among those listed, so assuring with the English alone was not sufficient to be charged.[175] Some of the men may have been those who laboured on the English fortifications, though given that at least 146 out of the 193 charged were burgesses, it is unlikely that they would have agreed to do manual labour for five pennies a day.[176] It seems likely, therefore, that those charged either traded with the enemy or were involved with the attacks organised by Henry Durham and John Charteris. Of course, it may be that as with the heresy prosecutions of the 1530s, the crown thought the Dundonians were worth more alive than dead.

Conclusion

Following the devastation caused by the English, one can imagine that the townspeople of Haddington and Dundee were thoroughly fed up with the invaders, who did not follow through on their promises to promote Protestantism, failed to defend their towns against Scottish and French forces, and were finally themselves responsible for their destruction. In Dundee especially they were enraged with the Scots who sided with the invaders, especially those such as Durham, Whitelaw and Stewart who fled and left the others to deal with both reconstruction and government reprisals. In addition to the important individuals identified, this hardline Protestant faction included the kin and clients gathered around Scrimgeour and Lord Gray, who in 1543 mustered 300 followers.[177] The opprobrium which fell upon this group following the burning of Dundee by the English neutralised many of the more active early Protestants, and contrasts with the support the burgh gave to those targeted by the earlier anti-heresy campaigns. It would take a few years for the Protestant movement to find new momentum again, under men who had been loyal to the government.

By the end of the 1540s, the Scots must have been emotionally and physically shattered. All towns experienced the devastating effects of the plague. The wartime experiences of Dundee and Haddington were extreme, but other burghs such as Kelso, Peebles, Leith, St Andrews and even Edinburgh suffered as well. Towns such as Stirling which had avoided the direct effects of the destruction still had to build defences and pay extra contributions, and, most importantly, send their men off to fight and die. Civic harmony would have to be rebuilt, after both the suspicion directed at those suspected of bringing in the plague, either directly or spiritually, and the collaboration of some with the English. It is not surprising that in the following years many Scots were reluctant to create new divisions and conflict.

Notes

1. Wedderburn, *The Complaynt*, 1.
2. For a discussion of different Scottish attitudes to the expedition against Wark Castle, see Neil Murphy, 'The Duke of Albany's Invasion of England in 1523 and Military Mobilisation in Sixteenth-century Scotland', *The Scottish Historical Review* 99 (2020): 1–25.
3. Gervase Phillips, *The Anglo-Scots Wars 1513–50* (Woodbridge, 1999), 138–48.
4. Phillips, *Anglo-Scots Wars*, 138–43; *TA*, 5:201, 211, 229.
5. Phillips, *Anglo-Scots Wars*, 146–7; *ALC*, 391; *TA*, 6:106, 108, 109, 136.
6. See figure 1.3.
7. *TA*, 8:116; Phillips, *Anglo-Scots Wars*, 148.
8. HAD/4/6/5, fl73, 175.
9. *TA*, 8:137; Phillips, *Anglo-Scots Wars*, 150.
10. *TA*, 8:139.
11. HAD/4/6/5, f175.
12. HAD/4/6/5, f175, 175v, f185.
13. Phillips, *Anglo-Scots Wars*, 157.
14. HAD/4/6/5, f188v.
15. Phillips, *Anglo-Scots Wars*, 162; *TA*, 8:284.
16. Phillips, *Anglo-Scots Wars*, 167.
17. *LP*, 19, part 1, no. 188.
18. Phillips, *Anglo-Scots Wars*, 170–1.
19. *TA*, 8:284, 332, 339, 351, 353, 362, 374, 397, 401, 407; Phillips, *Anglo-Scots Wars*, 173.
20. *TA*, 8:480; 9:31, 32, 41.
21. *TA*, 9:76.
22. *TA*, 5:231. In 1523 towns were told to send provisions rather than men to the army. Murphy, 'The Duke of Albany's Invasion of England', 20.
23. *ALC*, 391.
24. *RCRBS*, 518; *TA*, 7:249.
25. *TA*, 8:293.
26. *TA*, 8:402, 431.
27. *TA*, 8:408–9.
28. *Extracts . . . Stirling*, 41–2; *RCRBS*, 518.
29. *TA*, 8:249.
30. *TA*, 8:252.
31. J. F. D. Shrewsbury, *A History of Bubonic Plague in the British Isles* (London, 1970), 157, 166.
32. William Naphy and Andrew Spicer, *Plague: Black Death and Pestilence in Europe* (Stroud, 2004), 86. Although Audrey-Beth Fitch suggested that pneumonic plague, which has a mortality rate of almost 100 per cent, may have been more common in Scotland than elsewhere. Audrey-Beth Fitch, 'Assumptions about Plague in Medieval Scotland', *Scotia* 11 (1987): 30.
33. Paul Slack, *The Impact of Plague in Tudor and Stuart England* (London, 1985), 66, 84; Shrewsbury, *Bubonic Plague*, 178–9, 188.
34. *A Diurnal of Remarkable Occurrents*, 39.
35. Shrewsbury, *Bubonic Plague*, 188.

36. Slack, *The Impact of Plague*, 16, 26, 87, 108; Naphy and Spicer, *Black Death*, 10, 11, 13, 20: Karen Jillings, *An Urban History of the Plague: socio-economic, political and medical impacts in a Scottish community, 1550–1650* (Milton, 2018), 54.
37. Gilbert Skene. *Ane Breve Descriptioun of the Pest Quhair in the Causis, Signis and Sum Speciall Preseruatioun and Cure Thairof Ar Contenit / Set Furth be Maister Gilbert Skene, Doctoure in Medicine.* Edinburgh, 1568 (EEBO).
38. Slack, *The Impact of Plague*, 29 (citing T. Paynel, *A most profitable treatise against the pestilence* [? 1534], sig. Avr); Jillings, *An Urban History*, 54.
39. John Aberth, *From the Brink of the Apocalypse: Confronting famine, war plague and death in the later Middle Ages*, 2nd edn (London, 2010), 153–66; Shrewsbury, *Bubonic Plague*, 209, 256.
40. HAD/4/6/5, f2v.
41. Shrewsbury, *Bubonic Plague*, 185–6.
42. Slack, *The Impact of Plague*, 8; Shrewsbury, *Bubonic Plague*, 157.
43. HAD/4/6/5, f209v; for a discussion of national plague regulations, Jillings, *An Urban History*, 58–60.
44. HAD/4/6/5, f213v.
45. Shrewsbury, *Bubonic Plague*, 186.
46. HAD/4/6/5, f213v.
47. HAD/4/6/5, f214.
48. HAD/2/1/2/1, f38.
49. *Extracts . . . Stirling*, 40.
50. *Extracts . . . Stirling*, 44; SCA SBCB 1544–50 29/10/1546.
51. SCA SBCB 1544–50 92/6/1545.
52. *Extracts . . . Stirling*, 41.
53. *Extracts . . . Stirling*, 43.
54. *Extracts . . . Stirling*, 44; SCA SBCB 1544–50 13/10/1546.
55. SCA SCBC 1544–50 29/10/1546.
56. SCA SBCB 1544–50 2/12/1546.
57. *Extracts . . . Stirling*, 43.
58. *Extracts . . . Stirling*, 48.
59. *Extracts . . . Stirling*, 48.
60. SCA SBCB 1544–50 28/4/1547.
61. Knox, *Works*, 1:126.
62. Dawson, *John Knox*, 34–5.
63. Knox, *Works*, 1:129–30.
64. Marcus Merriman, 'The assured Scots: Scottish collaborators with England during the Rough Wooing', *Scottish History Review* 47 (1968): 11.
65. Although Merriman concludes in his study of assurances that there was not a strong connection between assuring and interest in reforming ideas, in both Dundee and Haddington those who were most involved in collaboration appear to have had Protestant sympathies, or at least, connections to those who did. Merriman, 'The assured Scots', 13–14.
66. Calderwood, *History*, 1:194; Knox, *Works*, 1:138.
67. Pittscottie, *The historie and cronicles*, 2:79.
68. Laing, 'Introductory Notice', in Knox, *Works*, 1:xxviii.
69. Most historians working on prophecies focus on political prophecies, attributed to ancient prophets. More work needs to be done on 'local' prophecies in the early modern period. Michael B. Riordan, 'Scottish political prophecies

and the crowns of Britain, 1500–1840', in *The Supernatural in Early Modern Scotland*, eds Julian Goodare and Martha McGill (Manchester, 2020); Bertrand Taithe and Tim Thornton, 'The language of history: past and future in prophecy', and Lesley Coote, 'A language of power: prophecy and public affairs in later medieval England', in *Prophecy: The Power of Inspired Language in History, 1300–2000*, eds Bertrand Taithe and Tim Thornton (Stroud, 1997); Sharon Jansen, *Political Protest and Prophecy under Henry VIII* (Rochester, 1991); Tim Thornton, *Prophecy, Politics and the People in Early Modern England* (Woodbridge, 2006), discusses prophecies circulating in Scotland, 45–9.
70. Phillips, *Anglo-Scots Wars*, 218.
71. *CSP*, 1: 111.
72. Phillips, *Anglo-Scots Wars*, 218.
73. *CSP*, 1:114, 123, 125, 135–6.
74. *CSP*, 1:111, 122–3.
75. *CSP*, 1:133, 137.
76. Calderwood, *History*, 1:256.
77. Phillips, *Anglo-Scots Wars*, 228.
78. Phillips, *Anglo-Scots Wars*, 233–7.
79. Merriman, *The Rough Wooings*, 321; Phillips, *Anglo-Scots Wars*, 239–40.
80. Phillips, *Anglo-Scots Wars*, 241.
81. Phillips, *Anglo-Scots Wars*, 239–41.
82. *A Diurnal of Remarkable Occurrents*, 48; Marshall, *Ruin and Restoration*, 19; Phillips, *Anglo-Scots Wars*, 251.
83. *CSP*, 1:24.
84. *CSP*, 1:33.
85. *CSP*, 1:35, 50, 61.
86. *TA*, 9:134–9.
87. *RPC*, 1:79.
88. *CSP*, 1:49–51.
89. *CSP*, 1:51.
90. *CSP*, 1:48.
91. *CSP*, 1:49–54; *The Scottish Correspondence of Mary of Lorraine*, ed. Annie I. Cameron (Edinburgh, 1927), 209.
92. *CSP*, 1:53, 61.
93. *CSP*, 1:53.
94. *CSP*, 1:60.
95. *CSP*, 1:67.
96. *CSP*, 1:67.
97. *CSP*, 1:71–4.
98. *CSP*, 1:78.
99. *CSP*, 1:86–7.
100. *CSP*, 1:91.
101. *TA*, 9:192.
102. DCA BHCB 1561–2, 75–75v.
103. *Scottish Correspondence*, 273.
104. *Scottish Correspondence*, 243.
105. *CSP*, 1:167, 168.
106. DCA BHCB 1550–4, f15.
107. *Scottish Correspondence*, 275–8.

108. *TA*, 9:266.
109. *CSP*, 1:172; *TA*, 9:303.
110. *TA*, 9:363–86.
111. *TA*, 9:392–3.
112. *TA*, 10:68–9.
113. *Extracts . . . Stirling*, 50.
114. *Extracts . . . Stirling*, 51.
115. *Extracts . . . Stirling*, 51.
116. *Extracts . . . Stirling*, 52.
117. SCA SBCB 1554–7 19/12/1554.
118. *Extracts . . . Stirling*, 49; *TA*, 9:153, 169.
119. *Privy Seal*, 3:450.
120. *TA*, 9:273, 368.
121. SCA SBCB 1544–50 18/5/1548.
122. *Privy Seal*, 3:449.
123. SCA SBCB 1544–50, 16/11/1548.
124. SCA SBCB 1544–50 7/5/1548.
125. SCA SBCB 1544–50 21/2/1547–8.
126. SCA SBCB 1544–50 9/5/1549.
127. Merriman, 'The assured Scots'. See also Donaldson who highlights the peak of English success at recruiting Scots but passes over how easily many returned to the Scottish side. Gordon Donaldson, *Scotland: James V–VII* (New York, 1966), 76–8.
128. *Scottish Correspondence*, 240.
129. *CSP*, 1:80.
130. *CSP*, 1:111.
131. *Privy Seal*, 3:427.
132. Marshall, *Ruin and Restoration*,19; *CSP*, 166.
133. *Privy Seal*, 3:183, 329–30.
134. *Privy Seal*, 3:448.
135. *CSP*, 1:117.
136. Calderwood, *History*, 1:261.
137. *Privy Seal*, 4:101.
138. *Privy Seal*, 4:73, 151, 332.
139. *Privy Seal*, 4:452.
140. Maxwell, *Old Dundee*, 98.
141. *CSP*, 1:102; *Scottish Correspondence*, 203; Bardgett, *Scotland Reformed*, 27.
142. *CSP*, 1:38–9; Maxwell, *The History of Old Dundee*, 25.
143. *TA*, 9:270.
144. *TA*, 9:15, 270; Merriman, *The Rough Wooings*, 332.
145. Bardgett, *Scotland Reformed*, 55.
146. *Privy Seal*, 3:389; *TA*, 9:12; *CSP*, 1:102.
147. DCA BHCB 1561–2, f75–75v.
148. *CSP*, 1:52.
149. *TA*, 9:287, 294; *Privy Seal*, 4:21.
150. Merriman, 'The assured Scots', 24.
151. *CSP*, 1:67; *Privy Seal*, 4:22.
152. *Scottish Correspondence*, 225.
153. *Scottish Correspondence*, 270.

154. *Privy Seal*, 4:48; DCA Burgess Roll, f25v.
155. DCA BHCB 1550–4, f171v.
156. At that time an inquest found him to be son of William Stewart; this inquest may have occurred for other reasons without his presence, however. DCA BHCB 1558–61, f50.
157. *Privy Seal*, 4:20.
158. If we assume that he was not the same person as David Gardin, litster.
159. *Privy Seal*, 4:33.
160. *TA*, 9:12, 13; *Privy Seal*, 4:14.
161. *Privy Seal*, 4:17; DCA Burgess Roll, 34v.
162. Maxwell, *Old Dundee*, 234; Bardgett, *Scotland Reformed*, 55.
163. *CSP*, 1:124.
164. *Privy Seal*, 3:449.
165. *RCRBS*, 515; *TA*, 9:214; DCA Burgess Roll, 29; DCA BHCB 1550–4, f80.
166. *TA*, 9:274.
167. *Privy Seal*, 4:12.
168. DCA BHCB 1550–4, f10; DCA BHCB 1558–61, f132.
169. *Privy Seal*, 4:130; *TA*, 10:9.
170. A Robert Anderson had been convicted of heresy in 1538. George Lovell had been suspected of hanging an image of St Francis in 1536, was summoned in July 1558 to Edinburgh to face charges of 'wrongful using and [discussing] of Scripture, and for disputing upon erroneous opinions and eating of flesh in Lent and other forbidden times' and at some point in 1559–60 would lend £120 to the Lords of the Congregation. James Lovell had been forced to abjure heresy in 1539. *Privy Seal*, 2:396, 447; *TA*, 6:307; 10:369; DCA BHCB 1561–2, f12v.
171. *CSP*, 1:35.
172. 'Indictment', 393–5; DCA, TC/CC 1/54.
173. By comparison, a skilled labourer could earn about ten to fifteen pounds a year, and twenty pounds seems to have been the minimum salary for a 'professional' such as a priest.
174. 'Indictment'.
175. 'Indictment'.
176. Although five pence in English money would have been good pay in a war-ravaged town.
177. Bardgett, *Scotland Reformed*, 30.

CHAPTER SEVEN

Recovery and Reaction: 1550–1558

By 1550 many Scots were exhausted as the chaos of war and plague had left a great deal of destruction behind. Men and women were dead, land was laid waste and public buildings and private homes alike were in ruins. The economies of the towns would not regain the heights of the 1530s and early 1540s for several decades – indeed, Haddington's export trade was almost completely wiped out, and Stirling's gravely damaged, even despite the lack of physical destruction there. Burgh court records were destroyed or lost, making the enforcement of agreements and rent collection difficult.[1] The devastation to the towns was such that in 1551 Parliament passed an act concerning 'burnt lands and tenements within the burgh of Edinburgh and other burghs', specifying the deductions rent and annual holders were required to allow from damaged and destroyed properties.[2] This act would govern much court business over the following years, as burghs tried to figure out who owed what. The towns would also put considerable resources into repairing the damage, prioritising churches along with critical infrastructure as best they could. Townspeople continued to worry about a recurrence of the troubles as Scotland risked being drawn into renewed war, this time as part of the Habsburg-Valois conflict. The Scots also thought about why these events had happened. Some voices made a connection between their sins and the disasters that had come upon them, and urged their countrymen to mend their ways. These warnings came from reformers of all types, from Protestants to the leadership of the Scottish Catholic Church, creating or reflecting a widespread sense that change of some form was necessary to avert continued divine punishment. Though the 1550s seem like a quiet pause between the disruptions of the 1540s and the drama of 1559–60 and then Queen Mary's reign, it is during this period that we can see the concerns of many Scots and appreciate how badly shaken they were. While in a political sense the Reformation of 1559–60 may have come from a 'blue sky', as Ryrie put it, the status quo was clearly untenable for many Scottish townspeople.

Recovery

Both Dundee and Haddington were among the most damaged towns in Scotland. The inhabitants of Haddington had suffered particularly badly as the English occupation had physically devastated the town, forced many of them to flee through a dangerous war zone, and inflicted an additional outbreak of disease within the town. Haddington, in fact, was the most badly ruined town in Scotland. The Convention of Royal Burghs in 1555 acknowledged that several towns in the country, because of 'war, pest, and troubles, that are depaupered and poor and decayed at this time'.[3] As a result, Haddington had its tax contribution reduced by almost two-thirds in 1557.[4] Inside the town attempts to recover rents and other valuables reflected the toll of war and plague. Of the thirty-one property repossession cases brought before Haddington's burgh court in 1554, at the end of the grace period specified in the act on burnt tenements, twenty-three were for tenements or lands whose owners were dead.[5] Rents had gone unpaid since the arrival of the English, a sign of the disruption of normal life; George Symson, in giving his account for the hangman's acres which he rented from the town, deducted three pounds because 'in the Englismen's time they lying waste'.[6] In other cases, where evidence was lost, witnesses testified about the rent paid until 'the coming of ye Englishmen to this burgh'.[7] As late as 1557 Katherine Wilson was pursuing Alane Bell for a meat almonry withheld 'since the English were in this town'.[8] Despite precautions taken before the fighting began, valuable goods were lost or damaged. The baxter craft had to go to court to recover its silver chalice, which they had entrusted to Martin Wilson. After almost a year of wrangling they still had not recovered it, most likely because Wilson had lost it or allowed it to be damaged.[9] As a small recompense for their losses, in August 1559 the burgh received from the central government the gift of all gear left behind by the English, artillery excepted.[10]

The townspeople put immediate effort into reversing the damage. Buildings, both private homes and civic infrastructure, were rebuilt at considerable expense. In November 1552 the town council prohibited the export of stone or slates from the town, as well as the moving of stone from one tenement to another.[11] The parish church, which was the product of a century of rebuilding following the fourteenth-century English invasions, had lost its roof, suffered broken windows and damage to the steeple, received a hole in the wall of the north aisle, and was scarred by cannon and bullet marks.[12] It would take twelve years to rebuild, and at that only part of the church was repaired. The council also had to find money to repair other common property. John Forrest, one of the renters of the town's mills, was paid £170 10s by the burgh for rebuilding the mills and dams 'after the departing of the Englismen'; John Ayton, the other feuar, received £201 23d for the same work, as well as for building trenches and putting up pavilions before the arrival of the English, a futile effort at defending the town.[13] In 1554, they paid thirty-eight pounds to repair the clockhouse, along with two pounds for a clockface.[14] In 1557, the burgh spent another thirty pounds on a bell for the clock.[15] The townspeople were called upon to contribute their labour as well. In April 1557, the town was divided into four quarters and each householder was required to come on a festival day to clear the passage of the 'loch burn' behind St Anne's chapel.[16] Work repairing the tolbooth also took place in 1557, 1558 and 1559.[17] It is not hard to imagine the apprehension the Haddingtonians must have felt in 1559–60 as war, and accompanying English and French armies, reappeared just as these rebuilding efforts reached fruition.

Dundee also suffered considerable damage from the wars, though it was likely not as extensive as in Haddington. The disruption during the years of fighting was such that while the English commanders were pleading with their government for Protestant books with which to win the allegiance of the population, the local printer left town and moved to Edinburgh.[18] As in Haddington, the reconstruction efforts give us a sense of what was lost. St Mary's had suffered particularly badly. The nave and transept had been destroyed, the chancel was defaced and spoiled, and the tower, while still standing, had been burnt and was much damaged. War damage to the ornaments and valuable possessions of the church, however, was minimal, as these items had been hidden before the start of fighting. The council sought to resume divine services as soon as possible despite the damage. Measures to restore the pre-war functioning of the church were taken on 31 December 1551, when the council, provost and craft deacons, meeting in Provost Haliburton's lodging, passed acts concerning the 'reparing and decoration of their mother kirk' and resolved to restore the old privileges of burying people in the church and choir with bells ringing 'not with standing the spoliation and away taking of our bells be our old ennemies of England'.[19] Some fines for breaking burgh statutes were directed to church repairs, and others were directed to the harbour work.[20] The council started importing wood from the Baltic and, in October 1552, hired Patton Blak, wright, to build cuppils (connected rafters) in the church.[21] Shortly after, in November, they convinced the Abbot of Lindores to contribute £500 towards church repairs, to be paid in instalments.[22] The next month, eight men were ordered to make themselves available, summer or winter, to work on the church.[23]

This reconstruction must have proceeded quite quickly, for on 31 January 1553, Blak was given a bonus of ten merks for having completed the work he was contracted for the previous October.[24] The council then ordered the Dean of Guild to prepare the Holy Blood altar to receive divine service, 'where it was of before' and to name a chaplain to serve at the altar. At the same time, the crafts were ordered to prepare their altars to be used as indicated in their letters of craft.[25] The crafts, who had difficulty funding their altars even during prosperous times, took longer to recover from the damage, and as late as March 1557 the bakers diverted craft fines to the repair of St Cobett's altar.[26] The final touch in restoring the church, decreed at the January 1554 Head Court meeting, was the decision to levy a tax of £200 for the purchase of a new bell. Once installed, in a spirit of civic-minded generosity and inclusiveness the council proclaimed that the bell was to ring freely for the death of any neighbour, not just burgesses; the only fee was to be twelve pence paid to the sacristan.[27] Obtaining a satisfactory bell was a complicated matter, however, and in September 1557 the council ordered James Forester, the kirkmaster, to exchange the bell which had been purchased by James Rollok (III) for a bigger one, either in Flanders or wherever he thought best.[28] Though the damage was severe, repairing St Mary's and returning to their previous forms of worship was a clear priority for Dundee's council.

Damage to the rest of the town was likely significant as well. The council was anxious to return to a form of normality in local affairs as well, and on 11 January 1552 ordered all burgesses to return and live in the burgh, in order to participate in their duties of taxation, walking and warding, under threat of losing their burgess rights.[29] Dundee did not benefit from the same reduction in tax contributions that Haddington did, and its share remained at roughly half Edinburgh's.[30] Customs receipts throughout the 1550s stabilised at roughly the same level they were at in the 1520s and early 1530s, though tending to decline, and there were no boom years.[31] Though the losses and scars of the war remained visible, Dundee's economy returned to a stable, if not prosperous, footing.

Having not experienced the destruction suffered by Haddington and Dundee, Stirling did not go through the same desperate effort to rebuild. There was some lasting economic damage as the town's trade did suffer during this period. The customs were initially rented for a set annual fee of forty pounds, half of the level of the peak years of the late 1530s, and despite a slight rebound in 1555–6, settled at fifty pounds through the late 1550s and the 1560s. It is possible that the failure to recover economically during the 1550s was a result of the wars, as the herds of livestock, likely culled by English raiding parties or to supply Scottish forces, needed to be restocked before they could once again be slaughtered for export on a large scale. This caused the collapse of Stirling's export trade which was heavily dependent on animal skins. These difficulties were reflected in Stirling's relative decline in national tax contributions, from eighth to eleventh place nationwide.

Otherwise, the routine affairs of the town continued during this decade, and the establishment of Marie of Guise's household and administration in Stirling Castle created business opportunities for the burgesses. The frequent presence of the court brought townspeople into contact with both the royal household and those of the great nobles. Burgesses, notably Walter Cousland, continued to have commercial and financial dealings with the royal court.[32] Minor frictions occurred as well. Thomas Ryton was summoned to answer for troublance he committed against a servant of the Earl of Argyll.[33] John Graham was expelled for a year, by the Queen Regent's command, 'for the handling of ane Francheman's bag'.[34] Small incidents such as these did not lead to any significant tension between the town and court.

There was greater politicisation of the burgh council. The 1550s saw the increasing prominence of landed men on the council, which peaked with seven lairds sitting in various positions, from provost to councillor, in 1560–1. This period also saw factional disputes on the council, which became implicated in a dispute between Henry Livingston of Falkirk and John Forester of Craginelt. In nearby Perth, outside lairds joined with craftsmen inside the town in an alliance against the merchants who dominated the town council (although the craftsmen were, in effect if not in status, wealthy merchants themselves). A similar situation seems to have played out in Stirling in 1555 when Mary of Guise ordered the townspeople to elect a burgess as provost, after the crafts had conspired to have an outsider elected (likely Henry Livingston of Falkirk).[35] Although Verschuur identifies the alliance of craftsmen and lairds as having a Protestant (or proto-Protestant) dimension, no such religious element is apparent in Stirling's burgh politics.[36] The burgh may have escaped physical damage during the 1540s, but throughout the 1550s it was still suffering economically and going through some turmoil in burgh affairs.

1550s: The Threat of War Persists

The Scots still had reason to worry about the return of war even after the English were defeated in 1550. Despite the harrowing experience of the 1540s, demands for military contributions were still being made on the towns throughout the 1550s as war and war scares arose. The tensions this time were due to Mary Tudor's England joining the Habsburgs in their struggles against the French, once more making the Anglo-Scottish border a theatre in broader European conflicts.[37] The men of Haddington in particular were summoned many times, despite their recent sufferings. Only months after the English occupation was ended, in December 1549 'all manner of men' were once again called up from Haddington to resist the English.[38] In January 1550, they were ordered to the siege at Broughty, and in March to muster with the governor at Edinburgh.[39] Demands on the manpower of the burgh continued to be frequent during a fragile peace. In 1552, an army was assembled at Haddington, and in December the Haddingtonians, along with the rest of Scotland, were ordered to contribute one footman to a delegation to France for every forty merks of land, although this order was rescinded the next month.[40] In September 1553, 'lords, lairds, gentilmen and other substancious yeomen, both to burgh and to land' were to meet the governor in Jedburgh with twenty days provisions.[41] In July 1554, the inhabitants of Haddington, along with those of North of Berwick and Lauderdale, were ordered to join the lord of Yester, apparently on an expedition against unruly subjects in the Borders.[42]

Fears of English invasion continued throughout the decade; when John Ayton and John Forrest rented the burgh mills in 1557, the agreement included a clause that the council would rebate the fee for each day left in the term should 'the said mills or any of them to be burnt and destroyed by Englismen'.[43] Sir Adam Brown, chaplain, along with some others, captured two Englishmen in Haddington in the winter of 1556–7, seizing their weapons, horse and a dog.[44] The threat of war increased in 1557 and 1558, with conflict with England simmering.[45] In March 1558, all men between the ages of sixteen and sixty were summoned to gather at Langton with fifteen days' provisions, and at the same time the brewers and bakers of Haddington and other burghs were to provide the army with bread and ale.[46] Further summonses went out in June, July, August and September.[47] In 1558, the town spent a total of nine pounds on a watchman on the tolbooth head, who served nightly from Michelmas to Candlemas.[48] The following March, the regent's government ordered Haddington and other towns to shelter 'certain men of war with their captains' and indeed from 10 March to 18 May 1559 the Haddingtonians found themselves hosting a detachment of French soldiers. That April the council provided five legs of beef and two swine 'to the French men' for which they were still trying to reclaim £320 in August.[49] Although in retrospect the decade was nowhere as violent as the 1540s, this was still a marked increase in defence spending over the activity of the 1520s and 1530s. The constant stream of summonses, warnings and demands for supplies must have been exhausting, especially for a burgh still struggling to recover.

The Dundonians also had to pay significant tax contributions and accept defensive burdens, especially putting up with French soldiers. As early as August 1550, the burgh paid £274 4s 1d towards the peace embassy.[50] Throughout the decade French soldiers were garrisoned at Broughty, and occasionally had disputes with the townspeople; in December 1551 some Frenchmen were accused of stealing some kale and threatening the burgh's officer at sword point when he intervened. Provost Haliburton presumably reached a diplomatic solution, as nothing more is recorded of the incident.[51] Sometimes it was the inhabitants who were in the wrong; in January 1555, the bailies ordered Patrick Gray to pay £11 10s to 'John du Wykace, Frenchmen of the fort' to settle a debt.[52] A more violent episode was recorded in May of 1555 when the Lyon herald, Bute pursuivant and other royal servants travelled to Broughty to hold a trial of 'the slaughter between the Scots and Frenchmen'.[53] It is possible that the Dundonians were growing weary of the French garrison, making them willing to return to war in 1559, running the risk of renewed violence to rid themselves of the nearby soldiers.

There are few records of demands being made on Stirling during this period, but it is unlikely that the burgh escaped the obligations placed on other towns. As before, the proximity of the burgh to the central administration in the castle most likely meant that requests and summonses could be issued informally and cheaply, thus leaving no traces in the written records.

Reactions

As the Scots assessed the damage, they also considered the causes of, and solutions to, the ongoing series of disasters. All over Europe medieval and early modern Christians saw God's hand in the events surrounding them. Plagues, comets, storms, even the casting of lots were commonly interpreted as signs from God.[54] Disasters which clearly had a human cause could also, ultimately, be ascribed to God's will. As John Hale points out concerning war, people took for granted that specific wars or military actions were done for political reasons, but it was 'when war dragged on bringing increasing desolation, or when one war was followed by another, that men were tempted to revert to non-secular explanations of international conflict and see it as the painful working out of God's inscrutable purpose', with both commoners and intellectuals interpreting war as punishment for sin.[55] The sixteenth-century Scottish academic John Mair (Major) for example, writing in about 1520, explained the destruction of his hometown of Haddington by English troops during the 'Burnt Candlemas' of 1356 by attributing it to divine punishment and wrote 'it may well be for their [Franciscan friars] sins, and the sins of the town itself, God willed that it should be given to the flames.'[56] He saw the English soldiers as instruments of God's will, just as their sixteenth-century counterparts would be.

All of these beliefs were evident in Scotland during the 1550s. Two writers in particular expressed views that may have been more widespread: Sir David Lindsay, a courtier and playwright whose work commented on the political situation of mid-sixteenth-century Scotland, and the author of *The Complaynt of Scotland*, plausibly identified as Robert Wedderburn, Vicar of Dundee, who wrote to urge the Scots to unite behind the French. Both authors saw the disasters as God's punishment for the sins of the Scots, and both proposed remedies to lead the Scots back to better times. Similar interpretations could also be found among the senior Catholic clergy, Scotland's political leadership, and likely among Protestant preachers as well.

Sir David Lindsay and The Complaynt

Sir David Lindsay, a Fife laird and royal herald, was an observer and participant in Scottish politics and diplomacy in the first half of the sixteenth century. His works, among other topics, critiqued the corruption of the Catholic Church and urged religious reform, though his silence around theological points such as the mass means that he cannot be considered a firm Protestant, either Lutheran or Zwinglian/Calvinist.[57] In his later works, written during his retirement in Fife during the 1550s, Lindsay clearly thought that there was a religious moral to be derived from recent events: the Scots' suffering was divine punishment that they had brought upon themselves by their own sins. Old enough that his memory went back as far as the battle of Flodden and its aftermath, he was especially struck by the wars that ruined Scotland:

> In lande quhare ony Weris bene,
> Gret Miserrie thare may be sene:

> All thyng on erth that God hes wrocht
> Weir doith distroye, and puttis at nocht:
> Ceteis, with mony strang Dungeon,
> Ar brynte, and to the erth doung doun;
> Virginis and Matronis ar deflorit;
> Templis that Rychelie bene decorit
> Ar brynt, and all thare Preistis spulʒeit;
> Pure Orphelenis under feit ar fulʒeit,
> Mony auld men maid childerles
> And mony childer fatherles.[58]

Given the destruction that took place in Haddington, Dundee and throughout southern and eastern Scotland, many Scots would have recognised this as an accurate description of their experiences. In *Dialogue Betwix Experience and ane Courteour*, written about 1554 and described as his 'magnum opus', Lindsay used biblical examples to make an extended argument against idolatry. He made a direct link between the disasters that had befallen Scotland and the sins of its people, identifying especially war, plague and famine as divine punishments.[59] Lindsay wrote:

> That, for the brekyng of the Lordis command,
> His Thrynfald wande of Flagellatioun
> Hes Scurgit this pure Realm of Scotland,
> Be mortall weris baith be sey and land,
> With many terrabyll trybulatioun.
> Therefor mak to thame trew narratioun,
> That al thir weris, this derth, hunger, and Pest
> Was nocht bot for our Synis manifest.[60]

As Carol Edington observes about political thought in this period 'moral failings were perceived as the cause of socioeconomic problems, and political and ethical goals were largely interchangeable.'[61] Though the immediate cause of Scotland's troubles may have been human, ultimately they had been sent by God who, in turn, was reacting to human sin. As such, better behaviour, pleasing to God, offered a way out of Scotland's troubles. An end to sin would cause God to withdraw his instruments of punishment, in this case the English, and bring better times to Scotland:

> Thoucht God with mony terrabyll effrayis
> Hes done this cuntrie scruge by divers wayis,
> Be Iuste Iugement, for our grevous offence,
> Declare to tham thay sall have mery dayis
> Efter this trubyll, as the Propheit sayis:
> Quhen God sall se our humyll Repentence,
> Tyll strange pepyll thoucht he hes gevin lycence
> To be our scurge Infuryng his desyre,
> Wyll, quhen he lyste, that Scurge cast in the fyre[62]

Among Scotland's sins, Lindsay specified idolatry and sexual misconduct, particularly among the nobility and the clergy, as the causes of God's anger which would continue until they mended their ways. If the people repented, however, God would look favourably on them:

> Declare to thame, this mortall miserie,
> Be sweird and fyre, derth, pest, and pouertie,
> Procedis of Syn, gyf I can rycht discryve,
> For laik of Faith, and for Ydolatrye,
> For fornicatioun, and for Adultrye,
> Off Princis, Prelatis, with mony ane mari & wyve.
> Expell the cause, than effect belyve
> Sall cease; quhen that the people doith repent,
> Than God sall slak his bow, quhilk 3it is bent.[63]

Lindsay's explanation of cause, effect and remedy are quite blunt. The disasters are clearly linked to the sins of the ruling classes, including lack of faith and idolatry and sexual offences. In *Dialogue Betwix Experience and ane Courteour*, idolatry comes in for further strong criticism from Lindsay, who describes the various images to which the Scots pray and the justifications of the clergy for the practice. Once again, these sins will lead directly to God's punishment, which the clerics should particularly fear, though there is hope that some of them are ready to reform and avoid the coming disaster:

> Unmercifull memberis of the Antichrist,
> Extolland 3our humane traditione
> Contrar the Institutione of Christ,
> Effeir 3e nocht Divine punytione?
> Thoucht sum of 3ow be of gude conditione,
> Reddy for to ressave new recent wyne,
> I speik to 3ow auld bosis of perditione:
> Returne in tyme, or 3e ryn to rewyne[64]

Lindsay goes on to recall the biblical punishments of King Ahab of Israel, an idolater, and Sodom and Gomorrah, demonstrating both precedent for the punishment of the Scots and a warning for them to change their ways. While *Ane Dialogue* focuses its criticism on the ruling classes, other works, such as *Ane Satyre of the Three Estatis* (1552), made clear that other social groups were guilty as well. Lindsay's later work was aimed at a wide audience, and *Ane Satyre* was performed publicly at least twice, in Cupar in 1552 and in Edinburgh in 1554.[65] It is likely that many Scots already shared Lindsay's assumptions about divine punishment, though his work would surely have reinforced the sentiment. Lindsay's focus on idolatry and sexual morality foreshadows two of the immediate concerns of the Protestants of 1559 and after, and either reflected or inspired concern about these topics throughout the population. Many Scots, like Lindsay, would have perceived a connection between idolatry, sexual misconduct, their sufferings from plague, war and dearth, and the hope of better days brought about through repentance and reform.

The Complaynt of Scotland is a response to pro-union English propaganda written in 1549 and 1550. Scotland will only successfully resist the English, the author contends, if the Scots forget their quarrels and discords and unite, with the support of Mary of Guise and the French. The author points to recent and historical events as God's judgments on the sins of the Scots.[66] Repenting of these sins, therefore, will lead to God's mercy, expressed as an end to the plagues and wars suffered by Scotland and victory over the English.[67] *The Complaynt* may also be considered the text of a reform-minded Catholic who is open to a variety of influences, favourably citing, for instance, the Lutheran *Clarion's Chronicle*. Published anonymously, it was catalogued in the eighteenth century as *Wedderburn's Complaint*. A. M. Stewart argues persuasively if not conclusively that the author's concerns and knowledge fit the known career of Robert Wedderburn, Vicar of Dundee during the early 1550s.[68]

The author clearly describes his belief in divine providence, writing in the first chapter

> As the high monarchs, lords and authorities are established by the infinite divine providence, and maintained by the 'sempeternal' providence such like their ruin comes by the sovereign counsel of the divine sapiens, the which things done [flings] them from the high throne.[69]

He further asserted that 'there is no thing in this world, that comes on mankind, as prosperity or adversity, but all proceeds from the divine power', supporting his arguments with ancient and biblical examples.[70] This is a very direct view of divine providence, in which all earthly events can be attributed to God.

Having established God's direct intervention in the world as a general principle, the author considered the specific case of Scotland. He refuted the notion that the disasters which have befallen Scotland, including defeat at the battle of Pinkie, plague and the occupation of the land by the English, were due to 'fortune' rather than divine providence.[71] Considering that

> the cruel dolorous destruction of our noble barons, and of many others of the three estates, by cruel and unmerciful slaughter, and also by most extreme violent spoiling and hardship of their movable goods in great quantity, and also our old enemies, by treasonable sedition, taking violent possession of an part of the strengths and castle of the border of our realm, and also remain within the plain man lands far with in our country, and violently possessing an certain of our burghs, villages and castles

The author was inspired to study the Bible, desiring to know 'whether this dolorous affliction be an wand of the father to correct and chastise the son by mercy, or if it be a rigours merciless decreet of a judge, to execute on us a final extermination'.[72] After a study of Deuteronomy, Leviticus and Isaiah, he came to understand that 'the divine indignation has decreed an extreme ruin on our realm but if that we retire from our vice, and also to become vigilant to seek hasty remedy and medicine at him who gives all grace and comfort to them that are most destitute'.[73] In other words, this is not the Apocalypse, the end of the current world and its replacement by a new divine order, but rather God's almost automatic response to the sinful functioning of the present earthly realm.[74] While all events are God's will, there is yet room for human agency; human action can cause God to either inflict more suffering, or to bring benefits to the people. This belief is expressed repeatedly throughout the book, as when the author writes

> I have as great cause to deplore the calamities that rings presently in our realm through the vice of the people, and how be it that the threatening of God against us be very severe and extreme, yet nonetheless I hope that his awful scourge of apparent extermination shall change in a fatherly correction so that we will know his majesty, and to retire from our vice, for he has promised grace to all them that repents.[75]

If the Scots repent and regain God's favour, then the author hopes 'that five of us shall chase a hundred of our old enemies'.[76]

The author's ultimate purpose is to call on the Scots to unite, and for the three estates to stop mistreating each other. The commoners are given a sympathetic hearing of their troubles, but are ultimately condemned as ignorant, unfaithful and uncivil, and therefore not worthy of governing themselves.[77] The nobles are reminded that their virtue should be earned, and not merely inherited, while the clergy are condemned for not showing a better example, which is the only effective remedy against the spreading heresy.[78] They are to reform their own abuses and negligence of their duties, failings which were the cause of reformations in other countries. Executing heretics will only cause more to join the Protestant cause, so only improved behaviour among the clergy will eliminate heresy.[79] Here again is the voice of a reform-minded Catholic, even a 'Protestantising Catholic' with his emphases on studying the Bible and openness to Lutheran works.

Again and again *The Complaynt* emphasises that the sufferings of the Scots are the result of divine anger. Indeed, the author is careful to explain that the English are merely agents of God's will, and not favoured by God or otherwise justified in their actions. God's anger is aimed at the sins of the Scots, especially their mistreatment of each other. Significantly, given the emphasis on the performance of the mass in Scottish religion, there is no suggestion that the way back to God's good grace is through worship. Rather, it is by reforming their behaviour and working towards national unity that the Scots will bring an end to their suffering. Unlike Lindsay, there is no focus on idolatry and less material that would lend itself directly to a Protestant way of thinking. By so repeatedly emphasising God's direct, angry intervention against the Scots, however, and calling for unity among them as part of the solution, the author creates the conditions in which many people might wish to avoid conflict, because of both the immediate damage and dangers and the possibility that God might react by sending yet more punishments.

These literary ideas likely received some popular circulation. Sir David Lindsay's plays were performed before audiences at least twice. Robert Wedderburn was active in Dundee, and, if he was indeed the author, may be presumed to have shared some of his thoughts. The apparently random deaths from the plague and the brutal devastation of the war must have inspired many Scots to think about the causes and about how to avoid them in future. Through the works of Lindsey and *The Complaynt*, the suggestion was planted that sin, idolatry, and the misbehaviour of both the political and ecclesiastical hierarchies were directly linked to the disasters of the 1540s and the poverty and ruin of the 1550s. These sentiments most likely were also played upon by Protestant preachers. John Knox wrote, concerning this period, that 'The maist parte of Lothiane, from Edinburgh east, was eyther assured or laid wast. Thus did God plague everie qwarter; butt men war blynd and wold nott, nor could nott, considder the cause.'[80] Knox composed this some years after the 1540s, yet it is likely that he and other preachers would have been happy to spread that same message earlier.

Church and Parliament

The Scottish Catholic Church also recognised that the situation during the 1550s was precarious and took measures to meet some of the challenges posed by the religious reformers. Just like Lindsay and the author of *The Complaynt*, church leaders made a connection between broader problems – in their case, the challenge of Protestantism – and individual failings in morals and behaviours. As a result, beginning in the late 1540s they initiated a series of reforms. John Hamilton, sympathetic to reforming ideas, was appointed Archbishop of St Andrews by his half-brother, the Earl of Arran, following the assassination of Cardinal Beaton in 1547.[81] His efforts to implement changes in the church to counter the criticisms of reformers and Protestants and to improve the religious understanding of both clerics and lay people is evident in the surviving records of the meetings of the provincial church council during his tenure. The focus on heresy began with the council of 1549 which stated its desire 'utterly to extirpate the same, as it were, from the very roots'. The main problems, the attendees declared, were 'the corruption of morals and profane lewdness of life' of the clergy and their 'crass ignorance of literature and of all the liberal arts'.[82] The council addressed these problems by requiring priests to be more austere and focused on their vocation, enacting legislation against priests who kept concubines, who engaged in trade or farming, or who dressed and ate extravagantly. They tried to increase lay religious knowledge by requiring clerics to reside near their posts and ordering bishops, rectors and designated preachers to preach more frequently.[83] Inquisitors were instructed to look out for those who criticised the mass, the existence of purgatory, the intercession of saints, the usefulness of prayers and good works, and those who opposed religious 'fasts and feasts' and images in churches. The church authorities were also aware of popular criticisms that were being made and ordered searches for 'books of rhymes or popular songs containing calumnies and slanders defamatory of churchmen and church institutions', an indication of the popularity of the type of songs contained in the *Godlie Ballatis*.[84] As in previous decades, much of the discussion of these new ideas came from the clergy. The council gave bishops powers to silence preachers within monasteries, and ordered the monks' cells to be searched for heretical books.[85] The preaching of reforming ideas by and amongst Catholic clergy would have emphasised the need for changes even to Scots who considered themselves loyal Catholics.

The next council in 1552 shifted its attention to the laity and aimed to increase the seriousness of their devotion. The attendees complained of low attendance at mass and called on curates to note the names of the absent.[86] Those who misbehaved or who took mass lightly were to be punished by the bishops' officials, and trade in churchyards and at church doors was also prohibited on Sundays, a move which some town councils had already taken on their own authority.[87] The most significant move by the council, however, was to commission a catechism to further educate the laity.[88] Priests were to read this catechism to the parishioners for thirty minutes each week.

The authors composed the resulting text to reinforce the faith of the laity in the traditional religion, but it also reflected the providentialism of the moment.[89] The catechism was written in Scots and its' authors supported their points with frequent biblical references, which might be seen as a response to calls for preaching based on Scripture. It discussed the Commandments, the Creed, the seven sacraments, the Pater Noster and, briefly, the Ave Maria. The catechism also accords with George Wishart, Sir David Lindsay and the author of *The Complaynt* in emphasising the physical, earthly consequences of disobeying God: 'what are the plagues which God is wont and uses to send to the people for transgression of his commands? They are three in special, hunger, pestilence, and the sword, and repeated in sundry places of the auld testament.'[90] On the other hand the catechism quoted Leviticus 26 and promised, on God's behalf, that

> If that you go in my laws, and keep my commands and do them, I shall give you rain in time convenient, the earth shall bring forth the corn, the trees shall be full of fruit, you shall eat your bread with fouth [abundance], and shall dwell in your land without fear.[91]

The catechism emphasises that images were acceptable so long as they encouraged Christians to pray to God, rather than to the image itself.[92]

Those who listened attentively may nonetheless have caught the passage that 'God almighty plagued the old Gentiles for their abominable idolatry'.[93] It is possible that some listeners did not grasp the careful distinctions around images and focused instead on the dire warnings of misfortune to fall on idolaters. The catechism was also concerned with behaviour, emphasising that 'dancing, unnecessary drinking, wantonness, lecherous songs and touching, whoredom, card [playing] and dicing and specially caroling and wanton singing in the kirk' should be avoided on Sundays.[94] The sin of ignoring the Sabbath was 'no doubt is one of the special causes of the calamites and great plagues and miseries which we feel daily among us send be the hand of God'.[95] Whether they listened attentively or not, surely many would have understood the point that their sins had brought on their current physical misery. Although the text was designed to reinforce the Catholic faith of the laity, it brought up anxieties and hopes which Protestant preachers likely addressed just as, if not more, emphatically than the Catholic clergy.

Despite or perhaps encouraged by these efforts from the Catholic hierarchy, reformers and Protestants became more active and confident during the second half of the 1550s. The Catholic provincial council of 1559 therefore opened with an increased sense of urgency. They began their session by ordering public processions three times a week inside the churches to pray for the success of the council, 'for the peace and tranquility of the commonwealth of this realm, and for the removal of errors and heresies'.[96] Such processions may have actually conveyed a lack of confidence to any laypeople who happened to notice them. The council slightly modified the hated mortuary dues, reducing the burden on the very poorest, but retaining the usual usage for those with estates over ten pounds as well as for burgesses and barons, two groups who were turning against them.[97] The order that all parishioners attend the mass was also repeated. Paul Methven, the Protestant preacher in Dundee, and several other men were mentioned by name as having introduced a new form of baptism. In response the council introduced a special formula to be used by priests when baptising those children who had received the Protestant sacrament, to ensure their proper christening.[98] The council also emphasised that the Eucharist and marriage could also only be performed by priests. These measures are indications that some Protestants were establishing a separate church with its own clergy, freed from a reliance on priests ordained in the Catholic Church who hovered on an unclear boundary between reformer and Protestant.

The hierarchy's efforts aimed to appeal to those who were interested in reform but reluctant to leave the Catholic Church.[99] In introducing the reforming statutes and the catechism Archbishop Hamilton and his advisors modelled themselves on Archbishop Hermann von Weid of Cologne, who in the 1530s attempted to reform Catholic practices in Cologne so as to include Protestants. Von Weid went so far as to commission Philip

Melanchthon and Martin Bucer to establish a set of mutually acceptable religious practices and beliefs.[100] The major flaw in the Catholic effort was that Protestants could offer more vehement and better-defined solutions to the same problems of inadequate preaching, lay sin and misbehaviour, the role of scriptural primacy, the meaning of the sacraments, and ultimately the vital question of how to abate God's wrath. Their focus on idolatry in particular could not be matched or defused by the Catholics, and it would become the key issue of the early stages of the Reformation. Many of the measures directed at lay behaviour, meanwhile, would be rapidly introduced by the newly reformed town councils. Burgh governments would find ministers and kirk sessions to be more effective partners than vicars and church courts.

Parliament was also concerned with sin among the Scottish population. The Parliament of 1552 introduced legislation against 'execrations and blasphemy of the name of God' and those who disturbed divine service and preaching in the kirk, with a sliding scale of penalties from earls and prelates all the way down to children.[101] A further act concerned adultery, focusing especially on 'incorrigible' offenders who ignored spiritual sanctions 'to the great peril of their own souls', who were to be outlawed.[102] We do not know much about what specifically Protestant preachers were discussing during the 1550s, but if they were anything like Wishart's prophecies or Knox's writings, it is not surprising that between them, writers such as Lindsay and the author of *The Complaynt*, the leadership of the Catholic Church, and the parliamentary representatives of Scotland, there was an urgent sense that the Scots had to reform themselves to avoid God's anger.

It was in this climate of concern about God's wrath that reformers began to push for changes to religious worship throughout Scotland. During the second half of the 1550s, Protestant preachers spread the word in urban 'privy kirks' and noble and lairdly households. Although the church hierarchy intermittently prosecuted some Protestants, the temporal authorities protected others. It was Mary of Guise who had protected Knox from heresy charges in 1556, and Knox subsequently wrote to her to request that she consider how to implement true worship and restrain the bishops' persecution of Protestants.[103] Despite Mary of Guise's apparent rejection of this letter, the Protestant nobles – the Earl of Glencairne, Lords Lorne and Erskine and James Stewart – wrote to Knox to report that they were indeed no longer persecuted and that 'we see daily the friars, enemies to Christ's Evangel, in less estimation, both with the Queen's grace and the rest of the nobility of our realm'. indicating the isolation of the conservative friars from a growing moderate group.[104] These nobles and lairds, in turn, corresponded and negotiated with Mary of Guise, and set out their relatively modest initial hopes in the First Band of the Congregation, a pledge signed in December 1557.[105] The Heads which accompanied the Band requested that public worship feature prayers and readings taken from the English Book of Common Prayer. They desired that discussion and preaching of Scripture be allowed in private homes until the regent would permit it publicly.[106] The signers of the Band declared themselves hostile to idolatry, though they did not yet call for the abolition of the mass specifically. This was not the new church hoped for by Knox and Calvin, but it expressed a mood for some clear reforms to the existing church. More committed Protestants, meanwhile, of whom Knox is only the best remembered, did begin to advocate for the elimination of the mass and the introduction of new forms of sacraments.[107] Starting in 1558, some of them even began to administer sacraments themselves, a significant step in creating a new church, the development which had alarmed the Catholic Provincial council.

Conclusion

The Scottish townspeople, surveying their burnt towns and decimated communities, must have wondered what they had done to bring such misfortunes upon themselves. In common with the Scottish writers and leaders of the 1550s, and other sixteenth-century Europeans in general, they likely thought that their tribulations were, to a large extent, punishments from God. These punishments were not necessarily over. Through the 1550s, the pace of economic recovery was miserable, the threat of war remained and the plague threatened to come back at any moment. Though the inhabitants immediately restored their Catholic religious services, they must have pondered Wishart's prophecies from the 1540s, which had foretold devastation for those who ignored God's word, and listened a little more attentively to those who identified idolatry and misbehaviour as the source of God's anger.

Notes

1. DCA BHCB 1550–4, f105.
2. *RPS*, A1552/2/30 (accessed 15 November 2013).
3. *RCRBS*, 6–7.
4. *RCRBS*, 525–6.
5. *RPS*, A1552/2/30 (accessed 17 January 2022).
6. HAD/4/6/5, f258.
7. HAD/4/2/3/1, f13v, 41.
8. HAD/4/2/3/1, f110.
9. HAD/4/6/5, f270, 271, 273, 288v; HAD/4/2/3/1, f8v, 10.
10. *Privy Seal*, 5:138.
11. HAD/4/6/5, f234.
12. Marshall, *Ruin and Restoration*, 21.
13. Paton, 'Books of the Common Good', 50.
14. Paton, 'Books of the Common Good', 49.
15. Paton, 'Books of the Common Good', 54.
16. HAD/2/1/2/1, f12v.

17. Paton, 'Books of the Common Good', 53, 57, 58.
18. Maxwell, *Old Dundee*, 69.
19. DCA BHCB 1550–4, f126; Maxwell, *Old Dundee*, 74, 248.
20. DCA BHCB 1550–4, f94v.
21. Maxwell, *Old Dundee*, 125; DCA BHCB 1550–4, f190v.
22. DCA BHCB 1550–4, f197v.
23. DCA BHCB 1550–4, f202v.
24. DCA BHCB 1550–4, f210v.
25. DCA BHCB 1550–4, f205v.
26. DCA Baxter Craft Lockit Book, f7.
27. DCA BHCB 1550–4, f277v.
28. DCA BHCB 1555–8, f69v.
29. DCA Head Court Laws 1550–1612, f2v. Throughout the 1550s Peebles, another town burnt during the wars, appealed for their clergy to return to their posts. *Charters and Documents relating to the Burgh of Peebles, with extracts from the records of the burgh. A.D. 1165–1710* (Edinburgh, 1872), 208, 227, 242.
30. *RCRBS*, 514, 518, 519, 522–3, 526.
31. See Chapter One.
32. *TA*, 10:104, 118, 237.
33. SCA SBCB 1554–7, 17/2/1556.
34. *Extracts . . . Stirling*, 67.
35. SCA SBCB 1554–7, 25/9/1556.
36. Verschuur, *Politics or Religion?*, 37, 48, 54.
37. See Dawson, *Scotland Re-formed*, 182.
38. *TA*, 9:362.
39. *TA*, 9:369, 389.
40. *TA*, 10:147, 154.
41. *TA*, 10:211.
42. *TA*, 10:226.
43. HAD/2/1/2/1, f15.
44. HAD/4/1/5, f168v.
45. Amy Blakeway, 'The Anglo-Scottish war of 1558 and the Scottish Reformation', *History* 102 (2017), 201–25, especially 203–11.
46. *TA*, 10:342.
47. *TA*, 10:359, 375, 383, 388.
48. Paton, 'Books of the Common Good', 57.
49. *TA*, 10:419; HAD/2/1/2/1, f20v.
50. *RCRBS*, 519.
51. DCA BHCB 1550–4, f130.
52. DCA BHCB 1550–4, f362v.
53. *TA*, 10:277.
54. On providence as a decisive factor in the decision-making of early modern people, see Keith Thomas, *Religion and the Decline of Magic* (New York, 1971) chap. 4; Martha McGill and Alasdair Raffe, 'The uses of providence in early modern Scotland', in *The Supernatural in Early Modern Scotland*, eds Julian Goodare and Martha McGill (Manchester, 2020); Alexandra Walsham, *Providence in Early Modern England* (Oxford, 1999); David Randall, 'Providence, fortune and the experience of combat: English printed battlefield reports, circa 1570–1637.' *Sixteenth Century Journal* 35 (2004): 1053–77; Blair Worden,

'Providence and politics in Cromwellian England', *Past and Present* 109 (1985): 55–99; Margo Todd, 'Providence, chance and the new science in early Stuart Cambridge', *Historical Journal* 29 (1986): 697–711; Ronald J. Vandermolen, 'Providence as mystery, providence as revelation: Puritan and Anglican modifications of John Calvin's doctrine of providence', *Church History* 47 (1978): 27–47.

55. John Hale, 'Sixteenth-century explanations of war', in J. R. Hale, *Renaissance War Studies* (London, 1983), 422.
56. Major, *A History of Greater Britain*, 297; Alexander Brodie, 'Mair [Major] John (1467–1550), historian, philosopher and theologian', *ODNB*, Oxford, 2004 (accessed 14 January 2022).
57. Carol Edington, *Court and Culture in Renaissance Scotland: Sir David Lindsay of the Mount* (Amherst, 1994), 53.
58. Sir David Lindsay, *The Monarche and other Poems, Part 1*, ed. Fitzedward Hall (London: 1865), 1:62.
59. Edington, *Court and Culture*, 69.
60. Lindsay, *The Monarche and other Poems*, 1:2.
61. Edington, *Court and Culture*, 132; R. J. Lyall, 'Complaint, satire and invective in Middle Scots literature', in *Church, Politics and Society: Scotland 1409–1929*, ed. Norman Macdougall (Edinburgh, 1983), 49.
62. Lindsay, *The Monarche and other Poems*, 3.
63. Lindsay, *The Monarche and other Poems*, 3.
64. Lindsay, *The Monarche and other Poems*, 84.
65. Edington, *Court and Culture*, 65–6.
66. Stewart, 'Introduction', *The Complaynt*, xxxiii–xxxv.
67. Wedderburn, *The Complaynt*, 147.
68. Stewart, 'Introduction', viii–x.
69. Wedderburn, *The Complaynt*, 15.
70. Wedderburn, *The Complaynt*, 17.
71. Wedderburn, *The Complaynt*, 17.
72. Wedderburn, *The Complaynt*, 18.
73. Wedderburn, *The Complaynt*, 18.
74. Wedderburn, *The Complaynt*, 28; Katharine R. Firth, *The Apocalyptic Tradition in Reformation Britain, 1530–1645* (Oxford, 1979), 15.
75. Wedderburn, *The Complaynt*, 20.
76. Wedderburn, *The Complaynt*, 21.
77. Wedderburn, *The Complaynt*, 96–110, 112.
78. Wedderburn, *The Complaynt*, 119–22, 124–9.
79. Wedderburn, *The Complaynt*, 25–7.
80. Knox, *Works*, 1:215.
81. James K. Cameron, '"Catholic Reform" in Germany and the pre-1560 church in Scotland', *Records of the Scottish Church History Society* (1979), 105–17. The second Earl of Arran became known as the Duke of Chatelherault after being awarded the French duchy in 1554.
82. *Statutes of the Scottish Church*, 84.
83. *Statutes of the Scottish Church*, 89–91, 92, 98–101, 104–5.
84. *Statutes of the Scottish Church*, 126–7.
85. *Statutes of the Scottish Church*, 123.
86. *Statutes of the Scottish Church*, 136–7, 139.

87. See Chapter Two. *Statutes of the Scottish Church*, 139.
88. *Statutes of the Scottish Church*, 143–7.
89. On authorship, see Ryrie, 'Reform without frontiers', 37.
90. *The Catechism of John Hamilton Archbishop of St Andrews*, ed. Thomas Graves Law (Oxford, 1884), 32.
91. *Catechism*, 35.
92. *Catechism*, 52–3.
93. *Catechism*, 33.
94. *Catechism*, 68.
95. *Catechism*, 69.
96. *Statutes of the Scottish Church*, 152.
97. *Statutes of the Scottish Church*, 178–9.
98. *Statutes of the Scottish Church*, 186.
99. Cowan, *The Scottish Reformation*, 79–83; Ryrie, 'Reform without frontiers', 41, 43, 47, 49–52; Cameron, '"Catholic Reform" in Germany'; Clare Kellar, *Scotland, England and the Reformation 1534–61* (Oxford, 2003), 121–35.
100. Cameron, '"Catholic Reform" in Germany', 105; Kellar, *Scotland, England and the Reformation*, 121.
101. *RPS*, A1552/2/7, A1552/2/8 (accessed 8 December 2013).
102. *RPS*, A1552/2/12 (accessed 17 January 2022).
103. Knox, *Works*, 4:82–3.
104. Knox, *Works*, 1:268.
105. Less James Stewart, and adding the Earls of Argyll and Morton.
106. Knox, *Works*, 1:273–6; Ryrie thinks that 1549 Prayer Books may have been most common in Scotland, because of English occupation of late 1540s. However, the English religious propaganda efforts were under-resourced (see Chapter Six) and Knox, who served in the Edwardian church, would surely have introduced them to the 1553 Prayer Book. Ryrie, 'Congregations', 73; Kellar, *Scotland, England and the Reformation*, 154.
107. Dawson, *Knox*, 114, 134.

PART THREE

Reformation from Within and Without

There is no doubt that, as twenty-first-century historians Pamela Ritchie, Jane Dawson and Alec Ryrie have demonstrated, the Protestant revolt of 1559 was caused by the tensions between, on one part, the religious convictions of a significant group of nobles, lairds and townspeople; on another, Mary of Guise's attempts to create a religious settlement; and finally, suspicion and resentment of growing French power in Scotland.[1] This understanding of the origins of the revolt is less helpful in explaining why Protestantism was so easily accepted by many ordinary Scots and why councillors in towns large and small so swiftly implemented the drastic changes to long-standing forms of practice and belief. Some burghs were turned into Calvinist polities in a matter of days, as Protestants cleansed churches of Catholic ornamentation, banned and replaced masses with preaching or prayer reading, and established kirk sessions. Though the Protestants were often only able to impose these reforms with military support, Scottish townspeople rarely attempted to restore Catholic worship once the militants had moved on.[2] Other burghs which were not in the path of the initial Protestant surge also reformed their civic churches, though they waited until the Reformation was made official policy by the Parliament of 1560.

It was in those moments, when they were left to themselves to either continue the changes, reform only superficially, or revert to the old ways, that townspeople and their councillors played a decisive role in the Reformation. In Dundee, Stirling, Haddington and burghs throughout Scotland, town councils began or continued the process of reforming their civic churches, despite the uncertainties surrounding the legality of the Parliament of 1560 and the possibility of a reversal of the religious changes under the personal rule of Queen Mary.[3] Provosts, bailies and councillors introduced Protestant services, supported Protestant clergy, cooperated with kirk sessions, passed tighter morality laws, took over church property and revenues for civic purposes, and found ways to support the former Catholic clergy. The councillors were quick to see the advantages of absorbing church revenues and imposing stricter disciplinary standards. The cooperation of burgh councils and a significant portion of townspeople was therefore crucial to the remarkable success of the Scottish Reformation. An explanation of why they did so must take into account the change in mood among many Scots during the 1550s which was partly responsible for the acceptance of Protestantism after 1560. It is clear that many Scots were seeking, and others must have expected, some kind of religious reform. These expectations coincided with or reflected anxiety about sin and misbehaviour in the wake of the plague and war that had struck Scotland during the 1540s. It is likely too that the councils had their eyes on some of the resources and revenues consumed by religious organisations, especially those outside the civic church such as friaries and abbeys, which likely eased some of the qualms they had about abandoning their traditional religion. Expecting reform, uneasy about Catholic practices, concerned about sin and misbehaviour, fearing further disaster, and frustrated by the religious orders, many Scots may have been willing to give Calvinism a chance.

The expectation of change was evident at all levels of Scottish government and politics, and meant that the Protestants received some benefit of the doubt during the initial stages of the Reformation. The regent, Mary of Guise, was considering some form of religious change during the mid- and late-1550s, although she never got around to calling an assembly or parliament specifically to establish a religious settlement. Ultimately, either through misunderstanding or deliberate provocation, the Dundonians, among others, introduced religious reforms beyond what she was willing to tolerate. The resulting confrontation played into the hands of those Protestants who followed Calvin's line from Geneva and who worked for the establishment of a new church rather than a modification of the old. It soon turned into a full rebellion, during which Dundee, along with Ayr and Perth, halted the civic practice of Catholicism and introduced burgh-sponsored Protestant regimes. Armed Protestants, calling themselves the Lords of the Congregation, reformed Stirling and other towns by force in June 1559. Many of these burghs rapidly adapted themselves to the new order, even after the Protestant army moved on. Haddington, which like many towns was evidently more content with Catholicism and less willing to engage in a confrontation, waited until after the Reformation Parliament of 1560 before reforming its civic church, as did other towns which were not central to the conflict of 1559–60.

Whether it took days or months, in all three burghs, and throughout Scotland, the councils acted to dismantle the structures of the Catholic civic church and replace it with a Calvinist kirk. In place of the administration of dozens of altars, they considerably expanded the forms of social discipline they enforced; in place of supervising a roster of priests they developed a new form of cooperation with a minister and the kirk session elders. Though some events and decisions were out of their control, the councils ultimately retained their responsibility for much of the religious practices in their towns. Indeed, the decentralised structure of Calvinism made it ideal for the religiously autonomous Scottish burghs, which were used to organising many of their civic practices, religion included, by looking horizontally to their neighbours rather than vertically to the central government or church hierarchy. Chapter Eight will identify three different types of urban reformation in Scotland and show that while Protestantism was introduced to each of our burghs in a different way, in each it became successfully established. Chapter Nine will then demonstrate that the burgh councils acted decisively to reform their own civic churches. Though the pace differed slightly, the councils all took the same steps to dismantle Catholicism and turn their towns into Calvinist societies while maintaining their control over the civic church.

Notes

1. Cowan, *The Scottish Reformation*, 109, 111; Dawson, *Scotland Re-formed*, 202; Ryrie, *The Origins*, 119–21, 129–35; Pamela E. Ritchie, *Mary of Guise in Scotland, 1548–1560: a political career* (East Linton, 2002), 206–16, who argues that Mary of Guise acted to promote Mary Stewart's claim to the English throne.
2. With the exception of Edinburgh and Perth, where changes were ordered by Mary of Guise. Lynch, *Edinburgh*, 78; Knox, 'Letter to Anna Locke 23 June 1559', *Works*, 6:24.
3. On the legality of the 1560 Parliament, see Knox, *Works*, 2:126–7; Julian Goodare, 'The First Parliament of Mary, Queen of Scots', *Sixteenth Century Journal* 36 (2005): 55–75; McNeil, 'Our Religion', 68–89.

CHAPTER EIGHT

Reformation: 1558–1560

The Burghs Become Protestant

Protestantism found its initial support in pockets throughout lowland Scotland: in Ayrshire, Edinburgh, Perth, Dundee and among the gentry, especially from Fife to Montrose. The campaigns of the Lords of the Congregation largely took place in a fairly restricted area centred around the Firth of Forth, from St Andrews west to Stirling and then south-east to Edinburgh and Leith. The Reformation process therefore was not uniform across the country, not even in the lowland regions. Consistent patterns of urban Reformation are nonetheless apparent, and the three towns studied here represent three distinct paths followed by Scottish towns. Thanks to more than a generation of local and regional studies, it can be determined that many Scottish towns reformed according to one of these patterns. The first group, represented by Dundee but also including Ayr and Perth, are burghs that reformed from within, beginning by introducing Protestant elements to civic worship while still retaining some Catholic rituals and services. They then completely reformed in the spring of 1559 under the inspiration of Protestant preachers and in alliance with local lairds.[1] The second group, which includes Edinburgh, Linlithgow, St Andrews and several smaller Fife towns along with Stirling, was reformed from without as armed Protestants entered the towns and forcibly dismantled the Catholic churches.[2] The third group, represented here by Haddington but including many other burghs across Scotland such as Inverness, Elgin and Peebles, also reformed from within but only after the Parliament of 1560 introduced Protestantism nationally.[3] An outlier may be Aberdeen, which shared some similarities with the second and third group but where the full implementation of Protestantism was notoriously slow.[4] In every burgh there was a choice made to accept Protestantism – actively in the first group, but burghs in the second group maintained the Protestant church even when the threat of physical violence grew more distant, while the third group chose to introduce Protestantism on their own terms rather than resisting or waiting for more direct compulsion. Throughout the towns, there was very little interpersonal violence between the inhabitants, despite the importance and drastic nature of the Reformation changes. These choices by the town councils to accept Protestantism, and by the clergy and townspeople to not inflame the situation, even if they were reluctant converts, were just as important to the success of the Reformation as the military victory of the Lords of the Congregation.

Early Reform from Within: Dundee

Dundee, Ayr and to a certain extent Perth, make up the group of burghs that initiated the Reformation from within. These burghs followed the development path of urban reform seen in towns from Wittenberg on, and especially in Swiss cities where councils controlled civic religion in a manner comparable to Scotland. There Protestant preaching 'generated concern for the moral purification of the community', first converting a sizable faction of the urban population, who then demanded the replacement of the mass by a new form of worship, the removal of religious images, and regulations on taverns and prostitution.[5] A similar pattern was taking shape in France during the late 1550s and early 1560s as Huguenot churches were established 'under the cross', with interested Christians gathering for prayer and scripture discussion, eventually being joined by a minister, establishing a consistory court (called a kirk session in Scotland) and then taking over existing Catholic churches to perform public services, and finally, if possible, expelling the Catholic clergy.[6] In Dundee and Ayr, the early sympathy and support of the town councils meant that the replacement of the Catholic Church by the Protestant was more orderly and less violent than in many French towns, likely reducing (but not completely eliminating) opportunities for Catholic resentment and therefore polarisation and resistance.

The catalyst for reformation in Dundee was the arrival of the Protestant preacher Paul Methven in 1558. Methven had previously studied in England, been expelled under Mary Tudor, and then become a teacher in Edinburgh's privy kirk. The foundation of a Protestant congregation in Dundee under his leadership was a development that placed the town council in an awkward position. On one hand, they had a history of sheltering religious dissent, and at least one senior member of the council, George Lovell, soon joined Dundee's congregation. On the other hand, the council took seriously their task of maintaining the Catholic civic church. They also had to consider the attitude of Mary of Guise and do their best to protect the townspeople from reprisals. For a little over a year, the council tried to have it both ways, sheltering and even cooperating with the Protestant congregation while maintaining Catholic worship. When Mary of Guise began to take action against the Protestants, the burgh opted to defy her openly. Having embarked on a political rebellion, the council also broke with Catholicism and reformed the civic church.

Methven's presence either inspired or coincided with a new determination among Dundee's reformers. Throughout the early and mid-1550s there had been no sign of religious upheaval in Dundee; indeed the town placed its energy into restoring the infrastructure and ornaments necessary for Catholic services. Following Methven's arrival, however, there was a renewed interest in new religious ideas. Unlike in earlier years, this time some inhabitants began to act on some of the proposed changes, beginning with defying the Lenten fast in 1558. In July 1558, George Lovell, David Ferguson and other Dundonians were summoned to appear before the Justice-General in the tolbooth of Edinburgh, along with Methven, to answer 'for their wrongful using and discussing of the Scripture, and for disputing upon erroneous opinions and eating of flesh in Lent and other forbidden times contrary the acts of parliament'.[7] The Dundonians, however, were saved by the intervention of a group of Protestant-leaning nobles who were in Edinburgh, and Mary of Guise put off the proceedings.[8] In November 1558 Methven was cited again, this time by a clerical assembly in Edinburgh. When he failed to appear, he was banished (apparently with the approval of Mary of Guise), and sanctions were ordered against those who would shelter or feed him.[9] Methven, nonetheless, again received support from the townspeople of Dundee who, as they had done with a previous generation of reformers, 'supplied him with provisions, and harboured him from one house to another' even though their appeal to Mary had been denied. He was also backed by various gentlemen from Fife, Angus and the Mearns.[10]

First Steps: Regulating Social Nuisances

It was during the mid-winter of 1558–9 that Dundee's council started to officially implement reforms. Likely inspired by Methven's preaching, they began to impose disciplinary changes on the whole community at the semi-annual Head Court meeting held on 10 January 1559. Previous legislation in Dundee's book of burgh laws concerned matters of trade and business transactions, not individual behaviour. The court also took on cases of interpersonal violence, but was largely disinterested in individual behaviour that was neither violent nor violated trade regulations. In 1559 this changed, with the town council involving itself in a wider range of its inhabitants' affairs. At that meeting the bailies, councillors and craft inscribed a series of acts against social nuisances in their town. Panderers (pimps) who were reported to be seducing the wives, daughters and servants of honest men into prostitution were ordered to leave the burgh within twenty-four hours. The council also ordered prostitutes in bordellos to adopt a virtuous manner of living or leave the town. Other regulations targeted vagabonds, nightwalkers, dicers and carders. The magistrates instructed their officers to inquire into the 'maner of the[ir] conversation' before deciding on banishment or other forms of punishment. Inhabitants were ordered not to house such persons but to turn them over to the bailies. A 10 p.m. last call was introduced, enforced by fines for the drinkers and banishment for the tavern keepers. Beggars had to obtain notarised certificates of their inability to work or be branded on the cheek. Finally, the council scolded parents and schoolmasters who let children disrupt the time of preaching, although they at least were spared the threat of banishment, instead being warned that they would be punished 'with all rigour'.[11] Of these acts, only the one against disruption of divine service and preaching was the recent subject of an Act of Parliament (1552); the others were driven by local concerns.[12] As early as 1554, an assize had banished two women and ordered a third to stay out of the marketplace, which may have been an attempt to deal with prostitution.[13] Notably absent from this first list were measures against fornication, adultery and blasphemy against God, sins which would dominate the council's concerns as soon as Protestantism was fully established. For the moment, the focus was on behaviour that caused public disturbances.

Like all early modern (and indeed, modern) towns, Dundee's magistrates undoubtedly had always sought to regulate social nuisances. This burst of legislation in 1559 was unprecedented in the surviving burgh records however, as the town council moved beyond the acts of violence, slander and unpaid debts which had previously occupied them. The problems which Dundee's council set out to solve could have bothered a Catholic community as easily as a Protestant one. The specifics of the regulations and their timing nonetheless suggest that Dundee's council was influenced by the growing Calvinist movement. Dundonians were getting their Calvinist ideas not only from Paul Methven but also from Europe. In addition to their contacts with Lutheran Scandinavia, one of the town's most frequent trading partners was the French port of Dieppe. Dieppois merchants and sailors were frequently in Dundee, and Dundee merchants often travelled to the French town, where a Scottish colony, which included the exiled Protestant Dundonian merchant James Wedderburn, had been established.[14] Dieppe embraced Calvinism just slightly before Dundee did, with a small Protestant group meeting in August 1557 and growing throughout 1558. John Knox himself preached there for several weeks in the late winter of 1558–9. By April 1559, as a seventeenth-century Protestant history asserted, the Dieppois, especially the sailors, had stopped blaspheming, going to houses of ill repute, associating with 'public women' and participating in masquerades and gambling.[15] Given the close contacts between the two ports, it is likely that merchants and sailors were exchanging notes about the new religious ideas in circulation, that the flurry of legislation in January was connected to the desire for religious reform, and that the Dundonians shared with other European towns the wish to create a more godly society through changes in worship and behaviour.

Maintaining Balance: Coexistence of Catholic and Protestant Worship

During the first few months of 1559, the Protestants in Dundee rapidly became more established, again defying the Lenten fasts, administering their own sacraments and establishing a kirk session. Only 'several' Dundonians participated, however, suggesting that the number who opted to separate themselves from the Catholic Church was not very large. Methven performed similar acts in Montrose, a little over forty kilometres away.[16] In other places it was typical for ministers to be based in one town but travel to preach and minister in surrounding communities, so he may still have served principally as minister to Dundee's congregation despite his travels.[17] The kirk session was established by the end of winter. Its immediate incorporation into the structure of municipal government was demonstrated by a case in March 1559. The son and the widower of the late Agnes Branguthie had arrived at an impasse over who would continue to occupy her tenement, and the case was referred to both the bailies and the elders of the congregation. After consulting with the elders, the bailies finally rendered judgment in the case. Although the burgh court would continue to maintain its jurisdiction in other similar cases, the elders were already establishing themselves as an alternate mechanism for settling disputes and possibly enforcing discipline, and were recognised as such by the town council.[18]

Dundee's Protestant congregation was growing and becoming more assertive, but it was not yet the civic church. Knox would claim that Methven's preaching caused many to renounce idolatry, 'and to submit themselves to Christ Jesus, and to his blessed ordinances; insomuch as the town of Dundee began to erect the face of a public church reformed, in the which the word was openly preached, and Christ's sacraments truly ministered'.[19] Knox's chronology here is vague, but he appears to be referring to 1558 and the beginning of 1559. Parsing Knox's writings is always a fraught exercise, but the key term in the passage is 'began'. Dundee's Protestant congregation may have been increasingly open in its activities, but they had not yet reformed the town; Knox only mentions that individuals had renounced idolatry, and does not refer to purging idols and chasing priests from the town, as Protestants did in other European towns as soon as they gained sufficient strength.[20] Indeed, immediately after Knox reports that the Protestants in Edinburgh decided against a 'public Reformation', by which he clearly means acts of iconoclasm, instead hoping for a religious settlement, appealing to the regent for 'a godly Reformation' led by magistrates.[21] In neither town were the Protestants strong enough to launch a Reformation from below.

Through 1558 and the beginning of 1559, therefore, the Protestant congregation in Dundee was asserting an increasingly prominent place in the still Catholic burgh. During this period the councillors, whatever their individual sympathies, were still taking seriously their responsibility for overseeing traditional religious observance. On 7 November 1558, the bailies George Lovell and Andrew Fletcher required George Rollok, himself a former bailie and future associate of John Knox, to agree to pay five merks yearly because his son, having been appointed to the chaplaincy of Our Lady altar, was not yet qualified to serve at the altar.[22] Dundee's elites still expected someone to perform the mass. The same court session ordered that money be put aside for repairs to a chapel devoted to St Thomas.[23] Even though George Lovell was one of the most committed Protestants in the burgh, as bailie he still ensured that the mass was being properly performed at the altars within the town's gift. A couple of weeks later, on 23 November, the baker craft re-elected sir Thomas Wedderburn as their chaplain at their annual craft meeting.[24] Sir Thomas's position would not be renewed the next year, but it seems that at the time, if Paul Methven had been encouraging the Dundonians to renounce the mass and idolatry, the bakers at least were not yet completely convinced.

No arrangements were being made at this stage to confiscate any church revenue or reform the clergy in the town's employ. On 13 January 1559, just three days after passing their new disciplinary code, the bailies ordered the town's officers to accompany the choristers of St Mary's in visiting all those who owed rent in order to confiscate goods on the spot.[25] The choristers, along with all other property owners, appeared frequently in the burgh court to claim past rents, but this is the first time that the bailies ordered a systematic sweep of all their tenants. Far from being corrupt nuisances, the choristers were being treated as valuable public servants, at least by the council. Finally, on 25 April 1559, just a few days before the arrival of John Knox and two weeks before an iconoclastic outburst at Perth provoked open rebellion, the provost, bailies, councillors and deacons of craft convened a special meeting to appoint sir John Dene to St Severan's altar, ensuring that he be paid all duties belonging to it.[26] The fact that the whole town council convened a special meeting to appoint a priest to a chaplaincy indicates that they were neither planning to eliminate the mass in the near future nor developing an animosity towards the local priests.

At least some members of the burgh government must have had mixed feelings as they sought to maintain the delicate balance in the burgh. The council included men who were or who would become committed Protestants, but there is no indication that council policy was determined by religious factions, though attitudes may have been evolving over 1558 and the winter of 1559. James Haliburton was Provost, as he had been for every year since 1550, and while he would become a committed member of the Lords of the Congregation there is no evidence in the burgh records that he exerted specific influence on local religious affairs.[27] It is also difficult to discern whether there were factions on the council especially loyal or opposed to him. No lists of the councillors for 1558–9 exist, a particularly disappointing gap in the records, but the bailies that year were all experienced members of the town council. The most senior, George Lovell, was certainly a Protestant activist, suspected of hanging a statue of St Francis in 1536, and was one of those summoned in July 1558 to face accusations of erroneously disputing Scriptures and breaking the Lenten fast.[28] While it is tempting to attribute some of Dundee's religious changes to his influence, it should be noted that he had served as bailie four times since 1550. During his previous terms in office, the town council had repaired wartime damages to St Mary's, supported the town's chaplains in their pursuit of back rents, restored the Holy Blood altar, ordered the crafts to resume services at their altars, hired a mass singer, intervened to support their preferred candidate for post of vicar, and recovered church ritual equipment hidden during the wars.[29] His Protestant leanings had not interfered with administering Catholic religious observances in the burgh. Robert Kid had also served as bailie at least four times previously, and George Rollok had served as a councillor and as Master of the Almshouse, one of Dundee's most important civic institutions. Andrew Fletcher, the most junior bailie, had previously served at least one term as a councillor. The election of the bailies was wholly in keeping with burgh practice and marked no discontinuity with the councils of previous years. The religious changes that this council would implement were not the work of a particular faction, but were carried out by the same group which had spent much of the 1550s working to restore traditional worship. Some members of Dundee's congregation were doubtlessly waiting for their opportunity to purge the town of Catholic 'idolatry' but in the meantime, those councillors with Protestant sympathies had to balance enthusiasm and prudence.

The council's policy during 1558 and early 1559 of simultaneously tolerating or even promoting both practices was likely an attempt to play for time as they waited for a broader religious settlement.[30] Dundee's reforms in the winter of 1558–9 were motivated by desires from within the burgh itself, but it was not alone among Scottish towns. Ayr and Perth were also introducing Protestant reforms at the same time, Ayr's council having appointed a curate with Protestant leanings in 1558, and Perth saw growing support for Protestantism, especially among a faction of its craftsmen, under the watch of a pro-Protestant provost.[31] There was also growing support for major reforms among important parts of the nobility and gentry, and the balance that Dundee's council tried to achieve was similar to the kind of national compromises being proposed by both sides. Mary of Guise did intervene to discharge the Dundonians summoned in July 1558 and similarly acted on behalf of Paul Methven after appeals from the burgesses of Dundee. Despite Knox's invective, there is no reason to doubt her sincerity in promising to consider the demands of the Protestants after the Parliament of November 1558, when she favourably received a petition which called for all acts of Parliament to be suspended until a General Council on religious matters could convene, presumably ensuring in the meantime that Protestants could maintain the Scripture reading and ministration of the sacraments mentioned in the preamble.[32] Such a policy of discussion with the aim of creating religious concord was similar to the policies promoted in France by her brother, Charles the Cardinal of Lorraine. The policy of Lorraine during the late 1550s and 1560 was based around 'a pragmatic distinction between public worship and private conscience' resembling the Elizabethan settlement of 1558 (at least as it was understood in France). To this end, he advocated including Lutherans in negotiations to reach a new religious settlement, either at Trent or within France. The reverse of this policy, with private elite Catholicism and public Protestantism for everyone else, would be the basis for Mary Stewart's religious policy on her return.[33]

Confrontation and Reformation

Though Dundee's town council seemed convinced by Protestantism in the winter of 1558–9, they were initially cautious about open confrontation. The Dundonians had particularly good reason to hesitate in implementing religious changes. Twice in the previous fifteen years, in 1543–4 and 1552–3, the burgh had been visited by royal justice after it was implicated in acts of radical Protestantism, and individual burghers had frequently been summoned to answer charges of heresy. In all, between 1538 and 1552, Dundonians paid a total of £4,194 in fines for heresy or associated offences. To put that figure in perspective, Dundee as the second wealthiest burgh in Scotland, paid £2,527 17s 9d in direct taxes over the same period.[34] Despite contemporary affirmations of Dundee's 'zeal and boldness' in their support of Protestantism, it would be very surprising if the wealthy and experienced town councillors risked similar repercussions a third time, especially with a French garrison stationed in nearby Broughty Castle.[35] It was the conciliatory gestures by Mary of Guise that may have given the council the assurances it needed to openly recognise the Protestants and to try to establish a religious balance in the towns. The councillors appear to have been content to retain the mass as a civic institution, and an option for those who wanted it, at the same time as they increased the administration of discipline (which may not have even been controversial), and permitted vernacular preaching along with Calvinist baptism and communion. This is close to the offer Knox describes the bishops extending to the Lords of the Congregation in 1558, when they offered Protestant prayer and baptism in exchange for preserving the mass, Purgatory, prayers to saints and the retention of their benefices.[36] In following this model the council may have hoped to placate the Protestants while avoiding governmental reprisals. Despite the invective of Knox and other reformers directed against the evils of idolatry, it appears that at that moment in time, the Protestants on council were willing to accept the mass in public worship.

It is the administering of Protestant sacraments at Easter 1559 that appears to have finally driven Mary of Guise to act. Mary had promised to hold a convention on 7 March 1559 in Edinburgh, where 'she would send for the nobilitie and estates of the realme to advise for some Reformation in Religion'.[37] No record of a convocation exists for that date, although a council of the Catholic Church was held at around that time. At some point, however, decrees were sent out ordering the Catholic observance of Easter; Robert Lindsay of Pittscottie, a contemporary historian, wrote that the bishops issued a decree on 6 February, and George Buchanan asserted that Mary 'wrote also to the neighbouring assemblies, enjoining them to keep the Easter following after the popish manner. But the orders were generally disobeyed, at which she was soon enraged.'[38] This was not surprising; Mary might have been open to a religious settlement, but any settlement would be based on, and enforced through, her (and her daughter's) authority. As Stuart Carroll has pointed out, this concern with authority and disobedience was also at the heart of Guise reactions in the early phase of the religious wars in France.[39] Her decree regarding the Catholic observance of Easter was not necessarily a hardline imposition of Catholicism, but rather an attempt to set the boundaries pending a more permanent settlement. Disobeying her decree was not then a religious issue, but a matter of sedition: it was for rebellion, not heresy, that she summoned the preachers to Stirling on 10 May, and, when they refused to submit, outlawed them.[40] While she may not have been willing to include altering the Eucharist as part of a religious settlement, or at least was not willing to tolerate changes to the sacraments without permission, the co-existence of two forms of sacraments appears not to have caused any unrest within Dundee, at least as far as the burgh records reveal.

When it became clear, however, that Mary of Guise was serious about enforcing the Easter edict, the Dundonians chose the route of open defiance and accompanied the preachers to their gathering point at Perth, just as they had with Friar Dik in 1532. Once the majority of the town, or at least of the council, opted for Calvinism it was inevitable that Catholicism would be purged from the burgh, as happened in other places once the Calvinists gained political control.[41] At some point between 25 April, when the whole council appointed sir John Dene to a chaplainry, and 5 May, when John Knox arrived to find 'the kirk of Dundie reformed', the town did convert to Protestantism, with Protestant preaching, sacraments and the elimination of 'idolatrie'.[42] While there is no evidence available to tell if this was the act of the whole community or merely a determined minority, from then on the council remained largely united in supporting the Protestant cause. Dundee's reformation was not a Protestant coup, but was adopted by the existing, previously Catholic, town council. As in other places, Dundee likely contained a large number of people who were interested in new ideas but who would not commit until obliged to by events; once forced to decide by Mary of Guise, they chose Protestantism.[43]

From the gathering at Perth the Protestant laird John Erskine of Dun went on to Stirling, where negotiations with Mary of Guise failed. On 10 May she outlawed the preachers, which would prove to be the beginning of the Protestant rebellion. In Perth itself Protestant reforms seem to have been introduced over the winter of 1558–9, and the refusal of the provost to enforce the Catholic celebration of Easter was one of the provocations that had caused Mary of Guise to issue her summons. It was a sermon by Knox on 11 May that set off an iconoclastic riot, the first violent act in the open conflict between the Protestant Lords of the Congregation and the Catholic Mary of Guise.[44] If Perth's town council had acted earlier to suppress Catholicism, or Knox had been less vehement in his preaching, it is possible Scotland's Reformation may have been shaped by negotiation rather than war.

At Perth, the Dundonians were joined by their fellows from Ayr. Ayr reformed in the spring of 1559, banning masses and dismissing the chaplains in the burgh church.[45] John Willock preached publicly, and the Franciscans left peacefully on 14 May, while a delegation of townspeople marched to join the Lords of the Congregation at the end of the month. At the same time, the congregation of Dundee signed the political agreement made among Protestants known as the Second Band of the Congregation, which included the provision that they would 'destroy, and put away, all things that do dishonour to his name, so that God may be truly and purely worshipped'.[46] Though they may have at one time thought that a religious settlement under Mary of Guise was possible, from this point on the Dundonians were effectively fighting for their survival and for a complete Protestant Reformation.

Reformation from Without: Stirling

Stirling, along with towns such as St Andrews, Linlithgow and Edinburgh, was violently reformed by outside forces from the Lords of the Congregation.[47] Though there is no evidence that most townspeople desired this change they quickly adopted it and established a Protestant congregation. The new religion had a bumpy start, as Stirling's central strategic location meant that both sides sought to hold it during the conflict of 1559–60, and periods of occupation by forces loyal to Mary of Guise alternated with those of the Congregation. Though this instability may have disrupted any initial momentum the reformers had, it did not ultimately stop them and their sympathisers in the town. As the conflict began to peter out, the townspeople, and especially their leadership on the town council, quickly started to build a Protestant civic church.

Stirling's Reformation began abruptly when the Earl of Argyll and Lord James Stewart, leading a detachment of the army of the Lords of the Congregation, came to the burgh in late June 1559. Their aim was to pre-empt Mary of Guise from stationing soldiers there, which would have prevented the Protestants from crossing into southern and western Scotland.[48] On their arrival they subsequently 'purged religious places from monuments of idolatry' in Stirling and the surrounding region. Buchanan and Pittscottie emphasised that their primary targets were the friaries and secondly 'the other churches in and about the city'. As in other towns the friaries were seen as the main site of potential Catholic resistance. Although the Lords of the Congregation also dealt with the parish church, the fact that it was a secondary target suggests that they were less concerned about the civic church as a focal point for the defence of traditional religion. Once the friaries, isolated from the civic church, had been neutralised, then the civic church could be dealt with more leisurely. Conversely, this might run the risk that the inhabitants would have time to organise a defence of their own church, but presumably the presence of an armed force and the demonstration of violence against the friaries would be enough to dampen opposition. Possibly also the attack on the friars bought time for discussion and arrangements between the Protestant leadership and the town council. The Congregation stayed two or three days and then moved on to Linlithgow, which was similarly reformed.[49] It is likely that during the two or three days they were in Stirling they appointed preachers and established a Protestant church, but only the anonymous author of 'A Historie of the Estate of Scotland', an Edinburgh-based contemporary, says so clearly.[50] The initial priority seems to have been the destruction of the Catholic Church rather than the establishment of a Protestant one, and so it may have been left to the townspeople to sort themselves out.

The town of Stirling would change hands repeatedly over the following year.[51] The Congregation gathered there several times in autumn 1559, using it as a base for their campaigns around Edinburgh, finally leaving in December just before French soldiers arrived to reoccupy it. The French remained until the end of March 1560, at one point gathering as many as 1,200 soldiers prior to their march into Fife. Buchanan claims that the French pillaged the town, and indeed during the spring of 1561 the burgh court was still resolving cases concerning goods taken by the French. The small number of these cases suggests that the damage was nowhere near the scale experienced by Dundee and Haddington in the 1540s, yet the events were still frustrating and likely even terrifying for the inhabitants. In one incident fourteen French soldiers entered the house of Helen Smith, took her goods, including hides and skins, and 'wald not lat hir enter in hir awin houss again'.[52] The French forces left at the end of March 1560, having repulsed an attempt by the Congregation to take the town around 26 March.[53]

In the midst of this turmoil the townspeople bided their time until they could establish a Protestant congregation. In early September 1559, Knox included Stirling in his list of towns where congregations had been established and sacraments administered, which likely means that there was a session, a reader and at least occasional visits by a minister.[54] This Protestant congregation went into hibernation during the French occupation, but re-emerged at Easter 1560, two weeks after the French soldiers left, when Thomas Duncanson took up his duties as reader.[55] It is not known if Catholic services were restored during the French occupation. Once Protestantism was established, not everyone in the burgh immediately converted. Three months later, on 8 July 1560, in a burgh court case concerning a claim to the revenues of St Michael's altar, a litigant tried to have his opponent's claim thrown out of court as 'he hes nocht as yot recantit his auld traditionis'.[56] The case demonstrated that the townspeople were paying close attention to who among their neighbours attended the new Protestant services. Though the town, and country, were rapidly moving in a Protestant direction and at least one person felt (or hoped) that those who had not yet adopted Protestantism should be deprived of legal rights, in the early months it seems that people were not yet conforming out of duress or feeling obliged to follow the dominant religious practice of the burgh. The continued uncertainty about the new order was even evident in the appointment of Thomas Duncanson as reader on 14 October, backdated to April, as the council specified that his appointment was 'quhill ordour be put thereto be the lordis' leaving themselves room to manoeuvre in the event of future changes.[57]

Stirling's town council cooperated with the establishment of a Protestant civic church, though the Reformation coincided with a turnover of the councillors. While there is little evidence of active Protestant sympathies in Stirling during the 1550s, the period around 1560 saw a noticeable change in the composition of Stirling's burgh council, as a generation of experienced councillors was suddenly replaced by new men. Though we do not know enough about the religious sympathies of these men to conclusively demonstrate that the changes occurred for religious reasons, the circumstantial evidence is suggestive. Two thirds of the men who had been most involved in council affairs during the late 1550s and who might have been expected to serve several further terms stopped participating in the period around 1560, a higher than expected turnover. In their place new men quickly obtained senior positions as bailies or deans of guild.[58] Given that the case of John Bethok indicates that the inhabitants were aware of each others' religious positions, and that a January 1561 slander case lumped together both elders and magistrates, it is plausible that the period around 1560 saw the departure of Catholic sympathisers from council and their replacement by men, who if not necessarily militant Protestants, were willing to work with and develop an enthusiasm for the new order.

The provostship also changed hands during the initial Reformation period. Stirling's provosts were an important link between the burgh and the region's major landholders. The provost from 1559 to 1562 was James Stirling of Keir. Also prominent in burgh affairs, serving as provost before and after Stirling's turn, was John Forrester of Craginelt, who was part of the entourage of the Sixth Lord Erskine, later Earl of Mar. The Erskine family had important landholdings in the Stirling area based on their seat at nearby Alloa, and were the keepers of Stirling Castle. The Sixth Earl was one of those interested in Protestantism during the 1550s, meeting with Knox in 1555 and attaching his name to the 1557 letter to the preacher. He remained neutral during the war of 1559–60, and while there is no evidence of his promoting Protestantism in the burgh of Stirling, surely prominent men in the area, such as John Forrester and James Stirling, would have known of his interest and taken their cues accordingly.[59]

Stirling's path in this period was likely similar to those of St Andrews and Edinburgh. There is stronger evidence for Protestant activists or sympathisers in those two burghs prior to 1559, though they had not succeeded in influencing the town councils to start reforming the burghs. Edinburgh, like Stirling, would have been closely watched by Mary of Guise and her administration, and St Andrews was the headquarters of the Scottish Catholic Church, so their burgh councils would have been unable to start internal reforms without attracting attention, even if they had wished to do so. Like Stirling, once the Reformation was imposed by outsiders, local sympathisers came to the fore and supporters of Catholicism were subject to intimidation and forms of disenfranchisement, though there is no evidence of violence to persons.

In St Andrews, the Lords of the Congregation, including Lord James Stewart and the Earl of Argyll (who were also responsible for reforming Stirling), as well as James Haliburton Provost of Dundee, and others, organised the reform of the town, which began with four days of preaching by Knox. This drove the Archbishop of St Andrews from the town, and the council and 'the commonalty for the most part' adopted the Reformation (how willingly, with the Lords of the Congregation occupying the burgh, is unknown). Catholic ornaments were removed from local churches and the friaries rapidly ruined or demolished – in the case of the Dominicans, within a week of the beginning of the burgh's reform.[60] A kirk session was established, and a concerted effort was made to convert the local population. Catholic priests were especially targeted: they were publicly summoned to convert, had revenues withheld, and at least one was imprisoned and eventually threatened with expulsion.[61] The burgh would remain in Protestant hands, though as Rhodes puts it, 'to contemporaries the permanence of this transition was not necessarily as obvious as it is with hindsight', especially as the regent's forces would make two attempts to recapture it.[62]

In Edinburgh, the Reformation went through several stages of Protestant and Catholic control; while there was an active Protestant faction within the town that launched an attack on the friaries in June 1559, it took outside intervention to establish a burgh Protestant church.[63] The first occupation of the Lords of the Congregation in July 1559 created a situation where both Catholic and Protestant preaching took place in the burgh at the same time. With the retreat of the Protestants in the autumn of 1559 Mary of Guise reimposed Catholicism, and it was only in April 1560 that Protestants regained control and imposed a radically Protestant town council who stopped paying chaplains in favour of ministers.[64]

Protestant sympathisers existed in all three places, and had these towns been less important to the government and Catholic leadership earlier reform efforts might have taken place, similarly to the first group of towns. As it stood Protestant sympathisers in these burghs were not strong enough to attempt reformation on their own, but were eager to take over with outside help. Once they had been established in power, they moved confidently to drive out Catholicism and build a Protestant civic church, though there was significant foot-dragging by unconvinced inhabitants.[65]

Late Reformation from Within: Haddington

The Reformation in Haddington and other towns in the third group contrasts starkly to Dundee and Stirling's, as the townspeople expressed no interest in religious change and stayed out of the Wars of the Congregation. East Lothian in general was quiet, as the confrontations, iconoclasm and fighting of 1559–60 mostly took place in other regions of Scotland. Though the English army passed nearby on their way to join the Lords of the Congregation, there is no evidence of forced iconoclasm in the town. Any local Protestant adherents, such as David Forrest, seem to have left to join the Lords of the Congregation rather than staying to reform the burgh.[66] This does not necessarily mean that there was a strong attachment to the traditional religion, however, neither is there obvious evidence of resistance to Protestantism. After 1560, the town cooperated with the Protestant regime and hired a minister and reader and dismantled some of the physical and administrative structure of the Catholic civic church, though with far less gusto than the other two towns. The Reformation process in Haddington thus represents a process that took place in many Scottish towns, such as Peebles, Elgin and Inverness, where moves to establish a Protestant church only took place after the Reformation Parliament of 1560.[67]

The uneventful transition to Protestantism in Haddington was helped by the stability of the town council. During the period of crisis, from October 1558 to October 1561, the town council was dominated by a small group of eleven men. They were a very experienced group of town councillors; eight had served at least four times already, with Thomas Dikson and John Ayton having served thirteen and ten times respectively. Three men had already served as bailie, three as provost, and John Ayton had held both positions. Only James Ayton had not served as a councillor before 1558, though he had served as deacon of the bakers. They were also fairly wealthy; eight of them had or would contribute financially to the town, though the group was a mixture of craftsmen and merchants.[68] Nothing in these men's biographies suggests that they held particularly strong religious opinions. Haddington's reaction to the crisis was to ensure unity and continuity by entrusting town government to a group of experienced councillors who continued the town's trend of uncontroversial government.[69]

The full implementation of the new religion in Haddington and other similar towns was slower than in Dundee and Stirling. It is not known when Catholic masses ended and Protestant services began in Haddington but in June 1560 there is a reference to payment being made on the high altar of the parish church.[70] This does not prove that mass was still being said, but it does indicate that the church had not yet been 'cleansed' by Protestants. As Bardgett points out about Inverness, it is possible that Haddington's actions were at least partly motivated by the desire to avoid outside attention and interference with burgh affairs, and that they therefore introduced reform measures slowly, avoiding internal disruption and perhaps keeping their options open in case the national Protestant movement would be reversed, but avoiding outright refusal or resistance.[71] Haddington's experience during the Reformation was also likely similar to that of Peebles, a border town that had also been hard-hit during the fighting of the 1540s. Through the summer of 1559, Peebles's town council continued to make appointments to the Catholic civic church as normal, with the assumption that young men could still be ordained as priests. In March 1560, they prohibited 'John Wallace als appostat' from preaching or using the common prayers, and sent a delegation to join the regent's army. It was only in the autumn of 1560, after the Reformation Parliament, that Peebles and Haddington introduced Protestant reforms to their burghs.[72]

Reluctant Reformation: Aberdeen

Aberdeen, which has the reputation of being the most religiously conservative burgh in Scotland, still shares many characteristics with other towns which reformed slowly from within.[73] The burgh had local leadership which was both traditional in its own beliefs and reluctant to offend the local magnate, the firmly Catholic Earl of Huntly.[74] The combination of tight control over burgh politics by the conservative Menzies family, the nearby presence of the Earl of Huntly, and the clergy gathered around the bishop, cathedral and university hindered a swift implementation of the Reformation, and some Catholics, former clergy and teachers at the University as well as ordinary people, continued to live undisturbed in Aberdeen into the 1570s, especially in the heavily clerical Old Aberdeen.[75] An attempted Protestant takeover in January 1560, featuring both outsider Protestants from further south and a local Protestant in the person of the council's treasurer, was rebuffed politically as the provost and town council ultimately retained control. As elsewhere, the Protestant force inflicted the worst damage on the friaries, and did succeed in removing all ornamentation from the interior of the parish church. Unlike in other burghs however, there was recorded resistance from townspeople which prevented further structural damage to the church, and the intervention of Huntly similarly prevented extensive damage to St Machar's cathedral, and the Principal, students and staff of the university defended their chapel.[76] The council did nonetheless make the same reforms as other towns, even preceding the Parliament of 1560, such as the dismissal of the choristers in 1559 and the granting of a salary to a preacher in 1560.[77] A kirk session was appointed in 1562 (just before the visit of the heavily Protestant Privy Council), but the council kept tight control over both it and the minister, in doing so further establishing its authority over discipline, as did other burghs.[78] As Nicholas White puts it, in terms that could apply to many Scottish towns, 'The inhabitants of Aberdeen found that they had exchanged one jurisdiction for a sterner and tighter form of discipline. The Reformation increased the power of the council, rather than diminished it.'[79] The kirk session throughout the 1560s issued decrees aimed at protecting the Sabbath and obliging attendance at preaching, as did Dundee's town council. As in Dundee, these laws had to be adjusted and re-issued as compliance was neither immediate nor total.[80]

What Aberdeen reveals is that even though the burgh contained clearly identifiable groups which remained either devoutly Catholic or at least unconverted, there too the structure of the Reformed church was implemented in a manner similar to the other burghs that were reformed from the outside, or slowly from within. Aberdeen had the noble support, town council factions, and motivated clergy to resist the Reformation – and indeed all three groups did resist Protestant iconoclasts in January 1560 – but still acquiesced in the Reformation nonetheless, and even abandoned their own choristers before any significant pressure was applied. The well-kept burgh records and researchers who studied them have demonstrated that a fair number of Catholic sympathisers lived in the town, but while it may have been a slightly lighter and more gradual approach to Protestantism than elsewhere, the broad outlines of the Reformation in Aberdeen were not so different than in many other Scottish towns. Better placed than anywhere else to offer a strong resistance to Protestantism, the Aberdonians declined to do so, the traditionalists on council orchestrating, at most, a passive recusancy.

Conclusion

Three widespread types of Reformation thus existed in Scotland's towns. First, in some towns, far enough from the close attention of the central government, Protestant preachers were able to establish factions of supporters, who eventually persuaded the town council to introduce elements of Protestantism and to start to eliminate Catholicism. After a period of religious co-existence, the Reformation process was accelerated when the towns had to pick sides in a national conflict and acted to suppress Catholicism. Second, other towns were forcibly reformed from outside, but a combination of Protestant sympathisers and weak attachment to Catholicism created the conditions for town councils to continue implementing Protestantism once the Lords of the Congregation departed. Third, in burghs which had neither strong internal Protestant factions nor outside intervention, there were no moves to reform until the autumn of 1560. As the following chapter will demonstrate, the third group of burghs also eventually actively participated in the introduction of Protestantism, their town councils maintaining control of civic religion through the Reformation process. In all towns, Protestantism was implemented without significant interpersonal violence. In a few cases this might be due to overwhelming Protestant military strength on the spot, but in many place the religious changes occurred without direct intimidation. Many Scottish townspeople may not have been eager Protestants, but nor were they willing to spill blood, either their own or others', to defend their Catholic ornaments, statues or masses.

Notes

1. Sanderson, *Ayrshire*; Verschuur, *Politics or Religion?*
2. Lynch, *Edinburgh*; Dawson, 'The face of Ane Perfyt Reformed Kirk'; McCallum, *Reforming the Scottish Parish*.
3. Frank D. Bardgett, 'The Reformation in Moray: precursors and initiation', *Journal of Scottish Historical Studies* 41 (2021): 1–37.
4. McLennan, 'The Reformation in the Burgh of Aberdeen'; White, 'The Menzies Era'; Lynch *et al.*, 'The faith of the people'.
5. Benedict, *Christ's Churches*, 16; see also Gordon, *The Swiss Reformation*, 53–67, 91, 111–12; Eire, *The War Against the Idols*, 63–4.
6. Benedict, 'Dynamics', 41, 47–8; *L'organisation et l'action*, Benedict and Fornerod, viii.
7. *TA*, 10:373. Given that the Justice-General was the openly Protestant Earl of Argyll, this would have been an interesting encounter. Most likely however the case would have been handled by a deputy. Jane E. A. Dawson, 'Campbell, Archibald, fourth earl of Argyll (1498–1558), magnate', *ODNB* 2004 (accessed 26 September 2020).
8. 'A Historie of the Estate of Scotland from July 1558 to April 1560', in *Miscellany of the Wodrow Society I*, ed. D. Laing (Edinburgh, 1844), 53–4. The author starts their narrative of the Reformation with this incident, evidently feeling it was the first of an important sequence of events. Buchanan, *History of Scotland*, 2:395.
9. Buchanan, *History of Scotland*, 2:396; Spottiswood, *History*, 266.
10. Buchanan, *History of Scotland*, 2:396; Pittscottie, *The historie and cronicles*, 2:138; Calderwood, *History*, 1:347.
11. DCA BHCB 1558–61, f41; DCA Head Court Laws, f5–6.
12. In 1564 acts would be passed by the Privy Council against bordellos and adulterers. *RPC*, 1:295–8. McIntosh points out that in England local concerns were often aroused before Acts of Parliament were passed. Marjorie McIntosh, *Controlling Misbehavior in England, 1370–1600* (Cambridge, 1998), 40.
13. DCA BHCB 1550–4, f328–328v.
14. DCA BHCB 1550–4, 59, 146, 155v, 156v; DCA BHCB 1558–61, 40v, 51, 64, 73; Michel Mollat, *Le commerce maritime normand à la fin du Moyen Âge: étude d'histoire économique et sociale* (Paris, 1952), 158, 508. My thanks to Philip Benedict for this reference.
15. Guillaume Daval and Jean Daval, *Histoire de la Réformation à Dieppe 1557–1657*, ed. Émile Lesens (Rouen, 1878–9), 7–12.
16. *Statutes of the Scottish Church*, 186; Pitcairn, *Ancient Criminal Trials*, 2:406–7.
17. Philip Benedict and Nicholas Fornerod, 'Les 2150 Églises réformées de France de 1561-2', *Revue Historique* CCCXI (2009): 548. Even after the Reformation this continued to be the case; McCallum, *Reforming the Scottish Parish*, 17–22.
18. DCA BHCB 1558–61, f61, 63v. The relationship between the composition of the elders and the town council would certainly merit further study, although the lack of sixteenth-century kirk session minutes for our towns makes it impossible in this case.
19. Knox, *Works*, 1:300.
20. Eire, *The War Against the Idols*, chap. 4; Denis Crouzet, *La genèse de la Réforme française* (Paris, 1996), 572–3; Marnef, *Antwerp in the Age of Reformation*, 89;

Conner, *Huguenot Heartland*, 24; Judith Pollmann, *Catholic Identity and the Revolt of the Netherlands 1520–1635* (Oxford, 2011), 108–110.
21. Knox, *Works*, 1:301.
22. DCA BHCB 1558–61, f28v; Knox, 'Letter to Anna Locke, 23 June 1559', *Works*, 6:27.
23. DCA BHCB 1558–61, f30.
24. DCA Baxter Craft Lockit Book, f14, 16.
25. DCA BHCB 1558–61, f42. A similar arrangement was made in St Andrews in May 1557. Rhodes, *Riches and Reform*, 64.
26. DCA BHCB 1558–61, f71.
27. For a more positive view of Haliburton's influence, see Flett, 'The Conflict of the Reformation and Democracy', 70.
28. DCA BHCB 1558–61, f25.
29. DCA BHCB 1550–4, f3v, 32, 39v, 40v, 42–42v, 81v, 84, 92v, 134v, 205v, 239, 244v.
30. In Edinburgh, during the summer of 1559 there was both Protestant preaching in St Giles' and Catholic mass being held in Holyrood. Lynch, *Edinburgh*, 76.
31. Sanderson, *Ayrshire*, 90; *The Perth kirk session books, 1577–1590*, ed. Margo Todd (Woodbridge, 2012), 19–23; Verschuur, *Politics or Religion?*, 72–111.
32. 'A Historie of the Estate of Scotland', 53–6; Buchanan, *History of Scotland*, 1:395–7; Pittscottie, *The historie and cronicles of Scotland*, 2:136–8.
33. Ryrie, 'Reform without frontiers', 54; Ritchie, *Mary of Guise*, 198, 201–4; Stuart Carroll, *Martyrs and Murderers: The Guise Family and the makings of Europe* (Oxford, 2009), 37, 119–20, 128–59.
34. *RCRBS*, 514, 518, 519, 521, 522, 526; *TA*, 6:376, 377; 7:74, 77, 78, 79; *Privy Seal*, 2:403, 407, 408; DCA TC/CC 1/54.
35. My thanks to Roger Mason for indicating this point.
36. Knox, *Works*, 1:306; Ryrie, 'Reform without frontiers', 41.
37. 'A Historie of the Estate of Scotland', 55.
38. Buchanan, *History of Scotland*, 2:398; Knox, *Works*, 1:315–16.
39. Carroll, *Martyrs and Murderers*, 14–15, 19, 45.
40. Pitcairn, *Ancient Criminal Trials*, 1:406–7; Buchanan, *History of Scotland*, 2:398; the extent to which the confrontation was also about who had the social status to negotiate religious change was evident in the instructions of the bishops, as recorded by Pittscottie, to not listen to the 'new preaching and doctrine of soutteris tailzeouris skynneris baksteris'. Pittscottie, *The historie and cronicles of Scotland*, 2:142. This explanation fits Carroll's argument that Guise policy during the late 1550s and 1560, in France as well as Scotland, was to distinguish between those who used religion as a means of sedition, who must be crushed, from those who merely wished to worship differently, who were to be tolerated so long as they behaved. Carroll, *Martyrs and Murderers*, 109. Note, however, that Sir James Melville, a Scottish member of the household of the Constable of France, the Duke de Montmorency, a rival to the Guise, blames them for the crackdown and the eventual loss of Scotland. He claims that at the signing of the treaty, Cardinal Lorraine sent to Mary of Guise instructions that in accordance with the first article of the Treaty of Cateau-Cambrésis, the Pope, the Emperor, the kings of Spain and France, should join together 'to reduce again the most part of Europe to the Roman Catholik religion, and to pursue and punish with fire and sword all heretiks who would not condescend to the same, desiring the Queen

Regent to do the same in Scotland'. Despite Mary's reluctance to challenge the Protestant lords who otherwise supported her, 'the instructions which Bettancourt brought to her, and to Monsieur d'Osel in Scotland for the Kings of France, were so strict, and mixed with some threatenings, that she determined to follow them' commanding the observance of Catholic Easter, even showing the letter to Protestant lords to convince them to comply. Sir James Melville of Halhill, *Memoirs of his own life* (London: Chapman and Dodd, 1922). It is possible that Mary did indeed use these instructions to put pressure on the Protestant-leaning nobles. However, her actions at the time are more consistent with an attempt to impose a political settlement rather than to suppress heresy. There were no attempts, for example, to prosecute suspected Protestants in areas under her control.

41. *L'organisation et l'action*, Benedict and Fornerod, vii; Eire, *The War Against the Idols*, chap. 4.
42. Knox, 'Letter to Anna Locke, 23 June 1559', *Works* 6:22.
43. Note Marnef's findings that there existed in Antwerp 'a broad, religious middle group, which could lean, under the pressure of events, one way or another'. Marnef, *Antwerp in the Age of Reformation*, xi, 56–8, 97; Marnef, 'Dynamics', 53.
44. *The Perth kirk session books*, 19–23; Verschuur, *Politics or Religion?*, 100–1.
45. Sanderson, *Ayrshire*, 97–9.
46. Knox, *Works*, 1:344.
47. Rhodes, *Riches and Reform*, 97–8; Dawson, 'The Face of Ane Perfyt Reformed Kyrk'; Lynch, *Edinburgh*, 76–9; *A History of the Estate of Scotland*, 61–2.
48. Knox, *Works*, 1:362.
49. Calderwood, *History*, 474; Buchanan, *History of Scotland*, 1:403; Pittscottie, *The historie and cronicles*, 2:159.
50. 'A Historie of the Estate of Scotland', 61.
51. *CSP*, 281; see also Elizabeth Elsie Brain, 'John Erskine, earl of Mar: advocate of the middle way, 1548–72', unpublished MA Thesis, McGill University, 1965.
52. Buchanan, *History of Scotland*, 1:408; SCA SBCB 1560-4 25/4/15/1.
53. 'A Historie of the Estate of Scotland', 67, 72, 3, 75; *CSP*, 263, 266, 272, 300, 302, 313, 340, 343; *Scottish Correspondence*, 424; Pittscottie, *The historie and cronicles*, 2:168.
54. Knox, 'Knox to Anna Locke, 2 September 1559', *Works*, 6:78.
55. *Extracts . . . Stirling*, 74.
56. SCA SBCB 1560-4 8/7/1560; *Extracts . . . Stirling*, 73.
57. *Extracts . . . Stirling*, 74.
58. Timothy Slonosky, 'Burgh Government and Reformation: Stirling, c.1530–1565', in *Scotland's Long Reformation: New Perspectives on Scottish Religion, c.1500–c.1660*, ed. John McCallum (Leiden, 2016), 58–60, 62–7.
59. Henry Summerson, 'John Erskine, Seventeenth or first Earl of Mar', *ODNB* (accessed 17 March 2022); Slonosky, 'Burgh Government', 61.
60. Rhodes, *Riches and Reform*, 101–2.
61. Dawson, 'The Face of Ane Perfyt Reformed Kyrk', 413–19.
62. Rhodes, *Riches and Reform*, 97–8.
63. Lynch, *Edinburgh*, chap. five.
64. Lynch, *Edinburgh*, 76–9.
65. Lynch, *Edinburgh*, 108; Michael F. Graham, *The Uses of Reform: 'godly discipline' and popular behaviour in Scotland and beyond, 1560–1610* (New York, 1996), 55–6;

The Register of the minister, elders and deacons of the Christian congregation of St Andrews, 2 vols, ed. David Hay Fleming (Edinburgh, 1889–90), 1:36.

66. HAD/2/1/2/1, f20v; though the presence of French soldiers in 1558–9 may have forced caution on any local adherents.
67. It is possible that in Inverness, like Stirling, a pro-Protestant group came to dominate the council in 1560, and was then reinforced with the appointment of a provost with a connection to Lord James Stewart. Bardgett, 'The Reformation in Moray', 23, 31; *Charters . . . Peebles*, 263, 264–8, 268–9.
68. Thomas Dikson guaranteed Archibald Borthwick's service in 1533, while James Ayton received twenty pounds from the profits of the parish clerkship and was responsible for recovering the silver chalice owned, and presumably hidden, by the baker craft. Several of the men took a turn collecting with the kirkboard. Others were involved in routine disputes with clerics; Thomas Punton, for example, went to arbitration with a chaplain of Preston over the rent owed by his tenement following the burning of the town. After the Reformation, John Ayton, John Douglas mason, James Oliphant and William Gibson would all rent parts of the friars' lands, though taking advantage of the opportunity does not necessarily imply that they supported the Reformation for material gain. Alex Barnis and Thomas Punton had been found guilty of assuring and assisting with the English during the occupation of Haddington, though there is no evidence that they were religiously motivated. HAD/4/6/73, f3–6; HAD/4/2/3/1, f110; *Privy Seal*, 4:131, 332.
69. Even John Ayton stayed out of trouble during this period.
70. HAD/4/1/5, f277v.
71. Bardgett, 'The Reformation in Moray', 31.
72. *Charters . . . Peebles*, 255–6, 258, 260, 263–4, 268–9.
73. McLennan, 'The Reformation in the Burgh of Aberdeen', 144; White, 'The Menzies Era', 230; Lynch *et al.*, 'The faith of the people', 294.
74. White, 'The Menzies Era', 228.
75. McLennan, 'The Reformation in the Burgh of Aberdeen', 133, 137–9; White, 'The Menzies Era', 230.
76. McLennan, 'The Reformation in the Burgh of Aberdeen', 136.
77. McLennan, 'The Reformation in the Burgh of Aberdeen', 134, 136.
78. Lynch *et al.*, 'The faith of the people', 294.
79. White, 'The Menzies Era', 231; Lynch *et al.*, 'The faith of the people', 294.
80. McLennan, 'The Reformation in the Burgh of Aberdeen', 141.

CHAPTER NINE

Creating Protestant Towns: 1560–1565

Once Protestantism had been introduced to Scotland's towns, either from within or without, the councils took on the responsibility of thoroughly reforming their civic churches. Some burghs started these changes as early as spring 1559, as seen in the previous chapter, while others waited until after the Parliament of August 1560 banned Catholicism and adopted the Scots Confession. No matter when and how they reformed, the burghs took similar actions to turn their towns into Protestant societies. Town councils advanced the Protestant reformation in three different ways: firstly by participating in the struggle for a national reformation, dispatching both contingents to the Protestant army and delegates to Parliament and General Assemblies of the church; secondly by converting the burgh's civic church to Protestantism and suppressing Catholic institutions that were not part of the civic church; and thirdly by legislating and enforcing social discipline on the townspeople to create a godly town. By participating in some or all of these aspects on their own initiative, Scotland's towns helped drive the Reformation process. In doing so they maintained control over their civic churches and even used the Reformation to make desired changes. The motives for their enthusiasm were mixed – there was certainly an eagerness to apply revenues and resources tied up in supporting Catholic clergy and worship for other burgh projects. Fear and intimidation played a role, as burghs wished to avoid violence at the hands of Protestant forces and to preserve communal harmony. The desire to create a more godly society, though, was real, as demonstrated by the attempts to recruit and pay ministers and to introduce stricter standards of individual behaviour in the burghs. The diligence and promptness with which many towns implemented these measures demonstrate that the Reformation tapped into already existing desires for general social reform.

Participation in the National Reformation

Of our three towns, only Dundee fully participated in the national reformation process, though it was joined by other towns such as Perth and Ayr. Once Dundee's councillors had fully embraced Protestantism at the beginning of May 1559, the summer of that year was spent reforming the burgh's civic church and fighting in the war to implement the Reformation throughout Scotland.[1] The Dundonians were strongly motivated to secure a national reformation because doing so would protect them from prosecution for their indisputable support of Protestantism. Many prominent Dundonians therefore spent a good deal of time outside the burgh as they served with the Lords of the Congregation, the army composed of Protestant nobles and townspeople.

After the initial confrontation in May between Mary of Guise and the Lords of the Congregation in Perth, the Dundonians may have been involved in the iconoclasm which took place in St Andrews and other Fife towns.[2] In the meantime, Mary of Guise gathered troops to confront the Congregation, and the two sides met outside Cupar, armed and drawn up in battle array. The Dundonians were led by their provost, James Haliburton, who had proved an able military leader in the war of 1547–50, and along with contingents from St Andrews and Cupar were deployed behind the horsemen and gentry. The confrontation ended peacefully after Mary's French commanders agreed to withdraw.[3] A contingent of Dundonians then returned to Perth, where between 24 and 26 June they participated in the sacking of the Abbey of Scone. Provost Haliburton, his brother Captain Alexander Haliburton, and John Knox all apparently tried to halt the violence, which exceeded the bounds of accepted iconoclastic destruction, but eventually it was the Earl of Argyll and Lord James Stewart who succeeded in calming the crowd.[4] The sacking was resumed the next day however, after a Dundonian was killed by one of the abbey guards.[5] Even though the Dundonian was the victim, the incident still demonstrates something of the confrontational attitude of the townspeople, who were determined to remove Catholic ornaments from other burghs as well.[6] It is possible that they were more aggressive with outside institutions than they would have been with their own burgh churches.

The town council was fully behind these efforts. While pausing in Dundee to reorganise in between these expeditions, on 21 June 1559 the bailies 'with the most part of council deacons and community' borrowed £500 from William Carmichael, David Ramsay and James Fletcher for the 'defence of the liberty of their conscience and of their own common will'.[7] The phrasing, recorded amongst the routine entries of the burgh court book rather than in a propagandistic piece of rhetoric, gives a hint of the passions aroused. The council clearly acknowledged that this was a religious conflict, and asserted their right to make their own religious decisions. William Carmichael, along with George Lovell and George Rollok (II) were identified by Knox as associates, and George Lovell would also contribute financially to the Lords of the Congregation.[8] The formulation 'the most part' indicates that this was not a unanimous decision, though it is unclear if that demonstrates the existence of a Catholic opposition. If so, it was not a decisive player in burgh affairs. Dundee's council had clearly chosen sides in the war and was actively involved in helping to organise the military effort of the Lords of the Congregation, as was Ayr, and much as French Protestant towns and congregations would become part of the Huguenot military effort in the French Wars of Religion.[9]

The Dundonians continued to participate in the conflict and in the establishment of the national Protestant Church that followed. Later in the summer, Provost Haliburton and some of the Dundonians were involved in the fighting around Leith, and again in the occupation of Edinburgh in October 1559.[10] George Lovell, the Protestant bailie, was reportedly hurt during that campaign.[11] In the autumn Broughty Castle was taken by the Congregation, though it would turn out to be less strategically important than during the war of 1547–50.[12] By the early summer of 1560, Mary of Guise had died and an English army had arrived to reinforce the Congregation. Giving up on their investment of the previous decades (and as it turned out, centuries), the French signed the Treaty of Edinburgh and withdrew from Scotland. The Lords of the Congregation seized their moment and at the Reformation Parliament of 1560 imposed a Protestant Church across the country.

The burghs continued to play a role in national religious politics after the fighting ended. Dundee, Stirling, Haddington and eighteen other towns sent commissioners to the Reformation Parliament of 1560.[13] Burghs, especially those in the south and west, also dispatched representatives to the meetings of the Protestant kirk's governing body, the General Assembly. Dundee sent a particularly strong delegation on 13 December 1561 when seven men, mostly prominent councillors, accompanied the minister William Christeson to Edinburgh for a disputation with the 'papists'. This debate was likely part of the December 1561 General Assembly of the kirk, and the delegates were granted twenty-one pounds in expenses for the trip.[14] Two years later, sixteen burghs were represented at the 1563 General Assembly. Eleven sent at least one burgess, the rest being represented by nearby lairds.[15] Given the usually hands-off approach by Scottish burghs to political questions which did not directly affect them, the diligent attendance and size of the delegations is a strong indication of the townspeople's confidence in their religious position, their authority to express it, and their desire to shape the national Reformation.[16]

Reforming the Civic Church

The disruption caused by the Reformation created an opportunity for the burghs to reform their own civic structures, enacting changes at least some of which had probably been mooted for some time. The towns all moved quickly to reform their own civic churches, hiring and funding ministers and readers, dismantling friaries, redirecting the income that supported the Catholic civic church to new projects, and renewing their commitment to poor relief and other communal support. The burghs were united in their enthusiasm for these transformational works, though the available evidence shows that they had slightly different priorities.

Just as they had with many of the burgh's Catholic chaplains, the town councils hired and paid the Protestant ministers and readers, though they received recommendations from the leaders of the Protestant movement. Though it took some time for ministers to be appointed to all Scottish parishes, the burghs were among the first posts filled, and the men chosen were of a high quality whom the councils were eager to welcome and support. In Dundee, the formal appointments happened as early as 7 July 1559 when, in the presence of Provost Haliburton and many of the deacons, the council promised Master John Young, chaplain of the Song School and reader in the Congregation, twenty pounds annually.[17] Readers were to recite prayers and scripture passages, but could not preach or perform sacraments, and Master Young was to do so while Paul Methven, the minister, was otherwise occupied. A month later, on 4 August, they specified that he was to receive the revenues of St John's chaplainry, presumably as a contribution towards the twenty pounds.[18] At the same meeting the bailie George Lovell was commanded to provide Methven with 'necessary furnishings' while he was in the parish, paid out of the tolbooth revenues. Methven, however, soon went on to become minister at Jedburgh. His replacement William Christison was appointed by the Lords of the Congregation in July 1560, and on 24 September 1561 the council agreed to pay him 250 merks annually.[19] Christison had been a friar, but then spent time in Scandinavia where he associated with Protestants. He had returned to Scotland in March 1558.[20]

In Stirling, the establishment of a Calvinist church continued at a steady pace once the French withdrew for good in spring 1560. The new council elected in October 1560 confirmed Thomas Duncanson as reader and granted him a salary of forty merks, comparable to the better benefices of the pre-Reformation clergy. Two weeks later the council provided a house for the minister John Duncanson (relation unknown).[21] The minister would become a fairly prominent member of burgh society, as demonstrated in February 1562 when he became guarantor to James Archibald for money owed to the Queen.[22] A kirk session was established, perhaps more than once between the summers of 1559 and 1560, and cooperated with the town council. In one January 1561 case included in the burgh records, four men appeared before the elders and confessed firstly to slandering the elders and magistrates, and secondly to blaspheming the name of God. In this early stage of establishing their authority, it is noteworthy that the elders prioritised criticism of themselves over blasphemy. It is possible that the men's offences were minor, for they were let off with a promise to not repeat their actions; should they reoffend they would be corrected by the elders and minister.[23] The inclusion of this case in the burgh court books is an indication that during the early years of the Reformation, in Stirling as in other burghs, the division of responsibilities between the council and the kirk session was still being worked out.

Haddington and other towns which reformed after the Parliament of 1560 were not immediate priorities when it came to assigning ministers. The sincere desire of these towns to obtain a minister was demonstrated by

Peebles, which banned Protestant preaching as late as 3 March 1560, but sent representatives to the Lords of the Congregation on 20 November 1560 and then again on 20 December to request that a minister be appointed to them.[24] One trip would have sufficed to demonstrate compliance: two, a month apart, suggests real urgency. In Haddington the first appointment was the reader, Walter Balcanquhall, who was to read the common prayers in the morning on Sundays, Wednesdays and Fridays.[25] The eminently qualified Patrick Cokburn was appointed minister in 1562, still earlier than in many parishes.[26] He had long-standing connections to the burgh, having been appointed chaplain of the Trinity altar in 1531, though by that time he may have already been in Paris where he was a professor of Oriental languages.[27] He was present in the burgh in 1537, when he witnessed the apology of sir Mungo Millar to sir John Tait.[28] He then acquired the patronage of Lord James Stewart, commendator of St Andrews priory, which owned the vicarage of St Mary's church, and accompanied him to France in 1548.[29] Lord James granted him a pension of fifty pounds a year from the kirk of Leuchars, and likely arranged for his later appointment as minister to Haddington.[30] It is unclear when he developed Protestant sympathies, whether it was as far back as his student days during the 1520s at St Leonard's college in St Andrews or during his service with James Stewart. He was later considered for the superintendency of Jedburgh, before dying in 1568.[31]

Haddington filled other positions more gradually. The role of the parish clerk had been suspended at the Reformation, but William Wilson, who had originally been appointed parish clerk in 1533 alongside Archibald Borthwick, appeared before the town council in March 1567 saying that 'now since all Clerkships are restored to their offices, with such additions as accords to religion at this present' he was willing to serve in a Protestant manner, to 'minister in the parish church with water at baptism' as well as cleaning the kirk and opening it at appropriate times. In return he requested permission to resume collecting twelve pennies a year from 'each fine house' in the town, as he had done from 1533 until the time that the 'Imitation of Religion' had been introduced. The council agreed to let him resume collecting his twelve pennies, throwing in forty shillings for keeping the kirk clean and adding the conditions that he sing the psalms on Sunday and serve as chanter.[32] Wilson's use of the expression 'Imitation of Religion' demonstrates that, seven years after the Reformation, he was far from a convinced Protestant, although financial necessity meant that he was willing to take on the tasks in a Protestant manner. Similarly, the council was willing to overlook his grumpiness about the new religion and keep him employed, likely at a barely subsistence level. In this case neighbourly obligations proved more important in Haddington than religious allegiance.

An obvious move for many of the burghs was to take over the friaries which had always been outside the civic church. The towns were enthusiastic about taking over the friars' revenues and properties, which was easiest in the towns where militant Protestants drove the friars out at the very beginning of the Reformation, and more awkward and complicated in the towns where the councils had to evict the orders themselves. All the burghs eventually did so nonetheless, renting out the lands and absorbing the revenue into their general funds, and either taking over the friars' buildings for their own use or dismantling them for new projects.

As the Reformation began, some congregations of friars, rightly worried about the threat posed by militant Protestants, transferred ownership of their buildings and lands to town councils or other hopefully sympathetic figures. These transfers were often by feu charters which granted ownership or use to the new possessor under specific terms, which could include provisions for the friars to reclaim or even remain in their convents. The dates when the transfers were made shows how threatened the various groups of friars were by Protestant reformers in their region. In St Andrews for example, the Franciscans acted quickly, just after the iconoclasm in Perth, and granted their property to the burgh in May 1559. In Inverness, the friars placed their ornaments in the safekeeping of the town council.[33] In Haddington, the friars only felt the need to make protective arrangements in October 1559.[34] In practice, the careful provisions the friars made to retain some rights turned out to be futile, though the towns did eventually respect the requirement to pay them a pension of sixteen pounds a year.

In Dundee, the Reformation came too quickly for the friars to prepare, and their properties were likely seized by the burgh in early May, at about the same time as Ayr's friars left their convent.[35] In August 1559, the friars' tenants testified to the burgh court about rents they paid to the Dominicans, which would be paid to the town from then on, with the burgh treasurer becoming responsible for collecting the rents formerly owed to the orders. At the same meeting, the council auctioned off the crops growing on the Franciscan lands for twenty-two pounds.[36] In October 1560, with the Reformation an established fact, Dundee's town council moved to physically obliterate the friaries and nearby abbeys. As part of a civic rebuilding project they assigned the stones of the Dominicans to a new bulwark to be built in the harbour, the stones from the Franciscan friary to a new building for the butchers, and the timber from Lindores Abbey to a new tolbooth.[37] The same month they rented the Dominican lands to Thomas Thomson, mason, for a period of three years, for nine merks and ten pounds, and they sold the stones and lime from the Dominican kirk and the Franciscan Sisters' walls for a total of 143 merks and ten shillings.[38] In December 1560, the council instructed James Lovell, treasurer, to take down the stones of the kirk and steeple of the Franciscans, which were to be applied to the common good of the burgh. By the beginning of 1561 the process of dismantling the physical structures of the religious orders, buildings which had not been under the burgh's control prior to the Reformation and which served as a base for the Catholic hierarchy in the town, was well underway.[39]

In Stirling, the town council was not able to benefit from the dissolution to the same extent, as the Dominicans feued a significant parcel of lands and rights to Alexander Erskine, brother of John Lord Erskine. The agreement, dated May 1560, was likely confirmation of a deal which had been struck earlier.[40] This transaction is another indication of the loose bonds between the friars and the burgh of Stirling, as in Haddington and elsewhere the friars made their deals with the burghs. In Stirling, they preferred to deal with a local magnate. The town did take over some land belonging to the Franciscans, and in April 1561 the council authorised the treasurer to pay for a pair of archery butts to be built there.[41]

The calm atmosphere in Haddington is demonstrated by the fact that it was not until the autumn of 1559 that the Franciscan friars took steps to avoid the fate of their colleagues elsewhere in Scotland, feuing their lands, gardens, buildings, dovecots and church to the town council on 8 and 9 October.[42] The contract specified the 'favour and help' provided by the town council in the friars' hour of need, during 'this present [calumny] urged against religious orders and ecclesiastics in this kingdom'.[43] It is not specified what the friars received in return for giving up their buildings and lands. A notarial charter of 11 October 1559, confirmed on 18 April 1560, included a provision that they would be able to take up their possessions again when 'they are permitted to live in the habit and under the rule of the Conventual friars as they have heretofore done'.[44] The process was fairly leisurely even though the friars must have known for some time that they were being targeted by the Protestants, given that the seizures of friaries elsewhere had begun in late spring 1559.[45] In Haddington, though the friaries were unmolested and able to cooperate with the town council to protect their interests, they do not seem to have been able to organise resistance to the Protestants. They may not have even attempted to do so. Instead, they meekly, if disgruntledly, accepted their fate. In Peebles, despite their similar loyalty to the old religion, in December 1560, almost as soon as Catholicism was abolished and Protestantism introduced, the town council politely but quite firmly took over the friars' kirk to use for Protestant preaching, the parish church having been destroyed during the wars of the 1540s.[46] Good cooperation with town councils delayed the friars' fates but did not change it.

Good relations notwithstanding, not even Haddington was going to ignore the revenue to be had, and by March 1561 had begun renting out the friars' lands, mostly to prominent men in the burgh, which brought in at least £10 16s 8d – and likely more, considering the revenue gained by Dundee.[47] Haddington, perhaps not convinced that the Reformation was permanent, was not as quick as Dundee or Stirling to physically dismantle the friary. The town council first acted to protect the buildings, legislating in October 1561 against the taking of stone from the friars' kirk and waiting until 1572 to decide to use the stones in the rebuilding of St Mary's.[48] Some of Haddington's former friars remained in the community. In July 1560, the former friar William Hepburn was found to have broken the lock on the door to the warden's chamber in the friary, which was now in the town's possession, though Hepburn evidently thought he still had some claim to it. Provost James Oliphant as a result demanded compensation from Hepburn.[49] Personal tensions cannot have been too strong, however, for the next month friar John Auchinlek, warden of the friary of Haddington, appointed Oliphant as his business agent.[50]

Haddington's council had a harder time gaining control over the revenues of the friars than the physical buildings. Despite the initial cordial relations, the council did eventually try to claim the revenues, which Auchinlek fiercely resisted. The council and he spent a decade tussling over the income. In March 1567, he obtained a letter of the Privy Seal awarding him a yearly pension of sixteen pounds from the rents of the friary, which had been granted to all friars, in addition to the six merks from Ralph Eglington's acres that the burgh had long paid to the friars, and a clothing allowance.[51] The burgh received the remainder of the revenues for sustaining a minister and a hospital for the poor, infirm and orphans.[52] The burgh would not gain full control over the friary accounts until 1572, when Auchinlek finally handed over the whole title and revenues to the burgh in exchange for twenty-two pounds annually, supposedly to be shared with the one remaining friar, Patrick Allen.[53] His obstinate defence of his privileges did not prevent his subsequent appointment as reader in nearby Athelstaneford, an indication that despite the conflicts over money he still seemed to be personally well-regarded in the region.[54] Readers, who were not required or allowed to preach about doctrine, were often recruited from the pre-Reformation clergy, especially from local religious orders.[55]

In all the burghs, even the less enthusiastic Haddington, the buildings and revenues of the friars were eagerly absorbed and put towards the common good of the burgh. Though the Protestants may have struck first and hardest at the friaries for tactical purposes, the towns gladly did their share to literally dismantle their presence. This acquisitive attitude did not necessarily extend to personal animosity towards the friars themselves.

The burghs also disposed of the parts of their burgh churches which had been used for Catholic worship. They sold off Catholic ornaments and asserted their rights to revenues which had been used to support the priests of the civic church. These items and properties had originally been granted by the towns and individual inhabitants, and the councils had few qualms about reappropriating and redirecting the wealth they represented, though as in all aspects of the Reformation process some acted more swiftly than others. The Catholic ritual equipment belonging to Dundee was very rapidly disposed of, as one would expect from committed Calvinists with wartime expenses to pay. In August 1559, the council sold twelve sets of vestments and ornaments used by the priests to John Fletchour for £125, on condition that he alter the vestments so that they could never be used in 'papistry' thereafter.[56] It may have been suspicions about the rapid dispersal of other church equipment that provoked Alexander Carnegy, on behalf of the craftsmen of the burgh, to complain on 10 October 1560 that common goods or plates of the burgh should not be sold privately but rather publicly auctioned for three days, as was custom.[57] Meanwhile, in November 1560, at the same time as the friaries were sold off, the council feued the kirk and kirkyard of St Clement's to George Lovell in exchange for twenty merks annually of feu mail and a promise to build a weigh-house.[58] Stirling's council also diverted some of the revenues and possessions of the civic church to new uses, though not as rapidly as their counterparts in Dundee. In April 1561 for example, the council ordered that the chalices of St James and St Peter's altars be sold for the price of twenty shillings an ounce, the funds to be spent on the repair of the street.[59] There is no surviving evidence to indicate what Haddington did with their Catholic ornaments and ritual equipment, though Peebles sold off their vestments in March 1562, the money going to the poor householders.[60]

The disposal of these items was unsentimental, with no recorded objections, but it was done carefully, with an eye to the value of the equipment and property and the ongoing physical needs of the burgh. Some of the items, such as the chalices, would have once had sacred status, while others, such as the kirkyards and stones from the friaries, were more mundane. Nonetheless, the pragmatic attitude of the councillors and community in disposing of these items and investing in burgh infrastructure was a sudden shift away from perceiving the burghs as a places in which the sacred might manifest itself in the ordinary world, and instead focusing more of the council's attention on physical infrastructure and creating a human community that would be physically prosperous, purged of idolatrous elements that might anger God, and better organised at providing Christian charity. No longer would common resources be spent on trying to bring the divine into the burgh – instead they would be spent on creating a society that might be spared disaster sent by God's wrath.

The church buildings themselves were of course part of the council's ongoing responsibilities for physical infrastructure, and Protestant or Catholic, were constantly in need of attention. On 10 December 1561, Dundee's council called for 'an honest godly and famous man and an most notable within this burgh' to be appointed kirkmaster. The council also continued to restore to the church the dignity it had lost during the wars, and ordered that the kirk gate and wall be put up again, the repairs begun after the English invasions continued, and that all stones, timber and waste in the kirkyard be removed. Fines of forty shillings were to be levied on those who stored timber, stones or malt in the kirkyard.[61] Stirling's council also continued to look after the physical space of their church, sorting out new rules about graves in the church, for example, though without the many different altars and ornaments to look after their responsibilities were somewhat simplified.[62] In Haddington the council continued to repair the damage caused by the fighting in the 1540s.[63]

Many of the legal obligations and financial structures of the old church remained, though the situation throughout Scotland was 'chaotic'.[64] As Bess Rhodes has shown, disputes about whether annuals and rents owed to clerics still had to be paid took place in St Andrews and throughout Scotland.[65] The councils insisted that agreements made by officials of the former church be upheld, along with payments due to the chaplains, though over time they appropriated most of the revenue for civic purposes. The rents owed to the burgh churches and friaries were exempted from the settlements of the Thirds of Benefices and theoretically went straight to the crown for use on schools and hospitals, but in practice the council still retained much of their authority over the distribution of the revenues.[66] Contracts which were registered with the Archbishop of St Andrews were still regarded as valid, as demonstrated on 13 December 1560 when Robert Barre produced in Dundee's burgh court 'ane cursing or sentence of the officials of St Andrews' as evidence in the case between him and John Walson in Newtyle.[67] The assumption of revenues belonging to the civic church was more gradual than the seizure of the friars' property. When vacancies opened up as the chaplains either died or moved away, the revenues were taken over by the burghs.[68] In May 1560, for example, David Davidson paid his rent, which was due to St Thomas's chaplainry, directly to Dundee's bailies who were the patrons of the altar.[69] Some of these revenues continued to be put towards the support of the now-Protestant church. In March 1562, two annual rents which had belonged to the choristers, worth twenty-five shillings and six pence, were assigned to James Blyth, the bellman, for his 'ordering of the kirk as use has been in times past'.[70] The council granted some annuals which had belonged to the Abbey of Scone to George Lovell to compensate him for the £120 he had loaned to the Lords of the Congregation.[71]

The burghs had to stand firm to ensure that the financial obligations owed to the old church continued to be respected, though in many cases the money no longer went to the clerics. With the end of the Catholic masses in the parish church, some tenants and feuers hoped to save the money that had previously gone to the chaplains. As part of his feu rent, John Waclie owed twenty-two pence annually to the chaplains of Stirling's parish church, and with the Reformation simply deducted it from his yearly feu rent of four pounds. The council was having none of it, and in July 1561 told him to pay the twenty-two pence to Walter Cowan and Jonet Tennand, who he had feued the property from.[72] David Barnage had similarly tried to avoid paying a two-shilling annual to the Cordiners' altar, arguing that the money was for the upkeep of the altar and was paid directly to the craft chaplain, not to the craft itself. Unfortunately for him, the cordiners provided documentation that the chaplain had received the annual on behalf of the craft, and David was obliged to resume paying the money to them.[73] His acceptance of this decision was quite reluctant however, for in October the council authorised the cordiner craft to seize six schillings' worth of goods from his land to make up his debt.[74] As elsewhere in Europe, the hope that the dismantling of the Catholic Church would lead to savings for the common people was thwarted, though at least some of the revenues in Scotland's burghs were directed to civic projects – 'the common good'.

The burgh councils often continued to protect the rights and respectability of the former clerics. Former priests were still respected in the community, retaining the title 'sir' and the designation of 'chaplain'. In March 1562, for example, 'sir Alexander Vye, chapellane' in Haddington provided testimony in a dispute between John Lyle and Thomas Millar.[75] The courts upheld their property rights, and the clergy appeared in burgh court to claim their rents as usual, though less frequently than during the peak years of the mid-1550s.[76] The councillors continued to support retired clergy: in Haddington, sir James Mauchlin was awarded a pension of six pounds in 1560 to supplement the four pounds annually he received for handing over his benefice to the council.[77] In December 1562, Dundee's cordiners agreed to supply their former chaplain, Robert Dunorand, with meat and drink for his lifetime.[78] Clerics also continued to engage in financial transactions as they had before. Sir John Tait, for example, rented out lands that belonged to him through personal inheritance.[79] In 1562, a new rental agreement between George Bruche and sir John Tait specified that as well as an annual rent of twenty-four shillings, sir John was to receive a new pair of shoes every year.[80] Such measures are absent from Stirling, however, where the council appeared less sympathetic to the former clergy. Their role as divine intercessors may have been eliminated, but the former Catholic clergy were still very much present and a part of the burgh communities. Though Dundee was most fervently Protestant, it was Stirling's town council that was most harsh towards the former Catholic clergy, possibly because the post-1560 town council was largely composed of new men, possibly akin to the radical Protestants who were part of the Kilspindie council in Edinburgh, who lacked the personal connections and sense of communal obligations that Dundee's councillors would have had.[81]

The post-Reformation disputes were not just about the status of property, but about the status of people as well. In 1564 Archibald Smyth appeared in Stirling's court and attempted to have the court rule that his brother, James Smyth, should not be allowed to inherit from their father as he had been a Dominican friar and when he had entered the convent he had 'grantit hym self deid of this warld'. The council, perhaps sympathetic to the fact that it was the world which had reclaimed James, refused Archibald's claim as well as his subsequent effort to have James disinherited because he had spent seven years in England.[82] Though Stirling council did not seem too concerned with preserving the clergy's ecclesiastical income, even there the magistrates recognised the right and need for former clergy to be able to claim personal property, perhaps ensuring that they would make no claim on the burgh for support.

Dundee's council had taken over church revenues as early as the summer of 1559, but as the 1560s progressed they were able to order the arrangements more formally.[83] In December 1565, the town council took a closer look at the altars in its patronage and drew up an inventory of the dues owed to the town.[84] In 1567, Queen Mary officially granted to the town control over many of the revenues owed to the Franciscans, Dominicans, Franciscan nuns and choristers of the burgh church. The town created a new position of collector of the Queen's donation to gather those incomes.[85] Thomas Ducher, who had continued to collect some rents for the choristers, transferred them to the town at that point in return for a lifetime pension of forty pounds. It is likely that this generous settlement was to be shared with other former choristers. Essentially the council replaced their role of managing the chaplains with direct administration of the revenues. This system was not necessarily any simpler, however, and as late as the nineteenth century the presbytery and town appealed to the Court of Session to sort out the revenues which were owing to the almshouse (hospital).[86]

Throughout the Reformation process, burgh councils moved to eliminate the physical infrastructure of Catholic worship and wipe out all traces of Catholic organisations that were not part of the civic church. The friars were chased out, their crops confiscated, and their buildings dismantled. The process was most swift and complete in Dundee and Stirling and other burghs that were reformed by militant Protestants, but Haddington and the other burghs in the third group were not too far behind. In contrast, the civic church was treated more moderately; the church physically altered for the new worship and the priests stripped of their sacred status but not of their position as members of the burgh community. The councils gradually took control of the revenues of the urban clergy, though they were not in a position to untangle all the legal and financial obligations owed to the old church immediately. In a time of uncertainty, when the future of the Reformation looked tenuous, the enthusiastically Protestant towns acted as quickly as they could to make a restoration of Catholicism impossible, while burghs such as Haddington moved only when the course of events became clear – though even then, it is important to remember how unsettled the 1560s would have appeared to contemporaries, and that more reluctance or resistance by these burghs would have shaped events differently. The swift change in theological allegiance by the burgh councils played an important role in undermining widespread adherence to Catholicism among Scotland's townspeople and in creating the conditions for the Protestant church to put down firm roots.

New Municipal Activism

The dismantling of Catholic institutions, the acquisition of new revenues, and the commitment to creating a new kind of godly society which was more concerned with communal responsibilities and less with individual good works also created the conditions for councils to become more active in looking after the poor. Poor relief had always been a communal concern under the supervision of the council, as demonstrated by the attention paid to the weekly kirkboard collections, but the halt to the funding of friaries, hospitals and almshouses as acts of religious charity led to new efforts to organise municipal institutions and poor relief. Stirling established a municipal almshouse under the supervision of the town's treasurer, which replaced the hospital which had been run as a religious foundation. Fines which previously would have been directed to the kirkwork were now directed to the hospital.[87] In Haddington, the town also took on a more active role in distributing welfare. Alms were not frequent entries in the surviving accounts from the 1550s, although six pounds was distributed to the poor in the almshouse in 1558.[88] Prior to November 1563, a regular alms collection at the church doors on Sunday was instituted, substituting for the kirkboard collections which would have been passed around inside the church. The council also decided how to distribute the alms, granting between five and ten shillings to five men, one woman and one boy.[89] Similar moves took place elsewhere. In Peebles, an inquest regretted in December 1560 that there was no money available to distribute to the poor, and hoped that the bailies would start a collection.[90] By the following June the council regularised the collection of charity and was preparing a mini-almshouse under the tolbooth to shelter the poor.[91] Kirk sessions also played a role in poor relief, as conclusively demonstrated by John McCallum, though the division of responsibilities between them and the burghs requires further study. In Inverness for example, it was the newly elected provost John Ross who ordered the deacons to collect alms, indicating that the town council regarded the kirk officials as part of the municipal government.[92]

The council also took steps to help the young and vulnerable in their community. A Dundee council meeting of 10 December 1561 concerned legal proceedings and recognised that 'the poor and their actions has in time bygone been frustrated and heavily hurt with cost and expense' which cost more than the sums at stake, and therefore ordered that the judges hear their cases first. This is reminiscent of the Catholic Church statutes from 1552 which condemned unjust legal actions, obstructive arguments and excessive delays, demonstrating that the need for reforms was apparent to all religious opinions, but that it was the energy unleashed by the Reformation which put renewed force behind these intentions.[93] A further act was made appointing two honest and godly men to visit the dying to make a testament to prevent their goods from being hidden from their children.[94] The councils continued to exercise authority over schoolmasters, and the bailie George Wishart was assigned to supervise Dundee's grammar school. When a new schoolmaster was hired in December 1560, the appointment was made by the bailies, councillors and craft deacons, with no evident participation by the minister or elders.[95] Haddington as always was a bit slower, and there by 1571 annuities that had belonged to the chaplains were diverted to support a schoolmaster.[96] In these measures, town councils used the opportunity provided by the Reformation to introduce new and better funded projects to benefit their whole communities and the most vulnerable among them. The town councils were ready to take on new responsibilities, and/or improve upon the tasks of the suppressed Catholic institutions.

Discipline: Creating an Orderly and Godly Burgh

The third area where the councils actively worked to advance the Protestant reformation and to create a new kind of godly community was in imposing stricter standards of behaviour on the laity. Discipline was an important feature of the Calvinist movement and in Scotland in particular it was one of the three marks of the true church, after preaching and administering sacraments.[97] The founding document of the new religion was *The Confession of Faith* (Scots Confession) adopted by the Scottish Parliament on 17 August 1560, although surely informal advice and directives also circulated through the country. *The Confession* discussed various aspects of belief, among them 'ecclesiastical discipline', the means 'whereby vice is repressed and virtue nourished'. Burgh officials were among those authorities charged with carrying out God's orders: 'they are the lieutenants of God' responsible 'to revenge and punish all open malefactors' and for the 'maintenance of the true religion and for the suppression of idolatry and superstition'. *The Confession* made specific mention of adulterers, drunkards and idolaters on the same level as murderers and thieves, demonstrating the utter abhorrence of the Calvinist reformers for these acts, and by listing them with existing crimes made them the responsibility of town councils. *The Confession* emphasises that such offences did not merely endanger the offender, but were the means by which 'God's hate and displeasure is kindled against the proud, unthankful world'.[98] Individuals who trusted in their own good works were guilty of idolatry; communities, however, must clamp down on sin to avoid God's anger.[99] With this mandate, it is no surprise that burgh governments felt able, or obliged, to extend their authority to new categories of misbehaviour. The speed and thoroughness with which they introduced and implemented the new measures shows than many urban magistrates did not need much persuading about this aspect of the new religion.

In our three burghs, the level of attention to discipline is clearly linked to their enthusiasm for the Reformation – it is a major pre-occupation of the burgh council in Dundee, somewhat important in Stirling, but was not of much concern in Haddington. Discipline has frequently been studied as a function of the ecclesiastical system, but the burgh records reveal that town councils also saw the imposition of religiously inspired disciplinary measures as their concern.[100] The burgh records show that from 1559 on Dundee's council took a much greater interest in behaviour than they had in previous years, especially Sabbath observance, adultery and fornication but also drunkenness and swearing. Though town councils had always been interested in disorder, the emphasis on protecting preaching and on sexual offences, largely absent from burgh legislation and court records until then, is a strong indication that this round of legislation was religiously inspired.[101] As Marjory McIntosh has pointed out for English towns, accompanying the emphasis on discipline was a fear of God's anger.[102] In Dundee and other Scottish towns which swiftly introduced disciplinary measures, this effort to curb sin quite likely was an attempt to assuage divine wrath and prevent a return to the disasters of the 1540s. It could be that it was this desire for tighter discipline that led people to the Calvinist variety of Protestantism, which bound clergy, magistrates and laity together in a common effort to create more godly towns than was possible in the late medieval Catholic, or even Lutheran, structure. A desire for stricter standards of public and private behaviour had been one of the concerns of the Swiss, German and French towns that opted for the Reformed variety of Protestantism, where measures against prostitution, taverns, card-playing, dancing and other perceived sins were among the first measures introduced by town councils when they reformed their churches.[103] Similar concerns in Dundee and throughout much of Scotland, either already simmering among the town's magistrates or stirred up by preachers, may explain why Calvinism took root more firmly than Lutheranism had in an earlier generation.

Dundee's council hurried to put these new measures into effect as soon as possible. At the Head Court meeting of 2 October 1559, when the Reformation had been established in Dundee but not yet secured across Scotland, the burgh passed a new set of laws which intensified the disciplinary structure introduced the previous January. The laws dealt with adultery, fornication (specifically, sex outside marriage), Sabbath observance and the respect due to the town council, minister and elders of the congregation. The adultery law required that any adulterer, man or woman, on their first offence be placed in the iron stocks for three hours, during 'the most notable time of day', after which they were to be taken to the shore and dunked in the sea three times, before being brought back to the market cross and formally banished from the burgh forever.[104] This was a much harsher penalty than that enacted by Parliament in 1552, which called only for obstinate offenders to be outlawed. The council would have the opportunity to put its act against adultery into action on 14 May 1560, when an assize found Agnes Bluk, the wife of David Park, and Nycolas Mason guilty of adultery, and ordered that 'the acts of the town maid anent [concerning] adulterers to be executed upon them both'.[105]

The second law passed by Dundee's council addressed fornication, for which first time offenders were to be punished and admonished by the preacher and then perform repentance in front of the whole congregation. For a second offence they were to stand for three hours in the stocks and then be dunked three times in the sea. A further offence was to be punished by perpetual banishment.[106] Any master who concealed their servant's fornication from the deacons or elders was to pay forty shillings to the burgh's common works. Other laws passed extended the acts against blaspheming the provost or bailies to cover the ministers, elders or deacons of the congregation, and specified penalties for misbehaviour in court. Merchants, craftsmen (in particular butchers) were to close on Sunday, which was 'to be kept in the meditation of god's word', and brewers and tavern keepers were not to sell ale or wine during the time of preaching on Sunday, all on pain of an eight-shillings fine.[107] The laws on protecting preaching and the ministers and elders were necessary to assert the authority of the new church but also to create the conditions for the new doctrine to be spread through the population.

In Stirling, just like in Dundee, the council took responsibility for enforcing religious discipline on the townspeople, especially in sexual matters. In June 1561, sir John Paterson, a former priest, agreed not to 'be found or taken with harloterie or whoredom' under pain of banishment from the town.[108] In September 1562, John Cameron from Kynnowll was found in adultery with Jonnet Gourlay, the wife of a burgess, who also happened to be the aunt of his own wife. Cameron promised to end his adultery, and 'to flee and abhor hir companye lik as he wald do the accumpanye of the evill spreitt'. Should he be found in adultery again, the magistrates wherever he be found were to be allowed to put 'him to the maist schamfull deid with all regour without merceye'. It is unknown what punishment was to fall to Jonnet Gourlay.[109] At the same time, Jonet Lyndsay of Cambus and her daughter Isabell Keir were said to have been involved in witchcraft; however, as no man would accuse them the burgh court was unable to pursue the case as vigorously as they would have liked. The two women were ordered not to be found in the town again, on pain of death.[110]

Evidence for these kinds of disciplinary efforts is absent from Haddington, but in other towns which adopted the Reformation only after the Parliament of 1560, disciplinary measures were among the first elements of Calvinism that were introduced. Peebles had firmly supported the old religion throughout the tumult of 1559 and the summer of 1560, but rapidly introduced Protestant disciplinary measures once Protestantism was established by the Parliament of 1560. In December 1560, an inquest ordered the bailies to go through the town to call on those guilty of 'public faults' 'to reforme thameseffis conforme to the law of God'. Those who disobeyed were to be punished in public, according to the practice followed in other burghs. Twenty-eight adulterers, fornicators/unmarried couples and blasphemers were brought before the court on 20 December, under orders to either abstain, or in the case of fornicators, marry. Those who were obstinate were carted to the market cross. Work on the Sabbath was banned.[111] Peebles demonstrates that a town that remained loyal to the traditional church as long as possible was nonetheless capable of adopting Protestantism quickly and enthusiastically once it became the law of the land, and it is striking how eager they were to start implementing increased disciplinary measures, especially concerning sexuality. In Inverness, burgh ordinances against adultery and fornication were introduced in February 1561, followed by more extensive measures in October 1562.[112] A late Reformation was not necessarily an unwelcome one, as town councils quickly saw the advantages of the Calvinist order.

Over the following months and years Dundee's council continued to refine its legislation, as the expansion of the burgh's jurisdiction over behaviour that was thought likely to offend God continued. Dundee's records from the period are the best organised of our burghs, with a register of legislation separate from the regular records of burgh business. The existing council records include very few disciplinary cases, suggesting that most cases were recorded in documents that are not extant, which might also be true for the other burghs. The continual adjustment of the laws and enforcement mechanisms shows that misbehaviour continued to vex the magistrates.[113] Repeated revisions of the laws suggest that it was easier to pass rules than to consistently enforce them.[114] The Head Court meeting held on 4 October 1560 added a penalty for blaspheming; offenders were to pay two shillings for a first fault or stand in the branks (a form of bridle used for punishment) for two hours if unable to pay, an alternative provision which suggests that swearing was perceived to be a problem among the lower orders. For a second offence, they were either to pay twenty shillings or to stand in the branks for six hours; a third offence was to be punished by banishment.[115] The same meeting amended the laws concerning adultery. On the one hand the bailies were reluctant to inflict the harsh punishment of banishment, but on the other some of those convicted were not as eager to repent as the council had hoped, and further sanctions were necessary to bring about a more satisfactory contrition. Those who were 'obstinate in repenting' were now to stand in the branks for six hours, and if that was not sufficient were to be dunked in the sea.[116] One surviving prosecution where a severe penalty was inflicted dates from 8 October 1560, shortly after the new laws were passed, when the court found Jonet Myln to be 'sometime the concubine of William Welscher' and ordered her banished from the burgh forever. As it was proven, somehow, that it was she who had sought out William, he escaped with being 'marked'.[117] Perhaps it was this couple whose obstinacy had aggravated the council.

As time went by, those convicted of fornication were still not demonstrating appropriate guilt, and so in January 1562 the town council ordered offenders to be imprisoned for two days before they made their repentance. Pregnant women, to spare them the danger of prison, were to be banished for a year and not readmitted to the town until they publicly repented.[118] In 1564, however, the Head Court meeting expressed frustration that pregnant women were getting off too easily – evidently, the immediate sentence of banishment, a harsh penalty in the circumstances, was not being imposed. The revised laws called for a woman who was caught 'of whatever estate that she be' to be brought to the market place to have her hair cut off and nailed to the cukstool, before she made public repentance in the kirk. For a second fault, the woman's hair was to be again cut off, then she was to be carried in a cart through the town, for which expense she was to pay two shillings, before being banished from the burgh for a year and day. Men were to be held in the steeple for forty-eight hours on bread and water, with the additional specification that no one was to keep the offender company except the burgh officers.[119] The constant adjustment of these laws indicates both the bailies' reluctance to actually impose severe punishments on their neighbours and a determination to come to grips with the problem nonetheless.

The council's mission to create a godly community was made explicit in their crackdown on drunkards in 1562, when they noted that 'we know to be the command of god that there shall not be any drunks and blasphemers of his holy name among his people'. Anyone found drunk in a 'drink-house' was to pay five merks for their first fault, the money to be distributed to the poor, ten merks for a second fault and ten pounds for a third.[120] If he or she continued in misbehaviour, they were to appear before an assize, which could banish them for a year and a day, receiving them back only with their open repentance. A drunkard without money was to spend two days and nights in the stocks for a first offence, four days and nights for a second, and for the third offence be placed in the thieves' hole, before facing an assize and the possibility of banishment.[121] Blasphemers 'of the holy name of god' were to be judged by an assize and face the same penalties as drunkards.[122] Not all drunkards were inhabitants of Dundee and outsiders were blamed for provoking whoredom and drawing people away from preaching and prayers 'to the great slander of religion'.[123] The council also ordered that sweeps for vagabonds be conducted four times a year. Those who housed vagabonds were to lose their freedom if they were burgesses and be banished from the burgh if they were not.[124] These regulations bring together both everyday social nuisances, threats to community cohesion, and acts which had no direct human victims but which might bring down God's displeasure on all. The theological concerns of the reformers, particularly about idolatry and disrespect for God, the exasperation of the inhabitants at bad behaviour, the need for improved care of the vulnerable, and fear of widespread catastrophe, all found possible solutions in the new order. The Reformation had created the opportunity for the councils to implement a social and religious programme which combined preventing offence to God, eliminating social nuisances, and looking after the poor.

Just as with adultery and fornication, the burgh courts could not always bring themselves to apply these harsh sentences and so the councillors continually adjusted their approach.[125] In April 1562, Andrew Monter and David Davidson, who seemed to be accustomed to hosting some raucous characters, were warned by Dundee's bailies who threatened banishment for a future offence.[126] The same threat was made against Robert Makkeltir and William Robertson, who confessed 'that they blasphemed god and his religion'.[127] The October 1564 Head Court meeting revised punishments to be less drastic but presumably more likely to be enforced, mandating that those who were caught swearing or blaspheming the name of God were to be immediately put in the stocks for one hour.[128] This approach to summary punishment proved popular, for in 1568 the laws were amended to include the provision that the officers of the burgh should be ready at all times to take 'command and charge' of drunkards and blasphemers from 'any honest man inhabitant of this burgh that apprehends' them and place them in ward in the tolbooth. Some Dundonians were evidently interested in curbing these behaviours among their neighbours, demonstrating that this concern for discipline was not just a top-down imposition and that there was some popular interest in enforcing collective standards.

Cooperation between Council and Kirk

Dundee's council explicitly sought to cooperate with the disciplinary structures of the new church. In October 1562, the Head Court passed an ordinance lending their support to ecclesiastical authority, adding to their previous acts (not found in the existing records) that a person who twice refused to appear before the session was to be placed in the steeple for twenty-four hours and not released until he found caution for the sum of ten pounds.[129] Some townspeople continued to avoid the authority of the session, and in February 1563 the penalties increased to twenty shillings for a first time appearance, which was to be given to the poor, and imprisonment for forty-eight hours, the offender only to be released on ten pounds security. Those without means were to be imprisoned for eight days on bread and water.

The council's continued concern for civic religion was also demonstrated by legislation protecting divine services. In January 1562, they ordered wine and ale sellers not to serve after nine at night or in the morning during prayers and preaching, nor during Sunday afternoon preaching, on penalty of being deprived of the right to sell ale or wine for a year.[130] By 1564 they had taken on the enforcement of attendance at Sunday services. The council commanded that anyone who stayed away from either the morning or afternoon preaching be admonished by the minister and assembly for the first three faults. For a fourth absence they were to pay a fine of twenty shillings or stand four hours in the stocks.[131] This ordinance proved to be perhaps too effective, and in 1567 it was decreed that women were not to bring any children under the age of five to the kirk, on penalty of eight shillings. By 1568, the town council had extended its interpretation of Sabbath keeping and ordered the town's gates to be closed on Saturday evening and not opened until Sunday afternoon. The same meeting ordered that those who disputed 'the good true religion and discipline in the kirk' face the penalties contained in the acts of Parliament and that those who heard these opinions to report them, on pain of being deprived of the freedom of the burgh.[132] Though the council was unwavering in its implementation of the Reformation and was supported by 'honest' men, not everyone was pleased by Protestantism or the new disciplinary measures. The evidence suggests, though, that opposition was limited to complaints and the council was not obliged to take action against actual militant Catholics. These rules imposed and enforced by Dundee's town council reflect both an interest in maintaining moral standards that they considered appropriate to a devout community, and a sense that there was a division between 'honest' Dundonians and their less-devout neighbours and outsiders.

The disciplinary offences prosecuted by the council overlapped with those addressed by kirk sessions. Extant Scottish kirk session records from the 1560s and 1570s were largely concerned with adultery and fornication, and occasionally blasphemy, disturbance of divine services and attachment to Catholicism.[133] It is likely that there were close ties between the sessions and councils, though the absence of kirk session records for the towns studied here means we cannot know who the elders were. In Edinburgh, it was infrequent for men to be members of the town council and session at the same time. They did sit on the session before or after their terms on council, and meetings were scheduled so that people might conveniently attend both.[134] In other Scottish towns there was a high degree of overlap between the town council and the kirk sessions, though admittedly the figures date from later periods.[135] In Dundee and Stirling the elders were clearly regarded as an arm of municipal government, due the same respect as the councillors. The councillors, for their part, seemed increasingly comfortable legislating against not just practices which disturbed the public but anything which might be against the godly order. This is similar to measures taken in French towns under firm Calvinist control, where the magistrates were considered to be one of the orders of the church and the Huguenots went to some effort to ensure that Protestants were elected or appointed to key positions.[136]

Though Dundee was undoubtedly a leader in implementing the Reformation, evidence from both other towns and kirk sessions indicates that similar processes were taking place throughout Scotland. Communities required little prompting to put these disciplinary measures in practice and to modify laws and practices to achieve the best results locally. The Scottish townspeople of the mid-sixteenth century were clearly predisposed to take the Calvinist concern for discipline and make it central to their urban communal culture.

Conclusion: Embracing the Opportunity for Reform

Scottish towns adopted the Reformation at different times and in response to different pressures, yet they all fairly quickly took on the task of reforming civic religion. The Reformation in Dundee took less than a year, from the imposition of new disciplinary measures in January 1559 to the selling of the burgh's Catholic ritual equipment that August. The ease with which the committed Protestants won over the whole burgh to the Reformation in late April and early May 1559 is partly explained by the fact that they and their less enthusiastically Protestant fellows had heard the same religious discussions, suffered through the same disasters, and probably shared the conviction that better behaviour was necessary to regain God's favour. Once the rupture with the central government made conflict inevitable, those who desired reform but were more moderate chose to stand with their neighbours rather than the undermined old religion and the external forces supporting it. It may have taken some time for the entire population to regard themselves as a Protestant nation, but the speed and ease of the Reformation of Dundee's council and civic church is due to the popularity or acceptance of the new ideas by a significant part of the population.

The Dundee town council continued to play a major role in civic religion after the Reformation. Before and after 1559–60 pleasing God was an essential part of their mandate, but they rapidly changed the focus of their concern. The new Protestant church, with a drastically reduced clergy and schedule of religious services, was undoubtedly easier to maintain and administer, and freed up the bailies' and councillors' time to expand their jurisdiction beyond business disputes and violence to acts more offensive to God than to their fellow inhabitants. In place of managing an extensive roster of chaplains and an elaborate infrastructure of churches, hospitals, chapels and altars intended to maximise divine services, the town council, in conjunction with the elders of the congregation, now focused on enforcing behaviour among the entire population. The same men who oversaw Catholic masses also supervised the Protestant, Calvinist disciplinary regime. The civic church remained, but its practices and theology changed.

The Protestant church in Stirling, though initially established by force from above, was swiftly adopted by the townspeople with little looking back. The town was quick to halt payments to the Catholic clergy, and no evidence survives of pensions or other forms of subsidies to the former priests, though they continued to own property. The councillors made arrangements to support the Protestant minister and reader, and worked with the session to impose stricter religious discipline on the townspeople. These measures were all administered, supported and even encouraged by the town council, which was made up of new men who may have had Protestant sympathies and who certainly felt little obligation or nostalgia towards the staff and structures of the old church. The example of Stirling demonstrates that those towns which were reformed by outsiders could still implement the religious changes with enthusiasm.

The Reformation process in Haddington and similar towns was longer and calmer than in Dundee and Stirling. The Haddingtonians were slow to give up Catholic practices and embrace Protestantism, and were not involved, on either side, in the Wars of the Congregation. The Earl of Bothwell, the local magnate, was on the regent's side but does not appear to have enlisted any support from the town.[137] The town's friaries were not sacked, but nor did the friars attempt to incite the population to resist Protestantism. The Haddingtonians clearly recognised that it was a time of crisis, as demonstrated by their retaining the same council for three years running, but as in the 1540s the greatest threats came from outside forces, not internal division. Perhaps because Haddington was a smaller burgh there was not the increased urgency for religious reform based around stricter standards of behaviour, though other similar towns adopted disciplinary measures fairly quickly. It appears, nonetheless, that while the townspeople were not enthusiastic about embracing Protestantism they were not so devoted to Catholicism as to feel inspired to defend it. The slower imposition may have helped ensure the establishment of Protestantism and dampened active resistance in the long run.[138] Doubts about Catholicism and the fear of God's wrath likely played a role in Haddington's orderly Reformation, but weariness, the desire to avoid conflict, and the necessity of preserving civic unity may have been more significant.

The Reformation's steady progress in Dundee, Stirling, Haddington and throughout much of Scotland, the willingness of the councillors supervising the civic church to change drastically their religious practices and introduce new disciplinary measures, and the absence of much resistance and complaint, can be explained at least partially by the events of the previous decades. Discussion of new religious ideas, and relations with Protestant trading partners on the Continent and England, prepared Scots, especially those who matured between 1540 and 1560, for the idea that different religious regimes were possible. These discussions would have slowly familiarised Scots with the idea that the late medieval Catholic religious practices, based heavily on masses to help avoid purgatory and to secure the intercession of saints, were perhaps misguided, or at least ineffective. The plague and wars of the 1540s planted in their minds the idea that contemporary religious practices were not pleasing God. Like many Christians before and after them, they may have concluded that their misfortunes were God's punishment for their sins, a sentiment reinforced by the Catholic clergy. They may have perceived the logical solution to be to place less emphasis on repeating masses, which were not having the desired effect, and more on individual faith and communal behaviour, especially offences which were disruptive to the whole community, such as extramarital sex and drunkenness. Attachment to the established Catholicism was therefore loosened, but the church and urban clergy were nonetheless not rejected or held in contempt by the majority of the townspeople. They were however, rejected by Protestant activists inspired by the Genevan example, who had no patience for even civic Catholicism.

Town councils and national politicians alike, therefore, spent much of the 1550s trying to establish a settlement which could incorporate new practices without disturbing established worship too much. When the effort was derailed by Mary of Guise's attempt to re-establish her authority over religious affairs, Protestants seized the opportunity to establish a completely new doctrinal regime, which the burghs either supported or accepted. In the burghs, the priests may have been replaced by a minister and the many masses for the dead by kirk sessions, but it was still the councillors who were responsible for supervising the civic church. All three burghs eagerly took over property belonging to the friars, and redirected the revenues that were already part of the civic church. Establishing the Protestant church would have been impossible without local cooperation, cooperation which came because the Reformation provided an opportunity for towns to achieve some of their own goals.

It was the Protestant nobles and lairds who won the war and changed the national religion at the Parliament of 1560, but it was the townspeople and magistrates who actually implemented the Reformation and ensured Protestantism's success at the local level. It was their actions, consistent across burghs in different situations, that gave the initial Protestant victory its staying power, and led to the transformation of Scottish urban society.

Notes

1. For accounts of the war, see Ryrie, *The Origins*, 161–3; Dawson, *Scotland Re-formed*, 204–12.
2. Knox, 'Letter to Anna Locke, 23 June 1559', *Works*, 6:25; Dawson, *Scotland Re-formed*, 205.
3. Spottiswood, *History*, 277; Knox, *Works*, 1:351–2; 6:25–6; Calderwood, *History*, 1:459–65.
4. It is hard to know how much of the efforts of the Protestant leadership was a desire to keep political control and prevent the common people from seizing the initiative, and how much was about the value of the seized ornaments.
5. Knox, *Works*, 1:360–1. See Eire for a discussion of how Reformation leaders inspired religious violence but avoided taking direct responsibility. Eire, *The War Against the Idols*, 74.
6. It is impossible to know whether this destruction was purely religiously motivated or if the Dundonians were hoping for an opportunity for plunder.
7. DCA BHCB 1558–61, f73v.
8. Knox, 'Letter to Anna Locke, 23 June 1559', *Works*, 6:27; DCA BHCB 1561–2, f12v.
9. Sanderson, *Ayrshire*, 99; *L'organisation et l'action*, Benedict and Fornerod, liv, lxxxiv; Conner, *Huguenot Heartland*, 149.

10. Buchanan, *History of Scotland*, 2:407; Calderwood, *History*, 1:549; Spottiswood, *History*, 305.
11. Calderwood, *History*, 1:552.
12. St Andrews Castle was taken at about the same time, suggesting that the Lords of the Congregation were shoring up their seaward defences against French intervention. Calderwood, *History*, 1:524–8; Rhodes, *Riches and Reform*, 102.
13. *RPS*, A1560/8/1 (accessed 12 November 2013); Peter G. B. McNeill, Hector L. MacQueen and Anona May Lyons, *Atlas of Scottish History to 1707* (Edinburgh, 1996), 130.
14. DCA BHCB 1561–2, f37; Knox, *Works*, 2:294.
15. Gordon Donaldson, 'The General Assembly of 1563', in Gordon Donaldson, *Scottish Church History* (Edinburgh, 1985), 116–17.
16. MacDonald, *The Burghs and Parliament in Scotland*, 102; in France Huguenot consistories became involved in regional, if not national, military and political planning and organising. *L'organisation et l'action*, Benedict and Fornerod, lvi.
17. DCA BHCB 1558–61, f74v.
18. DCA BHCB 1558–61, f75v.
19. DCA Laws, f18.
20. Richard L. Greaves, 'Christison, William (d. 1599)', in *ODNB* (accessed 14 November 2013).
21. *Extracts . . . Stirling*, 74, 75.
22. SCA SBCB 1560–4 20/2/1562.
23. *Extracts . . . Stirling*, 77.
24. *Charters . . . Peebles*, 258, 263, 268.
25. Forbes Gray, *Short History*, 32–3.
26. For Fife, see McCallum, *Reforming the Scottish Parish*, 11–12.
27. Hew Scott, *Fasti ecclesiæ Scoticanæ: The succession of ministers in the Church of Scotland from the reformation*, 11 vols (Edinburgh, 1915–), 1:368; Anderson, *Early records*, 116, 222; HAD/4/1/2, f22v.
28. HAD/4/1/2, f95v.
29. Scott, *Fasti ecclesiæ Scoticanæ*, 1:368.
30. Scott, *Fasti ecclesiæ Scoticanæ*, 1:368.
31. Scott, *Fasti ecclesiæ Scoticanæ*, 1:368.
32. Marshall, *Ruin and Restoration*, 23–4.
33. Bardgett, 'The Reformation in Moray', 18–19.
34. HAD/4/1/5, f253v.
35. Sanderson, *Ayrshire*, 96.
36. DCA BHCB 1558–61, f72v, f76.
37. DCA BHCB 1558–61, f134v, 135v.
38. DCA BHCB 1558–61, f146v, f148.
39. Rhodes, *Riches and Reform*, 122.
40. The lands included the burgh mill and St Mihillis hill, the Friar's croft, the Balbowis croft, the Brown yard and mill outside Stirling, fishing rights on the Forth, and the lands called Halbuke outside Stirling. SCA B66/1/4 Protocol Book of Robert Ramsay 1556–63, f119–119b; *Privy Seal*, 5:180.
41. *Extracts . . . Stirling*, 78.
42. HAD/4/1/5, f253v.
43. Bryce believes that their lands were originally feued on 10 October 1555, in a document now lost but included in a list of charters handed over to the burgh

on 21 April 1574. This, he holds, was part of a general strategy of the Scottish Conventuals, who feued their friaries throughout Scotland. There survives a charter from 15 October 1555, when the friars feued a parcel of land to Thomas Dykest, though one feu charter unfortunately cannot tell much about a trend. HAD/4/1/5, 110v, f253v. See HAD 1/16 Haddington Charters, for a charter issued 9 October 1559, and a charter issued 11 October 1559. Forbes Gray, *Short History*, 32–3; Bryce, *Scottish Grey Friars*, 1:150, 178, 187.
44. Translation Bryce. Original rendered as 'ad vinendum sub habitu et regula conventualem fratum prout hactennis vixbenit', HAD 1/16 Haddington Charters; HAD/4/1/5, f269.
45. Lynch, *Edinburgh*, 75.
46. *Charters . . . Peebles*, 263.
47. John Ayton, James Oliphant, Walter Gibson, George Crag; HAD/2/1/2/1, f27.
48. Marshall, *Ruin and Restoration*, 26.
49. HAD/4/1/5, f278v.
50. HAD/4/1/5, f279.
51. *Privy Seal*, 5:2:325.
52. *RGS*, 4:443. St Andrews received a similar grant at the same time. Rhodes, *Riches and Reform*, 123.
53. Bryce, *Scottish Grey Friars*, 1:189.
54. Bryce, *Scottish Grey Friars*, 1:190.
55. McCallum, *Reforming the Scottish Parish*, 87–8; Sanderson, *Scottish Curates*, xxviii–xxxii.
56. DCA BHCB 1558–61, f76v.
57. DCA BHCB 1558–61, f132v.
58. DCA BHCB 1558–61, f145.
59. *Extracts . . . Stirling*, 78.
60. *Charters . . . Peebles*, 277.
61. DCA Laws, f20.
62. *Extracts . . . Stirling*, 80.
63. HAD/2/1/2/1, f31v.
64. Rhodes, *Riches and Reform*, 119.
65. Rhodes, *Riches and Reform*, 116, 137.
66. Rhodes, *Riches and Reform*, 120; *RPC*, 1:201–3.
67. DCA BHCB 1558–61, f165.
68. Rhodes demonstrates that in St Andrews, the Lords of the Congregation used the seizure of clerical incomes to force the clergy to convert. Rhodes, *Riches and Reform*, 102–3.
69. DCA BHCB 1558–61, f92v.
70. DCA BHCB 1561–2, f108v.
71. DCA BHCB 1561–2, f12v.
72. SCA SBCB 1560–4 14/7/1561.
73. SCA SBCB 1560–4 28/7/1561.
74. SCA SBCB 1560–4 20/10/1561.
75. HAD/4/2/3/2, f218.
76. HAD/4/2/3/2, f278; HAD/2/1/2/1, f35v.
77. HAD/2/1/2/1, f24v, f18.
78. DCA BHCB 1562–3, f29v.
79. HAD/4/2/3/2 f255v, 257, 274v.

80. HAD/4/2/3/2, f225v.
81. Lynch, *Edinburgh*, chap. 5.
82. *Extracts . . . Stirling*, 82; SCA SBCB 1560-4 24/11/1564.
83. See Rhodes, *Riches and Reform*, 119-36, for an excellent discussion of this process in St Andrews.
84. James Froster, John Fothringham, Robert Kyd and Alex Carnegie. Warden, *Burgh Laws*, 31.
85. DCA Head Court Laws, f46, f50; DCA BHCB 1561-2, f42; *Charters, Writs and Public Documents of Dundee*, 41, 42-3, 55-85; Rhodes, *Riches and Reform*, 124.
86. *Charters, Writs and Public Documents of Dundee*, 233-5.
87. *Extracts . . . Stirling*, 81. See also John McCallum, 'Nurseries of the poor: hospitals and almshouses in early modern Scotland', *Journal of Social History* 48 (2014): 435, 440. He suggests that the hospital and almshouse may have continued as separate institutions, or were re-founded at some point, as by the turn of the seventeenth century both the town council and session had a role in administering the hospital.
88. Paton, 'Books of the Common Good', 57.
89. HAD/2/1/2/1, f35.
90. *Charters . . . Peebles*, 263.
91. *Charters . . . Peebles*, 272-3.
92. For the activities of a kirk session during the 1560s, see McCallum's discussion of the poor relief organised by the Canongate kirk session. McCallum, *Poor Relief*, 54; Bardgett, 'The Reformation in Moray', 23.
93. *Statutes of the Scottish Church*, 128-130, 182-3.
94. DCA Laws, f23.
95. DCA BHCB 1561-2, f173.
96. Marshall, *Ruin and Restoration*, 25.
97. Donaldson, *Scottish Reformation*, 78-9; Graham, *The Uses of Reform*, 38-40; Benedict, *Christ's Churches*.
98. *RPS*, A1560/8/3 (accessed 13 July 2010).
99. See also Graham, *The Uses of Reform*, 42.
100. Graham, *The Uses of Reform*, 1-3, 51-64; Todd, *The Culture of Protestantism*, esp. 29-44, 128-80. For the example of Geneva, see William G. Naphy, *Calvin and the Consolidation of the Genevan Reformation*, 2nd edn (Louisville, 2003), 32, 41.
101. The idea of the reformation of manners, by which elites used the disciplinary emphasis of Protestantism to impose stricter social control over the population, was classically developed by Wrightson and Levine in their study of Terling, and has been echoed by Scottish historians. Keith Wrightson and David Levine, *Poverty and Piety in an English Village: Terling, 1525-1700* (New York, 1979); Lynch *et al.*, 'The faith of the people', 295; Graham, *The Uses of Reform*, 343. McCallum, on the other hand, indicates that discipline in the early Protestant kirk 'was not an attempt to control any particular group of offenders; rather it was an attempt to uphold biblical standards of church government and behavior as far as possible', a position this study supports: McCallum, *Reforming the Scottish Parish*, 220. Graham has pointed out that sexual matters were a focus of many kirk sessions between 1560 and 1580, and speculates that it was an effort to reduce the burden unwed mothers placed on the community. Though this could very well be the case, the burgh records

offer no specific evidence that unwed mothers were a particular problem. Graham, *The Uses of Reform*, 69, 95,100–1, 112, 119, 125, 129.
102. McIntosh, *Controlling Misbehavior in England*, 205.
103. Benedict, *Christ's Churches*, 13–14, 25, 32, 44; Naphy, *Genevan Reformation*, 30.
104. DCA Laws, f6.
105. DCA BHCB 1558–61, f84v.
106. DCA Laws, f6.
107. DCA Laws, f12.
108. SCA SBCB 1560–4 17/6/1561.
109. *Extracts . . . Stirling*, 80.
110. *Extracts . . . Stirling*, 80.
111. *Charters . . . Peebles*, 268–9.
112. Bardgett, 'The Reformation in Moray', 24–5.
113. In 1556–7, for example, there is only one recorded case of violence and one of injurious speech. The busiest year, 1560–1, had six cases of violence, three of injurious speech and one of adultery. These numbers of offences are no justification for the constant introduction of legislation and adjustment of existing laws, and many cases must have been recorded elsewhere.
114. See Graham, *The Uses of Reform*, 44.
115. DCA Laws, f16.
116. DCA Laws, f17.
117. DCA BHCB 1558–61, f131.
118. DCA Laws, f26.
119. DCA Laws, f39.
120. DCA Laws, f26.
121. DCA Laws, f26–7.
122. DCA Laws, f27–8.
123. DCA Laws, f53.
124. DCA Laws, f22.
125. See also Graham, *The Uses of Reform*, 49.
126. DCA BHCB 1561–2, f140.
127. DCA BHCB 1561–2, f160.
128. DCA Laws, f39.
129. DCA Laws, f31.
130. DCA Laws, f28.
131. DCA Laws, f39.
132. DCA Laws, f55; possibly a reference to the Act passed in December 1567, banning the mass, on pain of death for the third offence, specifying that those who denied the religion were not to be included in the kirk or receive any ecclesiastical revenues. *RPS* 1567/12/4 (accessed 27 July 2012). This could also be a reference to Queen Mary's decree of 30 May 1562, forbidding any alteration to the state of religion that existed on her arrival in the country, on pain of death. *RPC*, 1:208–9.
133. *The Perth kirk session books*, 108, 183–4; *The Register . . . of St Andrews*.
134. Lynch, *Edinburgh*, 40–2.
135. McCallum, *Reforming the Scottish Parish*, 161–5; Graham, *The Uses of Reform*, 80, 95.
136. The synod of the Dauphiné, for example, held that the magistrates were to uphold peace and public tranquility, promote a public order conforming to

Scripture and the glory of God, and to punish heretics, schismatics and those who defy church discipline: *L'organisation et l'action*, Benedict and Fornerod, lxii. Similar rules were put in place across Huguenot-controlled France: 'Actes du synode du Haut-Languedoc', 40; 'Reglement Général des États Protestants du Dauphiné', 264–5, 267; 'Discipline de L'Église de Saint-Lo', all in *L'organization et l'action*, 300, 307; Conner, *Huguenot Heartland*, 52, 64, 70–83, 118. See also Naphy, *Genevan Reformation*, chapter 7, for the electoral takeover of Geneva's town council system by Calvinists.
137. Gordon Donaldson, *All the Queen's Men* (New York, 1983), 43.
138. McCallum, *Reforming the Scottish Parish*, 232, though his form of gradual change takes place over decades.

Conclusion

Haddington, Stirling and Dundee followed different paths to the Reformation, paths shared by towns throughout Scotland, yet the similarities in the actions of their councillors and townspeople provide some explanations for why Scotland became the only successful national Calvinist Reformation. The three towns had different levels of enthusiasm for Protestantism but in each one the council implemented religious change with support from the community. The burgh councils supervised and promoted Catholic religious services right up until the Reformation, and then oversaw the dismantling of the Catholic civic church and its replacement by a Protestant one. In Dundee, the town council took the initiative and reformed the civic church out of its own free will; in Stirling the process was started by the forceful intervention of the Lords of the Congregation; in Haddington the council waited until the Reformation Parliament of 1560, but then steadily implemented the changes. Throughout the process, the councils retained their responsibility for the civic church, even as the practice, structures and underlying beliefs of that church changed.

In each of the three towns individuals grumbled about the religious alterations, yet there is no evidence of division or popular violence among the townspeople. This aversion to conflict can be found in burghs throughout Scotland. The Scottish Reformation was certainly a violent process, with destructive acts of iconoclasm, intimidation by armed groups, and outright war carried out mostly by professional soldiers, but there was very little interpersonal religious violence amongst Scots. Specifically, there was little physical resistance to Protestants from those loyal to the traditional religion, even though, as seen in Dundee, Haddington and Stirling, townspeople were committed and willing to put their money into Catholic worship right up to 1559. That pattern held throughout the country.[1] In towns such as Perth, St Andrews, Edinburgh and Ayr, which were all reformed in the spring or summer of 1559, nothing stronger than passive Catholic resistance occurred, with the exception of the sacking of the abbey at Scone, where one Protestant was stabbed to death.[2] In Edinburgh, for example, the Protestants were not opposed during their first occupation in 1559, though they were mocked as they retreated.[3] The strongest opposition among Scottish towns came from Aberdeen, where the provost, Thomas Menzies, remained Catholic and protected Catholic recusants in the burgh well until the 1570s. Even there, Protestant iconoclasts faced only limited resistance; in January 1560, the townspeople did not stop the sacking of the interior of St Nicholas church, and St Machar's cathedral was only saved from complete destruction by the arrival of the Earl of Huntly. At the university, the staff and students defended their own chapels, but there is little evidence of violence against individuals by either side.[4]

Elsewhere in Scotland resistance was either muted, such as the complaints recorded in the St Andrews kirk session records, or took the form of continuing Catholic services without interfering with Protestant ones, as in Ayrshire, Teviotdale and elsewhere.[5] This passivity might simply have been prudence in the face of superior force, as the Lords of the Congregation were certainly stronger than anything traditionalists in any given town might have been able to muster, but there is no evidence of defensive preparations once the pattern of Protestant militancy became obvious, nor of local initiatives to re-impose Catholicism once the Protestant forces moved on.[6] Given that most Scottish townspeople were not especially dissatisfied with their civic church, this lack of active resistance to a drastic reformation is remarkable, especially compared with the popular religious violence that would tear apart France just two years later.[7]

Four factors may be proposed to explain why Scottish townspeople avoided popular violence and division, and in doing so created the conditions in which a new and not widely popular religion could be established. Firstly, many people in Scotland had long expected some kind of religious change to happen, even if the exact form it would take was unclear. Reforming ideas of various sorts had been spreading through the country for thirty years, and Scots would have gotten used to the idea that different religious interpretations and opinions were held. Many of these ideas were spread by clergy, such as the friars William Arth and Alexander Seton in Dundee and priests such as sir Duncan Symson in Stirling and, possibly, sir John Tait in Haddington, who had access to church pulpits and civic protection.[8] For many lay people, and indeed, for some of the clergy as well, it would not have been clear which reforming ideas could be considered heretical and which were not. Mainstream opinion, as expressed by Sir David Lindsey, the author of *The Complaynt*, the kind of songs circulated in the *Ballatis* and even the Catholic Church's own reform efforts, emphasised the dangers of idolatry and clerical corruption, especially in the higher clergy of the church. These mutually reinforcing messages likely weakened the attachment of Scots to religious ornamentation and to the idea of an institutional church with their best interests at heart (if they had ever believed that). The preliminary efforts of Mary of Guise and others to establish a new religious settlement during the 1550s and expectations that the Council of Trent might lead to a pan-European compromise further reinforced the sentiment that the contemporary religious structure was outmoded and not particularly worth defending.

The combination of expectation of change and uncertainty about its course also likely inhibited the widespread formation of a distinctly partisan Catholic religious identity, a process which took several decades and confusing switches in royal policy to develop in England, which in France was linked to the sacred conception of the Most Christian king, and which in the southern Netherlands did not develop until the end of the sixteenth century.[9] The strongest confessional identity in the late 1550s belonged to the Calvinists who thus had a wide-open opportunity, even if they were few in number. In the initial stages of the Reformation therefore, many Scots may have decided to take a wait and see approach to the new religion. Once some of them decided that they did not care for it, Calvinism was too firmly in place to be opposed; it could only be avoided, for a while at least.[10] Others meanwhile embraced the opportunity to impose stricter order on the towns and benefit from the takeover of the friaries.

Secondly, the town councils' control of urban religion gave them an opportunity to head off dangerous rabble-rousing. Town councils everywhere prioritised civic peace and unity, and this was especially the case in Scotland during the 1550s, as the inhabitants sought to recover from plagues and wars, rebuild their civic infrastructure and private homes and regain economic prosperity all the while hoping that there would be no further destruction. Writers such as the author of *The Complaynt* had identified dissention rather than heresy as a cause of God's wrath.[11] In small towns where the inhabitants knew each other and lived in close quarters, the pressure to remain civil was intense.[12] Indeed, preserving civic harmony was the priority of the burgh courts, and Dundee's efforts from the 1530s through to 1559 to protect their own from heresy prosecution demonstrate that townspeople placed a higher value on civic peace and mutual protection than on ridding their towns of differing opinions.[13]

In these conditions, Catholic priests who sought to create more conflict by inciting their followers against a faction of the townspeople would have been dimly viewed by both their employers in the municipal administration and their neighbours. In France and regions of the Low Countries where there was resistance to Protestant takeovers, the clergy were very often the instigators.[14] The vast majority of urban priests in Scotland, however, were firmly under civic control. They were often born in the places they served and depended on the town councils and their neighbours for their positions, for their assistance in collecting rents and dues, for side employment, and for everyday neighbourly relations. Priests would have had to be very sure of support of the town council to risk all that, and it appears that in the unsettled mood of the late 1550s, not many were certain of receiving that backing. As early as 1543, Ayr's council had imprisoned a friar who objected too strongly to a reformist preacher.[15] In some places such as St Andrews and Edinburgh, once the Protestants gained control priests who refused to conform were even expelled from the towns, a dangerous prospect for men so embedded in urban life.[16]

Thirdly, one religious group who may have been able to mobilise the population against the militant Protestants were the friars. Their swift neutralisation, however, was due to both the success of Protestant tactics and the failure of the friars to develop good relations with the burghs. Preachers from the orders played a role in instigating violence in France, and the Jesuits inspired some resistance in the Low Countries.[17] Most of the recorded confrontations between Scottish Protestants and clergy in the years leading up to the Reformation involved friars rather than secular priests. Both Dominicans and Franciscans were strong opponents of Protestantism, though both orders also produced reformers and Protestants.[18] The Dominicans had been involved in heresy prosecutions in the years leading up to 1559, beginning with the trial and execution of Patrick Hamilton.[19] The Observant house in St Andrews seemed particularly active in pursuing Protestants.[20] The Franciscans also stood up to the reformers, confronting George Wishart when he preached at Inveresk for example.[21] Reformers returned the animosity, vandalising statues outside Franciscan friaries in Dundee and Ayr in the 1530s, sacking friaries in Perth and Dundee in 1543 and making the friaries the first targets of the urban Reformations of 1559 and 1560.[22] When Mary of Guise offered concessions during the negotiations at Cupar in 1559, she specified that the Lords of the Congregation should refrain from assaults against 'friers and abbeyes', an indication of the deliberate violence the Protestants were deploying against these targets, and the damage it was doing to the cause of traditional religion.[23] Their attacks were especially focused on the stricter Observant Franciscans – the laxer but wealthier Conventuals were largely left alone.[24] The Protestant actions, as Foggie argued regarding the attacks of 1543, were tactical strikes against their strongest opponents. As such, they did indeed succeed in silencing an important source of opposition.[25]

The fierce attacks against the friars were possible because they were not part of the civic church and thus denied the protection afforded by town councils, and so more exposed to insult and damage by locals and outsiders alike, as the repeated targeting of the friary at Dundee demonstrates. To a large extent the friars themselves created their own isolation. The Dominicans especially relied on royal favour, which may have discouraged them from establishing closer ties to the townspeople.[26] In Stirling, the Franciscans also relied on financial support from the central government and seemed to have few positive links with the burgh council. Relations between the Franciscans and the people of Haddington seemed good, though the friars belonged to the Conventual movement, which was not as active against heresy as the Observants, and there may have been as few as two friars left by 1559. The Haddington house, therefore, seems an unlikely base for anti-Protestant resistance. In Dundee, however, the oft-targeted Franciscans were clearly representatives of outside religious authority, in opposition to the town council and the civic church, hosting interventions by the central government and the disliked Bishop of Brechin. This isolation limited the friars' ability to defend themselves or obtain protection. As Pollmann points out, in the Low Countries, without town council approval to make strong attacks on Protestants, the preaching of the friars was reduced to urging believers to make individual reform and repentance to stave off the spread of heresy.[27] A similar dynamic may have played out in Scottish burghs. Exposed, isolated or weak, the friars would have had difficulty in mobilising the population without the support of the councillors, and so became early and easy targets for the reformers.

Fourthly, the slow growth of Scottish Protestantism in the late 1550s may have prevented any determined Catholics from developing an undue sense of alarm. Though people did begin to form themselves into groups of Protestant believers or privy kirks, these groups were small and conservative.[28] Studies from France show that the most spectacular violence occurred when one group was a minority, yet large enough that the majority felt threatened. Especially dangerous incidents occurred when Protestants returning from preaching encountered Catholic processions.[29] In Scotland, there was likely some public Protestant preaching in the late 1550s but there is little evidence of the kind of mass field preaching seen in France and the Low Countries.[30] The Scottish structure of a single urban parish, tightly controlled by the council, meant that there were few opportunities for separate churches to develop openly or for religious ceremonies to be used provocatively and for clashes to occur. Instead, there were likely meetings in private homes, especially those of lairds, which would have been difficult to confront.[31] Aggressive anti-Catholic acts between the early 1540s and 1559 were rare. The country's civic churches, which townspeople might have been motivated to defend, were largely left alone. Some incidents did occur in Edinburgh in the late 1550s and 1560s, such as the attacks on the St Giles procession in 1558 and on those attending Catholic services in Holyrood palace in 1563. These episodes did not develop into extensive violence, the 1563 disturbance being notably quelled by the intervention of the provost and bailies.[32] Likewise, though the conditions that sparked conflict in French towns also existed in Dundee during the winter and spring of 1558–9, no incidents were recorded. Finally, as Scotland was the first country to experience a national Calvinist 'revolutionary reformation' outside of Geneva itself, its Catholics had little precedent to draw on to understand how drastically and quickly their traditional worship would be altered.[33]

The lack of popular violence was an important element of the success of the Reformation, as without violence there was less polarisation.[34] There were certainly Scots who stayed loyal to the mass and who did not care for the new religion; there were certainly Protestant activists who were impatient with them and sought harsh measures to ensure conformity and compliance. Neither group succeeded in creating a sustained disruption to the public peace. This lack of polarisation had important implications for the development of the Reformation. It meant that change in personal affiliation could be gradual, and therefore more successful, a peaceful process due in large part to the control exercised by the burghs over their religious life.[35] Violence was undoubtedly an important aspect of the Scottish Reformation, as individual towns were reformed by force and the religious settlement secured by military victory. Despite this, interpersonal violence among Scots was very largely absent. In the midst of a very turbulent period of war, plague and disruption, significant religious changes were accepted, if not always happily, at least calmly. The Scottish Reformation is another example therefore, that the religious violence that took place in France was, in the European context, not the norm.[36]

The course of the Scottish Reformation was significantly shaped by the nature of Scottish urban religion. The political factors developed by twenty-first century historians explain the timing of the Reformation and how the Protestants achieved a national victory. Recent studies of the Scottish Catholic Church itself show that it was not a rotting institution about to collapse under its own weight, and that there was popular enthusiasm for late medieval Catholicism.[37] To understand why the Scottish Reformation was such a rapid success on the ground, the experiences, fears and choices of the townspeople provide important answers. The control exerted by townspeople over their religious practices, and the distinction between the civic church they controlled and the outside elements represented by the friars and hierarchy, gave them cover to protect those with new ideas and practices and ensure that their churches met their needs. These needs included individual but also collective salvation: from disease, war, dearth, economic collapse and internal division. Religious changes were intended to please God and help achieve this salvation, and there was a general desire to not exacerbate already difficult times. With the expectation of coming religious change, and a fear of further conflict, disruption and divine wrath, what mattered to many Scots was not necessarily the exact form of the change but that it be carried out as peacefully as possible.

Notes

1. The siege of Castle Sempill in October 1560 can be considered an episode of religious violence, though it does not seem to have involved Catholics beyond Lord Sempill's retinue. Knox, *Works*, 2:130–1; *CSP*, 480–1, 486, 489.
2. Knox, *Works*, 1:359; Verschuur, *Politics or Religion?*, 122; Dawson, 'The Face of Ane Perfyt Reformed Kyrk', 417; Lynch, *Edinburgh*, 36–7, 92; Sanderson, *Ayrshire*, 90–7; Cowan, *The Scottish Reformation*, 71.
3. Knox wrote that 'everie ane provoked other to cast stones at us' without specifying if any stones were actually thrown. Knox, *Works*, 1:464–5; Cowan, *Regional Aspects*, 26. Some riots occurred during the early 1560s, though Lynch argues that some of these were more motivated by economic rather than religious complaints. Lynch, *Edinburgh*, 92, 95.
4. McLennan, 'The Reformation in the Burgh of Aberdeen', 135–6; White, 'The Menzies Era', 231.
5. *Register . . . St Andrews* 1:36; Lynch, *Edinburgh*, 190–2; Cowan, *Regional Aspects*, 31–4; Knox, *Works*, 2: 370–1, 379; *A Diurnal of Remarkable Occurrents*, 75–6;

Pitcairn, *Ancient Criminal Trials*, 420, 427–40; Sanderson, *Scottish Curates*, xxix–xxx; Pollmann notes that in the Low Countries, faced with the increasing confidence and prominence of the Protestants, 'Catholics were feeling angry, but rarely did that spur them on to active resistance, let alone the violence that we saw in France'. Pollmann, 'Countering the Reformation in France and the Netherlands', 96.

6. With the exception of Perth and Edinburgh, where Mary of Guise intervened to reintroduce Catholic services. Lynch, *Edinburgh*, 78; Knox, 'Letter to Anna Locke', *Works*, 6:24. Peebles strengthened its defences and maintained watchmen in 1559–60, and was loyally Catholic during the period but there is nothing to indicate if these measures were aimed at keeping out Protestants or simply aimed at securing the town during an unsettled period.

7. The classic study of religious violence in France is of course Natalie Zemon Davis, 'The Rites of Violence: Religious Riot in Sixteenth-Century France', *Past and Present* 59 (1973): 53–91; but see also Denis Crouzet, *Les Guerriers du Dieu: La violence au temps des troubles de religion vers 1525–vers 1610* (Seyssel, 1990); and the collection of articles in the 2012 supplementary edition of *Past and Present*, especially Stuart Carroll, 'The Rights of Violence'; Mack P. Holt, 'Religious Violence in Sixteenth-Century France: Moving Beyond Pollution and Purification'; Alan Tulchin, 'Massacres during the French Wars of Religion', who suggests that the extent of popular, as opposed to military violence, was perhaps exaggerated; *Past and Present* 217 (2012). See also Barbara Diefendorf, *Beneath the Cross: Catholics and Huguenots in Sixteenth Century Paris* (Oxford, 1991) and Philip Benedict, *Rouen during the Wars of Religion* (Cambridge, 1981) for accounts of popular violence in major cities. Comparative studies between France and the Netherlands have pointed out that there was much less popular resistance to Protestantism in the Low Countries than in France. Reasons proposed for the differences include a more internalised religious devotion, a cultural disposition against persecution, and a clergy less able, or willing, to mobilise popular resistance in the Netherlands, compared to clergy who actively chose to mobilise the lay population in France. J. J. Woltjer, 'Violence during the Wars of Religion in France and the Netherlands: A Comparison', *Nederlands archeif voor kerkgeschiedenis/Dutch Review of Church History* 76 (1996): 26–45; Pollmann, 'Countering the Reformation in France and the Netherlands'; Pollmann, *Catholic Identity*.

8. Knox, *Works*, 1:46–52, 62–3.

9. Peter Marshall, *Heretics and Believers: A history of the English Reformation* (New Haven, 2017), 204, 225, 266, 288, 316; Roelker, *One king, one faith*, 161; Mack P. Holt, *The French Wars of Religion, 1562–1629*, 2nd edn (Cambridge, 2005), 8–10, 26; Pollmann, *Catholic Identity*, 131, 133, 142.

10. Cowan, *Regional Aspects*, 30–5.

11. Wedderburn, *The Complaynt*, 125–8.

12. See Mark Konnert, *Local Politics in the French Wars of Religion* (Burlington, 2006), 123; Lynch, *Edinburgh*, 6.

13. While an important strand of scholarship, starting with Natalie Zemon Davis, has identified the religious violence in France as designed to remove sources of pollution that threatened to bring down God's wrath, in Scotland, idolatry and the sins of the clergy, not the dangers of heresy, were the focus of reformers of all persuasions which is surely part of the explanation for why

Scottish Protestants were so willing to engage in iconoclasm but lay Scottish Catholics were less willing to attack Protestants. Davis, 'Rites of Violence'. See also commentaries by Holt, 'Religious Violence in Sixteenth-Century France', and Carroll, 'Rights of Violence'.

14. Pollmann points out that Catholic violence in France was inspired by the clergy, and that some of the few incidents of Catholic violence in the Netherlands were linked to Catholic priests. Widespread violence in France, Pollmann concludes, was the exception not the norm because French priests developed an 'innovative' strategy to fight heresy by rallying lay people to the defence of their traditional religion. Pollmann, 'Countering the Reformation in France and the Netherlands', 96–7; Crouzet, *Guerriers du Dieu*, 209, 211, 412; Larissa Taylor, 'Dangerous Vocations: Preaching in France in the late Middle Ages and Reformations', in *Preachers and People in the Reformation and early modern period* ed. Larissa Taylor (Brill, 2000).
15. Sanderson, *Ayrshire*, 61
16. Dawson, 'The Face of Ane Perfyt Reformed Kyrk', 429; Lynch, *Edinburgh*, 36–7. There is no specific evidence of this practice in the three burghs studied here; while expulsions may have been carried out in Dundee or Stirling, they were certainly not in Haddington, based on the continued presence of unreformed clergy such as Wolson and Auchinlek.
17. For example, Benedict observes that after a Protestant coup captured Rouen, Catholics were allowed to continue celebrating mass but 'the often incendiary members of the mendicant orders were warned that they would be expelled if they stirred up any trouble, and some fled the city'. Benedict, *Rouen*, 97; Pollmann, 'Countering the Reformation in France and the Netherlands', 105–6.
18. Knox, *Works*, 1:268; 4:257.
19. Foggie, *Renaissance Religion*, 73, 122–4.
20. Bryce, *Scottish Grey Friars*, 1:80, 81, 100, 103, 106; Knox, *Works*: 1:135.
21. Knox, *Works*, 1:135.
22. Verschuur, *Politics or Religion?*, 83; Lynch, *Edinburgh*, 75; Dawson. 'The Face of Ane Perfyt Reformed Kyrk', 417; White, 'The Menzies Era', 231; Sanderson, *Ayrshire*, 50, 96; Knox, 'Letter to Anna Locke, 23 June 1559', *Works*, 6:23.
23. Knox, 'Letter to Anna Locke', *Works*, 6:26.
24. Bryce, *The Scottish Grey Friars*, 1:149; Cowan, *The Scottish Reformation*, 47–8.
25. Foggie, *Renaissance Religion*, 43; McRoberts, 'Material Destruction', 419.
26. Eight out of thirteen Scottish Dominican houses were founded by the crown, for example. Note, however, that Foggie argues that they were very much integrated into urban life, though her examples are scattered in time and place: this study has not been able to demonstrate sustained connections. Foggie, *Renaissance Religion*, 41, 54, 128–33; *TA*, 6:32; 10:21, 66, 95, 97, 101, 106, 166, 167, 189, 195.
27. Pollmann, 'Countering the Reformation in France and the Netherlands', 116.
28. Lynch, *Edinburgh*, 85; Ryrie suggests that many of these groups could be thought of as discussion groups rather than organised congregations. Ryrie, 'Congregations', 61–2.
29. Crouzet, *Guerriers du Dieu*, 344–50, 356–7; Tulchin, 'Massacres during the French Wars of Religion', 116. See also Holt, 'Religious Violence in Sixteenth-Century France'.

30. Although see Row, for one possible example. John Row, *The History of the Kirk of Scotland: from the year 1558 to August 1637* (Edinburgh, 1842), 4.
31. Ryrie, 'Congregations', 66.
32. Ryrie, 'Congregations', 49; Knox, *Works*, 1:127–8, 260; Lynch, *Edinburgh*, 108; Knox, *Works*, 2:393–4.
33. The experiences of the Swiss cities may have offered some hints, though. Benedict, *Christ's Churches*, 123.
34. Barbara Diefendorf, 'Rites of Repair: Restoring Community in the French Wars of Religion', *Past and Present* 217 (2012): 30–51; Lynch, *Edinburgh*, 86.
35. McCallum, *Reforming the Scottish Parish*, 232. See for example, Lynch who points out that Catholics were not excluded from public life after the Reformation. Lynch, *Edinburgh*, 80.
36. Pollmann, 'Countering the Reformation in France and the Netherlands', 119–20.
37. Rhodes, *Riches and Reform*; Holmes, *Sacred Signs*; Fitch, *The Search for Salvation*; M. Cowan, *Life, Death and Religious Change*.

Works Cited

MANUSCRIPTS

National Records of Scotland (NRS):
  CC6/5/1/319
  CC8/8/1/72–4
  CC8/8/1/93
  CC8/8/1/140
  CC8/8/1/149
  CC8/8/1/160
  CC8/8/1/193
  CC8/8/1/217
  CC8/8/1/225
  CC8/8/1/232
  CC8/8/1/297
  CC8/8/1/390
  CC8/8/1/393
  CC8/8/1/420
  CC8/8/1/470
  CC8/8/1/493
  CC8/8/2/14
  CC8/8/2/57
  CC8/8/2/200
  CC8/8/2/212
  CC8/8/2/228
  CC8/8/2/609
  CC8/8/2/688
  CC8/8/3/268
  CC8/8/3/436
  CC8/8/3/465
  CC8/8/3/517
  CC8/8/11/167
  E71/12/1–5
  E82/27/1
  GD45/13/119

Dundee City Archives (DCA):
  Baxter Craft Lockit Book

Burgh and Head Court Book 1454–1524
Burgh and Head Court Book 1550–4
Burgh and Head Court Book 1555–8
Burgh and Head Court Book 1558–61
Burgh and Head Court Book 1561–2
Burgh and Head Court Book 1562–3
Burgess Roll
Head Court Laws 1550–1612
Protocol Book 1518–34
Protocol Book of Alexander Wedderburn vol. 1 (1554–65)
Town Charters TC/CC 1/54
Transcript of Rental Roll (ed. Cosmo Innes)

Dundee City Library Rare Books Collection:
  Ane Compendius Buik of Godloe Psalms (1567)

East Lothian Council Archives:
  HAD/1/15 Charters and other writs and papers 1409–1606 (formerly NRS B30/21/39)
  HAD/1/16 Haddington Charters (formerly NRS B30/21/39/3; NRS B30/21/40/5; NRS B30/21/40/9; NRS B30/21/40/1; NRS B30/21/40/17; NRS B30/21/40/18; NRS B30/21/40/19; NRS B30/21/40/21; NRS B30/21/40/22; NRS B30/21/40/27; NRS B30/21/40/28; NRS B30/21/40/29; NRS B30/21/40/30; NRS B30/21/40/31; NRS B30/21/40/33; NRS B30/21/39/15)
  HAD/2/1/2/1 Burgh Minutes 1554–80
  HAD/4/1/2 Protocol Book of Alexander Symson 1529–44
  HAD/4/1/3 Protocol Book Alexander Symson 1539–42
  HAD/4/1/4 Protocol Book Alexander Symson 1542–44
  HAD/4/1/5 Protocol Book Thomas Stevin 1548–65
  HAD/4/2/3/1 Haddington Court Book 1555–60
  HAD/4/2/3/2 Haddington Court Book 1560–71
  HAD/4/6/5 Haddington Court Book 1530–55
  HAD/4/6/73 Treasurer's Account 1558

Stirling City Archives (SCA):
  B66/1/4 Protocol Book of Robert Ramsay 1556–63
  B66/25 Charters by Burgh, Protocol and Saisines, 1544–90
  Stirling Burgh Court Book 1519–30
  Stirling Burgh Court Book 1544–50
  Stirling Burgh Court Book 1554–7
  Stirling Burgh Court Book 1560–4

PRINTED PRIMARY SOURCES

Abstract of Inventory of Charters and Other Writings belonging to the Corporation of Weavers of the Royal Burgh of Dundee. Dundee, 1881.

Accounts of the Lord High Treasurer of Scotland, 13 vols, edited by Thomas Dickson *et al.* Edinburgh, 1877–1916.

Acts of the Lords of Council in Public Affairs, 1501–1554: Selections from the Acta dominorum concilli, edited by Robert Kerr Hannay. Edinburgh, 1932.

Anderson, James Maitland. *Early records of the university of St Andrews; the graduation roll, 1413–1579, and the matriculation roll, 1473–1579.* Edinburgh, 1926.

The Books of Assumption of the Thirds of Benefices, edited by James Kirk. Oxford, 1995.

Buchanan, George. *History of Scotland*, 3 vols, translated by John Watkins. London: 1900.

Calderwood, David. *History of the Kirk of Scotland*, 8 vols, edited by Rev. Thomas Thomson. Edinburgh, 1842–9.

Calendar of State Papers relating to Scotland and Mary Queen of Scots, 1547–1563, 12 vols, edited by Joseph Bain *et al.* Edinburgh, 1898–.

The Catechism of John Hamilton Archbishop of St Andrews, edited by Thomas Graves Law. Oxford, 1884.

Charters and Documents relating to the Burgh of Peebles, with extracts from the records of the burgh. A.D. *1165–1710*. Edinburgh, 1872.

Charters and other Documents relating to the Royal Burgh of Stirling A.D. *1124–1705*, edited by Robert Renwick. Glasgow, 1854.

Charters, Writs and Public Documents of the Burgh of Dundee, edited by William Hay. Dundee, 1880.

The Chartulary of the Abbey of Lindores, edited by John Dowden. Edinburgh, 1903.

A Compendius Book of Godly and Spiritual Songs, edited by A. F. Mitchell. Edinburgh, 1897.

'The Confession of faith of the Swezerlandes', translated by George Wishart. In *Miscellany of the Wodrow Society I*, edited by David Laing. Edinburgh, 1844.

A Diurnal of Remarkable Occurrents that have passed within the country of Scotland since the death of King James the Fourth till the year MDLXXV, edited by T. Thomson. Edinburgh, 1833.

'Documents relating to Haddington.' *Transactions of the East Lothian Antiquarian and Field Naturalists Society* 5 (1952): 67–80.

The Exchequer Rolls of Scotland, 23 vols, edited by John Stuart, George Burnett and George Powell McNeill. Edinburgh, 1878–1908.

Extracts from the Records of the Royal Burgh of Stirling, 2 vols, edited by Robert Renwick. Glasgow, 1887–9.

The Hamilton Papers: Letters and Papers Illustrating the Political Relations of England and Scotland in the XVIth Century, 2 vols, edited by Joseph Bains. Edinburgh, 1890–2.

'A Historie of the Estate of Scotland from July 1558 to April 1560.' In *Miscellany of the Wodrow Society I*, edited by David Laing. Edinburgh, 1844.

'Indictment of Certain Dundee Burgesses on Charges of Riot and Treason', translated by Alexander Maxwell. In *Old Dundee, ecclesiastical, burghal and social, prior to the Reformation*, Alexander Maxwell. Dundee, 1891.

Knox, John. *The Works of John Knox*, edited by David Laing. Edinburgh, 1895.

Letters and papers, foreign and domestic, of the reign of Henry VIII, 21 vols, edited by J. S. Brewer, R. H. Brodie and James Gairdner. London, 1862–1910.

Lindsay, Sir David. *The Monarche and other Poems, Part 1*, edited by Fitzedward Hall. London, 1865.

Lindsay, David. *Sir David Lyndesay's Works*, edited by J. Small and F. Hall. Early English Text Society, 1871; reprint: New York: Greenwood Press, 1969.

Lindsay of Pittscottie, Robert. *The historie and cronicles of Scotland: from the slauchter of King James the First to the ane thousand fyve hundreith thrie scoir fyftein zeir*, 3 vols, edited by Robert Lindsay and A. J. G. Mackay. Edinburgh, 1899–1911.

Major, John. *A History of Greater Britain*, translated by Archibald Constable. Edinburgh, 1892.

Melville of Halhill, Sir James. *Memoirs of his own life*. Introduction by W. M. Mackenzie. London, 1922.

Miscellany of the Wodrow Society, edited by David Laing. Edinburgh, 1844.

Munimenta alme Universitatis glasguensis. Records of the University of Glasgow from its foundation till 1727, 4 vols, edited by Cosmo Innes and Joseph Robertson. Glasgow, 1853.

L'organisation et l'action des Églises Réformées de France, edited by Philip Benedict and Nicolas Fornerod. Geneva, 2012.

Papal negotiations with Mary Queen of Scots during her reign in Scotland 1561–67, edited by John Hungerford Pollen. Edinburgh, 1901.

Paton, Henry M. 'Haddington Records: Books of the Common Good.' *Transactions of the East Lothian Antiquarian and Field Naturalist Society* 7 (1958): 46–80.

The Perth kirk session books, 1577–1590, edited by Margo Todd. Woodbridge, 2012.

Pitcairn, Robert. *Ancient Criminal Trials in Scotland*. Edinburgh, 1833.

Records of the Convention of Royal Burghs of Scotland, with extracts from other record relating to the affairs of the burghs of Scotland, 1295–1597. Edinburgh, 1866.

Register of Privy Council of Scotland (first series), 14 vols, edited by John Hill Burton and David Masson. Edinburgh, 1877.

The Register of the minister, elders and deacons of the Christian congregation of St Andrews, 2 vols, edited by David Hay Fleming. Edinburgh, 1889–90.

Registrum episcopatus Brechinensis, 2 vols, edited by Patrick Chalmers, John Inglis Chalmers and Cosmo Innes. Edinburgh, 1856.

Registrum Magni Sigilli Regum Scotorum: The Register of the Great Seal of Scotland, 11 vols., edited by J. M. Thomson *et al.* Edinburgh, 1886–1914).

Registrum secreti sigilli regum Scotorum. The register of the Privy Seal of Scotland, edited by David Hay Fleming and James Beveridge. Edinburgh, 1908–.

Row, John. *The History of the Kirk of Scotland: from the year 1558 to August 1637*. Edinburgh, 1842.

The Scottish Correspondence of Mary of Lorraine, edited by Annie I. Cameron. Edinburgh, 1927.

Skene, Gilbert. *Ane Breve Description of the Pest Quhair in the Causis, Signis and sum Speciall Preservatioun and Cure thairof Ar Contenit/Set furth be Maister Gilbert Skene, Doctoure in Medicine*. Edinburgh: 1568 [Early English Books Online].

Spottiswood, John. *The History of the Church of Scotland*. Edinburgh, 1847–51; reprint: New York, 1973.

Statutes of the Scottish Church 1225–1559, edited by David Patrick. Edinburgh, 1907.

Wedderburn, Robert. *The Complaynt of Scotland*, introduction by A. M. Stewart. Edinburgh, 1979.

SECONDARY LITERATURE

Aberth, John. *From the Brink of the Apocalypse: Confronting famine, war, plague and death during the later Middle Age*, 2nd edn. London, 2010.

Archer, Ian A. 'Politics and government 1540–1700.' In *The Cambridge Urban History of Britain*, vol. II, edited by Peter Clark. Cambridge, 2008.

Bardgett, Frank D. 'The Reformation in Moray: precursors and initiation.' *Journal of Scottish Historical Studies* 41 (2021): 1–37.

Bardgett, Frank D. *Scotland Reformed: The Reformation in Angus and the Mearns*. Edinburgh, 1989.

Baxter, J. H. *Dundee and the Reformation*. Dundee, 1960.

Benedict, Philip. *Christ's Churches Purely Reformed: A Social History of Calvinism*. New Haven, 2002.

Benedict, Philip. 'Dynamics of Protestant militancy, France 1555–1563.' In *Reformation, Revolt and Civil War in France and the Netherlands*, edited by Philip Benedict, Guido Marnef, Henk von Nierop and Marc Venard. Amsterdam, 1999.

Benedict, Philip. 'Introduction.' In *Reformation, Revolt and Civil War in France and the Netherlands*, edited by Philip Benedict, Guido Marnef, Henk von Nierop and Marc Venard. Amsterdam, 1999.

Benedict, Philip. *Rouen during the Wars of Religion*. Cambridge, 1981.

Benedict, Philip, and Nicholas Fornerod. 'Les 2150 Églises réformées de France de 1561-2', *Revue Historique* CCCXI (2009): 529–60.

Bernard, G. W. *The Late Medieval English Church: Vitality and Vulnerability before the Break with Rome*. New Haven, 2012.

Blakeway, Amy. 'The Anglo-Scottish war of 1558 and the Scottish Reformation.' *History* 102 (2017): 201–25.
Blanchard, Ian, Elizabeth Gemmill, Nicholas Mayhew and Ian D. White. 'The Economy, Town and Country.' In *Aberdeen before 1800: A New History*, edited by E. Patricia Dennison, David Ditchburn and Michael Lynch. East Linton, 2002.
Bossy, John. *Christianity in the West 1400–1700*. Oxford, 1985.
Bossy, John. 'The mass as a social institution 1200–1700.' *Past and Present* 100 (1983): 29–61.
Brodie, Alexander. 'Mair [Major] John (1467–1550) historian, philosopher and theologian.' *Oxford Dictionary of National Biography*. Oxford, 2004.
Brown, Andrew. *Civic Ceremony and Religion in Medieval Bruges, c.1300–1520*. Cambridge, 2011.
Brown, Keith. 'The Reformation Parliament.' In *History of the Scottish Parliament*, vol. I, edited by Keith M. Brown and Roland J. Tanner. Edinburgh, 2004.
Brown, Peter. *The Rise of Western Christendom*, 2nd edn. Oxford, 2003.
Bryce, W. M. *The Scottish Grey Friars*. 2 vols. Edinburgh, 1909.
Cameron, James K. '"Catholic Reform" in Germany and the pre-1560 church in Scotland.' *Records of the Scottish Church History Society* 20 (1979): 105–17.
Cant, R. G. *The University of St Andrews: A Short History*. Edinburgh, 1946.
Carroll, Stuart. *Martyrs and Murderers: The Guise Family and the Makings of Europe*. Oxford, 2009.
Carroll, Stuart. 'The Rights of Violence.' *Past and Present* 214 (2012): 127–62.
Conner, Philip. *Huguenot Heartland: Montauban and Southern French Calvinism during the Wars of Religion*. Burlington, 2002.
Coote, Lesley. 'A language of power: prophecy and public affairs in later medieval England.' In *Prophecy: The Power of Inspired Language in History, 1300–2000*, edited by Bertrand Taithe and Tim Thornton. Stroud, 1997.
Cowan, Ian B. *The Medieval Church in Scotland*, edited by James Kirk. Edinburgh, 1995.
Cowan, Ian B. *Regional Aspects of the Scottish Reformation*. London, 1978.
Cowan, Ian B. *The Scottish Reformation: Church and Society in sixteenth century Scotland*. New York, 1982.
Cowan Ian B., and David E. Easson. *Medieval Religious Houses: Scotland*, 2nd edn. London, 1976.
Cowan, Mairi. *Death, Life and Religious Change in Scottish Towns c.1530–1560*. Manchester, 2014.
Crouzet, Denis. *La genèse de la Réforme française*. Paris, 1996.
Crouzet, Denis. *Les Guerriers du Dieu: La violence au temps des troubles de religion vers 1525–vers 1610*. Seyssel, 1990.
Daval, Guillaume, and Jean Daval. *Histoire de la Réformation à Dieppe 1557–1657*, edited by Émile Lesens. Rouen, 1878–9.

Davis, Natalie Zemon. 'The Rites of Violence: Religious Riot in Sixteenth-Century France.' *Past and Present* 59 (1973): 53–91.

Dawson, Jane E. A. 'Campbell, Archibald, fourth earl of Argyll (1498–1558) magnate.' *Oxford Dictionary of National Biography*. Oxford, 2004.

Dawson, Jane E. A. 'The face of Ane Perfyt Reformed Kyrk: St Andrews and the Early Scottish Reformation.' In *Humanism and Reform: The Church in Europe, England and Scotland, 1400–1643: essays in honour of James K. Cameron*, edited by James Kirk. Oxford, 1991.

Dawson, Jane E. A. *John Knox*. New Haven, 2015.

Dawson, Jane E. A. *Scotland Re-formed, 1488–1587*. Edinburgh, 2007.

Dawson, Jane E. A. 'The Scottish Reformation and the Theatre of Martyrdom.' In *Martyrs and Martyrologies*, edited by Diana Wood. Oxford, 1993.

Dennison, E. Patricia. *The Evolution of Scotland's Towns: Creation, Growth and Fragmentation*. Edinburgh, 2018.

Dennison Torrie, Patricia E. *Medieval Dundee: a Town and its People*. Dundee, 1990.

Dennison, Patricia E. 'Power to the people? The myth of the medieval burgh community.' In *Scottish Power Centres from the Early Middle Ages to the Twentieth Century*, edited by Sally Foster, Allan Macinnes and Ranald MacInnes. Glasgow, 1998.

Dennison, E. Patricia, and Grant G. Simpson, 'Scotland.' In *The Cambridge Urban History of Britain*, vol. I, edited by D. M. Pallister. Cambridge, 2008.

Dennison, E. Patricia, Gordon DesBrisay and H. Lesley Diack, 'Health in the two towns.' In *Aberdeen before 1800: A New History*, edited by E. Patricia Dennison, David Ditchburn and Michael Lynch. East Linton, 2002.

Dennison, E. Patricia, David Ditchburn and Michael Lynch, 'Preface.' In *Aberdeen before 1800: A New History*, edited by E. Patricia Dennison, David Ditchburn and Michael Lynch. East Linton, 2002.

Des Brisay, Gordon, Elizabeth Ewan and H. Lesley Diack. 'Life in the towns.' In *Aberdeen before 1800: A New History*, edited by E. Patricia Dennison, David Ditchburn and Michael Lynch. East Linton, 2002.

Devine, T. M. 'Scotland.' In *The Cambridge Urban History of Britain*, vol. II, edited by Peter Clark. Cambridge, 2008.

Diefendorf, Barbara. *Beneath the Cross: Catholics and Huguenots in Sixteenth-Century Paris*. Oxford, 1991.

Diefendorf, Barbara. 'Rites of Repair: Restoring Community in the French Wars of Religion.' *Past and Present* 214 (2012): 30–51.

Ditchburn. David. 'Religion, ritual and the rhythm of the year in later medieval St Andrews.' In *Medieval St Andrews: Church, Cult, City*, edited by Katie Steveson and Michael Brown. Woodbridge, 2017.

Dollinger, Philip. *The German Hanse*, translated and edited by D. S. Ault and S. H. Steinberg. London, 1970.

Donaldson, Gordon. *All The Queen's Men.* New York, 1983.
Donaldson, Gordon. *Scotland: James V–VII.* New York, 1966.
Donaldson, Gordon. *Scottish Church History.* Edinburgh, 1985.
Donaldson, Gordon. *The Scottish Reformation.* Cambridge, 1960.
Dotterweich, Martin Holt. 'Sacraments and the Church in the Scottish evangelical mind 1528–1555.' *Records of the Scottish Church History Society* 36 (2006): 41–71.
Dotterweich, Martin Holt. 'Wishart, George (c.1513?–1546).' *Oxford Dictionary of National Biography.* Oxford, 2004.
Duffy, Eamon. *The Stripping of the Altars: Traditional Religion in England 1400–1580*, 2nd edn. New Haven, 2005.
Durkan, John. 'Chaplains in late medieval Scotland.' *Records of the Scottish Church History Society* 20 (1979): 91–103.
Durkan, John. 'Heresy in Scotland: the second phase 1546–1558.' *Records of the Scottish Church History Society* 24 (1992): 320–65.
Dyer, Christopher. 'Trade, towns and the Church: ecclesiastical consumers and the urban economy of the West Midlands.' In *The Church in the medieval town*, edited by Terry Slater and Gervase Rosser. Aldershot, 1998.
Edington, Carol. *Court and Culture in Renaissance Scotland: Sir David Lindsey of the Mount.* Amherst, 1994.
Eire, Carlos. *The War Against the Idols.* Cambridge, 1989.
Ewan, Elizabeth. 'The community of the burgh in the fourteenth century.' In *The Scottish Medieval Town*, edited by Michael Lynch, Michael Spearman and Geoffrey Stell. Edinburgh, 1988.
Fawcett, Richard. *The Architecture of the Scottish Medieval Church 1100–1560.* New Haven, 2011.
Fawcett, Richard. *Stirling Castle.* Edinburgh, 1995.
Firth, Katherine R. *The Apocalyptic Tradition in Reformation Britain, 1530–1645.* Oxford, 1979.
Fitch, Audrey-Beth. 'Assumptions about plague in medieval Scotland.' *Scotia* 11 (1987): 30–40.
Fitch, Audrey-Beth. *The Search for Salvation: Lay Faith in Scotland, 1480–1560*, edited by Elizabeth Ewan. Edinburgh, 2009.
Foggie, Janet P. *Renaissance Religion in Urban Scotland: The Dominican Order, 1450–1560.* Leiden, 2003.
Forbes Gray, W., assisted by James H. Jamieson. *Short History of Haddington.* Edinburgh, 1944.
Forrest, Martin A. 'David and Alexander Forrest and their part in the Scottish Reformation.' *Transactions of the East Lothian Antiquarian and Field Naturalists Society* 25 (2003): 13–24.
Fournié, Michelle. 'Confréries, bassins et fabriques dans le Sud-Ouest de la France: des oeuvres municipales.' In *La Religion Civique à L'Époque Médiévale et Moderne (Chrétienté et Islam)*, edited by André Vauchez. Rome, 1995.

Fox R. C. 'Stirling 1550–1700: the morphology and functions of a pre-industrial Scottish burgh.' In *Scottish Urban History*, edited by George Gordon and Brian Dicks. Aberdeen, 1983.

Fraser, William. *The Stirlings of Keir*. Edinburgh, 1858.

Friedrichs, Christopher R. *The Early Modern City 1450–1750*. Harlow, 1995.

Friedrichs, Christopher R. *Urban Politics in Early Modern Europe*. London, 2000.

Gibson, A. J. S., and T. C. Smout. *Prices, food and wages in Scotland 1550–1780*. Cambridge, 1995.

Goodare, Julian. 'The first parliament of Mary, Queen of Scots.' *Sixteenth Century Journal* 36 (2005): 55–75.

Goodare, Julian, and Martha McGill (eds). *The Supernatural in Early Modern Scotland*. Manchester, 2020.

Gordon, Bruce. *The Swiss Reformation*. Manchester, 2002.

Graham, Michael F. *The Uses of Reform: 'godly discipline' and popular behaviour in Scotland and beyond, 1560–1610*. New York, 1996.

Greaves, Richard L. 'Christison, William (d. 1599).' In *Oxford Dictionary of National Biography* (accessed 14 November 2013).

Grell, Ole Peter. 'Introduction.' In *The Scandinavian Reformation*, edited by Ole Preter Grell. Cambridge, 1995.

Haddington: Royal Burgh: A History and Guide. East Linton, 1997.

Haigh, Christopher. *English Reformations: Religion, Politics and Society under the Tudors*. Oxford, 1993.

Hale, John R. *Renaissance War Studies*. London, 1983.

Holmes, Stephen Mark. *Sacred Signs in Reformation Scotland: Interpreting Worship 1488–1590*. Oxford, 2015.

Holt, Mack P. *The French Wars of Religion, 1562–1629*, 2nd edn. Cambridge, 2005.

Holt, Mack P. 'Religious violence in sixteenth-century France: moving beyond pollution and purification.' *Past and Present* 217 (2012): 52–74.

Horn, Barbara L. H. 'List of references to the pre-Reformation altarages in the parish church of Haddington.' *Transactions of the East Lothian Antiquarian and Field Naturalist Society* 10 (1965): 55–91.

Jackson, Gordon. 'The economy: Aberdeen and the sea.' In *Aberdeen before 1800: A New History*, edited by E. Patricia Dennison, David Ditchburn and Michael Lynch. East Linton, 2002.

Jamieson, James H. 'John Knox and East Lothian.' *Transactions of the East Lothian Antiquarian and Field Naturalists Society* 3 (1934–8): 49–79.

Jansen, Sharon. *Political Protest and Prophecy under Henry VIII*. Rochester, 1991.

Jillings, Karen. *An Urban History of the Plague: socio-economic, political and medieval impacts in a Scottish community, 1550–1650*. Milton, 2018.

Kellar, Clare. *Scotland, England and the Reformation, 1534–61*. Oxford, 2003.

Kirby, David. *Northern Europe in the Early Modern Period: The Baltic World 1492–1772*. London, 1993.

Kirk, James. 'The religion of early Scottish Protestants.' In *Humanism and Reform: The Church in Europe, England and Scotland, 1400–1643: essays in honour of James K. Cameron*, edited by James Kirk. Oxford, 1991.

Konnert, Mark. *Local Politics in the French Wars of Religion*. Burlington, 2006.

Larson, James. *Reforming the North*. Cambridge, 2010.

Lyall, R. J. 'Complaint, satire and invective in Middle Scots literature.' In *Church, Politics and Society: Scotland 1409–1929*, edited by Norman Macdougall. Edinburgh, 1983.

Lynch, Michael (ed.). *The Early Modern Town in Scotland*. London, 1987.

Lynch, Michael. *Edinburgh and the Reformation*. Edinburgh, 1981.

Lynch, Michael. *Scotland: A New History*. London, 1992.

Lynch, Michael. 'The social and economic structure of the larger towns, 1450–1600.' In *The Scottish Medieval Town*, edited by Michael Lynch, Michael Spearman and Geoffrey Stell. Edinburgh, 1988.

Lynch, Michael, Gordon DesBrisay and Murray G. H. Pittock, 'The faith of the people.' In *Aberdeen before 1800: A New History*, edited by E. Patricia Dennison, David Ditchburn and Michael Lynch. East Linton, 2002.

Lynch, Michael, Michael Spearman and Geoffrey Stell (eds). *The Scottish Medieval Town*. Edinburgh, 1988.

Mair, Craig. *Stirling: The Royal Burgh*. Edinburgh, 1990.

Marnef, Guido. *Antwerp in the Age of Reformation, 1550–1577*, translated by J. C. Grayson. Baltimore, 1996.

Marnef, Guido. 'The dynamics of Reformed religious militancy: the Netherlands 1566–1585.' In *Reformation, Revolt and Civil War in France and the Netherlands*, edited by Philip Benedict, Guido Marnef, Henk von Nierop and Marc Venard. Amsterdam, 1999.

Marshall, Peter. *Heretics and Believers: A History of the English Reformation*. New Haven, 2017.

Marshall, Rosalind K. *Ruin and Restoration: St Mary's Church Haddington*. Haddington, 2001.

Maxwell, Alexander. *The History of Old Dundee, narrated out of the Town Council Register, with additions from contemporary annals*. Dundee, 1884.

Maxwell, Alexander. *Old Dundee, ecclesiastical, burghal and social, prior to the Reformation*. Dundee, 1891.

McCallum, John. 'Nurseries of the poor: hospitals and almshouses in early modern Scotland.' *Journal of Social History* 48 (2014): 427–49.

McCallum, John. *Poor Relief and the Church in Scotland 1560–1640*. Edinburgh, 2018.

McCallum, John. *Reforming the Scottish Parish: The Reformation in Fife, 1560–1640*. Burlington, 2010.

MacCulloch, Diarmaid. *Thomas Cranmer: A Life*. New Haven, 1996.

MacDonald, Alan R. *The Burghs and Parliament in Scotland 1550–1561*. Burlington, 2007.

Macfarlane, Leslie J. 'Chisholm, William (1493/4–1564), bishop of Dunblane.' *Oxford Dictionary of National Biography*. Oxford, 2004.

McGavin, John. 'Drama in sixteenth century Haddington.' In *European Medieval Drama* 1, edited by Sidney Higgins. Turnhout, 1997.
McGill, Martha, and Alasdair Raffe. 'The uses of providence in early modern Scotland.' In *The Supernatural in Early Modern Scotland*, edited by Julian Goodare and Martha McGill. Manchester, 2020.
McGinley, J. K. 'Wedderburn, James (1495–1553).' *Oxford Dictionary of National Biography*. Oxford, 2004.
McIntosh, Marjorie. *Controlling Misbehavior in England, 1370–1600*. Cambridge, 1998.
McKay, Denis. 'The duties of the medieval parish clerk.' *Innes Review* 19 (1968): 32–9.
McKay, Denis. 'The election of parish clerks in medieval Scotland.' *Innes Review* 18 (1967): 25–35.
McKay, Denis. 'Parish life in Scotland, 1500–1560.' In *Essays on the Scottish Reformation, 1513–1625*, edited by David McRoberts. Glasgow, 1962.
McLennan, Bruce. 'The Reformation in the burgh of Aberdeen.' *Northern Scotland* 2 (1976): 119–44.
McNeil, Peter G. B. '"Our Religion, established neither by law nor Parliament": was the Reformation legislation of 1560 valid?' *Scottish Church History* 35 (2005): 68–89.
McNeil, Peter G. B., Hector L. MacQueen and Anona May Lyons. *Atlas of Scottish History to 1707*. Edinburgh, 1996.
McRoberts, David, 'Material Destruction.' In *Essays on the Scottish Reformation, 1513–1625*, edited by David McRoberts. Glasgow, 1962.
Meehan, Andrew. 'Bination. In *The Catholic Encyclopedia* online (accessed 15 August 2013).
Merriman, Marcus. 'The assured Scots: Scottish collaborators with England during the Rough Wooing.' *Scottish History Review* 47 (1968): 10–34.
Merriman, Marcus. *The Rough Wooings: Mary Queen of Scots 1542–1551*. East Linton, 2000.
Mill, Anna Jean. *Mediaeval Plays in Scotland*. Edinburgh, 1927.
Mitchell, A. F. 'Introduction.' In *A Compendius Book of Godly and Spiritual Songs*, edited by A. F. Mitchell. Edinburgh, 1897.
Mollat, Michel. *Le commerce maritime normand à la fin du Moyen Âge: étude d'histoire économique et sociale*. Paris, 1952.
Mout, Nicolette. 'The historiographical traditions of France and the Netherlands.' In *Reformation, Revolt and Civil War in France and the Netherlands*, edited by Philip Benedict, Guido Marnef, Henk von Nierop and Marc Venard. Amsterdam, 1999.
Muller, Gerhard. 'Protestant theology in Scotland and Germany in the early days of the Reformation.' *Records of the Scottish Church History Society* 22 (1985): 103–7.
Murphy, Neil. 'The Duke of Albany's invasion of England in 1523 and military mobilization in sixteenth-century Scotland.' *The Scottish Historical Review* 99 (2020): 1–25.

Naphy, William G. *Calvin and the Consolidation of the Genevan Reformation*, 2nd edn. Louisville, 2003.
Naphy, William G., and Andrew Spicer. *Plague: Black Death and Pestilence in Europe.* Stroud, 2004.
Ollivant, Simon. *The Court of the Official in Pre-reformation Scotland.* Edinburgh, 1982.
Perry, David. *Dundee Rediscovered: The Archeology of Dundee Reconsidered.* Perth, 2005.
Phillips, Gervase. *The Anglo-Scots Wars 1513–50.* Woodbridge, 1999.
Pollmann, Judith. *Catholic Identity and the Revolt of the Netherlands 1520–1635.* Oxford, 2011.
Pollmann, Judith. 'Countering the Reformation in France and the Netherlands: clerical leadership and Catholic violence 1560–1585.' *Past and Present* 190 (2006): 83–120.
Pound, John. 'Clerical poverty in early sixteenth-century England: some East Anglian evidence.' *Journal of Ecclesiastical History* 37 (1986): 389–96.
Randall, David. 'Providence, fortune and the experience of combat: English printed battlefield reports circa 1570–1637.' *Sixteenth Century Journal* 35 (2004): 1053–77.
Rapp, Francis. *L'Église et la vie Religieuse en Occident à la fin du Moyen Âge.* Paris, 1971.
Reinburg, Virginia. 'Liturgy and the laity in late medieval and Reformation France.' *The Sixteenth Century Journal* 23 (1992): 526–47.
Rhodes, Bess. *Riches and Reform: Ecclesiastical Wealth in St Andrews c. 1520–1580.* Leiden, 2019.
Rhodes, Elizabeth. 'Property and Piety: Donations to Holy Trinity Church, St Andrews.' In *Scotland's Long Reformation: New Perspectives in Scottish Religion c.1550–1660*, edited by John McCallum. Leiden, 2016.
Rigby S. H., and Elizabeth Ewan. 'Government, power and authority 1300–1540.' In *The Cambridge Urban History of Britain*, vol. I, edited by D. M. Pallister. Cambridge, 2008.
Riis, Thomas. *Should auld acquaintance be forgot: Scottish–Danish relations c.1450–1707*, 2 vols. Odense, 1988.
Riordan, Michael B. 'Scottish political prophecies and the crowns of Britain, 1500–1840.' In *The Supernatural in Early Modern Scotland*, edited by Julian Goodare and Martha McGill. Manchester, 2020.
Ritchie, Pamela E. *Mary of Guise in Scotland, 1548–1560: a political career.* East Linton, 2002.
Roelker, Nancy. *One king, one faith: the Parlement of Paris and the religious reformations of the sixteenth century.* Berkeley, 1996.
Rorke, Martin. 'English and Scottish overseas trade 1300–1600.' *Economic History Review* 59 (2006): 265–88.
Rosser, Gervase, and E. Patricia Dennison. 'Urban Culture and the Church 1300–1540.' In *The Cambridge Urban History of Britain*, vol. I, edited by D. M. Pallister. Cambridge, 2008.

Rousseau, Marie-Hélène. *Saving the Souls of Medieval London: Perpetual Chantries at St Paul's Cathedral c.1200–1548*. Burlington, 2011.
Rubin, Miri. *Corpus Christi: The Eucharist in Late Medieval Culture*. Cambridge, 1991.
Rutherford, David S. *Biggar St Mary's: a medieval college kirk*. Biggar, 1946.
Ryrie, Alec. 'Congregations, conventicles and the nature of early Scottish Protestantism.' *Past and Present* 191 (2006): 45–76.
Ryrie, Alec. *The Origins of the Scottish Reformation*. Manchester, 2006.
Ryrie, Alec. 'Reform without frontiers in the last years of Catholic Scotland.' *English Historical Review* 119 (2004): 27–56.
Sanderson, Margaret H. B. *Ayrshire and the Reformation: People and Change, 1490–1600*. East Linton, 1997.
Sanderson, Margaret H. B. *Cardinal of Scotland, David Beaton c.1494–1546*. Edinburgh, 1986.
Sanderson, Margaret H. B. *Early Scottish Protestants 1407–1560*. Edinburgh, 2010.
Sanderson, Margaret H. B. *Scottish Curates and Parochial Chaplains 1429–1560*. Edinburgh, 2016.
Scarisbrick, J. J. *The Reformation and the English People*. Oxford, 1984.
Schmidt, J. 'A case of Bination Extra Loca Sacra.' *Jurist* (1945): 216–34.
Scott, Hew. *Fasti ecclesiæ Scoticanæ: The succession of ministers in the Church of Scotland from the Reformation*. 11 vols. Edinburgh, 1915–.
Scribner, R. W. *Popular Culture and Popular Movements in Reformation Germany*. London, 1987.
Shaw, Rev. Duncan. 'Zwinglian influences in the Scottish Reformation.' *Zwingliana* 17 (1988): 375–400.
Shrewsbury, J. F. D. *A History of Bubonic Plague in British Isles*. London, 1970.
Slack, Paul. *The Impact of Plague in Tudor and Stuart England*. London, 1985.
Slonosky, Timothy. 'Burgh Government and Reformation: Stirling c.1530–1565.' In *Scotland's Long Reformation: New Perspectives on Scottish Religion, c.1500–c.1660*, edited by John McCallum. Leiden, 2016.
Spearman, R. M. 'Evidence of Early Industries.' In *The Scottish Medieval Town*, edited by Michael Lynch, Michael Spearman and Geoffrey Stell. Edinburgh, 1988.
Stevenson, Alexander. 'Trade with the South, 1070–1513.' In *The Scottish Medieval Town*, edited by Michael Lynch, Michael Spearman and Geoffrey Stell. Edinburgh, 1988.
Stevenson, William. 'Patrick Hamilton's nine-part mass.' *Records of the Scottish Church History Society* 36 (2006): 29–39.
Stewart, A. M. 'Introduction.' In Robert Wedderburn, *The Complaynt of Scotland*, edited by A. M. Stewart. Edinburgh, 1979.
Summerson, Henry. 'John Erskine, seventeenth or first Earl of Mar.' *Oxford Dictionary of National Biography*, Oxford, 2018.
Taithe, Bertrand, and Tim Thornton. 'The language of history: past and future in prophecy.' In *Prophecy: The Power of Inspired Language in*

History, 1300–2000, edited by Bertrand Taithe and Tim Thornton. Stroud, 1997.

Tallon, Alain. *La France et le Concile de Trente (1518–1563)*. Rome, 1997.

Taylor, Larissa. 'Dangerous vocations: preaching in France in the late Middle Ages and Reformation.' In *Preachers and People in the Reformation and Early Modern Period*, edited by Larissa Taylor. Leiden: 2000.

Terpstra, Nicholas. *Lay Confraternities and Civic Religion in Renaissance Bologna*. Cambridge, 1995.

Thomas, Keith. *Religion and the Decline of Magic*. New York, 1971.

Thompson, Augustine O. P. *Cities of God*. University Park, 2005.

Thornton, Tim. *Prophecy, Politics and the People in Early Modern England*. Woodbridge, 2006.

Todd, Margo. *The Culture of Protestantism in Early Modern Scotland*. New Haven, 2002.

Todd, Margo. 'Providence, chance and the new science in early Stuart Cambridge.' *Historical Journal* 29 (1986): 697–711.

Torrie, Elizabeth P. D. 'The guild in fifteenth-century Dunfermline.' In *The Scottish Medieval Town*, edited by Michael Lynch, Michael Spearman and Geoffrey Stell. Edinburgh, 1988.

Tulchin, Alan. 'Massacres during the French Wars of Religion.' *Past and Present* 217 (2012): 100–26.

Vandermolen, Ronald J. 'Providence as mystery, providence as revelation: Puritan and Anglican modifications of John Calvin's doctrine of providence.' *Church History* 47 (1978): 27–47.

Vauchez, André. 'Introduction.' In *La Religion Civique à L'Époque Médiévale et Moderne (Chrétienté et Islam)*, edited by André Vauchez. Rome, 1995.

Venard, Marc. 'Catholicism and resistance to the Reformation in France, 1555–1585.' In *Reformation, Revolt and Civil War in France and the Netherlands*, edited by Philip Benedict, Guido Marnef, Henk von Nierop and Marc Venard. Amsterdam, 1999.

Verschuur, Mary. *Politics or Religion? The Reformation in Perth 1540–1570*. Edinburgh, 2006.

Walsham, Alexandra. *Providence in Early Modern England*. Oxford, 1999.

Warden, Alex J. *Burgh Laws of Dundee*. London, 1972.

White, Alan. 'The Menzies era: sixteenth-century politics.' In *Aberdeen before 1800: A New History*, edited by E. Patricia Dennison, David Ditchburn and Michael Lynch. East Linton, 2002.

Willock, Ian Douglas. *The Origins and Development of the Jury in Scotland*. Edinburgh, 1966.

Woltjer, Juliaan. 'Political moderates and religious moderates in the revolt of the Netherlands.' In *Reformation, Revolt and Civil War in France and the Netherlands*, edited by Philip Benedict, Guido Marnef, Henk von Nierop and Marc Venard. Amsterdam, 1999.

Woltjer, J. J. 'Violence during the Wars of Religion in France and the Netherlands: a comparison.' *Nederlands archeif voor kerkgeschiedenis/ Dutch Review of Church History* 76 (1996): 26–45.

Worden, Blair. 'Providence and politics in Cromwellian England.' *Past and Present* 109 (1985): 55–99.

Wrightson, Keith, and David Levine. *Poverty and Piety in an English Village: Terling, 1525–1700.* New York, 1979.

DIGITAL RESOURCES

The Catholic Encyclopedia: https://www.newadvent.org/cathen/
Dictionary of the Scots Language: https://dsl.ac.uk/
Early English Books Online: https://www.english-corpora.org/eebo/
National Library of Scotland: Town Plans and Views: https://maps.nls.uk/towns/
Oxford Dictionary of National Biography: https://www.oxforddnb.com/
Records of the Parliament of Scotland: https://rps.ac.uk/

UNPUBLISHED THESES

Brain, Elizabeth Elsie. 'John Erskine, earl of Mar: advocate of the middle way, 1548–72.' Unpublished MA thesis. McGill University, 1965.

Flett, Iain E. F. 'The conflict of the Reformation and democracy in the Geneva of Scotland, 1443–1610: an introduction to edited texts of documents relating to the burgh of Dundee.' Unpublished MPhil thesis. St Andrews, 1981.

Rorke, Martin. 'Scottish overseas trade 1275/86–1597.' Unpublished PhD thesis. University of Edinburgh, 2001.

Index

A Historie of the Estate of Scotland, 205
Abbot of Unreason, 72–3
Aberdeen, 14, 90, 120, 143n
   burgh council, 209
   plague in, 18–19
   Reformation in, 195, 209–10, 243
Aberlady, 17, 20, 154
Abircromby, James, 106
Adam, James, 106
adultery, 179, 185, 198, 228, 229, 230, 231, 234
Aikin, John, 69
Albany, Duke of, 145
Aldcorne, David, 93
Allane, Alexander, 118
Allen, Patrick, 222
almshouses, 6, 73
Anderson, Andrew, 158
Anderson, John, 24
Anderson, Robert, 122, 141n
Ane Satyre of the Three Estatis, 179
Angus, 123, 197
Annand, Alexander, 140n
Annand, Andrew, 55
Annand, family, 123
Annand, George, 122, 141n
Annand, James, 122, 140n, 141n
Annand, William, 163
appropriation of parish revenue, 49, 51
Arbroth Abbey, 129
Archibald, James, 218
Archibald, Watson, 93
Argyll, Fifth Earl of [Archibald Campbell], 185, 204, 207, 216
Argyll, Fourth Earl of [Archibald Campbell], 155, 156, 164, 174
Arran, Second Earl of, Governor of Scotland [James Hamilton], 76, 128, 129, 131, 132, 136, 146, 155–6, 157, 161, 163, 164, 174, 175, 182

Arth, William, 119, 244
assizes, 35, 38, 56
assured Scots, 152, 154, 156, 159, 160, 161, 163–4
Athelstaneford, 136, 222
Auchar, John, 45n, 98
Auchinlek, John, 222
Auchmurty, Robert, 89
Ayr, 148, 203–4, 245
   participation in Wars of the Congregation, 5
   Reformation in, 4, 192, 195, 196, 201, 203–4, 215, 243
Ayrshire, Reformation in, 4, 143n, 195, 244
Ayton, James, 19
Ayton, John, 20, 28n, 31, 32, 33, 56, 106, 150, 172, 175, 208, 214n

baillies
   complaints against, 36
   function of, 6, 30, 34–5, 66, 73
baker craft
   Dundee, 37, 42, 98, 173, 200
   Haddington, 72, 172
Balcanquhall, Walter, 219
Balfour, Andrew, 162
Balfour, James, 112n
Balfour, John, 111n
Balmerino Abbey, 52, 89, 155
Balnaves, Henry, 131, 132, 137
Balsom, John, 97
Barnage, David, 224
Barnes, Alexander, 18
Barnis, Alex, 105, 214n
Barnis, John, 105
Barnis, Robert, 42
Barre, Robert, 224
Barrie, Mark, 95
Barry, Andrew, 87

Barry, James, 66, 87
Barry, Janet, 87
Barry, John [Vicar of Dundee], 37, 62, 66, 87, 106
Barry, Robert, 105
baxter *see* baker
Beaton, David [Cardinal, Archbishop of St Andrews], 122, 123, 125, 127, 129, 131, 132, 138, 146, 148, 164
Beaton, James [Archbishop of St Andrews], 118–19, 120
Bell, Alane, 172
Bell, Lawrence, 75
Bell, Thomas, 96
Bell, William [of Spittal], 39
Bell, William, 158
Berwick, 148, 160
Bethok, John, 206
Beveridge, John, 127
Bible, 118, 155, 180, 183
bination, 111n
Black, John, 122, 123, 140n, 141n, 142n
Blackburn, John, 75
Blak, Patton, 173
blasphemy, 185, 198, 218, 230, 231, 233, 234
Bluk, Agnes, 229
Blyth, James, 64, 224
Book of Common Prayer [England], 185, 189n
Borders, 162, 175
Borthwick, Archibald, 61, 62, 63, 64, 91, 92, 214n, 219
Bothans college church, 89
Bothwell, Fourth Earl of [James Hepburn], 236
Bothwell, Third Earl of [Patrick Hepburn], 21, 133, 134, 146
Brechin, 14
  bishop of, 53, 65, 66, 119, 120, 132, 246
  diocese of, 52, 121
Broughty Castle, 13, 130, 148, 154–7, 161, 162, 164, 175, 176, 202, 217
Brouin, Isabell, 24
Brown, Adam, 61, 90–1, 98, 99, 103, 175–6
Brown, Alexander, 99

Brown, Edmund, 141n
Brown, Gilbert, 98
Brown, Janet, 99
Brown, John, 99
Brown, Katherine, 36
Brown, Margaret, 91
Brown, William of Stolencleuth, 31–2, 34
Brown, William, 21, 91, 98, 99
Brownfield, William, 136
Bruce, Marion, 105
Bruche, George, 225
Bubonic plague, 148; *see also* plague
Bucer, Martin, 185
Buchanan, George, 202, 204, 205
Bully, John, 63, 88
Bully, Thomas, 63, 106
burgesses, eligibility, 36
burgh council, 134, 192, 195, 232, 234, 235, 245
  supervision of clergy, 60, 61, 62–3, 245
burgh courts, 5, 34–5, 43, 245
burgh records, 6, 101, 171, 197, 218, 231
Burne, John, 105
Bute pursuivant, 176

Calderwood, David [historian], 121, 124, 134
Calvin, John, 117, 186, 192
Calvinism, 2, 8n, 191, 198, 203, 228, 229, 231, 243, 245, 247
Cambuskenneth Abbey, 21, 52, 89, 90, 123, 126, 127
Cameron, John, 230
Campbell, Henry, 56
Cant, Robert, 140n
Carale, Thomas, 66
Carale, William, 100
card playing *see* social discipline
Carmichael, William, 38, 216
Carnegy, Alexander, 223
Carnis, Thomas, 43
Carroll, Stuart, 203, 212n
Castillians *see* St Andrews (siege of)
Castle Sempill, 248n
Catholic church, 171, 177, 182–5, 196, 206; *see also* medieval church

Catholic hierarchy, 4, 49, 54, 76, 120–1, 130, 131, 135, 184, 185, 193, 220, 244, 248
Chapel Royal, Stirling Castle, 52, 89, 90
Charteris, John, 164–5
Chishlom, William [Bishop of Dunblane], 127
choristers
  Dundee, 60, 64, 66, 96, 105, 106, 200, 224, 226
  Haddington, 20, 58, 59, 64, 101, 103
  Stirling, 61
Church of St Clement, Dundee, 96, 97
Church of St John the Evangelist, Dundee, 96
civic church, 6, 77, 191, 192, 193, 196, 199, 204, 206, 208, 209, 215, 217–26, 236, 237, 243, 246, 247, 248
  Dundee, 18, 122, 124, 130, 132, 235
civic religion, 50–1, 53, 72, 76, 124, 132, 196, 210, 233, 235
Clapen, Elizabeth, 137
Clapen, William, 159
Clarion's Chronicle, 180
clergy, 2, 51, 86, 87, 225, 245
  celibacy, 91, 134
  connections to laity, 87, 91, 93, 97–100
  corruption, 86
  Dundee, 90, 93, 94, 95, 101, 102, 104
  duties, 58–60, 62, 63
  education and training, 87, 94
  Haddington, 90–3, 94, 95, 98, 101–2, 103, 105
  hiring, 61–2, 65
  income, 61–2, 63, 68, 69, 94, 95, 96, 97, 99
  litigiousness, 88, 91, 92, 100–7, 255
  Protestant ministers, 192, 206, 208, 217–18, 219
  Protestant readers, 192, 206, 208, 217–18, 219, 222
  Stirling, 90, 93, 94, 95, 98, 101, 102–3, 104
Clerk, John, 105
Clune, Andrew, 150–1

Cok, Marion, 104
Cokburn, Patrick, 219
Cokburn, William, 68, 71–2, 105
collaboration [with England], 123, 130, 131, 136, 137, 153, 155, 156, 158–65
collegiate churches, 6, 52, 58–9
commendators, 3, 49
Complaynt of Scotland, 124, 145, 177, 180–2
Confession of Faith *see Scots Confession*
Congilton, Sir John, 74
Convention of Royal Burghs, 172
cordiner craft
  Dundee, 225
  Stirling, 224
Corntoun, John, 64
Corpus Christi procession, 57, 72
councillors, function of, 6, 30, 35
Coupar Angus, Abbey, 89
court of the Official of Lothian, 43, 63, 88
Cousland, Robert, 127, 128
Cousland, Walter, 158, 174
Couson, Thomas, 105
Couttis, John, 54
Cowan, Ian B., 3, 49, 50, 86
Cowan, John, 128
Cowan, Mairi, 49, 86
Cowan, Walter, 224
Cowper, Andrew, 61, 112n
crafts, 41, 69–72
  Dundee, 16, 223
  Haddington, 18–19, 42, 71, 101
  Stirling, 23, 24, 40, 41–2, 175
Crag, James, 99
Crag, John, 89, 105
Craig, John, 140n
Craile, Alexander, 120, 140n
Cristeson, Alexander, 98
Cristeson, David, 98
Cristeson, James, 98
Cristeson, John, 93, 98
Cristeson, Robert, 61, 69
Cristeson, William, 106, 217, 218
Crosar, George, 92
Crosar, John, 92, 105
Cupar, 14, 179, 216, 246
curate, Dundee, 88, 93

curate, Haddington, 89
curates, 87
Curmannow, Robert, 162
Curmmanow, Wat, 105

dancing *see* social discipline
Danzig, 119
Darrow, James, 55
David I, King of Scotland, 21, 51, 52
Davidson, Alexander, 87
Davidson, David, 224, 233
Davidson, James, 163
Davidson, John, 163
Daw, David, 163
Daw, John, 163
Dawson, Jane, 3, 191
Dawson, Robert, 16
Dene, John, 200
Denmark, 118
Dennison, Patricia E., 30
Dialogue Betwix Experience and ane Courteour, 178–9
Dieppe, 37, 98, 198
Dik, Alexander, 120, 122
Dikson, Richard, 136
Dikson, Thomas, 208, 214n
Dirleton, 75
Diurnal of Remarkable Occurents, 148
divine providence, 149, 151, 177–82, 183, 184, 186, 228, 229
Dog, James, 148, 156–7
Dominican friary, Dundee, 13, 76, 129–30, 220, 226
Dominican friary, Stirling, 22, 93
Dominicans, 90, 246, 250n
    Dundee, 104
    Perth, 122
    St Andrews, 121
    Stirling, 127, 128, 221
Donaldson, Alex, 15
Donaldson, Gordon, 2, 49, 86
donations to religious institutions, 67
Dorrocht, William, 40
Dougal, William, 16
Douglas, Hew, 136
Douglas, John [mason], 214n
Douglas, John, 19
Drummond, Robert, 158
Drummond, William, 65

drunkenness *see* social discipline
Ducher, Thomas, 96, 98, 99, 103, 111n, 226
Duchok, William, 151
Dudley, Andrew, 155–6, 163–4
Duncan, John, 73
Duncanson, John, 118, 218
Duncanson, Thomas, 205, 206, 218
Dundee, 5, 13–16, 118, 119, 120, 121, 122, 126, 129–32, 133, 138, 145, 146–7, 151–2, 158, 159, 161–5, 191, 192, 195, 217, 234, 235, 243
    almshouse, 73
    bailies, 67, 120, 122, 199, 200, 201, 224, 231, 233
    burgh council, 33, 43–4, 53, 55, 118, 132, 161, 173–4, 196, 197–8, 200, 201, 202, 203, 216, 223, 228
    burgh council membership, 37, 39, 41, 46n, 87, 201
    burgh council supervision of clergy, 62, 64, 65, 66, 97
    burgh court, 104–5, 106, 197, 224, 227, 231–3
    burgh records, 7, 197, 198, 216
    craftsmen, 15, 87
    customs, 14–15
    Dean of Guild, 33, 41, 173
    Holy Blood guild, 41, 70, 87
    hospital, 13, 69, 73
    merchants, 15, 37, 87
    participation in Wars of the Congregation, 5, 203–4, 215–17
    plague, 151–2
    provost, 34, 120, 122, 156–7
    Reformation in, 192, 195, 196–204, 215–18, 226, 229–30, 234, 235, 250n
    schools, 62, 69, 76, 227
    taxation, 14, 176, 202
    war damage, 171, 173
    war in, 154–7
Dunfermline Abbey, 21, 22, 52, 53
Dunkeld, Bishop of, 127
Dunorand, Robert, 225
Durham, Henry, 40, 130, 131, 132, 154, 156, 161–2, 164–5
Durham, James, 130
Durham, Michael, 130

Durham, Patrick, 130
Durham, William, 130, 155, 162

ecclesiastical hierarchy, 50, 54, 86
Eddington, Patrick, 43
Edinburgh, 2, 14, 128, 143n, 149, 151, 154, 165, 179, 195, 205, 217, 234, 247, 249n
   Reformation in, 4, 14, 193n, 195, 204, 206, 243, 245
   shipping centre, 17, 21
   town council, 207
Edward VI, King of England, 146, 152
Elgin, Reformation in, 195, 208, 236, 245
England, 2, 17, 60, 95, 129, 148, 180
   military, 217
   Reformation in, 119
   war with, 4, 13, 17, 20, 31, 145–8, 152–8, 175–6
Erskin, James, 62
Erskine, fifth lord of [John Erskine], 35
Erskine, John, of Dun, 203
Erskine, sixth lord of [John Erskine], 34, 39, 185, 206

Fell, John, 88
Ferguson, David, 197
Ferne, John, 55
Ferny, Robert [son of Robert Ferny], 62
Ferny, Robert, 62
Fethy, John, 62, 65–6
Fife, 123, 197
Fife, Robert, 66
First Band of Congregation, 185–6
Fitch, Audrey-Beth, 49
flesher craft, Stirling, 42
Fleshour, Alexander, 122, 123
Fleshour, Andrew, 62, 199
Fleshour, family, 123
Fleshour, John, 122
Fletcher, Andrew, 199, 201
Fletcher, James, 47n, 216
Fletchour, John, 222
Flock, Friar, 75
Flodden, battle of, 145, 177
Foggie, Janet, 108n, 246

Forester, Alexander [Laird of Arngibbon], 127
Forester, Alexander of Garden, 34
Forester, family, 39, 40
Forester, James, 55, 174
Forester, John [merchant], 24, 127, 157
Forester, John of Craginelt [provost of Stirling], 34, 39, 40, 127, 158, 175
Forester, Sir Duncan of Garden, 61
Forester, Thomas, 163
Forester, William, 127, 128
Forfar, 14
fornication, 179, 198, 229–30, 231–2, 234
Forrest, Alexander, 137
Forrest, David [I], 136
Forrest, David [II], 133, 136, 137, 138, 208
Forrest, George, 136–7, 150, 160
Forrest, John, 137, 161, 172, 175
Forrest, William, 136
Forrester, John, 206
Forrois, John, 20
Forror, Alex, 112n
Forsitht, Alexander, 95
Forsyth, John, 163
Fothringham, John, 162
France, 2, 37, 118, 164, 175, 180, 201, 219, 229, 245, 246, 247
   influence in Scotland; *see also* Mary of Guise, 145, 191
   military, 145, 154, 157, 176, 202, 205, 218
   Reformation in, 2, 118, 196, 201, 234
   Wars of Religion, 203, 216, 244, 247, 249n, 250n
Franciscan friaries
   Ayr, 246
   Dundee, 13, 76, 121, 122, 129–30, 157, 220, 246
   Haddington, 51, 60, 74–5
   Stirling, 22, 93
Franciscan nunnery, Dundee, 13, 76, 220, 226
Franciscans
   Dundee, 76, 121, 138, 220, 226, 246
   Haddington, 20, 74–6, 101, 104, 120, 144n, 177, 220, 221, 222, 236, 238–9n, 246

François I, king of France, 118, 140n
François II, king of France, 2, 154
Friars, 2, 86, 104, 118, 119, 120, 122, 132, 185, 192, 209, 217, 219–22, 225, 246–7, 248, 250n
   Ayr, 220
   Edinburgh, 207
   Inverness, 220
   Peebles, 221
   Perth, 246
   records of, 7
   St Andrews, 207, 220
   Stirling, 204
   see also Franciscans, Dominicans
furrier craft, Haddington, 71

Galloway, Christopher [Cristell], 18
Gardin, David, 162
Gardineris, George, 106
Garheme, Annapill, 128
Geichay, Jonet, 93
General Assemblies, 215, 217
Geneva, 117, 131, 192, 237, 247
gentry *see* lairds
Germany, 118, 134, 229
Gethrason, Thomas, 105
Gibson, Philip [I], 32, 67, 111n, 160
Gibson, Philip [II], 111n
Gibson, William, 104, 106, 111n, 214n
Giffordgate, 17, 136
Gledstanis, Harbart, 37
Gothra, James, 57
Gourlay, Jonnet, 230
Graham, David, 40, 127, 128
Graham, John, 24, 174
Graham, Patrick, 88
Grange, Laird of *see* William Durham
Gray, family, 98, 130
Gray, George, 111n
Gray, Katherine, 43
Gray, Patrick Lord, 130, 131, 154, 161, 164, 165
Gray, Robert, 66, 88, 111n
Grey, of Wilton, 157, 160
Gude and Godlie Ballatis, 97, 125–6, 183, 244
guilds, records of, 7
Guise, Charles [Cardinal of Lorraine], 201, 212n

Guise, family, 203, 212n
Guise, Mary of, 2, 3, 34, 38, 39, 95, 158, 159, 175, 180, 185, 191, 192, 193n, 196, 197, 201, 202, 204, 206, 207, 212n, 216, 217, 237, 244, 246, 249n
Guise, Mary of, household, 24, 126, 128, 174
Gwilliam, Thomas [Williams], 129, 136

Haddington, 1, 5, 16–17, 118, 133, 135, 138, 145, 146–7, 152, 153–4, 158, 159–61, 165, 177, 191, 192, 217, 227, 228
   Abbey, 17, 21, 43, 51, 101, 154
   almshouse, 73, 75
   assizes, 31, 32, 33, 38
   baillies, 30, 31, 32, 33
   burgh court, 31, 43, 104, 105, 106
   burgh expenses, 21, 172–3, 176
   burgh records, 7
   burgh revenues, 20
   common mills, 20, 172, 175
   Corpus Christi procession, 42
   council, 20, 30, 31, 32, 33, 35, 43–4, 55, 58, 76, 172, 208, 222, 228
   council membership, 37, 38, 40, 41, 208
   council supervision of clergy, 63, 64–5, 68, 69, 91, 92, 219
   customs, 17–18, 21
   defensive preparations, 172, 176
   economy, 17–21, 171
   hospital, 73, 75
   leper hospital, 76
   merchants, 18, 19–20
   military obligations, 146–7, 175–6
   plague, 149
   plays, 42, 133
   provost, 31–2, 34
   Reformation in, 192, 195, 207–9, 218, 236, 250n
   siege of, 105, 136, 153–4, 158, 160, 171
   taxation, 18, 172
   treasurer, 32, 45n
   war damage, 171–2, 173
Hagy, Andrew, 68
Haliburton, Alexander, 39, 216
Haliburton, family, 39

Haliburton, James [provost], 34, 39, 42, 54, 200, 207, 216, 217, 218
Haliburton, John, 75, 95, 173
Haliburton, William, 74
Halys, Robert, 66
Hamburg, 119
Hamilton, John [Archbishop of St Andrews], 137, 182, 184, 207
Hamilton, John [vicar of Dundee], 88
Hamilton, Patrick, 118–19, 246
Hamilton, William, 88
Hawschaw, John, 105
Hay, James, 122, 140n, 141n, 142n, 163
Helvetic Confession, 134
Henderson, John, 150
Hendersoun, Agnes, 128, 151
Henry VIII, King of England, 119, 145
Hepburn, William, 222
Heresy, prosecution of, 118–19, 120, 121, 122, 123, 127–8, 131, 134, 135, 181, 185, 202, 246
Hertford, Earl of *see* Somerset, Protector
Hewat, James, 122, 124
Hobe, Robert, 158
Holmes, Stephen Mark, 8n
Holy Blood Altar, Dundee, 70, 173, 200
Holy Blood Altar, Haddington, 91, 92, 98, 105, 106
Holy Blood Altar, Stirling, 54, 94
Holy Roman Empire, 4, 13
Holy Rood Altar, Dundee, 66, 88, 96, 111n
Holy Rood Altar, Stirling, 68, 106
Holy Rude Church [Parish Church], Stirling, 22, 52, 54, 68, 223
Hunter, Christine, 36
Huntly, Fourth Earl of [George Gordon], 209, 244

iconoclasm, 2, 3, 130, 131, 143n, 196, 199, 200, 203, 204, 207, 216, 243, 250n
idolatry, 3, 125, 132, 178–80, 181, 182, 186, 199, 201, 202, 203, 204, 228, 244, 249n
inquests, 30, 31, 34–6, 43–4
Inveresk, 144n, 153
Invergowrie, 133

Inverness, Reformation in, 195, 208, 214n, 227, 231

Jakson, Richard, 97, 112n
James V, King, 18, 61, 64, 76, 117, 118, 120, 121, 124, 125, 127, 129, 145, 146
Jedburgh, 218
Jesuits, 246
Jesus Altar, Dundee, 87
Johnson, Gilbert, 106
justification by faith, 118, 121

Kay, Janet, 158
Keir, Isabell, 230
Kello, Cristiane, 105
Kelso, 165
Kemp, John, 62
Kemp, William, 61, 62, 92
Ker, Duncan, 24
Ker, Marion, 87
Kid, Robert, 201
Killore, John, 127
Kinloch, James, 61, 64, 96–7, 99–100
Kinloch, Robert, 100
Kinloch, William, 99–100
kirk session, 5, 7, 191, 192, 196, 198, 199, 207, 209, 218, 233, 234, 240n
kirkboard *see* poor relief
Kirkhill, castle of, 164
kirkmaster, 33, 54, 55, 64
kirkmaster, Dundee, 65, 174, 223
Knox, John, 17, 119, 121, 123, 129, 132, 133, 134, 136, 137, 138, 151–2, 153, 182, 185, 186, 198, 200, 201, 202, 203, 205, 206, 216, 248n
Kyd, Thomas, 140n
Kynneir, John, 15
Kynneris, Andrew, 141n

Laing, Friar, 120, 124
lairds [gentry], 4, 7, 34, 38–9, 44, 128, 129, 131–2, 155, 162, 174, 175, 185, 191, 195, 197, 201, 216, 217, 237, 247
Lammanson, Andrew, 98
Langlandis, William, 105
Lauta, family, 98
Lawta, Robert, 105

Leggat, William, 16
Leith, 119, 151, 165, 195, 217
leprosy, 36
Lethington, Laird of *see* Maitland, William
Leviston, Alex, 106
Lindores Abbey, 52, 55, 66, 89, 173, 220
Lindsay, David [playwright], 86, 177–80, 182, 183, 185, 244
Lindsay, David [priest], 131
Lindsay, Robert, of Pittscottie, 107n, 153, 202, 204
Linlithgow, Reformation in, 195, 204
Litstar, William, 105
Livingston, Henry, 39, 175
Logie, Gavin, 94, 118, 124, 125
Logie, Robert, 123, 126
Loigan, John, 99
London, 148
Longniddry, 136, 160
Lords of Council, 119–120, 146
Lords of the Congregation, 38, 137, 192, 200, 204, 205, 207, 216, 217, 218, 219, 224, 238n, 239n, 243, 244, 246, 248n
Lorne, Lord *see* fifth Earl of Argyll
Lothians, 17, 147, 154, 159, 182, 208–9
Lovell, Alexander, 65
Lovell, David, 162–3
Lovell, family, 39, 98
Lovell, George, 38, 55, 62, 122, 124, 141n, 142n, 196, 199, 200, 216, 217, 218, 223, 224
Lovell, Henry, laird of Balumbie, 155, 162
Lovell, James, 37, 163, 220
Low Countries, 2, 118, 138, 245, 246, 247, 249n, 250n
Lubeck, 119
Luther, Martin, 118
Lutheran, books, 119
Lutheranism, interest in, 121, 132, 181
Lutherans, 119, 201
Lutrell, John, 162, 163
Lwyd, David, 93
Lwyd, John, 100

Lwyd, William, 70, 88, 93, 100
Lyall, David, 97
Lyell, Patrick, 18
Lyle, John, 225
Lynch, Michael, 3, 30
Lyndsay, Jonet, 230
Lyne, John, 127
Lyngon, George, 75
Lyon herald, 176
Lyon, Patrick, 40, 47n, 156, 162
Lytle, John, 68

Magdalene altar, Dundee, 95, 112n
Mailer, John, 129, 142n
Mair, John [Major], 119, 177
Maitland, Robert, 21
Maitland, William of Lethington, 133, 137
Makinlay, Alexander, 130
Makkeltir, Robert, 233
Makynare, Duncan, 106
Malcolm, Lord Fleming, 58–9
Malmo, 119
malters, Haddington, 72
Mar, James, 35
Marischal, Earl, 132
Mary Stewart, Queen of Scotland, 2, 3, 18, 137, 146, 150, 152, 154, 191, 193n, 201, 218, 226
Mary Tudor, Queen of England, 137, 196
mason and wright craft, Haddington, 71, 72
Mason, Nycolas, 229
Mason, William, 57
mass *see* religious services, mass
Mauchlin, James, 56, 62, 68, 89, 92–3, 98, 105, 225
Mauchlin, Patrick, 54, 61, 64, 98, 105
Mauchlin, Robert [I], 98
Mauchlin, Robert [II], 98
Mauchlin, Thomas, 56, 91, 98, 103, 105
Maule, Thomas, 162
Mearns, 123, 197
medieval church, 1, 49, 100, 171
  criticism of, 119, 124, 125, 177–80
  failings of, 3, 77, 86, 248
Melanchthon, Philip, 184–5

Mentht, William, 24
Menzies, family, 209
Menzies, Thomas, 243
Merriman, Marcus, 159
Mertyne, John [Dundee], 60–1, 64, 97
Mertyne, John [Haddington], 60
Methven, Paul, 5, 184, 196, 197, 199, 200
Millar, Mungo, 117, 135, 219
Millar, Thomas, 225
Monter, Andrew, 233
Montrose, 132, 133, 198
Mur, Marion, 99
Murray, John, 95, 112n
Murray, Robert, 35
Myll, Robert, 65, 132
Myln, Andrew, 163
Myln, Jonet, 231
Myln, Robert, 163
Myrton, William, 106

Netherlands *see* Low Countries
New Testament, 129
New Testament [Tyndale translation], 119
Newbottle abbey, 17, 43
Newcastle, 147, 148
Nicolson, James, 68
nobles, 2, 128, 132, 174, 181, 195, 197, 216
Norrocht, Isabell, 99
North Berwick, church, 90
Norwell, William, 39
notarial protocol books, 92
Nungate, 17
Official of Lothian, 108n
Official Principal [St Andrews], 108n, 112n
Ogill, Agnes, 57
oligarchy, 30, 31, 33
Oliphant, James, 32, 98, 214n, 222
Oliphant, Janet, 98
Oliphant, Lord [Lawrence Oliphant, 3rd Lord Oliphant], 93
Ormeston, Laird of, 134
Our Lady Altar, Dundee, 40, 53, 62, 112n, 199
Our Lady in the Cowgait chapel, Dundee, 70, 96, 98

parish clerk, 1
  Dundee, 64, 65, 100
  Haddington, 61, 62, 63, 64, 92
  Stirling, 63
Park, David, 229
Parliament, 2
  Act on Burnt Lands, 95, 101, 102, 105, 106, 171, 172
  Legislation 1469, 33
  Legislation 1552, 185
  Legislation 1560, 5, 191, 195, 208, 209, 215, 217, 228, 243
Paterson, Duncan, 55
Paterson, family, 123
Paterson, John, 106, 140n, 142n, 230
Paterson, Robert, 140n
Peebles, 108n, 165, 187n, 227, 249n
  Reformation in, 195, 208, 219, 223, 230–1
Perth, 14, 100, 129, 131, 143n, 148, 154, 164, 175, 195, 203, 249n
  Reformation in, 192, 193n, 195, 196, 200, 201, 203, 215–16, 243
Phillip, John, 97
Pinkie Cleugh, battle of, 145, 147, 148, 153, 154, 158, 180
plague, 4, 15, 20, 36, 56, 101, 133, 145, 147, 165, 148–52, 172, 177, 178, 180, 182, 192
plays, 72–3, 124, 127, 133, 179, 182
pluralism, 70, 96
Poldrate, 17, 75
Pollmann, Judith, 246, 249n
poor relief, 73, 217, 222, 227
Pope, 118, 119, 120
popular violence, 2, 100, 130, 195, 197, 216, 243, 244, 246, 247
Poynton, Thomas, 18, 45n
preachers [Protestant], 2, 182, 184, 185, 195, 196, 203, 210; *see also* George Wishart, reformer
prebends *see* choristers
priests *see* clergy
privy kirk, 2, 185, 196, 247
procurator [prolocutor], 89, 91, 92, 93, 95
prophecy, 134, 151–2, 153, 167n, 168n, 186
prostitution, 196, 197, 198, 229

Protestant, definition, 8n
Protestantism, 86, 92, 119, 122, 155, 163, 165, 182, 185, 191, 193, 195, 198, 202, 204, 206, 210, 215, 231, 234, 235, 236, 237, 243, 244, 245, 246, 247
   interest in, 122, 124, 125, 126, 128, 129, 130, 136, 137
Protestants, 117, 118, 130, 134, 138, 159, 161, 171, 177, 179, 192, 195, 201, 209
provost, 33
punishment [burgh], 6, 31, 35, 36, 56, 57, 151, 197, 228, 231, 232, 233
Punton, Thomas, 105, 214n

Ramsay, David, 47n, 216
Ramsay, Elene, 64
Ramsay, James, 96, 100
Ramsay, Laurence, 106
Ray, Marion, 151
Reduacht, James, 99
Reformation, 185, 195, 215, 226, 227, 232, 235, 237, 243, 247, 248
   of 1559–60, 117, 126, 128, 171, 191, 192, 203–4, 246
Reidheuch, Henry, 105
religious identity, 244–5
religious services, 49, 50, 56, 57–60, 61, 77, 234
   Dundee, 76, 173–4
   Haddington, 67, 68, 71, 72, 74, 75
   mass, 1, 8n, 49, 53, 57, 58–60, 77, 118, 134, 135, 181, 183, 184, 186, 191, 196, 199, 200, 202, 203, 236, 247
   prayers, 219
   preaching, 49, 60, 132, 133, 191, 197–8, 207, 230, 233, 247
Renfrew, 150
Rhodes, Bess, 49
Richardson, Hector, 66
Richardson, John, 127
Richardson, Thomas, 18
Riclington, John, 137, 160
Ritchie, Pamela, 191
Robe, Robert, 24
Robertson, William, 233
Robesoun, William, 95
Robison, Gilbert, 71
Rog, William, 65
Rolland, John, 66, 69, 88, 89, 93
Rollok, Charles, 98
Rollok, David, 65
Rollok, family, 39, 98, 123
Rollok, George [I], 39, 57, 123
Rollok, George [II], 40, 47n, 62, 199, 201, 216
Rollok, George [III], 40, 47n, 97, 98
Rollok, James [in Veere], 129, 142n
Rollok, James [junior], 47n, 55, 124, 174
Rollok, James [senior], 47n, 120
Rollok, Richard, 47n, 140n, 141n
Rood altar, Dundee, 55, 93, 98
Rood altar, Haddington, 61, 64
Rood altar, Stirling, 62
Rouen, 125, 250n
Rough, John, 128, 129
Rycht, John, 28n
Ryklington, George, 92
Ryrie, Alec, 3, 49, 86, 191
Ryton, Thomas, 174

Sabbath observance, 229, 230
sacraments, 184, 186, 198, 202, 203
St Agatha's [and Erasmus] chapel, Dundee, 62, 96
St Andrews, 5, 49, 67, 118, 119, 121, 165, 195, 224, 238n
   Priory, 51, 53, 89
   Reformation in, 195, 204, 206, 207, 216, 239, 243–4, 245
   siege of, 129, 131, 136, 137, 146, 148, 164
St Andrews' altar, Haddington, 72
St Andrews' chapel, Dundee, 96
St Anne's chaplainry, Stirling, 93
St Clement's Church, Dundee, 13, 52, 53, 55, 223
St Cobett's altar, Dundee, 173
St Columba [Colanis] chaplainry, Dundee, 67, 69, 100
St Duthac's altar, Haddington, 74
St Giles procession, 247
St Gregory's chaplainry, Dundee, 106
St James' altar, Haddington, 62, 68, 93
St James' altar, Stirling, 95, 223

Index

St James the Apostle's chaplainry, Dundee, 97
St John's altar, Haddington, 71
St John's altar, Stirling, 58
St John's chaplainry, Dundee, 69, 218
St John the Baptist's altar, Haddington, 68
St John the Baptist's chapel, Dundee, 96
St Katherine the Virgin's chaplaincy, Dundee, 62, 96
St Katherine's altar, Stirling, 61, 68
St Katherine's chapel, Haddington, 56
St Leonard's altar, Stirling, 69
St Mary's Church, Biggar, 58–9
St Mary's Church, Dundee, 13, 52–3, 54, 56, 67, 68, 121, 132, 156, 173–4, 200, 223
St Mary's Church, Haddington, 17, 51, 54, 56, 74, 154, 172, 223
St Matthew's chaplainry, Dundee, 97, 111n
St Michael the Archangel altar, Stirling, 61, 94, 205
St Michael, Crispin and Crispianus altar, Haddington, 135
St Michael's chaplainry, Dundee, 70, 96, 97, 98
St Nicholas' chapel, Dundee, 111n
St Ninian's altar, Stirling, 62
St Ninian's chapel, Haddington, 56
St Ninian's chaplainry, Dundee, 55, 96, 112n
St Peter's altar, Stirling, 223
St Salvator's chaplainry, Dundee, 96, 97
St Severan's altar, Dundee, 200
St Severus the Bishop's altar, Dundee, 70
St Thomas the Martyr's chaplainry, Dundee, 61, 97
St Thomas' altar, Haddington, 68
St Thomas' chapel, Dundee, 96, 199, 224
St Traduan's chaplainry, Dundee, 97
Samuelston, 136
Sanderson, Margaret, 3, 4
Scharp, John, 57
Scone Abbey, 89, 216, 224, 243
Scot, George, 112n

Scot, Walter, 24
Scots Confession, 215, 228
Scottish export trade, 5
Scrimgeour, family, 14, 39, 98
Scrimgeour, James [chanter of Brechin], 121
Scrimgeour, James, 55, 97, 103, 120, 130
Scrimgeour, John, 163, 165
Scrimgeour, Walter, 121
Second Band of the Congregation, 204
Selkirk, 38
Sempill, lord, 248n
Seres, Robert, 53
Seres, Thomas, 53, 111n
Seton, Alexander, 121, 244
Sibbald, Alexander, 24
Sibbald, David, 24
Silver, Eufame, 99
Silver, William, 65
Simson, Duncan, 127
Sinclare, Elizabeth, 18
Skene, Gilbert, 149
skinner craft, Haddington, 71
Smart, William, 62
Smith, Agnes, 158
Smith, Helen, 205
smith craft
  Haddington, 42
  Stirling, 71
Smyth, Archibald, 225
Smyth, James, 225
social discipline, 184, 185, 192, 196, 197, 198, 215, 228–35, 236, 240n
Solway Moss, battle of, 146, 148, 161
Somerset, duke of [Protector], 146, 152, 160, 161
Spanky, David, 42
Spens, David, 15
Spens, John, 73, 111n
Spittell, Archibald, 127
Spotiswode, John [priest in Stirling], 68
Spottiswode, Thomas, 28n
Steton, Walter of Tucht, 43
Steward, Thomas, 162, 165
Stewart, A. M., 180
Stewart, Lord James, 51, 56, 185, 204, 207, 214n, 216, 219

Stirling, 5, 21–2, 118, 126, 128, 131, 138, 145, 147, 157–8, 159, 165, 191, 195, 203, 217, 234, 243
  almshouse, 73, 227
  assizes, 35
  burgh council supervision of clergy, 63, 68, 69, 218
  burgh council, 22, 24, 55, 88, 150, 157–8, 206, 223, 225, 228–9, 235
  burgh court, 36, 41, 106, 158, 205
  council membership, 38–9, 40, 41, 174
  defensive preparations, 157–8
  economy, 22–5, 171, 174
  government, 33, 35, 43–4
  hospital, 22, 240n
  leper colony, 73
  merchants, 24, 41, 175
  military obligations, 176
  plague, 150
  provost, 34, 206
  records, 7
  Reformation in, 192, 195, 204–7, 218, 225, 230, 235–6, 250n
  revenues, 23–4
  suppression of Protestantism in, 5, 126–9
  taxation, 22–3
Stirling Castle, 21, 22, 24, 34, 126, 174, 206
Stoddard, John, 62
Story, John, 64
swearing *see* social discipline
Switzerland, 2, 134, 196, 229
Swynton, John, 55
Swynton, Thomas, 95
Syld, Thomas, 105–6
Symson, Alexander, 92
Symson, Duncan, 244
Symson, George, 28n, 106, 172
Symson, Robert, 61, 64, 91

tailor craft
  Haddington, 71
  Stirling, 41, 71
Tailor, John, 158
Tait, Helen, 136, 160
Tait, John, 117, 135, 219, 225, 244
Tasker, William, 106

taverns, 196, 197, 229
Tennand, Joan, 224
Teviotdale, 244
Thane, Thomas, 162
The Catechism, 183
The Complaynt of Scotland, 107n, 183, 185, 244, 245
Thomas, Alexander, 28n
Thomas, Forret [Vicar of Dollar], 107n, 123, 127
Thomson, Bernard, 91
Thomson, John, 33
Thomson, Thomas, 220
tithes, 108n
town councils *see* burgh councils
Traprain Law, 153
Treaty of Edinburgh, 217
Treaty of Greenwich, 146, 152, 154
Trent, Council of, 201, 244
Trinity Altar, Haddington, 219
Tulloh, Margaret, 43
typhus, 148

University of Glasgow, 94, 110n
University of St Andrews, 87, 92, 94, 124, 125, 138, 219

Veere, 129
Verschuur, Mary, 9n, 175
vicars, 86, 87–8
  of Dollar *see* Forret, Thomas
  of Dundee, 66, 87–8, 97, 124, 145
  of Haddington, 89
  of Stirling, 88–9
  of Tullibody, 126
Virgin Mary and Three Kings of Cologne chaplainry, Haddington, 136, 137
Virgin Mary, 117, 126, 135
von Weid, Hermann [Archbishop of Cologne], 184
Vye, Alexander, 225

Waclie, John, 224
Wait, John, 121, 123, 140n, 141n
Walker, Andrew, 57
walker craft, Dundee, 70
Wallace, John, 209
Walson, William, 1, 4, 7, 62, 63

Wars of Rough Wooing, 15, 18, 145–7, 152–8, 159, 180, 192
Wars of the Congregation, 3, 5, 195, 204, 205, 208, 216–17
Watson, Alexander, 158
Watson, James [Stirling], 39, 127, 128, 142n
Watson, James [Invergowrie], 121, 133
Watson, John, 111n
Waus, Thomas, 62
weaver craft
  Dundee, 53, 70, 71, 93, 100
  Stirling, 41–2, 70
Wedderburn plays, 73, 124
Wedderburn, Elizabeth, 47n
Wedderburn, family, 39, 97, 123
Wedderburn, Gilbert, 140n, 141n, 142n
Wedderburn, James [b. 1495], 121, 124, 198, 141n
Wedderburn, James [b. 1450], 62, 87
Wedderburn, James [baillie], 66, 120
Wedderburn, John, 87, 97, 123, 124, 125, 141n, 142n
Wedderburn, Robert, 62, 87, 88, 97, 107n, 124, 145, 177, 180, 182
Wedderburn, Thomas, 70, 96, 97, 98, 200
Welscher, William, 231
Wemys, Robert, 89

Wenton, Margaret, 93
Whitelaw, Alexander, 162, 165
Wicht, James, 67
Wigton, John, 131, 133
Williamson, James, 130
Willock, John, 204
Wilson, James [alias Cristeson], 93, 106
Wilson, John, 97
Wilson, Katherine, 172
Wilson, Martin, 28n, 172
Wilson, William, 92, 219
Wishart, George [Dundee councillor], 38, 227
Wishart, George [reformer], 56, 72, 121, 125, 132–5, 136, 137, 138, 144n, 151–2, 153, 183, 185, 246
witchcraft, 230
Wittenberg, 118, 196
Wod, David, 122
Wolson, Martin *see* Wilson, Martin
Wre, John, 24
Wright, James, 112n
Wright, William, 158
Wyndham, Thomas, 155

Young, John, 94, 104, 218
Yule, 72, 73
Yule, John, 56

Zwinglianism, 132

EU representative:
Easy Access System Europe
Mustamäe tee 50, 10621 Tallinn, Estonia
Gpsr.requests@easproject.com

www.ingramcontent.com/pod-product-compliance
Lightning Source LLC
Chambersburg PA
CBHW050210240426
43671CB00013B/2280